Jewish Dimensions of Social Justice

Temple Beth-El of Great Neck

The **SHELDON MEISENBERG SERVICE AWARD**

is given to

Rachel Eve Lubert

June 18, 1999

Jewish Dimensions of Social Justice

Tough Moral Choices of Our Time

Albert Vorspan
and
David Saperstein

UAHC Press • New York, NY

Library of Congress Cataloging-in-Publications Data

Vorspan, Albert.
Jewish dimensions of social justice: tough moral choices of our time/Albert
Vorspan and David Saperstein.
   p. cm.
   ISBN 0-8074-0650-3 (alk. paper)
   1. Judaism and social problems. 2. Social justice. 3. Jews—United Sates—
Politics and government. 4. Bioethics. 5. Economics—Religious aspects—
Judaism. 6. Human ecology—Religious aspects—Judaism. 7. Jews—United
States—Attitudes toward Israel. 8. Peace—Religious aspects—Judaism. 9.
Civil rights—Religious aspects—Judaism. 10. United States—Race relations.
11. Afro-Americans—Relation with Jews. 12. Antisemitism—United States.
13. United States—Ethnic relations. I. Saperstein, David. II. Title.
   HN40.J5V589 1998
   306'.0973—dc21   98-34606
                                                     CIP

This book is printed on acid-free paper.

This book incorporates parts of the authors' previously published book,
Tough Choices: Jewish Perspectives on Social Justice, copyright © 1992 by the
UAHC Press.

Manufactured in the United States of America

10 9 8 7 6 5 4 3 2 1

We thank our wives, Ellen Weiss and Shirley Vorspan, whose wise observations about life and politics we steal incessantly and whose humor and patience help save us from each other.

CONTENTS

CONTENTS

CONTENTS

CONTENTS

CONTENTS

Contents

PREFACE

Not long ago, one of the coauthors of this volume was privileged to meet the Dalai Lama of Tibet at a Buddhist retreat center in New Jersey. He was part of a small delegation that wanted to convey its deep empathy with this great leader, living in exile since 1959, when China occupied his homeland. The recipient of the 1989 Nobel Peace Prize thanked the delegation for Jewish support of his efforts to place the tragedy of Tibet before the conscience of the world.

The Dalai Lama himself is colorful and engaging. Wearing brown and purple robes, perching comfortably on a couch with his legs crossed under him, with a warm smile lighting up his face despite the grimness of his situation, and displaying a puckish sense of humor, the Dalai Lama told us in a soft voice about the forty-year campaign of genocide his Tibetan people endured at the hands of the Chinese invaders and about the ongoing destruction of Tibetan religious, ethnic, and national identity. As Jews, we found it easy to commiserate. But the Tibetan leader had something on his mind. "Tell me," he said, "*what is your secret?* How can a people that has been persecuted and exiled and vilified throughout the centuries maintain its religion and its sense of national identity? No other people has done this except you. *I want to know your secret so that I might better help preserve my people.*"

We gave a variety of responses to the Dalai Lama. One told the story of Yochanan ben Zakkai and how his small school at Yavneh preserved Jewish values—values that outlasted the Roman conquest of Judea. Another explained the story of modern Israel itself, of how the Jewish people, exiled for centuries, achieved national liberation out of the ashes of the Holocaust. The miracle of Israel was a product of faith, memory, and peoplehood. Some of us said that the Dalai Lama had already learned our secret in his championship of the values of nonviolent resistance to evil, the quality for which he was honored by the entire civilized world. The power of the spirit, which he helps to symbolize in the world today, is ultimately more powerful than all the armies and weapons of repression. In that, both his people and our Jewish people share a common vision of peace, justice, and cooperative relations among all the brothers and sisters of the world.

One of our group said that persecution keeps a people alive. Another said that Judaism, as a way of life, was the key to Jewish survival and that the synagogue is the fount of Jewish immortality. Several added that the Jewish passion for social justice had made a difference not only to Jews but to all the world. The refusal to yield to despair, fatigue, or cynicism; the stubborn belief in *tikkun olam*, "repairing the shattered world"; the *chutzpadik* notion that we are copartners with God in refashioning a humane and civilized world—these Jewish compulsions, we said, have helped preserve the Jewish spirit.

This book is about that yearning for *tikkun olam*. It confronts the most compelling issues of social justice of our era—issues that will dominate the American political agenda well into the third century of American life. These issues involve complex dilemmas and require delicate choices. In this volume, we seek to place those tough choices into a context of Jewish tradition and ethics, to analyze the factual setting, and to lay out some real dilemmas for the reader to examine and resolve.

This book's "real dilemmas" are those confronting American Jewry generally and, more particularly, the Reform movement: the Commission on Social Action of Reform Judaism, which represents the Union of American Hebrew Congregations, the Central Conference of American Rabbis, and all the affiliated bodies of the Reform movement. The commission in 1962 created its Religious Action Center (RAC) in Washington, D.C., to apply Jewish ethics to issues of legislation and public policy in the nation's capital. The Religious Action Center has become a dynamic center of Jewish moral and political energy, immersed in issues of particular Jewish concern— Israel, Soviet Jewry, Ethiopian Jewry, anti-Semitism—as well as such issues of universal concern as the environment, church-state relations, civil liberties, and world peace. Augmenting its dedicated staff with brilliant and energetic legislative assistants, the RAC represents a unique Jewish enterprise: the only Jewish building in the world devoted exclusively to the pursuit of social justice.

The "real dilemmas" in this book, for the most part, were actually faced by the UAHC, the CCAR, the Commission on Social Action and/or its Religious Action Center, and the synagogues of America. We do not pretend that our responses stem from Sinai or from a dramatic epiphany, only that the questions arise from real experience and that the answers are guided by Jewish historical experience and informed by long-held Jewish values. We acknowledge at the outset that our answers are fallible and that some dilemmas may not even be resolvable.

Do Jews still have a passion for social justice? A young Jewish woman, a social activist in California, put it this way: "Most people in the world live heroic lives merely trying to survive for one more day. They are powerless to evoke change, let alone help others. That is why I feel so strongly that those of us who can make a difference *must* do so. And if we don't, we are depriving ourselves of perhaps the greatest opportunity life can offer: to help change the world and, in turn, give true meaning to our lives."

A postscript: In 1997, the Dalai Lama was a guest at an extraordinary Passover seder held at the RAC. National Jewish leaders from all streams of the community, prominent figures from Washington, including Supreme Court Justice Stephen Breyer, figures from the arts, and the Dalai Lama's entourage attended.

After participating in this age-old celebration, recounting the story of the journey from slavery to redemption, the Dalai Lama observed: "Now I understand a bit of your secret of survival and your passion for social justice—including our cause: this remarkable retelling of your journey from oppression to freedom."

That retelling takes many forms. Among them are the contemporary expressions of that journey that fill this book.

ACKNOWLEDGMENTS

This book has had several predecessors in the life of the social action movement. In the beginning (1956) was *Justice and Judaism* by Eugene J. Lipman and Albert Vorspan, followed by *Jewish Values and Social Crisis* (1967) by Vorspan, then *Great Jewish Debates and Dilemmas* (1980) by Vorspan, and *Tough Choices* (1992) by Saperstein and Vorspan. This new volume updates some of the earlier themes but basically focuses on the new and emergent issues that confront us in the life of a new millennium: biomedical ethics, ethnic cleansing, religious pluralism in Israel and America, the rise of Latino and Muslim communities, the changing family, and many other issues in addition to such continuing challenges as race relations, economic justice, civil liberties, and religious freedom.

This is not an encyclopedia of political hot-button issues. It is an earnest and searching effort to examine Jewish tradition and Jewish values to see what moral light they can shed on the great issues of our time—the very real issues confronting Jews, America, and the world. We try to do this by looking, in an open-ended way, at relevant Jewish texts and by analyzing some of the real dilemmas we have had to deal with in the work of the Religious Action Center, the Washington-based public policy arm of the Union of American Hebrew Congregations and the Central Conference of American Rabbis, as well as dilemmas faced by congregations and other institutions in our community.

It is because of the particular nature of the social justice movement within Reform Jewry that this book is the combined effort of scores of people. In synagogues throughout the United States and Canada, social action committees have created programs of social justice that touch every aspect of the domestic and international agenda of the Jewish community. Individual rabbis and lay leaders have taken positions of conscience—sometimes against the grain of popular opinion—that have made a real difference in the Jewish community and in America. At the local and national levels, laypeople and professionals are bound by the common thread and belief that to be a Jew is to be inexorably bound up with being a "light unto the nations," a partner with God in shaping a better world. In their totality, the voices and actions of these people have brought the Reform Jewish movement to the forefront of America's social justice agenda.

The work of many of those people is reflected throughout the book. The stories of synagogues and individuals who grappled with moral dilemmas are retold in our "Real Dilemma" sections. Speeches, sermons, and articles by social justice leaders, lay and rabbinic, are cited in many chapters.

Scattered throughout the book are the writings of several generations of Maurice N. Eisendrath legislative assistants (LAs) who serve at the Religious Action Center of Reform Judaism (RAC) in the nation's capital. These young people keep alive the memory of Rabbi Eisendrath, the UAHC president from 1946 to 1973, who presided over the creation of the Commission on Social Action and the Religious Action Center. Eisendrath's legacy was extended by Rabbi Alexander M. Schindler, president of the UAHC from 1973 to 1997, and is being enhanced by Rabbi Eric H. Yoffie, once himself director of the social action program, president since 1997.

While the number of people to whom we are indebted is too large for individual acknowledgment, there are several whose contributions simply cannot go unrecognized. Among those who drafted text or provided writings from which we have quoted at some length are:

- Rabbi Richard Hirsch, founding director, Religious Action Center of Reform Judaism; executive director, World Union for Progressive Judaism—Economic Justice
- Robert Greenstein, director, Center for Budget and Policy Priorities—Economic Justice
- Marc Saperstein, Charles E. Smith Professor of Jewish History, George Washington University—Gun Control, Bioethics, Anti-Semitism
- Rabbi Robert Kirschner, president, Skirball Cultural Center—HIV/AIDS
- Rabbi Sharon Kleinbaum, former director of congregational relations, RAC; rabbi, Congregation Beth Simchat Torah, New York—HIV/AIDS, Gay and Lesbian Rights
- Beckie Skelton, former legislative director, RAC—Economic Justice

- Ed Rehfeld, former Eisendrath LA; former director of development, writer-in-residence, RAC—Censorship, Religious Liberty
- Steve Derringer, former Eisendrath LA—Religious Liberty, Economic Justice
- Robin Katcher, former Eisendrath LA; legislative director, Coalition to Stop Gun Violence—Gun Control
- Brad Ortman, former Eisendrath LA—Environment
- Rabbi Fred Dobb, former Eisendrath rabbinic student LA—Environment
- William S. Meyers—*Cruzan* Case
- Ken Stern, program specialist, Anti-Semitism and Extremism, American Jewish Committee—Skinheads, Militias
- Aimee Zeltzer—Fetal Tissue Transplants
- Rabbi Marc Israel, director of congregational relations, RAC—Gender Language in Prayer
- Rabbi Richard Address, director, UAHC Department of Jewish Family Concerns/Committee on Bioethics—Bioethics
- Douglas B. Mishkin, Esq., McKenna & Cueno, Washington, D.C.—Bioethics
- Lauren Schumer, Eisendrath LA—Breast Cancer

We are equally grateful to Mark Pelavin, associate director, Religious Action Center of Reform Judaism; Rabbi Lynne Landsberg, former associate director, RAC; Dr. Leonard Fein, director, Commission on Social Action of Reform Judaism, founder of *Moment* magazine and Mazon: A Jewish Response to Hunger, whose contribution to the book is appreciated but whose larger contributions to Jewish ideals in this generation have been monumental; Temma Schaller, former RAC administrator; Rabbi Eric H. Yoffie, president, UAHC; Rabbi Leonard Thal, vice president, UAHC; Rabbi Dan Swartz, former director of congregational relations, RAC, assistant director of the National Religious Partnership for the Environment; Rabbi Amy Klein and Rabbi Marc Israel, former and current directors of congregational relations, RAC; Eisendrath legislative assistants who worked on the earlier version of *Tough Choices*: Julie Youdovin, Mickey Meyers, Adam Stock Spilker, Rachel Stock Spilker, Jennifer Marx, Rebecca Laibson, Michael Wigotsky, Jeff Danziger, Jamie Fleckner, Beth Wiener, Tamara

Cofman, Jessica Roth, David Rosen, Ryan Lilienthal, Debbie Banks, and Mitch Malkus; and those who worked on this book: Adeena Colbert, Danya Greenfield, Heather Kaplan, Laura Mutterperl, Lauren Schumer, Stacey Wions, Shara Abraham, David Abrams, Jennifer Morgan, Caryl Feldacker, Scott Dinsmore, Jordan Katz, Jeffrey Leininger, Jeremy Davidson, Nikki Horberg, Leah Malmon, Sam Rosenthal, Lysa Selfon, Rachel Smerd, and Liz Stark; and Eisendrath summer rabbinic student legislative assistants: Rabbi Fred Dobb, Rabbi Andi Fisher, Rabbi Marc Israel, Sherre Zwelling, and Dena Klein—all of whom drafted, edited, and checked the facts in the policy areas for which they were responsible while working at the RAC and have already transformed many of these chapters into educational and programmatic activities for synagogues; and especially for their endless passion and talents, Dvora Tager and Shelley Engel, former and current assistants to the director, RAC; Ian Marinoff, former special assistant to the director and associate director, RAC; and Lauren Schumer, Eisendrath legislative assistant, who was unflappable in compiling draft after draft of this book, editing and offering advice the whole way.

We also thank Rabbi Harold Saperstein and Marcia Saperstein for their advice on substance and style; Stuart Benick, director of publications at the UAHC, who skillfully oversaw the production of the publication itself, editors Bonny Fetterman and Annette Abramson, the late Kivie Kaplan, and the late Paul Kodimer, whose magnificent contributions to the cause of social justice and the RAC have inspired both authors.

Jewish
Dimensions
of Social Justice

··· 1 ···

Grappling with the Dilemmas of Social Justice in the 21st Century

In the days of the historic civil rights struggle, it seemed so easy to make a clear moral judgment on the big issues in American society. It seemed so easy to tell the good guys from the bad, to stand up and be counted. It did not require great ethical sophistication to distinguish right from wrong when witnessing black children in Birmingham being killed in church bombings and assaulted by police equipped with attack dogs, fire hoses, and electric cattle prods. It was not difficult to salute those fighting to win the elementary right to vote and to condemn those who sought to frustrate that right.

On the international scene, it was easy to shout "Let My People Go" on behalf of Soviet Jewry. And although making an initial judgment on the Vietnam War was less clear-cut than the civil rights issue, most Americans came to see the war as morally wrong.

The clear-cut issues of yesteryear have faded into the complex gray of today's dilemmas. While racial justice is still a high moral goal, through what methods is it to be achieved? Affirmative action? Busing? Quotas? Censorship and limitation of freedom of speech are contrary to American principles. Can the government, however, regulate hate-filled speech or speech on the Internet to protect children from pornography? Do American Nazis have the right to march through a community consisting largely of Holocaust survivors? Do newspapers have the right to refuse to place ads denying the truth of the Holocaust? And what limits, if any, do we set upon a woman's right to have an abortion? We still believe in economic justice, but is that furthered by our welfare system if, while helping the poor, it creates a dependency on government support and perpetuates economic injustice? All tough questions.

The certainties of yesterday have become the ambiguities and conflicts of today, especially when one right collides with another right. This is true for all Americans; for Jews *only more so.*

A snapshot of this dilemma: When Israeli Prime Minister Benjamin Netanyahu visited President Clinton in early 1998, at a pivotal moment in the peace process, he first stopped to visit Rev. Pat Robertson, Rev. Jerry Falwell, Senator Jesse Helms, and other prominent figures of the religious and secular Right—all friends of Israel but leaders of a domestic agenda that is anathema to most American Jews. Should those of us who object take a stand?

How do we reconcile our desire to redirect our nation's resources to meet domestic needs with our commitment to maintain strong foreign aid for Israel; the rights of gays and lesbians with the importance of the traditional Jewish family; our commitment to close Black-Jewish relations with our opposition to quotas; our efforts to find peaceful ways for nations to resolve differences with our need to contain Saddam Hussein's Iraq and to intervene in Bosnia and other places where genocidal activity takes place; our joy at the fall of the Communist empire with our concern about the resulting ethnic hatreds, nationalist fervor, and anti-Semitism; our support for the Middle East peace process with our pain at the price Israel must pay because of the increased terrorism that accompanies it; our commitment to the unity of the Jewish people and to *Klal Yisrael* with our determination to stand up for our rights as Reform and Conservative Jews in Israel? How should we balance our Jewish universal ethics and the ethics of our particular self-interest when they collide? That is the subject of this book.

What is the Jewish dimension in each of these issues? What is the Jewish stake? And what do Jewish values teach us about these issues? If Jewish tradition speaks to these conflicts, it does not always do so clearly. No "You shalls" and "You shall nots" were proclaimed at Sinai, no specific answers to our thorny political issues. There are no easy answers as we enter the twenty-first century.

But the complexity of these issues does not exempt us Jews from facing up to our moral challenges. We may have to walk a moral tightrope, yes, but we cannot escape our Jewish mission. With greater modesty and less certainty than in the past, with more tentativeness and greater tolerance for dissenting views, we still bear our historic Jewish burden: to face this world and its pain head-on; to engage in endless study and moral debate; to cherish human life and to pursue

justice; to enhance the life of the mind and to struggle to be God's
partner in repairing this broken and incomplete world. It was never
easy, even in the old days; it is more difficult today and will be even
harder tomorrow. But, if the agenda is more nuanced today, our duty to
do the right thing, to engage in *tikkun olam*, the "repair of our broken
world," is as compelling as ever.

USING THE JEWISH TRADITION IN POLITICAL DEBATE

Can the Jewish moral tradition contribute to a better America and a
more peaceful world? A new world is being fashioned before our eyes.
That new world has within it the seeds of great possibilities and also of
great dangers. The choices made now will shape the new century and
beyond. In these decisions, the historic insights and the moral resonance of a Jewish value system can make a vital contribution.

Will we find specific answers to current political debates in the Bible
or the Talmud? Rarely, if ever. Not even the rabbis of old could be sure
of the answers they fashioned—constantly revisiting them, testing
them in debate with other rabbis, ever striving to refashion more ethical and compassionate solutions to problems.

In more recent times, Reform Judaism, especially, felt our Jewish
tradition had to be constantly adapted to the fresh challenges of
modern life. The answer that Hillel may have given to the problem of
poverty in his time may provide a helpful ethical model, but it casts a
vote, not a veto, for the answer we choose for ours. In understanding
the halachic system that he applied, as well as the God-inspired values
that impelled him, we can certainly find guidance for our own moral
explorations.

While Jewish law, *halachah*, was not envisioned as applicable to a
non-Jewish society (Jewish law is a contract between God and the
Jewish people), many of its values, as well as those found in the *aggadah*
(the nonlegal component of the tradition), are applicable to all people
for all time.

What are these values? We suggest nine:

1. The inherent dignity and value of all human beings, derived from
   the belief that we are all made in the image of God.

2. The equality of all people, rooted in the tradition of our common descent from Eve and Adam.

3. The capacity of all people, given the will and the right educational opportunities, to improve themselves.

4. The concept of wealth ("The earth is *Adonai*'s, and the fullness thereof" [Psalms 24:1]) as lent by God in a trust relationship that requires sharing with the less fortunate. Hence, the special concern that God has mandated for the poor, the widowed, the hungry, and the orphaned.

5. The belief that out of that same trust relationship we have a responsibility of "stewardship" over the earth and must protect it.

6. The existence of certain fundamental laws (e.g., the seven Noachide Laws) that are regarded as basic to any civilized society, including prohibitions against murder, robbery, blasphemy, idolatry, sexual crimes, and the eating of living flesh, as well as requiring that every community establish courts of justice.

7. The rule of law to which even the highest human ruler is accountable.

8. Freedom of choice and the responsibility of each person for his or her own actions.

9. The paramount obligation of individuals and societies to pursue justice, righteousness, and *darchei shalom*, the "ways of peace" (i.e., to be involved in the work of social justice).

Our tradition, therefore, has not dictated specific answers but rather provided values to be applied to life. Judaism does not mandate for the nations of the world either monarchy or democracy, socialism or capitalism; nor has it endorsed food stamp programs or supply-side economics. These are human inventions and policies. Our role as Jews is to test these human theories and policies to see if they advance or impede the universal moral values of Judaism.

And, while good people—including good moral Jews—can and do debate the answers to these questions, a good person can never avoid the questions themselves. Indifference to the problems that confront society is the unforgivable Jewish sin. "Do not separate yourself from the community." (*Pirke Avot* 2:5) The Talmud teaches us: "Whoever has the ability to prevent his household [from committing a sin] and does not is accountable for the sins of his household; if he could do so with his fellow citizens [and does not], he is accountable for his fellow citizens; if the whole world, he is accountable for the whole world." (*Shabbat* 54b) We are Jews and thus we are mandated to dirty our hands in the gritty task of building a better world.

THE 21ST CENTURY: A UNIQUE CROSSROADS

Such a mandate could not be renewed at a more exciting or challenging time. The exploding technologies of the twenty-first century mean that, for the first time, we have the technological capability to cure disease, to feed the hungry, to restore the environment, to enhance the freedoms of all peoples, to eliminate illiteracy, and to build a peaceful world. But, if misused, the same technologies can visit destruction.

Will technology be used to find peaceful ways for nations to resolve their differences or to blow up the world in a nuclear war or accident? Will technology be used to clean up the environment or to destroy our ozone layer and permanently alter the climate of the earth? Will technology be used to enhance our freedoms or to make Orwell's nightmare of *1984* the reality of tomorrow? Will technology be used to distribute God's wealth fairly or to make the rich richer at the expense of the poor? Will the technology of genetics be used to engineer a cure for birth defects or to create a new "master race"? All this, we will decide. As we are commanded in the Bible: "Choose life and live." (Deuteronomy 30:19)

In each case, decisions will be made. Somebody will decide. The only choice is whether we will participate in shaping those decisions or allow ourselves to be passive spectators or victims of those decisions. If we remain silent, the outcome may wreck our values and poison our dreams. A handful of passionate people can change any community, for good or ill, because most people are too self-absorbed to get involved in public affairs.

Jewish theology teaches us that when God created the universe, one small part of creation was intentionally left undone. That part was social justice! God gave to human beings alone the ability to understand the difference between right and wrong, to choose between good and evil, to love, to empathize, and to dream. God entrusted to us, in our sacred texts, a blueprint for completing creation. By allowing us to be partners in completing the world, God has given to our lives destiny, meaning, and purpose.

To be involved in the work of social justice is to do God's work. Those who wrestle with the dilemmas of life and struggle for ethical solutions link their lives to the Jewish mission, which was set out so simply three thousand years ago in the words of the prophet Micah (6:8): "What does *Adonai* require of you? Only to do justly, to love mercy, and to walk humbly with your God."

A JEWISH SOCIODRAMA: THE THREE CHILDREN

Mr. Goldsmith is a fiction, but we will pretend that he was a leading Jew in this community and that he died last week.

I have before me the will of the late Simon Goldsmith. I am his attorney and I must, in the presence of his three children, read you his will: "Know all by those present that I, Simon Goldsmith, being of sound mind and testamentary capacity, do hereby make and publish this following instrument and direct the following disposition of my property. My entire estate shall be given to whichever one of my children shall be deemed to be the best Jew. My attorney shall select a committee of representative Jews to make this determination. If the committee cannot agree or finds that none of my children is worthy to be called a good Jew, the money shall be divided among reputable Jewish and general charities."

Richard, the eldest, owns a sports equipment manufacturing company. He became particularly wealthy when, years ago, he closed down his factories in the United States, which had employed 12,000 workers, and moved them to Pakistan. The newspaper has charged that he pays subnormal wages there and uses child laborers as young as eight years old. He is wealthy and is the largest single contributor in his community to the UJA and to the synagogue. He has endowed a generous scholarship fund at the nearby UAHC camp to subsidize children

who cannot afford to pay for camp. He and his wife have three children. They go to the temple regularly, and the children attend religious
school and join in celebrating the Sabbath and Jewish holidays at home
and in the synagogue.

When questioned about his business, he said: "Look, business deals
with the bottom line, not social justice. A global market means producing goods as cheaply as possible in order to compete and survive.
Business is business and I am not Mother Teresa."

Rachel is a lawyer who once worked for the Legal Aid Society (which
provides free legal assistance to poor people) and recently became
counsel for the American Civil Liberties Union, defending the rights
of minorities: African-Americans, the disabled, and gays and lesbians.
Rachel is an atheist and so is her husband, Mark, a teacher in an inner-
city public school. She explains that when she was small, her best
friend was hit by a car and Rachel prayed desperately for her life to be
saved. When she died, Rachel decided there was no God and refused
to go to the temple or to pray any longer. Her two children, therefore,
do not go to religious school.

At the same time, Rachel and Mark are passionate supporters of Israel
generally and have been particularly strong supporters of efforts to help
Ethiopian Jews settle in Israel. They raise large sums for Jewish causes.
While they do not send their children to religious school, by their
example they try to inculcate a love of Israel and of social justice in
their children. They are personally generous, inasmuch as their income
is supplemented by large gifts of stock from Richard and his company,
and they support a vast number of Israeli and social justice causes.

Harry, the youngest son, is a scholar, teacher, and writer on Jewish
themes. An inspiring teacher, he has enriched the Jewish lives of
countless students at the congregation. He is married to a non-Jewish
woman who remains actively committed to her own religion. They do
not have children yet and are not certain in what religion they will
raise them when they do have children. A serious person, Harry has
read the Bible in its entirety five times and reads Jewish literature
extensively. He writes a column in the local Jewish newspaper. In one
such column, he challenged his brother: "I believe the essence of Jewish
life is to do justly. Therefore, although I love my brother, I believe that
exploiting children in sweatshop conditions is irreconcilable with
Jewish values and that one identified with this evil should publicly

disavow such endeavors and end these policies."

Richard has not spoken to Harry since this episode. Harry's wife also disapproved of his action: "I thought that love of family was the most important Jewish value. And as you are so morally pure, how come we accepted money from Richard's stocks up until now and you never opened your mouth until it became a hot public issue?"

You need to decide. Which, if any, of the three children deserves the inheritance? Why?

··· 2 ···

Life-and-Death Issues: Policy on the Edge

T his chapter deals with controversial life-and-death questions that
are sure to continue to roil the national as well as the congressional agenda in the coming years: abortion, capital punishment, gun
control, AIDS, and substance (drug, alcohol, and tobacco) abuse.

Each one of these volatile issues has become a buzzword in American
politics, with the power to excite extremists to the heights of dema-
goguery and to seal the lips of nervous politicians who vote with a
finger to the wind. More than mere political hot potatoes, they are
urgent moral issues that cannot be omitted from the Jewish agenda.

ABORTION

A Real Dilemma: A Rabbi's Choice

In 1990, the state of Louisiana adopted a sweeping and highly
repressive anti-abortion law. A young rabbi in Shreveport,
Michael Matuson, had strongly opposed the bill, arguing that the
law violated women's rights and privacy. The night the law was
enacted, an official of the American Civil Liberties Union
(ACLU) visited the rabbi, asking him to be one of the defen-
dants in a lawsuit to enjoin the implementation of the law that
would criminalize doctors and health care workers as well as
women seeking abortions. Rabbi Matuson agreed. The local
newspapers plastered the story of the rabbi's role on the front
page. Community repercussions were severe. Indeed, the local
KKK group came to the parking lot of the temple in full regalia,
and threats to the rabbi's life were received daily.

The congregational leadership was upset that in a small town
in the South with a tiny Jewish population, the rabbi had placed
them in the eye of the storm without consulting them in

advance. If you had been a member of the temple board, what would you have said when an emergency meeting was called to discuss the matter?

Response

The board responded that they respected the rabbi's freedom of the pulpit and admired his courage. However, they said that the next time, the rabbi should inform the board before, and not after, making such a controversial decision and involving the synagogue in a heated public dispute.

This is a difficult decision for rabbis. On the one hand, rabbis have the same rights to express and act on their personal beliefs as do others. They have an obligation to provide leadership for the Jewish community based on their understanding of the values of the Jewish tradition. They are not merely the mouthpiece for the majority view of the temple board or membership. They have complete freedom of the pulpit. On the other hand, rabbis derive some of their authority from the perception that they speak for their synagogue and for the Jewish community. When a pulpit rabbi speaks out, based on personal convictions, the rabbi, to some degree, implicates the synagogue.

Rabbis walk a tightrope, balancing their conscience and their leadership role with community relations responsibilities. Trust must be placed in the rabbi's judgment on this. While tying the rabbi's hands by requiring approval of the board on specific issues would undermine the integrity and authority of the rabbi, informing the board in advance of controversial positions helps prepare the board members for questions from congregation members and affords an opportunity for gathering support. Both the UAHC and the CCAR commended Rabbi Matuson for fulfilling the resolutions adopted by the Reform movement and for his courage in upholding unpopular views. In the end, it was a source of great pride for the synagogue community.

In the political climate of the United States today, few issues are more divisive than abortion. This is true particularly in the wake of the *Webster* decision by the United States Supreme Court in 1989 (upholding state restrictions on when, where, and how women can exercise the right to have an abortion guaranteed in *Roe v. Wade*), the *Rust* decision in 1991 (upholding Congress's right to, in effect, gag doctors and counselors in publicly funded clinics from even mentioning abortion), and the *Casey* decision in 1992 (upholding requirements for parental notification, a twenty-four-hour waiting period, the reading of a prepared statement by the doctor concerning the risks of abortion, and a narrow definition for medical emergency exemptions). Legislative initiatives seeking to restrict abortion rights continued throughout the 1990s, most evident in the much debated "late-term (or so-called 'partial birth') abortion" legislation that has been gaining support since first being narrowly defeated in Congress in the fall of 1996.

The highly controversial late-term abortion bill would make a rarely used late-term abortion procedure, the dilation and extraction (D & E) method, a criminal act. On the one hand, this procedure, which dismembers the fetus while in the womb, is generally used in very limited circumstances, late in pregnancy, when the life of either the mother or the fetus would be at risk or there would be a serious threat to the mother's health if the pregnancy were to be carried to full term. On the other hand, evidence has emerged showing that this method was used more liberally and earlier than had been asserted by most advocates.

In 1996 and 1997, Congress voted to make this bill a landmark law that would be the first since *Roe v. Wade* to criminalize a form of abortion. Most pro-choice advocates argued that it should be left to the doctor to decide the safest and most appropriate form of abortion. President Clinton took a middle view, saying he would sign the bill if it included an exemption when the health of the mother was endangered. When the anti-choice forces in Congress refused, the president vetoed the bill. Although there was an attempt to override his veto, it was narrowly defeated. The late-term abortion issue produced a debate that continues to touch the entire country and concern pro-choice advocates.

More decisively than any other group in America, Jews favor the right of free choice in abortion. Some 87 percent (a number that is over 50 percent higher than among non-Jews) support reproductive choice. Nonetheless, there are differences even among Jewish groups, as there are among Protestants and Catholics. Reform and Conservative Judaism have taken a clear stand in favor of free choice for women, and rabbinic and lay leaders of these branches play prominent roles in groups like the Religious Coalition for Reproductive Choice. Some (but not the majority) in the Orthodox Jewish community side with the formal Roman Catholic Church and fundamentalist Protestant condemnation of abortion—albeit rejecting Catholic efforts to define human life as beginning at conception, a view incompatible with *halachah.*

During the fight to preserve a woman's right to choose, the UAHC was once again outspoken on behalf of women's rights. Its views were transmitted in a statement made by Rabbi Lynne Landsberg during a press conference after President Clinton's veto of the late-term abortion bill:

> In the recent debate over late-term abortions, some religious leaders have forgotten their commitment to compassion....
>
> In a full-page ad in the *Washington Post,* the Catholic Conference insinuated with a cynicism bordering on cruelty that women who must seek late-term abortions are motivated by the most petty of priorities. After the veto, eight cardinals then wrote a letter to President Clinton reiterating their contention that women regularly carry late into pregnancy and then capriciously choose to abort because their "boyfriends think they are too young" or because they "hate being fat."
>
> The bishops' ad says a woman might seek a late-term abortion in order to "fit into a prom dress." The reality is that when my colleague Rabbi Shira Stern discovered that her baby would be born without a brain, her decision to seek a late-term abortion was not a fashion consideration. It was a heartbreaking, soul-searching, horrible, life-changing decision that she and her husband suffered together.
>
> The bishops' ad and the cardinals' letter say that a woman might seek a late-term abortion because of career or money worries—because she "can't afford

both a baby and a new car." The reality is that when Karen Ham became critically ill with diabetes, she had to be flown 450 miles to find a doctor who would perform a late-term abortion in order to keep her alive. Karen Ham wasn't worried about saving money. She was worried about saving her life.

The bishops' ad says that a woman might seek a late-term abortion because she "doesn't want a baby with a cleft lip." The reality is that Anne Elfant sought a late-term abortion when she discovered that her baby would be born with a severely deformed heart and esophagus and when her doctors told her to hope the fetus would die in her womb. Late-term abortion is not about designer babies. It is about anguish and heart-break. It is about women who make very, very tough and painful decisions.

Religious leaders who promulgate these kinds of distortions defame the Shira Sterns and the Karen Hams and the Anne Elfants of the world, ridicule the pain and anguish women and families face in these circumstances, and confront these women and families with guilt rather than compassion.

While I respect and will defend any religious leader's right to add his or her voice of faith to the public debate, the tone and substance of the bishops' ad and the cardinals' letter have other religious leaders shaking our heads and sadly asking where is the compassion of the Catholic Church we have admired for decades? ...Are these women worthy only of your derision?

And to President Clinton, I join with other religious leaders of denominations and faith groups that hold pro-choice positions and say thank you, thank you for your compassion, thank you for your continued support, thank you for reminding the country that abortion is still legal and that there is no one moral authority on the issue. Thank you, President Clinton, for your trust in women's ability to make informed, religious decisions.

But Jewish dilemmas remain. Jewish law universally holds that a fetus may (in most cases should) be destroyed to save the mother's life. More liberal strands of *halachah* would justify an abortion simply to protect the mother's health, physical or mental. But is it not stretching the tradition to assert that it would support abortion on demand? Can Jewish tradition really sanction abortion on economic or social grounds?

Arguing for the right of free choice in the matter of abortion does not necessarily mean that the grave decision to abort a fetus is either ethical or wise. Abortion may be, and should be, a free choice, but it must be seen as one of the most serious moral decisions a person can ever face. Perhaps, as writer Roger Rosenblatt has urged, a moral position for America would be to permit but strongly discourage the practice of abortion. Consider the following fictional situation, a composite of real-life situations that happen across America every day:

A Real Dilemma: The Right to Choose—Right or Wrong?

Imagine you are sixteen years old. A month ago your boyfriend forced you to go farther sexually than you wanted to. It was a situation of acquaintance rape. You were embarrassed and scared and didn't want to tell anyone—especially your parents, who would punish you severely. Your mother drinks a lot under stress and when she does, she hits you. Your father demands that you meet his view of moral purity and always warned you against sexual activity, saying he would punish you severely if you had intercourse before marriage. You are miserable but decide to focus most of your energy on your schoolwork. You figure that there is a way out: you will go away to college and escape the pain.

You don't get your period on time. You don't know what to do. Panic strikes. You go to the drugstore and buy a home pregnancy test. You are pregnant. What are you going to do?

You know you are not prepared to be a mother. You don't know whom to ask for advice. You definitely can't tell your parents, who would probably say skeptically, "If you were raped, why didn't you say anything until now?"

You finally decide to tell an older friend. She takes you to the nearest family planning clinic three hours away. You talk to a counselor there. The two of you finally decide that abortion is the best option. Although the procedure terrifies you, becoming a sixteen-year-old mother in an unsupportive family is even more frightening.

The counselor tells you that in West Virginia, as in twenty-six other states, before the doctor can perform an abortion on a minor, one parent must consent. In some states, she tells you, both parents must give their permission.

What are you going to do? You wish you were able to tell your mother, to have her hold you in her arms and tell you that everything is going to be all right. However, you know that this is not going to happen.

You explain the situation to the counselor at the clinic. She explains that the Supreme Court has decided that in any state with a parental consent clause for minors in its abortion law, there is a "judicial bypass" mandate. This allows the pregnant teenager to go to a judge, who will determine if she is mature enough to make this decision on her own. If the judge decides that she is, she can get an abortion. Of course, the counselor explains, this is a complicated and time-consuming process. The longer you wait, she tells you, the more complicated the abortion would be.

Your head is swimming. You never wanted to have sex in the first place. You were raped. And now your entire life seems in danger. What should you do?

Response

While no organization can give a definitive answer to this kind of dilemma, rabbis and counseling groups like Planned Parenthood and, in the vast number of cases, parents can provide a young woman with invaluable information and advice both on the option of having an abortion and options for avoiding an abortion. Organizations can help by ensuring that the legal right to choose is preserved and by providing safe clinics for abortions *if* the woman does not otherwise have access to medical services.

The UAHC passed a resolution at its General Assembly in 1981 supporting minors' access to reproductive health care and, in 1989, endorsed a resolution proposed by the Women of Reform Judaism that included this clause:

> [We] support minors' access to reproductive health services, including contraceptives and abortion, unrestricted by parental notification, parental permission, or court order requirements.

There are several reasons why most Jewish organizations believe that this is the responsible stand to take. First, laws that mandate parental consent do nothing to improve parent-child communication or to prevent sexual activity among teenagers. Second, they can create dangerous delays in the decision-making process. Although the risks to a pregnant woman having a legal abortion never even approach the risks of childbirth, after the first eight weeks of pregnancy the risk of major complications from abortion increases about 15 to 30 percent for each week of delay. A study in Minnesota indicated that the parental notification law increased the percentage of minors who obtain second-trimester abortions by 26.5 percent.

Tragically, there have been cases in which women who feel they cannot go to their parents actually resort to attempts at self-abortion or rely on back-alley practitioners who use unsafe methods. This has resulted in great physical harm to the mother, at times even death. Most young women do turn to their parents when they find they are pregnant. When else are they more in need of parental love, support, and guidance?

Although good communication benefits both parent and child, we believe that compassion must be shown toward those young women who come from families that fail to nurture, and even terrorize, their children. Therefore, the UAHC opposes all parental consent or notification laws, even with judicial bypass.

Abortion presents other grave dilemmas both for opponents and proponents. Opponents, claiming fidelity to the right to life for the unborn, often care little about ensuring a decent quality of life for these children either before or after birth. They often show scarce concern for children on such matters as prenatal nutrition and health care programs, Head Start, and childcare and job programs for parents. They have not distinguished themselves in passionate concern for "life" beyond the womb on such issues as capital punishment or gun control (the Catholic Church is an obvious exception in this regard). They frequently help to elect politicians who vote "right" on abortion no matter how wrong they may be on everything else.

Similarly, those who wage war against abortion also tend to fight measures to alleviate the abortion crisis: sex education, free birth control clinics, and the support services required by poor pregnant women. Certainly, all Americans who do not have moral objections to birth control, whether they are pro-choice or anti-choice, should agree that we have a moral obligation to do everything possible through the dissemination of birth control technology and education about birth control options to avoid putting women into the position where they need to choose whether or not to have an abortion. That would certainly seem to accord with the values of the Jewish tradition that suggest that abortion is the most morally problematic form of birth control.

On the other hand, some proponents, for their part, have created an environment in which abortion, regarded as a profound and grave personal decision by most women and men, is too often made into an amoral decision. Today there are 1.4 million abortions performed annually in the United States. Sometimes abortion is used as another form of birth control by people who are somehow casually confident that the first manifestations of human life can be disposed of at will. It is one thing to defend the right of free choice; it is another to make a moral good of abortion. As has been the case with every woman who has had to consider abortion, all of us must pause and reconsider the moral and human implications of this persistent and painful dilemma.

A Real Dilemma: Calls for Violence

Militant anti-abortion groups argue that abortion clinics are the equivalent of Nazi death camps and believe they have a moral and religious obligation to prevent women from getting abortions. In this effort, many militant groups see themselves as being involved in a war and are willing, as is expected in times of war, to take extreme action. This has included hurling their bodies in front of cars, blocking entrances to clinics, harassing doctors and nurses involved in abortion procedures, both at their offices and even at their homes, and frightening women with threatening shouts and pictures of bleeding fetuses. This has also included threats of violence, as well as murderous assaults on doctors and clinics.

In December of 1994, a young man named John Salvi, who described himself as very religious and devoutly Catholic, walked into two abortion clinics in Brookline, Massachusetts, and began shooting wildly. The receptionist at one clinic was killed and a patient was wounded and eventually died. And, at the end of a week filled with celebrations in honor of the twenty-fifth anniversary of the historic Supreme Court decision of *Roe* v. *Wade*, America received a tragic reminder that some people will stop at nothing to deny a woman the right to choose. On January 29, 1998, a bomb exploded in the New Woman All Women Health Care clinic in Birmingham, Alabama, killing a security guard and critically injuring a nurse.

The Salvi tragedy occurred following months of rhetoric from the so-called "pro-life" community advocating extreme measures to prevent abortions. In July of 1994, Father David C. Trosch, a Catholic priest from Alabama, mailed a letter to members of Congress predicting "mass killing of abortionists and their staff" and included a list of those who would be "terminated as vermin are terminated." The list included members of the American Civil Liberties Union, Planned Parenthood, and the National Organization for Women. *Harper's* magazine quoted from a book entitled *The Army of God*, a manual for anti-abortion activists that clearly called for violence, saying, "Whatever activities are undertaken—torching, bombing, thumb removal, etc.—carry on with reckless abandon." Clinics surveyed during this time reported an increase in death and bomb threats. Pro-violence advocates argue: if you really believe that these are children being killed in the womb, is not such violence against the perpetrators morally justified?

With the evidence that this rhetoric would lead to violence becoming quite obvious in a growing number of tragedies, the UAHC felt it was absolutely necessary to make a statement. What should it have said and what should our synagogues have done?

Response

The UAHC issued a statement in response to the Salvi tragedy, saying:

> Once again, we mourn today for the latest victims of an anti-life act of terrorism and extremism apparently fueled by violent and inciteful rhetoric come home to roost. Once again, two of God's children lie wounded for doing nothing more than following the moral dictates of their consciences. As we grieve and offer support to the survivors, as we pray for the speedy and complete recovery of the wounded, we also pray for this nation. For every drop of blood shed in violence against abortion providers bleeds not only from the victims themselves, but from the nation's proud history of liberty and tolerance. Every wound inflicted on abortion providers wounds as well the very freedom of conscience that protects us all—regardless of what we may think of abortion.
>
> We call upon every religious leader and all religious people, whether pro-choice or pro-life, to condemn this brutal act, to end the silence that condones, and even encourages, such murder. We condemn as vicious, ungodly, and unholy any and all who would justify murder and other acts of violence in the name of God. We demand that those irresponsible religious leaders who regularly call for such violence end such calls. We humans have shed far too much blood in God's name; the God of Peace, of Life, demands of us that we all work together to stop violence, not to incite it.

At the time this statement was issued, many synagogues recruited members to participate in ongoing volunteer watch programs at reproductive health clinics across the nation. The programs helped deter harassment of patients and personnel at clinics. So did tough legislation aimed at curbing such violence.

Death Penalty

In 1976, the Supreme Court, reversing a trend of decisions that virtually barred the death penalty, gave the green light to the states to resume capital punishment. By March 1998, 444 persons had been put to death and over 3,300 more were on death row awaiting execution. Studies show that those executed are disproportionately poor minority persons and that in cases of murder, it is the race of the *victim* more than the race of the *defendant* that affects juries: cases of whites slain by blacks elicit the death penalty far more often than those of blacks slain by blacks or whites by whites.

The many national Jewish organizations opposed to capital punishment were shocked by the results of a number of polls showing that as many as 74 percent of all Jews *oppose* abolishing the death penalty. Jews, traditionally regarded as particularly liberal and humanitarian, voting in favor of capital punishment! What was going on?

Jews were demanding tougher measures to crack down on drug-related shootings, violence in the schools, and muggings on the streets that increased for many years until the early 1990s and, despite declining rates, remain too high. Some measure of law and order on the streets of our cities and safety in our homes had to be restored.

It is not "illiberal" to demand an end to such savagery. Like others, Jews are no longer content to articulate theories that the criminal is the product of society's failures and that reconstructing society is the surest way to reduce crime. Life and property are in jeopardy now. Daily life has become too anxiety-provoking.

Exasperated by the failure of other solutions, even Jews are tempted by politicians who exploit these anxieties. Reinstitution of the death penalty has become the vote-getting response of many politicians pandering to the public cry for law and order.

In some elections, politicians compete for the "bloody shirt" honor of promising to subject more criminals more quickly to the death penalty than their opponents. In 1991, the Senate passed a bill by a 71-to-26 margin expanding the death penalty to include over fifty new federal crimes, half of which do not involve murder. This trend is exacerbated by a 1991 Supreme Court decision and by the Effective Death Penalty and Public Safety Act of 1996, both drastically limiting the right of appeal by those on death row. The increasing frequency of executions has desensitized us and disappears into the back pages of newspapers, but there is no evidence whatsoever that state-sanctioned killing reduces crime.

Capital Punishment in the Jewish Perspective

In Judaism, the religious justification for the death penalty is found in the Hebrew Scriptures ("an eye for an eye"), but evolving Jewish law came to disdain the death penalty.

In early Hebrew society, capital punishment was instituted for crimes that later generations considered trivial. But those later generations could not simply repeal the ancient laws of divine origin. They could, however, create conditions whereby enforcement of the law became impossible. According to Deuteronomy 21:18–20, for example, a "stubborn and rebellious son" could be turned over to the elders of the city, who had the power to sentence him to death by stoning. Despite this law, there is not a single case cited in all of rabbinic literature of a "rebellious son" being executed. That law, like most legislation pertaining to capital punishment, remained purely theoretical.

Only deliberate murder was punishable by death, and proof of culpability had to be nearly absolute. Intent to commit the murder, treacherous lying in wait, and the use of a deadly weapon had to be proven. The murderer had to be warned specifically by two separate individuals and verbally acknowledge to each that he or she understood the nature of the act and the severity of punishment—prior to committing the crime. To establish guilt, two witnesses were required to give identical testimony against the accused in the commission of the murder. Such impediments to capital punishment reflected the dominant rabbinical view.

The most famous talmudic exposition on the limits of capital punishment appears in *Mishnah Makkot* 1:10.

> A Sanhedrin that executes [a criminal] once in seven years is known as destructive. Rabbi Eleazar son of Azariah says: Once in seventy years. Rabbi Tarfon and Rabbi Akiva say: If we had been members of the Sanhedrin, no man would ever have been executed.

Rabbi Simeon son of Gamaliel says: They [Rabbi
Tarfon and Rabbi Akiva] would have been responsible
for the proliferation of murderers in Israel.

Both of the viewpoints represented by the *Mishnah* continued in the
Jewish tradition. While it is true that the procedural obstacles were
significant and that, in fact, the death penalty was never imposed
during the past eighteen hundred years, it is also true that rarely did
Jews live with the political autonomy that would have allowed them to
implement the death penalty. Further, some rabbis, over many
centuries, wrote positively about the theoretical appropriateness of the
death penalty—particularly in cases involving extreme offenses, such
as treason against the Jewish community by informing against Jews to
non-Jewish authorities. Most modern rabbinic writers from all the
streams of Judaism have, however, focused primarily on the anti-death
penalty strands of the tradition.

As campaigns mount to restore the death penalty, we must recall
that in its origin, capital punishment was conceived as revenge.
Modern advocates of this practice stress, as did the last line of the
talmudic passage, that capital punishment is a deterrent to other
murderers and capital offenders. This contention was already challenged in 1923 by Dr. George W. Hirchwey, a renowned penologist
who looked at this argument throughout history. One illustration sums
up his argument: "On June 21, 1877, ten men were hanged in
Pennsylvania for murderous conspiracy. The *New York Herald* predicted
the wholesome effect of the terrible lesson. 'We may be certain,' it said,
editorially, 'that the pitiless severity of the law will deter the most
wicked from anything like the imitation of these crimes.' Yet the night
after this large-scale execution, two of the witnesses at the trial of these
men had been murdered and within two weeks, five of the prosecutors
had met the same fate." Some deterrence!

Capital punishment by hanging was practiced in England up to the
eighteenth century and often became a public spectacle. There was no
evidence that the crime rate lessened. Pocketpicking became so prevalent among the audiences gathered to watch the public hangings of
pickpockets that these spectacles were suspended.

There seems little, if any, correlation between the severity of punishment and the rate of crime. Minnesota and Michigan were just as safe

as Iowa and Illinois, states that have outlawed capital punishment.

Most problematic morally, the possibility of judicial error cannot be overlooked. Our system of justice is fallible because human beings are fallible. In 1955, in New York, Louis Hoffner, who had been convicted of murder and had already served twelve years of a life sentence, was pardoned on the basis of new evidence that had become available. Such grievous errors occur. But what if Hoffner had been given death instead of life imprisonment? Since 1900, approximately 350 innocent people have been sentenced to death; of these, 23 were executed.

Some have argued that gas, electrocution, and lethal injection have made execution painless. Others reject this assertion and point out that even aside from the physical pain, the mental torture preceding supposed "painless death" is beyond calculation. Too often, executions have gone awry: occasional need for multiple jolts from the electric chair; taking over half an hour to find a vein for lethal injection; in one state, the same electric chair has twice caused the person in the chair to burst into flames. In addition, they point to the torment and stigma inflicted upon innocent relatives of the executed. But the most important concern is what capital punishment does to society itself: it brutalizes the human spirit and arrogates to society God's life-taking power.

Until 1979, when Florida executed John Spenkelink, capital punishment seemed to have been fading from American life. No person was executed in the United States between 1967 and 1973; every state awaited the Supreme Court's decision on the constitutionality of the death penalty. Finally, in 1972 the High Court determined that the unequal application of the death penalty, which is usually reserved for the poor and minority group members, did represent a violation of equal protection under the law and was unconstitutional. It left open the question of whether the death penalty itself is unconstitutional.

Today, as advocates of capital punishment push the death penalty as a quick-fix answer to mounting crime, many states have drawn up laws that appear to satisfy the Supreme Court's strictures. The debate will continue in every state and community unless, at some future time, the Supreme Court decides that the death penalty is unconstitutional. Meanwhile, the door is now open to widespread executions by the state in the vain hope that these macabre spectacles will somehow deter violence. At the same time, the Western World—including Israel— has rejected the death penalty as uncivilized.

GUN CONTROL

The statistics are staggering, mind-numbing. Every two years, more people are killed by handguns in the United States than the total number of Americans killed during the entire Vietnam conflict. In 1995, firearms claimed the lives of 35,957 people in the U.S. There were 15,835 firearm homicides, 18,503 suicides, and 1,225 unintentional fatal shootings (National Center for Health Statistics, 1997). Every day, 15 children nineteen years old and under are killed by gunfire.

A study conducted by the Harvard School of Public Health in 1993 showed that 53 percent of the public supports a ban on the sale of handguns, and 81 percent of the public supports the registration of all handguns. Yet the wishes of the majority for a sensible control of firearm sales have been stymied by the formidable lobbying effort led by the National Rifle Association (NRA) and various gun manufacturers.

The proliferation of guns in the hands of Americans, abetted by easy access and availability, has been cited as a major cause of the soaring crime rate that afflicted our country for several decades until the 1990s. Then why, in light of this harsh reality, has so little been done over the years to control the ownership of guns?

Rabbi Jerome K. Davidson, religious leader of Temple Beth El of Great Neck, New York, is one of many Americans who brought the following 1979 incident to the attention of the *New York Times* with his published letter:

> To the Editor: Brenda Spencer, a San Diego sixteen-year-old, last week momentarily diverted our attention from the big news made by strife in Iran and visitors from China. She did it by opening fire with a .22-caliber rifle on an elementary school, killing two and wounding nine, including children ranging in age from seven to twelve. "I don't like Mondays. This livens up the day. I just started shooting for the fun of it...."

There is no excuse whatsoever for a .22-caliber rifle, with five hundred rounds of ammunition, to have fallen into that girl's hands. She didn't steal it. It isn't a trophy someone brought home from the war. She received it for Christmas! Someone gave it to her as a present.

Such tragic occurrences are not rare. Who does not recall the college student who gunned down forty-five people, killing fourteen, from the top of a tower at the University of Texas? Have we already forgotten the mass killing in New Rochelle by an American Nazi whose apartment contained an entire arsenal? Have we pushed the ugly memory of the "Son of Sam" killings out of our minds? Or, in 1997, the young man who gunned down Christian classmates because he was offended that they engaged in voluntary prayer during their free time? Or the 1998 killing of five students and a teacher and the wounding of eleven others in a Jonesboro, Arkansas, public school by two boys, ages eleven and thirteen? The local TV evening news is replete with variations of these tragedies, day after day.

These shattering events reflect the unwillingness of Americans to admit to the real danger that the private possession of guns represents to our very lives. Over 211 million firearms manufactured in the United States each year, of which 70 million are privately owned handguns. That is approximately one gun for each adult and half of the children in America. By the year 2003, firearm fatalities are expected to become the United States' leading cause of injury-related death. But it is evidently not enough to cause the American people to override the influence of the National Rifle Association and demand the enactment of effective controls.

It has already been said, "With all the violence and the murders and the killings we have in the United States…we must keep firearms from people who have no business with guns." Yet we do not heed the words despite the dramatic fact that they were spoken by Robert F. Kennedy five days before his assassination.

A few weeks after Rabbi Davidson wrote his letter to the *Times* demanding gun control, the gun lobby bought paid advertisements in several Long Island newspapers that consisted of an open letter signed by another rabbi. It read, in part:

> …The solution to the problem of violent crime cannot possibly be found in any panacea like gun control (prohibition) legislation.
>
> Firearms have often been the only hope of oppressed

and persecuted peoples. With but ten pistols, the Jews in the Warsaw Ghetto chased out the mechanized Nazi German war machine and forced the German army into house-by-house combat and the burning down of that ghetto in order to conquer it. Later in Budapest in 1944, the Nazis realized that they could not then afford a repetition of the Warsaw uprising.

For that reason they waited in their extermination of the Jewish community of Hungary until they were able to enlist the cooperation of the Hungarian Jewish leadership. This the Nazis were unfortunately able to do, to reassure the Jews and persuade them to go quietly to their extermination by keeping the horrible destination a secret. The Nazis perceived that armed resistance by even a handful of pistol-toting Jews in Budapest would necessitate house-to-house combat with troops they could not then afford.

Historically, Jews and other minorities have much to fear from gun control laws—laws that have been selectively enforced, inevitably against ethnic, religious, and political minorities all over the world. Therefore, any additional legislation on this subject must be approached with great reservations.

So the issue was joined. Which rabbi is most in accord with Jewish values? Would the possession of guns by Jews in Germany and Hungary really have prevented the Holocaust from taking place? Is gun control good or bad for the Jews?

HANDGUN CONTROL LEGISLATION

A background paper on firearms legislation, prepared for the Commission on Social Action of Reform Judaism, will help to clarify this issue:

What are the arguments of the opponents of firearms control legislation?

1. They maintain that the right "to keep and bear arms," guaranteed in the Second Amendment to the Constitution, would be violated by such legislation.
2. They are afraid that gun control laws would hurt the responsible sportsperson who uses guns for hunting and marksmanship.
3. They claim that the legislation would not lower crime rates, as criminals would still be able to obtain firearms illegally.

These arguments are unfounded.

1. The Second Amendment states: "A well-regulated militia being necessary to the security of a free state, the right of the people to keep and bear arms shall not be infringed." This obviously was written in order to guarantee each state a militia, and the Supreme Court has stated many times, in upholding the constitutionality of gun control laws, that it does not apply to individual citizens bearing arms. In 1939, in *United States* v. *Miller*, the Court held that "the Second Amendment applies only to those arms that have a reasonable relationship to the preservation of efficiency of a well-regulated militia." Furthermore, the courts have established that rights given by the Constitution are not absolute and have recognized the government's power to limit such rights in the face of compelling interests of the general welfare and domestic tranquillity. The right to bear arms must be subordinated to the right to life. There may be a legal right to own an automobile, but the automobile must still be registered and anyone who wants to drive it must be licensed, and its use must be regulated.

2. Sensible gun control legislation would not in any way interfere with the legitimate use of guns by the responsible hunter or marksperson. In nations with strict firearms laws, hunting still thrives. After the enactment of the laws controlling the purchase of guns in many states, the sale of hunting licenses increased. Legislative measures that would help eliminate the irresponsible firearms owners and set standards of competence for firearms usage, indeed, is likely to increase the prestige, and certainly the safety, of gun sports. The purpose of gun control legislation is not to prevent legitimate ownership of firearms but to keep such arms from those

who would misuse them. Furthermore, over the last few years, much gun control legislation has been aimed at stopping the proliferation of automatic weapons.

3. No one claims that gun control legislation is the neat and total solution to violence and crime. But the fact is that it does cut down both the incidence of crimes in which guns are involved and the general rate of violent crimes. In states with strong firearms laws, the percentage of homicides in which guns are used is significantly lower than in states without such laws. A comparison of our country with other nations that have stringent gun control is extremely revealing. In 1994, there were 72 firearm homicides in Great Britain, 76 in Spain, 176 in Canada, 96 in Australia, and 15,835 in the United States. Why is there such a discrepancy? One reason is that in several European countries, handguns and assault weapons are virtually banned from the general public. For example, as of July 1, 1997, all large-caliber handguns were banned in Britain.

What Rabbi Davidson could have only imagined in 1979—that the American public would stand up to the powerful NRA lobby—finally took place in the early 1990s. The NRA's opposition to legislation barring so-called cop-killer bullets actually cost them the support of law enforcement agencies. The NRA's opposition to legislation banning even assault weapons caused a severe backlash in public opinion.

The rabbi opposing gun control is right about one issue: violence in our cities and on our streets will not be solved by gun control legislation alone. Such legislation is a "necessary" component of the solution but not a panacea. The causes of violence are complex and therefore effective responses must be, too. But such responses can work. A coordination of tough gun control laws, strengthened police forces, "community" policing aimed at preventing crime rather than solving it after it happens, reducing the romanticism of guns, and breaking up gangs all have combined in recent years to contribute to a drop in violent crime in most larger cities (smaller cities have experienced increased drug- and gang-related violence). In Boston, for example, as opposed to approximately 70 youths gunned down by their peers between 1993 and 1995, a concerted attack on gun violence resulted in there being no teenagers shot to death from July 1995 through April

1998. That success has to do with the city's new approach to juvenile crime, making police officers and district attorneys act more like worried parents. They don't just wait for a crime to happen before dealing with a troubled youth; they actively seek out children who seem bound for trouble down the road. This program also includes a significant community and church involvement: the boys and girls clubs and school gymnasiums are open later at night, and local businesses have opened jobs for teenagers to make better use of free time. Those who don't comply with the rules face harsh treatments, such as a year in jail for illegally possessing a gun and two years for selling drugs near a school. Police officers walk through neighborhoods, keeping an eye on those who act suspiciously, and greater resources are given to the probation department to allow for more frequent checks on their parolees, with strict enforcement of parolee curfew.

THE "BRADY BILL"

In 1991, both houses of the U.S. Congress approved the "Brady Bill," handing the gun lobby a major defeat, although that lobby was able to block enactment of the law until February of 1994.

The history of the "Brady Bill" illustrates the tragedy of our failure to have enacted gun control legislation earlier. On March 30, 1981, when John Hinckley, Jr., attempted to assassinate President Ronald Reagan, he shot and forever changed the life of the president's press secretary, James Brady.

Today, Mr. Brady is permanently brain-damaged and partly paralyzed—doctors say that he will never walk again. After the shooting, Sarah Brady, his wife, courageously led the fight in lobbying for legislation, named after her husband, which imposed a national five-day waiting period before the purchase of a handgun. The intent is to give people who seek to buy a gun in a moment of anger time to cool off, as well as to provide time for local law enforcement to check if the prospective purchaser has a criminal record or is mentally ill. In 1997, the Supreme Court upheld the five-day waiting period but reserved to the states the decisions about background checks.

After former President Ronald Reagan himself, reversing his oft-repeated position against gun control, declared his support of the "Brady Bill," the measure was finally approved and signed.

In recognition of their heroic leadership in support of this legislation and their ability to overcome personal adversity to mobilize the public conscience, the UAHC bestowed upon Jim and Sarah Brady the Maurice N. Eisendrath "Bearer of Light" Award at its 1991 Biennial convention in Baltimore, Maryland.

AIDS

Another issue of life and death, which emerged less than two decades ago—acquired immunodeficiency syndrome (AIDS)—has already afflicted more people in the United States and throughout the world than have all of America's wars. AIDS is not a disease but a combination of several diseases that result when a person's immune system is gravely compromised. The impairment of the immune system is caused by a virus called the human immunodeficiency virus (HIV). The virus is transmitted through an exchange of bodily fluids, almost always by unprotected sexual relations, by sharing needles used by drug addicts, or by receiving contaminated blood accidentally in a transfusion (something that is *extraordinarily* rare in developed countries). On average, it takes five years (if the patient is untreated) to thirteen years or more (if aggressively treated) for HIV to progress to full-blown AIDS. There is, at this point, no "cure" for AIDS, but we are approaching the point at which aggressive treatment may prevent HIV from progressing to AIDS at all.

As of June 1997, eighteen years after it took root here, AIDS had claimed the lives of more than 362,000 people in the United States. In recent years, the fastest-growing group of people developing AIDS have been young women between the ages of eighteen and forty-four, and AIDS is the leading cause of death for African-Americans and Latinos twenty-five to forty-four years old. The Centers for Disease Control and Prevention estimate that about 40,000 to 60,000 Americans become newly infected with HIV each year. Since the beginning of the AIDS epidemic, between 650,000 and 900,000 Americans have been infected and are currently living with the virus.

Only in the past few years have medical scientists devised therapies, utilizing combinations of very expensive drugs, or "cocktails," that are proving to be successful in controlling, but not curing, HIV and AIDS. In 1997, the Centers for Disease Control and Prevention announced a

19 percent decline in total U.S. AIDS deaths, but the number of those living with AIDS continues to increase, with estimates of more than 239,000 people with full-blown AIDS. The new "cocktail therapies" raise poignant dilemmas about who can afford to purchase the drugs and who cannot. Those who can afford the new therapies, which average $15,000 per year, will have the capacity to add several years to their lives.

This raises particularly tragic dilemmas in other areas of the world, where funding and resources for HIV prevention and AIDS treatment are even more limited. The numbers of new HIV infections are occurring at an astronomical rate in the developing world, particularly Africa, India, China, and Southeast Asia. In sub-Saharan Africa, there are currently 14 million HIV-infected adults, which is approximately 63 percent of the world's total number of people infected. Even though the rate of HIV infections is decreasing in the United States, it is increasing in nearly every other place in the world, and those that bear the worst of this epidemic are the poorest countries, which can scarcely afford clean water and food, let alone expensive "cocktail" therapies.

For a generation of young people raised in the age of AIDS, it is difficult to comprehend the hysteria that swept America and the world when the epidemic first surfaced. In the early years, AIDS killed almost everyone who contracted it. While it was known to be contracted by contact with blood and bodily fluids, no one was certain whether more casual contact could spread the virus. Further, it emanated originally in the gay community and the drug addict community (among those sharing needles) and was looked upon by many as deserved punishment and a further reason to shun and resent people whom they denigrated to begin with—like the lepers of old.

The public response to AIDS was transformed overnight when Magic Johnson, the basketball superstar, told a stunned world that he was infected with the human immunodeficiency virus that causes AIDS. In an instant, for millions of people, the AIDS crisis was moved from the margins of public attention to the center of public concern.

The national habit of denial—"this is not my problem; it is a problem for gay men and drug users"—was challenged in an extraordinary moment of truth. Magic's courage and honesty illuminated one of America's most urgent and misunderstood problems.

That everybody is at risk from AIDS, that only abstinence and safe sex can begin to curb the escalating horror of AIDS, that sexual activity can be lethal, that much larger public funding is needed—all these truths came forward like a full court press when this gallant and smiling superhero addressed the American people. The Johnson story is a vivid reminder of the limitless power of one individual to make a difference in the world.

A Real Dilemma: Condoms at Kutz Camp

The UAHC/CCAR Joint Committee on AIDS was asked to take a stand regarding a proposal to combat AIDS by distributing condoms at all Reform Jewish camps in which teenagers, as campers or staff, participate. There are strong feelings on both sides of the issue.

The proponents of distribution argue that AIDS and other sexually transmitted diseases pose a serious risk to sexually active young people. To deny that our teenagers are sexually active is naive. As Jewish educators, we have a responsibility to educate our young people so that they can take the necessary precautions to prevent the transmission of HIV/AIDS. The distribution of condoms would take place only in the context of discussions of Jewish sexual ethics and responsible behavior.

Others argue that the distribution of condoms implies approval of sexual license at camp and youth group activities. Parents might not send their children to a summer camp that distributes condoms. It might be perceived that the camps are even encouraging sexual promiscuity.

What should the committee have recommended?

Response

The UAHC/CCAR Joint Committee on AIDS was split on the issue. Programs on sexual ethics and AIDS remain part of the youth movement's educational activity, but the provision of condoms is prohibited.

In 1998, the respected RAND Corporation, one of the nation's premier research institutes, came out with a comprehensive study of Los Angeles teenagers showing that providing condoms to high school students had no impact on sexual activity. The RAND study showed that before the program began, 55.8 percent of males and 45.4 percent of females reported having had sexual intercourse. A year later, after the distribution of condoms in classrooms, it was 55 percent of males and 46.1 percent of females. On the flip side, condom use for those who were already engaged in sexual activity the previous year jumped from 37 percent to 50 percent for males and 27 percent to 32 percent for females.

The Reform Jewish movement, partly upon the plea of its gay and lesbian congregants, has responded strongly to the AIDS crisis. Reform Judaism was the first national Jewish body to confront the challenge of AIDS. Its high-level commission of doctors, scientists, caregivers, and activists on the UAHC HIV/AIDS Committee serves as a resource for the movement and a conscience to the Jewish community. The Commission on Social Action presses for greater public funding; shapes UAHC policy; opposes discrimination against PLWAs (people living with AIDS); and trains rabbis and others in counseling AIDS patients. A panel honoring Jews who died from AIDS was unveiled at the 1989 UAHC Biennial convention and was added to the Names Project's AIDS Quilt. The quilt is a memorial to those who have died from AIDS, and, tragically, it has continued to grow over the years. It is now so big that it can no longer be displayed in its entirety; it has even outgrown the Mall in Washington, D.C.

The Jewish values that drive this concern—*pikuach nefesh* (the "saving of lives") and *bikkur cholim* (the *mitzvah* of "visiting the sick")—resonate eloquently in one of the earliest sermons given on this issue (1985) by Rabbi Robert Kirschner, then at Temple Emanu-El, San Francisco, California. The sermon, given at a time when hysteria about AIDS was at its highest, led to the establishment of an AIDS relief fund in the congregation, which has raised a significant amount of money for AIDS service agencies. It was republished by the UAHC and sent throughout the nation. The excerpt below captures the mood of the time and reflects the influence that rabbis, using the power of the pulpit, can have in raising social consciousness. They raise fascinating questions of how Jews should resolve situations in which Jewish values seem to conflict with specific biblical or later rabbinic writings.

Usually, when a rabbi quotes his ancient predecessors, he does so with approval, even reverence. Our sages of blessed memory were remarkably wise and perceptive, noble and compassionate. But not always. I quote from an ancient *midrash* on the thirteenth chapter of Leviticus, dealing with the subject of leprosy. The sages are discussing what they do when they see a leper. R. Yochanan says: I go no closer to a leper than four cubits. R. Shimon says: If the wind is blowing, I go no closer than one hundred cubits. R. Amnu and R. Assai say: We do not even go near a place where lepers are known to live. R. Eleazar b. Shimon was still afraid: If he heard that a leper was in the vicinity, he would hide. Then there was the great sage Resh Lakish: When he saw a leper, he would throw stones at him shouting: "Stop contaminating us and go back where you came from!" (*Leviticus Rabbah* 16:3)

I am not proud of this passage. I quote it now because I think it has something to teach us on Yom Kippur, when we ask forgiveness for our sins. Scholars have shown (*Encyclopaedia Judaica* 11:38) that by the time this passage was written, the segregation of lepers enjoined by the Bible was no longer required. In a case where a rabbi himself came down with leprosy, the decision was handed down that he could enter the synagogue together with everyone else.

No, the hostility of our passage does not arise merely from the fear of contagion. After all, to avoid a leper is one thing; to throw stones at him is another. In rabbinic literature, lepers are accused of everything from murder to incest, idolatry to robbery, perjury to blasphemy to slander. In the days of our sages, to be a leper was not only to be afflicted with a disease but to be despised for it. It was not only to die a terrible death but to be accused of deserving it.

Today, leprosy is called Hansen's disease, and those who suffer from it may walk among us without fear. No longer must they bear—as if their illness were not enough—the crushing weight of anathema. But now there is a new multitude of sufferers to fear and to shun. Theirs is the new dread affliction, the new mark of doom: AIDS.

The condition now known as AIDS, acquired immunodeficiency syndrome, was first recognized in 1981. Patients with AIDS have developed a severe loss of their natural immunity to disease, leaving them vulnerable to lethal infections and cancers. To date, no treatment has been able to restore the immune system of an AIDS patient to normal function.

Like the ancient rabbis, we prefer to keep our distance from the victims of this illness. Like them, we are afraid of catching it. But according to the medical experts, those outside the high-risk groups are highly unlikely to do so.

Only 1 percent of all reported cases involve a transfusion recipient or a child born with the mother's infection. Of over 13,000 cases nationwide, not one has been attributed to casual contact with AIDS patients. Of those caregivers who are constantly exposed to AIDS and frequently tested for it—doctors, nurses, hospital workers, family members—few outside the high-risk groups have caught it and those only after exposure to the blood of a carrier.

Yet, despite the evidence, we are still afraid. Not enough is yet known about AIDS. The fear of contagion is itself contagious and likely to persist. It explains, in part, why we stay away from people with AIDS. But, as in the case of the ancient lepers, it does not explain it all. Our aversion, too, goes beyond the fear of infection. We shrink from people with AIDS not only because they are sick but because we don't like how they got sick. When it comes to homosexuals and drug addicts, our sympathy for their affliction is diluted by the suspicion that they deserve it. Like the ancient leper, the AIDS patient suffers not only the torment of illness but the stigma of it. The patient's life and now death are alike regarded as a kind of disgrace.

Tomorrow afternoon, traditional Jews around the world will read the eighteenth chapter of Leviticus. This is where male homosexual sex is described as an abomination (18:22) punishable by death. (20:13) But Reform Judaism departs from the Torah on occasion. We do not stone adulterers; we do not ostracize children of forbidden marriages; we do not sprinkle lepers with blood. Such biblical legislation, we believe, is the work not of divine but of mortal and fallible hands, and we consign it to the antiquity from which it came.

The divine content of the Torah, we believe, is found in its transcendent vision of justice, peace, and compassion. The God we revere is the One who, as R. Akiva taught (*Mishnah Avot* 3:18), creates each of us because He loves us, who, as the *Mishnah* says (Babylonian Talmud, *Sanhedrin* 4:5), considers each life to be worth the life of the whole world. The God we revere is the One who, as the Torah itself insists, sides not with the mighty but with the forlorn, who hears the cry of the helpless and defends the defenseless. (Exodus 22:21ff.) The God we revere is the One who loved us when we were the unwanted, the unwelcome, the exiled, and the outcast. A belief in this God, to my way of thinking, simply cannot be reconciled with a judgment of anathema upon homosexuals, or lepers, or any other of God's children. "Blessed are You, O Eternal One," says our prayer book, "who has made me according to God's will."

Each of us, in our unique being, is the work of God's hands and the bearer of God's image; each of us—even someone with AIDS...

...A friend of mine, Father Michael Lopes, told me something that happened on a visit to ward 5B at San Francisco General Hospital. This is where the most desperately ill AIDS patients are treated and comforted before they die. Father Lopes walked into one of the rooms on the ward. The blinds were closed; only a little shaft of light penetrated the darkness. The patient lay in bed in agony. His entire body was covered with purple lesions of the cancer called Kaposi's sarcoma. His face was terribly swollen and disfigured and his mouth was infected with fungus. So appalled was Father Lopes that he could hardly bring himself to come near. But just then, the patient turned in his bed, and the little shaft of light came to rest on his eyes— bright blue eyes, clouded with pain but now suddenly filled with gratitude at the sight of his visitor. Looking into those eyes, Father Lopes said he remembered that beneath the mass of lesions was a person, a human being, hurting so badly that the mere presence of a visitor was a benediction.

My friends, surely as God is in heaven so is God with the patients on ward 5B. As surely as God's light shines above this ark, it shines above their beds. But God has no other hands than ours. (Dorothee Soelle, *Suffering* [Fortress, 1975], pp. 149, 174) If the sick are to be healed, it is our hands, not God's, that will heal them. If the lonely and frightened are to be comforted, it is our embrace, not God's, that will comfort them. The warmth of the sun travels on the air, but the warmth of God's love can travel only through each one of us....

...I return this time with great pride to the teaching of our ancient sages. "Where," they asked, "shall we look for the Messiah? Shall the Messiah come to us on clouds of glory, robed in majesty, and crowned with light?" The Talmud (Babylonian Talmud, *Sanhedrin* 98a) reports that R. Joshua b. Levi put this question to no less an authority than the prophet Elijah himself.

"Where," R. Joshua asked, "shall I find the Messiah?" "At the gate of the city," Elijah replied. "How shall I recognize him?" "He sits among the lepers." "Among the lepers!" cried R. Joshua. "What is he doing there?" "He changes their bandages," Elijah answered. "He changes them one by one."

> That may not seem like much for a Messiah to be
> doing. But apparently, in the eyes of God, it is a mighty
> thing indeed.

Given not so many years ago, in a city known for its tolerance, this sermon captures the fears and prejudices of the time, dramatizing how profoundly American attitudes about AIDS as well as about gays and lesbians have changed. It illustrates as well the approach to Jewish social justice delineated in chapter 1, an approach that can allow Jewish values to live and thrive in today's political and moral reality.

SUBSTANCE ABUSE

At least 12.8 million Americans currently use illicit drugs. More than 48 percent of high school graduates and 21 percent of eighth-graders have tried an illicit drug. In the United States, about 500,000 individuals use crack cocaine; and each week around 2 million use powder cocaine. In addition, 500,000 people are addicted to heroin (National Institute on Drug Abuse–National Household Survey 1995).

Our nation's drug policy is impotent at best. Some 50 percent of the federal drug-control budget is spent on law enforcement, border interdiction, and international antinarcotics activities. Only 30 percent is spent on prevention and treatment. As a result, as many as 6 million Americans in need of drug treatment are unable to receive proper treatment and rehabilitation care.

The age at which young people begin experimentation with beer, wine, and alcohol has dropped sharply. While the abuse of drugs has diminished slowly over the past few years, individual lives are distorted and sometimes wrecked by alcohol abuse, and legions of families are torn asunder by the spiraling conflicts set in motion by this abuse. The challenge of growing up in America is to ignore media hype and the seduction of advertising and to develop a lifestyle that is healthy and positive.

Of course, it is naive to expect slogans like "Just Say No" to make a real difference alone. But in a culture that is permeated with reliance on drugs (from Valium to aspirin) and that suggests in its advertising that whatever feels good must be morally OK, it is necessary to take charge of one's own life at an early age—and choose life! That applies to the choices we make about our own bodies—including those concerning drugs, alcohol, sex, and tobacco.

A Real Dilemma: Using the Synagogue for Alcoholics Anonymous Meetings

An Alcoholics Anonymous group asks permission to utilize the facilities of the synagogue. The proposal is submitted to the board. Some board members urge that the group be admitted just as other outside groups are able to use the synagogue facilities. One member of the board says this will look bad for the synagogue, their presence will "detract from the dignity of the institution," and, besides, very few Jews are alcoholics.

You are a member of the board. What do you say?

Response

Many synagogues welcome Alcoholics Anonymous and Narcotics Anonymous groups. Jewish alcoholism rates are only slightly lower than those of the general society, and participants in both groups include Jews. The presence of such groups in synagogues affirms the concept that the synagogue is an accepting and relevant institution to help members of the larger community, both Jews and non-Jews, receive the kind of support they need to overcome their addictions. Over the past few years, substance abuse programs with a more distinctive Jewish character have developed, making it even more comfortable for Jews to become involved in such programs. In 1992, the New York Division of Substance Abuse and Alcholism took a random sampling of 6,000 households and found the same incidence of addiction among Jews and non-Jews; both had rates of 12 percent. When Rutgers University asked the religion of the people who called into their cocaine hot line, they found that 18 percent of the callers were Jewish.

SMOKING

Most Americans agree that the problem of drug addiction is one of the most serious confronting the country today. Nevertheless, when people speak of drugs, they usually fail to mention or even recognize one of America's deadliest drugs. Tobacco is directly responsible for, or is a contributing factor in, the deaths of an estimated 419,000 Americans annually. *More Americans are killed by smoking than by all other illicit drugs, AIDS, alcohol, automobile accidents, homicides, and suicides combined!* Though still generally accepted in society, cigarettes represent, according to former Surgeon General C. Everett Koop, "the most lethal and addictive drug known."

Such societal acceptance has allowed the tobacco industry to flourish. In the process, it has established itself as a multibillion-dollar industry that will not easily disappear, regardless of the harm it leaves in its wake. Each year, the tobacco industry spends in excess of $6 billion on cigarette advertising and promotion. For the welfare of the tobacco industry, this is money well invested, as indicated by the annual sale of 30 billion packs of cigarettes. As for the nation's welfare, smoking contributes to medical bills and lost work hours, costing the country an estimated $60 billion annually.

When one pictures the average smoker, it is rarely the face of a young child that comes to mind. Yet approximately 4.5 million children under the age of eighteen smoke cigarettes or use smokeless tobacco in the United States. Every day almost 3,000 more children become regular smokers, a statistic achieved in large part by the influence of tobacco industry advertising aimed at children. Until its demise in 1997, over 90 percent of six-year-olds could identify Joe Camel, a tobacco industry cartoon character, as a symbol of smoking. Particular concern needs to be directed at children. If children do not smoke by age eighteen, then they are nine times less likely to smoke in adulthood.

More than any president who preceded him, President Clinton, during his time in office, has taken drastic steps to reduce the appeal and access of cigarettes to children. He gave the Food and Drug Administration (FDA) the power to limit advertising access of tobacco companies and has launched a mass media program aimed at educating the young about the risks of smoking. While these measures will help and may have long-term effects on smoking rates, it is only in conjunction with members and leaders of the community that such change will truly come about.

JUDAISM AND SMOKING

Cigarette smoking endangers not only the life of the smoker but also those who come into contact with the smoker, including children.

Still, there are those who say, "When I smoke, the only life I endanger is my own." Even if it were true that smoking causes no harm to others, it would still be difficult to reconcile with Jewish law. The *halachah* reflects a value system in which the intrinsic worth and preservation of human life is of paramount importance. Thus it is forbidden to harm any human being including oneself.

The Union of American Hebrew Congregations has taken a strong stance against smoking, banning the use of tobacco products in all its buildings. Many UAHC congregations have prohibited smoking in their facilities. In addition, congregations like Beth Israel of Hartford, Connecticut, have resolved not to invest in tobacco companies. (See the discussion "Socially Responsible Investment" in chapter 4, "The Elusive Search for Economic Justice in the World's Wealthiest Nation.")

In taking a long and hard look at the issue of smoking, the UAHC adopted the following resolution intended to bar smoking at its meetings, to mandate an educational campaign to raise the consciousness of Reform Jews on this issue, and to call upon its Religious Action Center to lobby against subsidizing the tobacco industry:

> In our time, cigarette smoking is the single most preventable cause of death and disease. Each year over 300,000 Americans and 75,000 Canadians die from causes associated with the use of tobacco. The American Cancer Society and the Surgeon General of the United States concur: smoking one or two packs of cigarettes a day decreases a smoker's life expectancy by at least six to eight years.
>
> Nonsmokers are also put in danger by the smokers around them. Indirect smoking...can cause disease, including lung cancer in healthy nonsmokers. Infants

and children exposed to tobacco smoke have increased respiratory infections and specific changes in lung function. The simple separation of smokers and nonsmokers in the same airspace does not decrease the hazards to nonsmokers.

Therefore be it resolved that the Union of American Hebrew Congregations

1. Ban smoking entirely at all its meetings, functions, and workplaces, and urge its affiliates and congregations to do likewise;
2. Establish educational programs that discourage the use of smoking and nonsmoking tobacco products and make those programs available to its congregations for use in their religious schools and youth group programs;
3. Support enactment of legislation to protect nonsmokers in public areas and workplaces;
4. Urge the United States and Canadian governments to phase out subsidies to the tobacco industry with steps taken to cushion adverse economic impact;
5. Urge parents who smoke to refrain from smoking when they are with or around their children.

The last item (5) was an amendment successfully proposed on the floor by the teenage delegates of the North American Federation of Temple Youth.

A Real Dilemma: Should Owners of Tobacco Companies Be Leaders of Jewish Organizations?

In 1990, a prominent and respected social activist came to the Religious Action Center (the Reform movement's social justice advocacy office in the nation's capital) with a generous but most unusual offer: he would contribute over $100,000 as an endowment fund to support the work of the center, provided that its leadership would agree never to allow as its chair, and never to honor in its events, any person who was an officer of a tobacco company. The first reaction was shock, mixed with irritation.

How dare he put such strings on his gift! What right did he have to dictate to an organization who its leaders should or should not be? And what kind of cockamamie condition was this man trying to impose? Why smoking? Why not also alcohol, adultery, income tax fraud, drugs, or any other on a long laundry list of personal and social sins?

Not so fast. The contributor explained the thinking behind his offer. Smoking is a *unique* problem, he argued. The tobacco industry is *sui generis* ("in a class by itself"). It is the only legal industry whose products are almost always addictive; smoking cannot be used safely and kills millions. (Furthermore, recent revelations indicate that the tobacco industry intentionally hid information about how addictive and dangerous the product was, even while targeting children in its advertisements.)

Recent statistics show that smoking is related to over 400,000 deaths in the United States each year. The number of deaths and disabilities that are connected to smoking throughout the world makes this a larger death industry than war itself.

Is it not a sad moral contradiction that the smoking industry is legal? As Jews, given our commitments to life and health, should we not, at the very least, withhold our moral sanction from those who profit from tempting the unknowing into a habit that leads only to death and tragedy? Jews should be in the forefront of efforts to end smoking, but at the very least we should not put our endorsement on this social evil by honoring its leaders. In any case, doesn't the donor have a right to insist that before his name is attached to an endowment to the center, he be ensured that it will not be associated with people involved in an industry he believes to be anathema to the values of Judaism?

What would you have decided if you were a commission member and had to vote whether to accept this gift? Should it matter whether this stipulation might be imposed on a Jewish social justice organization or an agency that deals with health and welfare issues directly affected by the tobacco industry, as opposed, for example, to a Jewish pro-Israel, educational, or defense (i.e., fights anti-Semitism) agency where these issues are less directly relevant?

Response

The Commission on Social Action rejected the offer not because it disagreed on the evil of smoking, but because it felt it wrong to address such issues in the context of a donor imposing such strings on a *gift* to the Religious Action Center. We wanted to avoid even the appearance of being "bought." Further, some members felt that as long as tobacco was lawful, the tobacco official's other good deeds should be weighed into the decision. Each case needed to be evaluated individually; no categorical limitation was appropriate. The donor, while disappointed with this decision, accepted it and has since contributed smaller amounts to specific programs of the center but did not proceed with the named endowment.

Similar questions have arisen in recent years over whether officers or principal stockholders of tobacco companies or their holding companies (many of whom are Jewish) should be allowed to head major local or Jewish organizations. What do you think? Does it make a difference whether the organization is one that deals directly with health issues or social justice issues as opposed to other less related issues—for example, Jewish education or the rescue of endangered Jewry?

··· 3 ···

Bioethics: Thinking the Unthinkable

THE IMPACT OF MODERN TECHNOLOGY

Several factors make the ethical challenges posed by modern technology the most formidable humanity has ever faced. Above all is the tremendous pace of technological advance. Because of this rapid pace in recent decades, it is no exaggeration to say that there has been as much change during our grandparents' lifetime as there had been during the entire previous history of civilization: transportation has been transformed by the jumbo jet plane; entertainment by VCRs; business by the computer and the fax; and the global community by the introduction of the Internet and the World Wide Web—all within the life span of most of our high school students. In a generation that has learned to split the atom, crack the genetic code, and pierce the veil of outer space, the question no longer seems to be "What can we do?" but "What *should* we do?" And this is, essentially, a moral question about which the Jewish tradition has much to say.

Our moral dilemmas are further exacerbated by the fact that each new invention, developed to solve a specific problem, tends to produce a series of new problems for which other innovations are needed. The result is a geometric expansion of technological development. In contrast, ethical thought, the development by society of humanistic or religious values, is a relatively glacial process. As a result, we face the central dilemma of our era: by the time society has realized the deepest implications of the technological innovation and sets for itself the task of formulating an ethical response, the innovation may already be firmly entrenched or even obsolete.

JEWISH ETHICS

In its biblical and rabbinic periods, Judaism never developed a systematic theory of ethics. Where Aristotle writes in the realm of abstractions, the prophets, the most authentic spokespersons for Jewish ethical ideals, speak about such mundane categories as widows, orphans, and the poor. When Jewish expression did give rise to a more abstract formulation, it produced not a coherently reasoned theory but a pithy sentence that condensed everything to a few short words: "It has been told to you...what is good, and what God requires of you: Only to do justly, to love mercy, and to walk humbly with your God" (Micah 6:8) or "The world is founded upon three things: upon truth, upon justice, and upon peace." (*Pirke Avot* 1:18)

Nevertheless, fundamental principles can be derived from the sacred Jewish literature of these periods, principles that speak to the issues of technological and biological ethics: human freedom, the infinite dignity of the human being, the supreme importance of human life.

MEDICAL ETHICS

In the Jewish view, God allows human beings to be partners in creating a better world and has given us the freedom of choice to do so.

We are expected to use our God-given wisdom to help create a better world. The philosopher-physician Maimonides in essence wrote: "God created food and water; we must use them in staving off hunger and thirst. God created drugs and compounds and gave us the intelligence necessary to discover their medicinal properties; we must use them in warding off illness and disease." (Maimonides' commentary to *Mishnah Pesachim* 4:9) But to what lengths must a doctor go to save a life (*pikuach nefesh*)? And how does Judaism's regard for the sanctity of life guide us in weighing the extraordinary financial costs involved in providing end-of-life care to relatively few people against what the same billions of dollars might provide in expanding primary and preventive health care to the millions of Americans who currently lack access to decent care?

Organ Transplants

Although the rabbis of the Talmud could not have imagined the transplantation of human organs, there seems little doubt that the Jewish commitment to the preservation of life would generally have approved such an advance in healing the sick. In analyzing the issue of organ transplants, the Jewish tradition brings to bear certain considerations that are distinctive from our modern secular perspective. Foremost among them is the assertion that each of us is made in the image of God and that our bodies, having been created by God, are not ours to do with as we please. From this principle we derive such varied prohibitions as substance abuse, asceticism, and suicide.

Even in death, we must treat the body as God's creation. This justifies the requirements for the immediate burial of corpses and the prohibition against desecrating a corpse. Nor are we permitted to derive economic benefit from a corpse. No body parts may be extracted and sold, not even hair for wigs.

On the other hand, almost any law may be broken to save a life. This commitment to *pikuach nefesh* would seem to justify one's voluntary decision to donate an organ if it can be done at a minimum risk to the donor, and it would seem to condone the removal of organs after death for the purpose of transplantation. Thus Orthodox scholars permitted cornea transplants, the first transplant perfected by medical science. The application of *pikuach nefesh* to the question of transplants is, however, limited in Jewish law by two other concepts: *holeh lefananu* (to justify transplants "we must have a sick person before us," i.e., someone for whom *emergency* treatment is needed) and *refu'ah bedukah* (the procedure must offer a good chance for success).

These two rules suggest that one may not remove organs solely for research purposes or when the life or at least the physical well-being of the recipient is not imminently threatened. These considerations underlie the prohibition of many Orthodox scholars against allowing autopsies except in a situation where there will be immediate benefit derived for the living (e.g., during an epidemic).

Increasingly, however, Orthodox scholars are joining their Reform and Conservative counterparts in recognizing that in a world where organs can be transported by jet across the globe in a matter of hours, where medical advances and breakthroughs are happening at breakneck speed, the old understanding of "an immediate need for the organ" must be reinterpreted more leniently.

Nevertheless, the progress of medicine in this area creates burning ethical questions. So far, the law is clear that the donor must consent to the transplant or, if the donor is dead, the next of kin must consent.

Will this principle always be applied? Are there any conceivable circumstances under which someone might justifiably be pressured to give an organ against his or her will? The acute shortages of available organs for approximately 56,000 people on transplant-waiting lists raise a number of other questions. Should the Jewish mandates to "save a life" and "not to stand idly by the blood of our neighbor" require that we assertively seek ways to increase the number of organs available for transplant? Could it justify a concept of "implied consent" whereby everyone is deemed to consent to donate their organs, unless there is a clear refusal?

What if a person is dying because both his kidneys are diseased and the only way to save his life is through the transplant of a healthy kidney from his brother? (A person can function normally with only one kidney.) And what if this brother with two healthy kidneys refuses to act as a donor? Is the brother morally or legally obligated to donate one kidney? Is it conceivable that an alternative to imprisonment for criminals might be to offer them the option of donating a kidney or a lung to save the life of another human being? Would such a deal be moral? Is it conceivable to find justification for the removal of a healthy kidney from a deeply retarded person who lives in an institution at taxpayers' expense for use in saving someone's life?

Conversely, do people have the right to be donors if by so doing they seriously endanger their own life or even end it? If someone has an incurable disease but a strong heart and wants to donate the heart to save the life of a loved one, should the person be permitted to do so? If the principle of human dignity conflicts with *pikuach nefesh*, where should the balance be struck?

Fetal Tissue Transplants

Similar questions arise in response to fetal tissue transplants. In 1988, a University of Colorado researcher transplanted "ten tiny bits of fetal brain tissue, sliced from a single piece the size of a grain of rice," into the right side of a patient with Parkinson's disease. That news burst on a country already embroiled in an intense debate over abortion. Opponents of abortion charged that such procedures would justify abortions as a means of obtaining human tissue for experimentation or transplant purposes.

Proponents of fetal tissue research and transplants responded that several formerly intractable diseases, including Parkinson's disease, diabetes, blood disorders, leukemia, and even AIDS, might be treated or cured through the use of fetal tissue. Fetal tissue is particularly suited to research and transplants because it multiplies extremely fast; it grows easily in the laboratory; it does not have an immune system and therefore will not be rejected in transplants; it can be used to achieve an extremely accurate evaluation of new vaccines and the toxicity of drugs; it can be used to produce large quantities of human growth hormone, insulin, and anticancer substances.

The first fetal-to-fetal tissue transplant was performed in April 1991. A couple who had already suffered two stillbirths because of a defective gene learned that the expected child would have the same malady. This time there was recourse to a new procedure that offered hope. The doctors performed an in-utero operation in which the five-month-old fetus was injected with the tissue of an aborted fetus in the hope that the healthy cells from the aborted fetus would cure the rare illness.

Even if one agrees in theory that these procedures should be allowed, problems arise: Who will regulate the process? Can individuals designate the recipients? Will mothers be permitted to sell the tissue of aborted fetuses?

In the spring of 1991, Mary Ayala gave birth to a baby girl, Marissa, with the hope that bone marrow from the newborn would be transplanted into Anissa Ayala, her nineteen-year-old daughter dying of leukemia. Fortunately, the bone marrow type was a perfect match and was promptly transplanted. But what would have happened if prenatal testing had found Marissa to be an imperfect match? Should ethics have allowed Mary Ayala to have an abortion so she could try again? What do you think?

Euthanasia

On a cold January night in 1983, a twenty-five-year-old woman named Nancy Beth Cruzan lost control of her car on a country road in Missouri. The car rolled over several times, and Nancy was hurled thirty-five feet. She landed facedown in a water-filled ditch. When paramedics arrived on the scene, they found no detectable respiratory or cardiac function. At the scene the paramedics were able to restore

Nancy's heartbeat and breathing by using multiple invasive methods. She was transported in an unconscious state to a local hospital. Doctors at the hospital determined that a fifteen-minute lack of oxygen had caused Nancy Cruzan to suffer permanent brain damage. She was in a "persistent vegetative state," which means that while she was able to exhibit motor reflexes like breathing and circulation, she showed no indication of cognitive function. She was completely oblivious of her surroundings; the parts of her brain that once thought, felt, and experienced sensations had deteriorated drastically and were continuing to deteriorate.

According to Nancy's doctors, the remaining cavities of her brain were filling with cerebrospinal fluid, and her cerebral cortical atrophy was "irreversible, permanent, progressive, and ongoing. Nancy would never interact meaningfully with her environment again and would remain in a persistent vegetative state until her death." Because she could not swallow, doctors implanted a tube in Nancy's stomach to deliver her nutrition and water.

Three years of treatment followed to no avail. After it had become apparent that Nancy had no chance of regaining her mental faculties, her parents requested that the hospital terminate the artificial nutrition and hydration procedures by removing the feeding tube. Because the hospital refused to honor the request without court approval, Nancy's parents went to the state trial court. The authorization to remove the feeding tube was granted. However, when the Supreme Court of Missouri reversed the lower court's decision, the matter reached the United States Supreme Court (1990) in the now celebrated case of *Cruzan v. Director, Missouri Department of Health*. For the first time in American history, the Supreme Court was presented with the issue of whether the Constitution grants an individual the so-called "right to die" or more precisely in this case, whether life-sustaining treatment could be terminated for a patient by a surrogate decision-maker.

The Supreme Court ruled: A competent person did have the right to refuse lifesaving hydration and nutrition. With an incompetent person, however, there had to be clear and convincing proof of that incompetent person's wishes not to be kept alive. While Nancy Cruzan had made some verbal statements to that effect, there was no formal statement of such intent, and, therefore, the Supreme Court would not authorize the removal of the feeding tube. This decision stirred millions of Americans to prepare a living will, affirming their wishes if they were ever to find themselves in Cruzan's situation.

In Nancy Cruzan's case, the issue was the withdrawal of life-sustaining treatment. Her life had all but ended and she was being kept alive solely by machines. According to the precedent established in the *Cruzan* case by the Supreme Court, an individual has, similarly, a constitutionally protected right to refuse treatment, even if that treatment would prolong or even save her life.

But what about the patient who is not imminently dying but is in tremendous pain and believes his suffering should end? What of the AIDS patient who has lived in unbearable pain for several years and knows the end of life is near? Do we allow that person to take active steps to shorten his own life? Can that individual's physician prescribe drugs for the purpose of hastening death? Where do our legal and ethical guidelines lead us?

Passive vs. Active Euthanasia

Euthanasia is the act of facilitating death either through active measures or by the passive cessation of treatment that keeps the patient alive at the request of the patient, or the family of the patient when the patient is not able to express her own wishes, e.g., brain death, coma, or vegetative state. Many experts in the field of medical ethics try to draw a clear legal and ethical distinction between passive euthanasia and voluntary active euthanasia, including physician-assisted death.

Following the logic of the *Cruzan* case, there is overwhelming consensus among medical personnel, legal authorities, and ethicists that passive euthanasia is permissible. No one should be forced to submit to medical treatments that would even prolong their life. However, there is significant dispute about active euthanasia and on just where the boundary is between active and passive euthanasia. Is cutting off feeding to a patient in a vegetative state passive or active euthanasia? (Authorities are split on this.) Is using a high-risk new procedure that has a 2 percent chance to cure an otherwise incurable disease and a 98 percent chance of killing the patient active or passive euthanasia? (Most believe this is passive euthanasia since its purpose is to cure, not kill.) Is providing high levels of painkiller to a patient with intense chronic pain—who might otherwise live another year—even though the painkiller may hasten death, passive or active euthanasia? (Most believe this is passive since its purpose is to comfort, not kill.) These and similar ambiguities have led a number of bioethicists to conclude that the argument over the boundaries between passive and active euthanasia distracts us from analyzing the ethical issues involved. Is it really necessary or even helpful to divide these situations into categories to decide what is right and what is wrong? While we will continue to discuss the issue in the more traditional terms, consider this question in wrestling with the dilemmas below.

Arguments for and against Active Euthanasia

The basic argument for voluntary active euthanasia—the purposeful hastening of death in order to end extreme suffering—rests in the commitment to the concept of individual autonomy: as long as an individual's choice does not infringe on anyone else's rights, that person should be able to decide whether to accept or to refuse medical treatment and to make decisions related to the end of life on their own terms. The spirit of that principle is used to suggest that someone in a vegetative state, with no hope of reversal, should have those decisions made for them by those they designate. In addition, families of those who are living in pain from a terminal illness often support the right of physicians to provide the most compassionate and palliative care, i.e., care aimed at easing pain and bringing as much comfort as possible for their loved ones, even if that relief would hasten their deaths. They argue that there is no real difference between, on the one hand, giving a terminal patient painkillers to ease pain and, on the other, giving pills to end life. You know that in both cases the impact on the patient, in terms of hastening death, is exactly the same. Many in the religious community argue that end-of-life decisions must be made by an individual according to that person's relationship with God and no state or lawmaking body has the right to interfere. Finally, on an economic basis, the cost of maintaining life through exorbitant treatments can be staggering, quickly wiping out a family's savings.

Those who oppose active euthanasia or assisted suicide argue that personal autonomy is secondary to the value of preserving life. Many believe that acting with the intention of cutting a life short for any reason is tantamount to murder. Others fear that legalizing this practice will put pressure on those who are sick, elderly, or disabled to choose to end their life to save their loved ones money, grief, and inconvenience. Furthermore, there is the "slippery slope" argument: if a society can decide that the lives of the terminally ill or vegetative patients are worth less than other lives, who else might be considered by some societies as unworthy of life—the retarded, the elderly, homosexuals, the disabled, gypsies, Jews?

Jewish Perspectives on Euthanasia and Assisted Death

The two statements on euthanasia in the Jewish tradition are summed up in the *Shulchan Aruch*, the sixteenth-century code of Jewish law (which was authoritative in the Sephardic Jewish communities), and in the commentary on the *Shulchan Aruch* by Moses Isserles (the authoritative equivalent in the Ashkenazic communities):

> Even if a patient has agonized for a long time, and he and his family are in great distress, it is forbidden to hasten his death by, for instance, closing his eyes, or removing a pillow from under his head, or placing an object such as feathers or a synagogue key under his head.
>
> (*Shulchan Aruch, Yoreh Deah,* 339:1)

> However, if there is an obstacle that prevents the departure of the soul [death], such as noise outside or salt present on the dying person's tongue, we may stop the noise or remove the salt so as not to hinder death.
>
> (Commentary of Rabbi Moses Isserles on
> *Shulchan Aruch, Yoreh Deah,* 339:1)

These passages essentially differentiate between active and passive euthanasia. While one should do nothing to actively kill someone, one is not required to begin or maintain a nonlifesaving treatment if death is imminent.

In Jewish law, these strictures referred only to one who is classified as a *goses* (i.e., someone who is likely to die in the next few days). In ancient times, there was no way of knowing if someone's disease was irreversible until the person was visibly near death. Today, we can know far in advance that someone's disease or injury is irreversible or irremediable. A major debate among Jewish scholars today is whether passive euthanasia should be allowed when death is certain—even if it is not imminent.

The *Cruzan* case provides a variant of this dilemma. She clearly would not die for a long time; yet there was no hope whatsoever for a recovery. Her life was being maintained by the miracles of modern medical technology. Although Jewish sources of old could not conceive of this scenario, they did notice the problem created by well-meaning, though useless, healing measures when the soul of the person is ready to depart. The Talmud, for instance, speaks of the slow and painful death of the great Rabbi Judah HaNasi and about his disciples who prayed continually for his recovery. It was said the rabbi's housekeeper dropped a clay jug in order to disrupt their prayers, allowing the tortured soul of the rabbi to depart (R. Nissim Gerondi, commentary on *Nedarim* 40a).

These discussions should be set in the context of Judaism's views on suicide. The Jewish tradition teaches that our bodies and souls are precious and we must take all measures possible to preserve the sanctity of ourselves and our lives (thus, for example, the clear Jewish prohibitions against substance abuse). Jewish opinion on suicide is reflective of this principle; it is a sin. It is not for us to decide when our time in this world is over. Our deaths, like our lives, belong to God. The holiness of all life is a core principle in Judaism, reflected in the rich details surrounding mourning and respecting the dead. In traditional Judaism, moreover, one who has committed suicide is denied the respect of the Jewish mourning rituals.

It is interesting to note that while the ritualized respect for the dead, which is so critical to Jewish values, should be withheld from one who takes her own life, there are important exceptions. Jewish texts take great pains to distinguish between intentional and forced suicide. Defining "intentional" suicide is a delicate nuance of words and circumstances. Those medieval Jews who died at their own hand rather than be forced to convert were such an exception. "A minor who commits suicide willfully is considered as though it were done unintentionally.

And likewise, one who was of age and committed suicide willfully, being under pressure as was King Saul, the law is that not a thing is withheld from him." (*Bereshit Rabbah* 34:13) King Saul's death is said to have occurred in battle. He was injured and lying in pain. He said to an Amalekite who was passing, "Stand over me, and finish me off, for I am in agony and am barely alive." The Amalekite gave the king his sword, explaining, "For I knew that he would never rise from where he was lying," and Saul threw himself on his sword. Thus the prohibition against suicide is not absolute and might well include those who acted out of severe psychological disease, although this is a point of disagreement among Jewish scholars and does not serve to justify suicide in most circumstances. Do we not venerate the memory of the martyrs of Masada even though that was a mass suicide?

Yet the question still remains—Who should make decisions regarding the end of life? The individual? The doctor? The family? The government? The Jewish halachic tradition, as interpreted by Orthodox Judaism, would suggest that such questions should be decided by a rabbi in accordance with *halachah* and that the family of an irreversibly comatose or terminally ill and suffering patient has no special role in the decision-making process. Given what we know about modern medicine, does the traditional Jewish approach make sense to you?

A Real Dilemma: Justice and Mercy—Roswell and Emily Gilbert

Roswell and Emily Gilbert had been married for many decades when Emily began to suffer from Alzheimer's disease and the degenerative bone disorder osteoporosis. Over the years, the pain and suffering became unbearable for Mrs. Gilbert, who finally begged her husband of fifty-one years to put an end to her agony and terminate her life. On March 4, 1985, Mr. Gilbert, following what he believed to be Mrs. Gilbert's wishes, shot and killed her.

Two months later, a jury found Mr. Gilbert guilty of first-degree murder. Judge Thomas Coker, Jr., sentenced Gilbert to twenty-five years in prison with no chance of parole. Judge Coker summarized the feelings of many when he said, "I am not without sympathies, but I am sworn to uphold the law."

Was this, as Roswell Gilbert testified, an act of love? Or was it simply murder, subject not to the fuzzy sentiment of human emotion but to the clear statutes of the state? If you had been on the jury, how would you have decided? The UAHC was asked to intervene to request a lenient sentence. What should the UAHC have done?

Response

In the aftermath of this decision, many people have looked carefully at this case and the very real dilemmas it poses. In fact, the case received such widespread notoriety that it became the subject of a 1987 television movie, *Mercy or Murder*, which focused national attention on the killing of a loved one.

The Commission on Social Action decided that Mr. Gilbert had been treated unfairly, saying the situation required justice *and* mercy but the court had applied only the letter of the law. The UAHC did not contest the verdict in light of the law and Jewish tradition's general opposition to euthanasia. However, the UAHC did become part of an effort to commute Mr. Gilbert's sentence, an effort that contributed to Mr. Gilbert's being granted clemency in 1990 by Florida's Governor Bob Martinez.

Physician-Assisted Death

The latest controversy to arise in the euthanasia debate is over physician-assisted death (often referred to as physician-assisted suicide). Physician-assisted death refers to the provision of life-ending means by a doctor at the request of the patient whereby either a patient is provided by the doctor with the means to take his own life or the doctor assists in administrating life-ending treatment.

The arguments that surround this issue are heated and charged with very strong emotions. The notion of a doctor helping someone to end a life offends many who believe in preserving the sanctity of the role of the physician in preserving life. On the other hand, those who are watching a loved one suffer in agony or who are suffering themselves look to their physicians for compassionate assistance. For some, this may include seeking to end their life with dignity and without pain.

The *halachic* position on this, with its effort to distinguish strictly between passive and active euthanasia, would seem to bar a physician from such action. But what about a physician's aiding a patient to end her life? To take another life is clearly one of the greatest wrongs a human being can commit. Physicians are, as are we all, imbued with the duty to heal the sick or when that is no longer possible, to care for them with compassion. We cannot, Jewish morality teaches us, include taking lives in the definition of "compassion" or "healing." The primary objective of the physician, in any and all circumstances, is to heal the sick and to engage only in activities that would further the saving of life and the bringing of comfort to the patient. In arguing for assisted death, some modern observers suggest that because the line between passive and active euthanasia in the texts is not really so clear, nonhalachic values such as mercy and compassion might justify medical assistance in more extreme situations.

A Real Dilemma: Should We Submit a Brief to the Supreme Court?

As of this writing, thirty-three states have statutes prohibiting physician-assisted death and ten others have banned them judicially. In 1997, the Supreme Court first considered whether there is a constitutional right to voluntary physician assistance when someone wants to die. This came after two lower courts, the Second and Ninth Circuit Courts of Appeal, handed down landmark decisions allowing for physician-assisted death in limited circumstances. While the outcome of the two cases was the same, the courts relied upon very different legal reasoning and precedent.

As the Supreme Court got ready to hear this landmark case, many organizations were writing amicus, or "friend of the court," briefs. These are written to inform the court what people in the country are thinking and feeling and are taken into consideration when the court is making its decision. Many entities wrote briefs against physician-assisted death, including the Clinton administration and Agudas Israel, the Orthodox Jewish movement. Other groups wrote in support of legalizing physician-assisted death, including the American College of Legal Medicine and a religious coalition led by the Unitarian

Universalist Church and the Leadership Conference of Secular and Humanistic Jews. The UAHC was approached by several organizations, including most of those mentioned above, to lend the voice of the Reform movement to their cause by signing its name to their respective briefs.

What should the UAHC have done?

Response

The Commission on Social Action of the UAHC, together with the UAHC Committee on Bioethics, spent an intensive two days hearing arguments about this issue. Jewish law and American law were taken into consideration, as well as the emotional arguments on both sides of the debate. After much discussion, no resolution was reached defining our position supporting or opposing physician-assisted death.

The members of the CSA did, however, feel that this was an important history-making court case and very much wanted to weigh in to help the Supreme Court reach its decision. They decided, therefore, not to write their own brief but to research existing briefs and sign on to one that most generally reflected some key points on which they did agree: that although physician-assisted death is not morally permissible in most cases and should be severely limited, the existing state laws were overbroad. In particular, the CSA members decided they would not at this time support a total ban on physician-assisted death and could not support the criminalization of such an act when a doctor in good conscience believes such assistance, in response to a patient's request, is morally and medically appropriate.

The search for a brief was, unfortunately, not successful and the CSA with the UAHC Bioethics Committee turned its efforts toward educating its community and constituents about the moral issues involved in making a decision regarding end-of-life choices. The Supreme Court upheld the state bans against physician-assisted death. It asserted that there was a rational basis for the state to differentiate between administering painkilling drugs knowing it will hasten death and giving drugs with the intent to kill.

The Definition of Death

Halachah generally defines death as the cessation of the heartbeat for several minutes (most variants include cessation of breathing). We know today that cessation of the heart no longer means that the person is dead. Even after the heart has stopped beating, a person can be revived, and if this is done within a very short period of time, there may be no ill effects. In other words, death is no longer considered to be a point in time but rather a process. The end of the process seems to be the absence of all electrical activity in the brain.

Among other obvious concerns, the point of death is a critical consideration with regard to organ transplants. For example, in order for the heart to be transplanted, to avoid damaging the organ, it must be removed from the body considerably before the end of the process. Some have argued that taking the heart before "brain death" is a kind of murder. Where is the end of the responsibility to keep alive the dying person, and where is the beginning of the responsibility to save the recipient?

A Real Dilemma: Defining Death

In the mid-1980s, Agudas Israel, a theologically and politically far-right Orthodox Jewish group, approached state legislators in California in an effort to block a proposed law that would have changed the definition of death. The old definitions were ambiguous and outdated. The proposed new definition, based mostly on "brain death" (with some provisions to allow for organ transplants), contradicted the halachic definition of death: the cessation of breathing and heartbeat for a period of time.

Without consulting any of the mainstream Jewish agencies or the Jewish Community Relations Councils (CRCs), Agudas told legislators that this proposed legislation violated "the rights of Jews" and was opposed by the Jewish community. The Los Angeles CRC criticized the effort of Agudas to have its religious definition of death enacted into law, calling it a violation of church-state separation.

The CRC called the Religious Action Center to ask its advice. What should it have recommended?

Response

Despite the general hostility of Agudas to the values and activities of Reform Judaism, the Center's staff recommended that the mainstream community groups should try to accommodate Agudas Israel's viewpoint. While the proposed legislation was better from both a public policy and a medical point of view, there should be a legal exemption providing for religious groups whose definition of death differs from that provided by the California law. The state could define death as the cessation of brain activity and when Orthodox Jews request such treatment could still recognize their definition based on the cessation of heart and breathing activity as an additional requirement. In this manner, the state would never declare death only on the fulfillment of the halachic definition; it would always have to wait for cessation of brain activity.

Asking for legal exemptions to accommodate differing religious beliefs, it should be noted, is not the same as imposing one's religious belief on the entire population. There are even some downsides to granting the religious exemption. In a number of situations, the additional time lag (and attendant deterioration of internal organs) in waiting for cessation of heart and breathing activity would eliminate the possibility of organs from that body being used for transplants even if the patient had indicated that intent. Furthermore, this doesn't resolve the dilemma of when to turn off heart-lung machines when a person is brain dead and the religious exemption applies. This raises keen moral problems when there are others waiting for the machine necessary to keep them alive.

At the same time, however, the Center's staff felt strongly that Agudas had erred by not consulting the broader Jewish community. It thus precipitated a situation in which the organized Jewish community felt it had been misrepresented by Agudas, which suggested that its view was "the" Jewish view. Thus the opportunity to evolve a common position on an important matter of public policy was lost. Since Judaism has a fairly well-developed body of law regarding medical and biological ethics, the need for such consultation is vital, lest we repeatedly face similar bioethical decisions that become needlessly divisive in the Jewish community.

Who Shall Live and Who Shall Die?

Every day, hospital staffs must decide whom to keep alive and whom to let die. There simply are not enough dialysis machines, heart-lung machines, or transplant donors to accommodate everyone who might need them. Who should be saved? Jewish tradition teaches: "You shall not render an unfair decision: do not favor the poor or show deference to the rich; judge your neighbor fairly." (Leviticus 19:15) Most Orthodox Jewish scholars argue that this leads to a first-come, first-served approach to triage (prioritizing who receives needed care), without regard to prospects for recovery or the patient's personal situation.

In addressing this issue, Rabbi Solomon B. Freehof, the most influential twentieth-century Reform Jewish interpreter of traditional Jewish sources, drew on a section in the Talmud (*Avodah Zarah* 27b): When there is a chance for a cure for a dying person, we are allowed to risk the patient's last hours to try out a new remedy that has the prospect of curing the patient or of adding a significant amount of time to the patient's life. Rabbi Freehof then summarized a number of responsa, concluding that a physician must strive to decide whether or not to save a patient solely on medical grounds rather than considering the personal situation of the patient. The doctor must select the patient who has the better prospect of survival and of leading a relatively healthy life. (*Modern Reform Responsa* [New York: Ktav, 1971], pp. 204–216)

Again, who should decide? And on what grounds should the decision be made? Should we choose to cure people who are rich because they have the money to pay for what is very expensive treatment? Who should pay the treatment costs for poor people who cannot themselves afford it? Should we choose to give care to those who hold the most responsible positions in society? Should we choose the middle-aged person in the prime of life or an adolescent on the threshold of adult life? Should the choice be random—a kind of life-and-death roulette— or based purely on medical grounds? Is it possible to arrive at a consensus that is objective, or would the chosen criteria inevitably reflect the prejudices and self-interest of the determining group?

Ethical Dilemmas in Altering Life

Genetic Engineering and Cloning

Perhaps the most far-reaching moral dilemmas in technology concern advances in genetics. No other technology so allows us to "play God." By altering the genetic structure of bacteria, plants, and animals, we can actually create new life forms, today even altering human life itself.

Genetic engineering began in the 1950s and 1960s with the lower organisms. By altering their genetic structure, scientists could "engineer" bacteria that consumed oil, fertilized plants, or killed harmful insects. Moving up the evolutionary ladder to plants and animals, researchers genetically altered plants to produce more fruit and cows to give more milk.

While use of genetic engineering to increase the world's food supply promises great benefit, the critics of this technology fear that it could lead to a catastrophe. Can we be certain that a newly engineered bacterium would not accidentally start a new disease in human beings—a bacterium that would multiply so fast we couldn't contain it? While scientists feel far more confident today than a decade ago of their ability to control such problems, we can never be sure. By the time we know enough about what the potential damage of a new technological development might be, it may be too late to prevent it.

In 1980, Genentech, a leader in the field of genetic engineering, developed a new strain of microorganism and applied for a patent from the United States Patent and Trademark Office. The application was challenged and the case reached the United States Supreme Court (*Diamond* v. *Chakrabarty*). The Court subsequently upheld Genentech's right to patent the new life form it had created. What does it mean to "own" a new form of life? Or even to reap a part of the financial benefits from each production and subsequent use of that life? If it applies to bacteria, should we also allow corporations to own new forms of plant or animal life? How do we draw these distinctions? Do corporations have the right to "play God"?

These questions have generated a heated debate on the topic of patenting genes. As the debate continues, genetic patenting increases and technological advances lead to more and more questions. In 1991, the Patent and Trademark Office changed the scope of this debate by granting a California company commercial ownership of human bone marrow "stem cells" whose DNA the company had discovered. This was the first patent to be given to an unaltered part of the human body. This launched further debate as to the concept of "ownership" of the human body. Should human genes be owned by a company? Does it matter whether the genes are simply located and identified by the company as opposed to altered by the company so as to create a new gene? What do our ethical guidelines say? Companies argue that giving patents provides economic incentives for them to do the costly research in the genetics field. Critics argue that they aren't inventing something but discovering (and therefore perhaps adopting) something God created that they could never create from scratch. Further, giving a patent will stifle research by other companies in using the discovered gene, thus impeding progress. How should we weigh the potential societal or medical benefits against our ethical and moral considerations?

Recent advances in biotechnology and genetics have presented various possibilities of controlling birth defects and deformities. Artificial insemination allows a woman to have a child by an anonymous donor whose sperm has been tested for genetic health. Today, for the first time, it is possible to detect genetic defects at a relatively early stage of pregnancy, allowing for the possibility of curing the fetus by replacing or repairing defective genes; where repair is not possible, parents are given time to prepare for proper care after birth or, if the other two options are not acceptable or available, to permit an abortion.

This would lead ultimately to the possibility of constructing whatever genetic makeup the parents might want. The fertilized egg with the appropriate genetic constitution could then be inserted in the uterus or even nurtured in the laboratory.

The idea of avoiding genetic diseases is not entirely new. In the Talmud (Babylonian Talmud, *Yevamot* 64b), we are instructed that one should not marry into a diseased family (e.g., a family in which three people have suffered from leprosy or epilepsy). While today we know that both diseases are treatable or controllable, this was clearly an early effort to avoid diseases that were thought to be genetic. The *Mishnah*, however, reminds us of limits in the altering of nature: A person may not pray to God that his pregnant wife bear a male child. Such prayers are considered *levatalah* ("wasted for foolish purpose") since the sex of the fetus has already been determined at the moment of conception. (*Mishnah Berachot* 54a)

Have we gone too far? Should we try to impose limits on human genetic experimentation?

Germ-Line Experimentation

Some critics of genetic engineering distinguish between altering genes related to a specific genetic disease and altering the genetic structure of a human being in such a way that the altered trait itself would be passed on through reproduction to the next generation. The latter, its critics say, should be prohibited because changing the human "germ line" through experimentation is truly "playing God." If, God forbid, we should make an error when changing the genes of an individual, the impact of that error is contained; when changing the germ line, the error will spread and expand as those progeny have children. Proponents of germ-line research respond that by correcting a genetic malfunction and allowing that correction to be passed on through the generations, we can eliminate the need for genetic surgery on the future offspring who would otherwise carry that trait.

The lines drawn between gene therapy, gene enhancement, and eugenics (improvement of the genetic constitution of the human species by selective breeding) are very fuzzy ones. Where is the line drawn between the "advantage" of being born without Down's syndrome or a predisposition for breast cancer and the "advantage" of being born with a genius-level intelligence or with the features of a supermodel?

What do you think?

Cloning

Consider "cloning," a process by which an entire organism is replicated from the original and contains the exact genetic makeup. This has been done with lower forms of life and in 1997 was used to clone an entire sheep named Dolly. Some day it may be possible to clone human beings. In theory, it is not inconceivable that from a single living cell of a Beethoven or an Einstein, a new Beethoven or Einstein could be produced. The same would, of course, apply to Attila the Hun or Hitler. Of course, despite our science fiction dramas, genetics alone will not create another Beethoven or another Hitler. Many factors—genes, culture, parents, circumstance, and free will—contribute to shaping a person's character or beliefs. How, then, should cloning technology be used? For example, parents whose six-month-old baby died could clone the baby and start anew. But then, of course, the different genetic baby they might have conceived will never be born.

Privacy and Genetic Engineering

In the early 1990s, scientists in the United States began an extraordinary scientific research project. In what is commonly referred to as the Human Genome Project, scientists are attempting to map out the entire genetic structure of the human being. Already they have made significant advances in determining DNA sequence data. This and further information will make it possible to understand completely, and perhaps even alter, the genetic structure of human beings—more accurately and completely than scientists even ten short years before could have dreamed about.

This raises an entirely new set of dilemmas involving individual privacy.

A Real Dilemma: Genetic Research and the Right to Privacy

If we begin to do regular genetic checkups on people to find out if they have diseases or if they have the genetic makeup that might possibly lead to diseases, how will that information be used? Some types of genetic problems always lead to certain results. Many others indicate the possibility of a particular result. For example, people who have a parent who died of Huntington's chorea have a 50 percent chance of developing the disease. Thus without very sophisticated genetic testing, we don't know who will live a healthy life. Who should have this information? Should it be given to insurance companies, which would be unlikely to provide a life or health insurance policy to such people—even though 50 percent will never have a problem? Should information about the presence of genes that indicate a propensity to alcoholism be given to a potential employer? Should information about a genetic tendency to emotional problems be given to a university admissions office? For that matter, if you were the patient, would you want to be told that you had a 50 percent chance of developing a disease that there is no way to prevent? Or would you choose not to be told?

What could the UAHC do to address these issues?

Response

In the late 1980s, several key UAHC leaders were part of a small coalition of prominent religious and scientific figures who began to raise ethical concerns regarding the intense pace of genetic research and application of such research. This coalition urged that testing and implementation of genetic research be slowed enough to ensure that these experiments are considered not only by scientists but by public officials, ethicists, and average citizens. The coalition was accused, in turn, of using scare tactics and trying to delay valuable genetic research.

Breast Cancer

In the United States today, breast cancer is the leading cause of death for women under fifty. One in every eight women will contract breast cancer in her lifetime, a dramatic increase from one in twenty women only twenty years ago. This staggering growth has the medical, genetics, and biotechnological communities desperately looking for causes, treatments, cures, and methods of early detection. Women whose breast cancer is diagnosed at the earliest stages stand a much higher chance of full recovery than those whose cancer is detected at later stages of development.

In late 1994, scientists isolated what are now known as the BRCA1 and BRCA2 genes. These genes are completely benign when normal or undamaged. When damaged or mutated, however, they indicate a susceptibility to breast and ovarian, and in men, prostate, colon, and men's breast cancer (the altered genes are often referred to as BRCA1+ and BRCA2+). A woman with BRCA1+ or BRCA2+ genes and a family history of breast cancer may stand as much as an 85 percent chance of developing breast cancer in her lifetime (in contrast to the average woman's chance of approximately 12.5 percent). Although much is still unknown about the causes of this genetic mutation, it is now possible to be tested for this genetic condition. This technology may, if used with sensitivity and full disclosure of information available to the patient, represent a milestone for breast cancer research, potentially saving the lives of many women.

However, genetic testing is not without significant downsides. As discussed with genetic information generally, a major problem facing women who opt to test for this genetic condition is discrimination from health insurance companies. Insurance companies, of course, are aware that individuals with a genetic predisposition to a particular disease are significantly more likely to develop the disease and thus be more expensive to insure. Women with this genetic mutation can, and do, face termination of their medical insurance or, at the very least, higher premiums and coverage discrimination from insurance companies. Their children may also face this problem, since this trait may be passed on in families. Fear of such discrimination may well prevent women from getting tested and therefore from taking prudent steps such as more careful self-examinations and more frequent mammograms.

Breast Cancer and the Jewish Community

These developments have been of particular concern for the Jewish community, since the mutations in the BRCA1 and BRCA2 genes are disproportionately prevalent in Ashkenazic Jewish women. In fact, it has been estimated that this genetic mutation occurs in approximately 1 percent of Ashkenazic Jewish women, a rate of occurrence three times higher than in the general population. This focus on Jewish women may make them more susceptible to insurance discrimination.

Many Jewish organizations, led by Jewish women's groups including the Women of Reform Judaism, have now joined the effort to urge Congress to pass new legislation. This legislation would prohibit health insurers from using genetic information to deny, refuse to renew, cancel, or change the terms and conditions of coverage, would prevent insurance companies from requesting or requiring genetic tests, and would require written informed consent before an insurer could disclose genetic information to a third party. Proponents of these bills believe that this type of discrimination is already taking place and that fear of such discrimination is already having serious ramifications for the positive advances that could come from advanced biomedical technology.

By the late 1990s, there was growing momentum behind such legislation.

These bills reflect a long struggle within the health advocacy community to alert the public to genetic discrimination problems. Of particular significance are references to health care denials going back to the early 1970s for African-Americans who were carriers of the gene for sickle-cell anemia. A recent survey conducted through Georgetown University in conjunction with the Alliance of Genetic Support Groups indicated that such discrimination has not stopped, finding that 22 percent of those with a known genetic condition in their families had been refused health insurance coverage.

Insurance companies repond that adjusting coverage and rates to reflect disease-related factors such as smoking or age—or genetic predisposition—is essential to the economic stability of the companies. They argue that if they can't charge higher rates or deny coverage to those most likely to become ill, the costs for covering those illnesses will be borne by the companies and passed on to all their healthy patients in the form of higher premiums.

Jewish Genetic Disorders

The understanding of the genetic likelihood of Jewish parents passing on one of a number of inherited genetic disorders to their children has been a major medical development presenting new challenges to the Jewish community worldwide. The fatal consequences of many of these diseases make recent advances in the field of genetics and genetic screening particularly important to Jews.

Specifically, there are six genetic diseases that are primarily, but not exclusively, found among Jews. Among the most prevalent:

- Bloom's syndrome stunts its victims' growth.

- Torsion dystonia is a muscle seizure disease.

- Gaucher's disease can result in blood abnormalities such as anemia, easy bruising, and impaired blood clotting.

- Tay-Sachs, the most well known of these diseases, is carried in the genes of some Jews of East European descent. The disease causes paralysis, blindness, and severe mental retardation, followed by death at the young age of three or four. The disease occurs in 1 out of 2,500 children born to Ashkenazic Jews.

Genetic Screening and Counseling

Until recently, these diseases were unpreventable. Every birth brought with it the risk that the newborn's life would be scarred by a debilitating genetic disorder. Today, however, a variety of screening measures can detect these genetic signals both in the parents and in the fetus. For example, a simple blood test given to anyone of reproductive age can identify carriers of the Tay-Sachs genetic disorder. In cases where both parents have the gene and a child would, therefore, definitely have it, the parents may decide to adopt instead. In cases where one parent has the gene and there is only a 50 percent chance, the decisions are yet more difficult. Further, during pregnancy an in utero diagnosis can be made through amniocentesis. If the fetus is affected, the parents may be prepared for what is to come or may decide to terminate the pregnancy.

Today, genetic screening tests give doctors the ability not only to predict who will be born with one of the known 4,000 inherited disorders but also which infants will be born with genes that are associated with—but do not necessarily result in—the more common illnesses like cancer and heart disease. And genetic screening will move from testing fetuses to testing children or adults and predicting who has a propensity toward diseases like cancer or certain types of mental illness.

This remarkable advance in medicine has already proven to be a potent weapon in fighting disease. After an intensive genetic screening program in New York, the incidence of Tay-Sachs, the fatal disease that hits the Jewish community hardest, was dramatically reduced.

A number of obvious moral and ethical dilemmas come to mind regarding genetic screening. In addition to the concerns about privacy, society must now deal with other questions. For example, once the genes for alcoholism or Alzheimer's are discovered, should an airline pilot *at risk* for these diseases be forced to stop flying or be forced to undergo more frequent and rigorous medical testing than other pilots? How about surgeons or nuclear power plant operators? Should insurance companies be allowed to charge higher rates to those at risk?

What happens when it is determined that a baby has genes associated with early heart disease? Should society still invest in the child's
education or professional career?

And what if the couple (or the government) is permitted to monitor
embryos so that any with an "undesirable" genetic trait may be aborted?
Is this social progress or the first step toward creating Hitler's master
race through eugenics (i.e., preserving only genetically "superior"
people)? What if tests show there is only a 50 percent possibility of
contracting an incurable debilitating disease? What if the disease is not
necessarily life-threatening, like cerebral palsy or multiple sclerosis?
What if genetic screening shows that the baby will be blind or deaf?
What if it shows the baby will be a boy and not the girl the couple
wants or if it will have brown eyes and black hair rather than the
desired blue eyes and blond hair? Under which of these situations
would abortion be moral? Where does a responsible society draw the
line?

The questions these changes raise are all but overwhelming in their
import. Who would decide what is "normal," what is preferable? Could
it be decided that all genes that controlled certain "antisocial" qualities
would be destroyed? Upon whom would such genetic engineering be
implemented? What is the morality of experimentation in genetics
when it may directly affect the nature of unborn human beings? Should
the government control the use of such techniques? Or would government control make it much easier to create a totalitarian society? What
are the implications of the new techniques—artificial insemination,
genetic restructuring, possibly even cloning—for the concept of parenthood? Does it make sense to speak any longer of natural parents?
Finally, is there a point beyond which we should not go in the creation
of, and tampering with, human life, or are all advances in the science
of genetics necessarily good?

A RADICAL PROPOSAL: ETHICAL IMPACT
STATEMENTS

There are few areas of public policy in which the Jewish tradition offers
a more systematic ethical analysis than bioethics. Each of the streams
of American Judaism has in recent years produced extensive Jewish
study materials. The UAHC's Committee on Bioethics has published a

broad range of guidelines, study resources, and sample legal documents, together with programmatic materials on these issues, and made them available to Jews nationwide.

A generation ago, public consensus about protecting the environment led the government to require environmental impact statements before any new projects that might negatively affect the environment could be undertaken. The result of these requirements was to reshape the kind of development America would undertake. It provided policymakers with sufficient time to assess the environmental implications of new undertakings and required that they be provided with the facts necessary to make an informed decision. Finally, it sent a message that the environmental integrity of our nation was a priority concern for Americans.

Perhaps it is time to demand similar *ethical* impact statements for new technological developments. Before any new major technological developments could be implemented, a study would have to be done by a panel of scientists, ethicists, politicians, economists, etc., on what the ethical (including the economic, environmental, privacy, social) impact of that development would be. The beneficial results would be the same: providing time and information necessary to assess the ethical implications of new technologies and their applications and sending a powerful message to the nation that America cares about its ethical integrity. Could such a system work—and perhaps save us from a catastrophic development—or would it simply impede the advancement of science and interfere with free enterprise? These questions will haunt us as we enter the twenty-first century.

··· 4 ···

The Elusive Search
for Economic Justice in the
World's Wealthiest Nation

*A Real Dilemma: Should a Synagogue Establish a Homeless
Shelter within Its Own Facility?*

During the 1980s and 1990s, the two domestic social justice
issues most frequently addressed by congregations were the problems of hunger and homelessness. Hundreds of congregations
across the nation collected food for local food pantries and
provided volunteers for soup kitchens and homeless shelters. As
congregations became more involved, one issue arose repeatedly:
should they set up food distribution programs and even homeless
shelters within their own congregational buildings?

Proponents of such measures argued that if the synagogue was
serious about social justice, it would have to do more than send
volunteers to other people's shelters; it would have to bring the
issue home. As the Reagan budget significantly cut back funding
for low-income housing and feeding programs in the 1980s and
the Contract with America cuts did the same in the mid-1990s,
it became incumbent upon synagogues and churches to help pick
up the slack.

Opponents expressed concerns that such activity would overwhelm the congregation. By taking on the responsibility of creating a facility in-house, they would have to ensure that the volunteers showed up and that there would be people to fill in if the
volunteers missed their shifts. They would be bringing in alcoholics and mentally disturbed persons. They would run the risk
that someone might get hurt, thus affecting the insurance of the

synagogue. They would have to devote a part of their synagogue building for the facility, possibly overtaxing the synagogue's structure and straining the budget.

What should our synagogues do? What would you have decided?

Response

This was an anguishing dilemma for many congregations. A surprisingly high number were willing to undertake the expense, the logistical difficulties, and the risks of providing just such programs. Like The Temple in Atlanta, which set up a shelter for homeless families, and Central Synagogue in New York, which set up a weekly breakfast program for the homeless, scores of synagogues opened their doors to put into practice the words of justice preached from the pulpit.

By the late 1980s, some of the more active congregations began to move beyond providing shelter, recognizing that shelters addressed only the symptom of the problem of homelessness. Some, like Temple Emanu-El in Dallas, helped to set up childcare programs for the children of homeless families, thus not only serving the needs of the children but making it possible for homeless parents to mount a serious effort to find a job—without worrying about their children. Others, like Rodeph Sholom in New York City, organized programs to assist homeless families in the transition from shelters to real apartments in the community.

A number of other congregations have undertaken efforts to build affordable low-income housing. In Westfield, New Jersey, such an effort is being undertaken jointly by Temple Emanu-El, a Reform synagogue, and a black church. In Los Angeles, an ambitious $7 million project was undertaken by a coalition of churches and synagogues led by an Episcopal church and the Leo Baeck Temple, resulting in the conversion of a dilapidated hotel to an affordable apartment building to house the previously homeless in downtown Los Angeles. Increasingly, congregations are exploring these types of approaches as a means to help people help themselves—the highest form of Jewish charity.

1994–1996: Dismantling the Social Safety Net

If these decisions were increasingly important for synagogues in the 1980s, the sweeping changes in our system of economic justice made by the 104th Congress in 1995 and 1996 brought this issue to the very forefront of the social justice agenda of churches and synagogues nationwide.

In the sixty years since the New Deal began, our nation had moved increasingly in the direction of a federally guaranteed safety net for the truly needy: food stamps for the hungry; Medicaid and Medicare for the ill; Supplemental Security Income (SSI) for the elderly and disabled; and aid for poor families with children (AFDC). Under a concept known as "entitlements," our nation said to its children, elderly, ill, hungry, and unemployed: If your income falls below a certain level, you are entitled to the help of your government. We may not have the financial resources to provide all you need or all we would like, but everyone who meets the eligibility criteria will get some help.

While a bipartisan coalition of Republicans and Democrats have brought about all the great social achievements of twentieth-century America, under the Contract with America beginning in 1994, one of the most conservative Republican-controlled Congresses of the century attempted to eliminate the concept of a federally guaranteed safety net for the truly needy. The religious community, which runs some of the largest and most successful social service agencies in the nation, successfully opposed efforts to end entitlement to food stamps or Medicaid. Those on the political Right, however, did manage to end the entitlement to cash welfare payments (Aid to Families with Dependent Children—AFDC) and disability payments (SSI); cut back funding for all programs; allow state matching funds to be used for a broad range of purposes beyond the programs for which they were intended; and relinquish control of most programs to the states. Millions of people have fallen through the holes in the safety net, and we are left with a patchwork quilt of government assistance to the poor.

TEN FACTS ABOUT ECONOMIC JUSTICE IN AMERICA

The efforts to help the poor and needy that began in the New Deal of the 1930s and accelerated during the Great Society programs of the 1960s made a significant difference in lifting tens of millions out of poverty. Several factors, however, left millions of others without resources to provide their families with a minimally decent standard of living. Those negative factors were:

- Most welfare programs focused on providing poor people with enough resources to eke out a minimal standard of living but not on educating them nor helping them to find jobs that would lift them out of poverty altogether.
- The $55 billion in federal cuts mandated under the 1996 Welfare Reform Act, coupled with the budget cuts instituted by the Reagan administration in the 1980s and steady state-level reductions in welfare benefits, have undermined some of our most successful social welfare programs.
- The value of wages and benefits has eroded, especially for low-income, minimum-wage jobs. In 1991, the average blue-collar wage, after adjusting for inflation, was lower than at any time since 1963. While wages have recovered slightly, we have seen a sustained "debenefitization" of American businesses.
- The purchasing power of the minimum wage has declined sharply. Although it has risen in recent years, the minimum wage would now have to be $7.33 an hour to reach the purchasing power it had in 1968. A single parent with two children working full-time at the minimum wage is now $2,600 below the poverty line, while in most of the 1960s and 1970s, such a job would have lifted the family above the poverty line. The current minimum wage is not a livable one, however, with minimum-wage earners making up a new class of working poor.
- A significant shortage of low-rent housing has developed. In 1970, there were 400,000 more low-rent units in the United States than there were low-income renters. By 1993, there were only fifty-eight affordable housing units for every one hundred low-income renters. As a result, rents have risen sharply and most low-income renters

spend very high percentages of their limited incomes for housing. Thirty-eight percent of rural households earning less than $10,000 pay 50 percent of their income for housing. Moreover, more than fifty percent of these households pay 70 percent of their income for housing costs.

Where has this left us in terms of poverty in America? Consider these facts:

1. In 1996, 13.7 percent of all Americans—some 36.5 million people—lived at or below the official poverty line. One in five of these were "working poor." This is the highest rate since 1963.
2. Minority poverty rates are almost three times that of whites. Despite the fact that two-thirds of poor Americans are white, 24.6 million poor whites represents only 11.2 percent of all whites. In contrast, the percentage for African-Americans is 28.4 and 29.4 for Hispanics. The typical white family earned about $47,000 in 1996, almost twice that of blacks. Worse, the typical black household had a net worth of only about $45,000, a tenth of the white figure.
3. A total of 14.5 million children under age eighteen were living below the poverty line in 1996. Among white children, 16.3 percent were poor. The poverty rate was 39.9 percent and 40.3 percent for African-American and Hispanic children, respectively.
4. In 1994, between 18 million and 20 million people were hungry year-round—that is, chronically short of the nutrients necessary for growth and good health. Of these hungry people, 5.5 million were children under the age of twelve. It is also estimated that another 6 million children under the age of twelve are at risk of facing hunger—meaning that one out of every four children in the United States is likely to experience at least one sustained period of food shortage during a lifetime.
5. In 1979, cash benefits from social insurance programs such as Social Security, unemployment insurance, and public assistance lifted from poverty an estimated 18.9 percent of families with children who otherwise would have been poor. By 1987, the Census Bureau estimated that cash benefits lifted only 10.5 percent of the families from poverty. In 1992, the percentage fell even further to only 8.1

percent of families who otherwise would have been poor. While these figures are no longer kept, it is estimated that the 8 percent figure has held steady in recent years but will fall further as welfare reform takes effect.

6. There is a widening gap between the rich and the poor, the largest since the 1930s. Ninety-eight percent of the gain in household income between 1979 and 1996 went to the top 20 percent—the wealthiest households. The remaining 2 percent of the wealth was spread thinly over the other 80 percent of the households. While the buying power of workers' hourly wages dropped 10 percent in the past two decades, the salaries of presidents and CEOs of corporations have skyrocketed. In 1973, CEO compensation was 40 times the average American worker's pay. In 1996, CEO compensation was 217 times the average worker's pay.

7. Families with incomes below the poverty level spend, on average, 60 percent of the income that remains after paying for shelter on food. Nonetheless, this amounts to an average of only $277 per month for food—just 68 cents per person per meal.

8. Malnutrition is a factor in approximately 16 million deaths worldwide each year, or about one-third of all deaths.

9. If infant mortality in the United States is broken down by race, white infant mortality is seen to be 8 per 1,000, putting it among the best in the world. Black infant mortality, by contrast, is 18 per 1,000, higher than the rate in Bulgaria, Poland, or Cuba.

10. Although the exact number of homeless people is not known, some estimates range from 600,000 to 3 million. On any given night, some 750,000 Americans are homeless. Over the course of a year, between 1.3 and 2 million people will experience homelessness.

A Real Dilemma: Should We Give Money to Homeless Beggars?

Walking in any American city, you will probably see numerous homeless persons, many of them begging. You can't ignore them. What should you do? Doesn't the Jewish tradition require us to give charity to the poor? But what good will it do to hand a beggar some change? Will it be used for food or for alcohol or drugs? Yet can you turn away without surrendering some of your humanity? Besides, even if you do want to help, isn't a handout really a cop-out? Shouldn't you be working on the fundamental problems of homelessness and poverty, of which these beggars are only pathetic symptoms? How do you resolve this dilemma?

Response

It is not a question of either/or. This unkempt and perhaps physically or mentally ill person needs the help of a fellow human being.

There are several ways to address this dilemma. First, use your instinct about giving money. If you sense the beggar will use your money for food, give the coins; if you think it will be used for alcohol or drugs, don't offer any money. If your donation is misused, it's the recipient's fault, not yours. A second approach is to take a few minutes and actually buy food for the street person. This ensures that it won't be misused. While too few of us will really go to this trouble, it is far and away the better way to help.

A third approach is to work with community groups that have set up mechanisms to ensure that the money given to the needy won't be misused. In Berkeley, California, a voucher system was designed to ensure that donations to homeless beggars are spent on necessities like food or laundry services. People can purchase vouchers for 25 cents each and offer them to the needy, who in turn redeem the vouchers at participating stores for food and other necessities. Would such a system work in your community?

However, all experts agree that taking time to chat occasionally with a homeless person and treating him or her like a human being rather than like an object to be avoided or a receptacle into which a quarter is dropped can be as important as the money given. Make eye contact, spend a few minutes and talk with the person; if it is someone whom you see regularly, learn his or her name and introduce yourself.

Liberals vs. Conservatives: Where Is the Jewish Community?

Beginning with the progressive reforms of the 1880s, conservatives have maintained that the capitalistic free enterprise system is inherently balanced and just. Government intervention, they argued, even when done for the best of purposes, inevitably causes more harm than good by upsetting that inherent balance and by infringing on the fundamental rights of individuals to regulate their business lives as they see fit.

Liberals take a very different approach, maintaining that our economic system is inherently neutral and therefore subject to the outside influence of the powerful. Since in this society power emanates from wealth, that influence has been used to further the interests of the privileged. In such a context, it is not only the right but the responsibility of government to intervene in the functioning of our economy and, where necessary, to regulate it to assure a more compassionate and just society for all people—the powerless as well as the powerful.

Is It Time to Say Kaddish for Jewish Liberalism?

Today, in America, liberalism is under attack. We live in a "What's in it for me?" culture, where the public mood is not interested in spending money for "them," where personal fulfillment is much more attractive than bold and costly social programs. We live in a time of political disillusionment with the efficacy of government itself and in a nation where, despite the fact that the budget is now balanced, the pressures of a staggering debt and fears of the resurgence of an annual deficit make it difficult to contemplate expensive social innovations.

Major Jewish voices, like the magazine *Commentary*, have for over two decades exhorted Jews to abandon "knee-jerk liberalism," which they say has run out of intellectual fuel. They challenge Jews to vote their real "interests" instead of their obsolete traditions and "values." "Is it good or bad for Jews?" became the new slogan of hard-nosed pragmatism, implying that automatic support for liberal programs—subsidized housing, military downsizing and nuclear disarmament, racial integration, church-state separation, affirmative action, abortion, civil liberties, assistance to the poor, gay and lesbian rights, etc.—is now contrary to Jewish interests.

These arguments shook and challenged a troubled Jewish community as neoconservative intellectuals began to dominate the debate on Jewish public policy. Unable to advance beyond the ideas of the New Deal and the Great Society, Jewish liberals went on the defensive. What new ideas did liberalism offer to meet the emerging challenges? It seemed only a matter of time before Jewish liberalism would disappear.

But as always, Jewish behavior defied all predictions. Institutionally, few Jewish organizations accepted the neoconservative line, which called for support for a stronger military, a foreign policy focused primarily on resisting communism, less government intervention in the economy, and the elimination of race-conscious remedies for discrimination. If one reviews the "Program Plan" of the Jewish Council of Public Affairs (JCPA), the largest umbrella organization of national and local Jewish organizations concerned with community relations, one will see that in the past twenty years none of these conservative positions were adopted by the Jewish umbrella group.

And it is against this backdrop that Jewish political behavior today must be viewed. Why were Jews the only white ethnic group to have consistently given a substantial majority of its votes to Democrats, joining only with America's Blacks in voting against Presidents Reagan and Bush in their 1984 and 1988 landslide victories and supporting President Clinton in both 1992 and 1996 by margins as high as 85 percent?

No other white group has displayed a similar propensity to vote against its own immediate pocketbook interests. Exit polls for thirty years found Jews more liberal in their attitudes than any other ethnic, racial, or religious group. Jews were most strongly in favor of abortion rights (including government aid to poor women) and civil rights for gays and lesbians. Jews overwhelmingly supported cuts in the defense budget and arms agreements with the Soviets, and they were, in general, far less interested than most Americans in a constitutional amendment requiring a balanced budget. In the massive 1990 National Jewish Population Survey, 43 percent of the Jews surveyed described themselves as liberal, more than twice the percentage of the general American population; only 19 percent of the Jews said they were conservative.

Why, then, is there a widespread impression of a Jewish turn toward conservativism? The answer isn't to be found in voting or attitudinal surveys but in the Jewish voices heard in political debates in America. What has happened is that the 20 to 30 percent of the community that has always held conservative views but was culturally intimidated, isolated, and unorganized during several decades of a strong liberal culture in American life is now far better organized, funded, and energized. Since the early 1980s, their voice has become far more powerful, confident, and assertive—thus altering the balance of Jewish voices heard in American politics to more accurately reflect the reality of our community. In other words, the number of Jewish conservatives has not changed; their effectiveness has.

Similarly, there has been persistent anecdotal evidence that younger Jews are becoming more conservative, but there is little statistical evidence to back up such claims. Indeed, increasing social activism in Jewish youth movements over the past few years belies that view. What do you think?

After two decades of conservative domination in American politics, Jews remain reluctant to join the new popular mood that insists that government cannot have much impact on social problems (e.g., poverty) and that it should stop wasting our tax resources by "throwing money at problems" that can only be solved by volunteer efforts.

This is a dilemma for Jews. We, too, are burdened by heavy taxes. We, too, are angered by the waste and corruption that frequently infect government at the local and national levels. Yet Jews still believe in government, still believe that government must be a primary instrument for achieving justice—and most Jews remain willing to pay taxes to support programs that work.

From where does this stubborn strain of Jewish liberalism stem? Is it a mindless, unexamined persistence in political attitudes appropriate to an earlier age? Is it a response to a widespread historic intuition that Jews are safer on the left side of the center than on the right? Is it a recognition that Jewish enlightened self-interest is best served in a compassionate society and that liberalism can best ensure such conditions? Is it a product of the Jewish ethical and religious heritage, which, in the context of American pluralism, is free to express itself more openly than at other times in Jewish history in the Diaspora? Is it the recognition in the Jewish tradition that taxes, when used well, repre-

sent an investment in the physical infrastructure and human capital of
this country that secures both long-term economic growth and social
justice? Perhaps the high level of education of Jews in America allows
us to feel more secure in this more sophisticated analysis of our long-
term "pocketbook interests" than do less educated segments of our society. Or is it a perverse Jewish instinct to vote against our own interests?
Either way, is it temporary, or is it ingrained in our group character?

Perhaps it is a bit of all of these, but there are two particularly strong
explanations for Jewish liberalism. The first is an enduring conviction
that in the long run, Jewish security is safeguarded by a decent and
compassionate society that actively seeks to help the disadvantaged,
the poor, the handicapped, and the elderly. Only in such a stable and
tranquil society can Jews be safe. Jews can never be secure in a divisive,
tormented, or unjust society that can explode in rage.

And if government doesn't care about the weak, who will? This is a
clue to Jewish liberal attitudes and the Jewish belief that government
must use its resources to diminish suffering and misery for those who
most need assistance. Our definition of enlightened Jewish self-interest
has helped to shape our social and political attitudes in democratic
America.

At the same time, Jewish conservatives have been among those who
have argued most effectively not that government is bad per se, but
that the goals of social justice can best be achieved through the private
sector and with less government interference in the lives of American
citizens and businesses. They point to the very statistics used in the
beginning of the chapter to show that liberalism has failed. What most
Jewish conservatives and liberals seem to have in common is an agreement that a just and fair society for all Americans, including the poor
and including minorities, is the moral test of our society.

The second explanation of Jewish liberalism goes to the heart of our
religious and historic heritage. Our Jewish ethical system *compels* us to
be concerned with the unfortunate and the stranger in our midst, rejecting the concept of "survival of the fittest." "The Earth is the Eternal's
and all that is therein." We are mandated to share God's wealth
entrusted to us with those of God's children who are less fortunate. We
are not engaged in a struggle for survival against our fellow human
beings. Our sages say, rather, "Not only do human beings sustain human
beings, but all nature does so. The stars and planets and even the angels

sustain one another." Human life is sacred, so sacred that saving one life is considered as if someone had saved the entire universe.

Biblical ethics are permeated with laws assuring protection of the poor. Indeed, many scholars believe that the first antipoverty program in human history was spelled out in the Hebrew Bible and Talmud. Our self-interest is reinforced by profound ethical impulses drawn from a Jewish religious value system that commands us to be copartners with God in building a just and peaceful world. It does not, of course, command us to be liberal or conservative, Republican or Democrat. It does command us to "know the heart of the stranger," to care, and to *act* to improve the world.

IS THE JEWISH POLITICAL TRADITION LIBERAL OR CONSERVATIVE?

If a key contemporary distinction between liberals and conservatives focuses on the economic justice role of government, the Jewish tradition is decidedly liberal or progressive (i.e., it always saw the public sector, the self-governing Jewish community as playing a primary role in ensuring economic justice). As discussed in depth below, by early talmudic times, at least four communal funds (plus communal schools for children) were required in every sizable community. These included a daily food distribution program, a clothing fund, a burial fund, and a communal money fund. By the Middle Ages, these had grown into a veritable bureaucracy of social welfare institutions. *Tzedakah* in Jewish history functioned as a system of taxation, not a voluntary philanthropic enterprise. Since members of the Jewish community were *compelled* to support these institutions, they are analogous in our own time to government institutions, not to voluntary private charities.

Indeed, most economic relations—including landlord-tenant, worker-employer, purchaser-seller, as well as regulation of business to protect the environment—were appropriate subjects for extensive communal regulation, not just matters of private contract law.

While the social welfare system evolved by the Jewish rabbinic authorities is obviously not the only model of an ethical economic framework, the pattern that emerged in Jewish history provides a standard against which the programs of our own society can be compared and judged.

HAS LIBERALISM WORKED?

This liberal approach has generally succeeded in contemporary American society as it did in historic Jewish communities, for America has made significant strides in the past sixty-five years toward achieving social justice. That is not to say that we have gone all the way, or even most of the way, or that there were not major reforms to be made in our economic justice and welfare programs. Some of the liberal solutions of yesterday have become the problems of today. But the unceasing politically inspired vilification of "liberal" programs threatened to drown the baby in the bathwater.

With all the problems besetting these programs, the fundamental truth of contemporary American life is that on the whole, liberal programs have helped make America a far more decent and caring society.

Consider the following: In 1959, before the birth of the modern social welfare program, 22 percent of American people lived in poverty; by 1965, it was down to 17 percent; in the 1970s, as a result of the Social Security and Great Society programs, the rate hovered in the 11-to-12-percent range. Since 1981, the trend has dramatically reversed itself, fluctuating higher than the 14-to-15-percent range. In 1996, the last year before "welfare reform," it had fallen to 13.7 percent. According to the Congressional Research Service, 49 million Americans would have sunk below the poverty line in 1989 if there had been no programs covering food and housing benefits, public assistance, and Social Security. Moreover, the vast majority of those in poverty were far better off than they would have been had there been no social welfare programs. Without Social Security, our elderly would be mired in poverty beyond imagining.

But there were also failures. The great failure of liberals in the 1970s and 1980s was their inability to recognize that major improvements could be made in social welfare programs, that a welfare culture was being passed from generation to generation, that there was extensive waste in some programs, and that other programs were counterproductive. The Welfare Reform Act, enacted in mid-1996, however, decimated rather than reformed these programs. These changes in federal welfare law have created undue hardships for those already buffeted most severely by economic problems. Rather than protecting the weak and the vulnerable, as our tradition requires, these programs exacted cruel sacrifices from those least able to sustain them.

THE 1996 WELFARE REFORM ACT

The Welfare Reform Act cut $55 billion in federal government spending on human needs programs over the following six years (while allowing states to withdraw an additional $40 billion in state funds) and made radical changes in federal cash assistance, childcare, disability assistance, and a wide range of other social service programs. While purporting to move people rapidly from welfare to work, the act in fact shredded the federal safety net of assistance for poor families and hindered the ability of community agencies to help provide for the needs of the poor.

The welfare act ended the sixty-year-old federal guarantee (entitlement) that all poor families who meet certain income eligibility guidelines would receive cash and childcare assistance. Instead, under the act, the federal government gave limited pools of money directly to *state* governments to use for a broad range of purposes, some of which may not benefit those families who are most in need of aid. If a state were to experience a recession, natural disaster, or other event that significantly raised human need, it nevertheless would find it very difficult to receive additional funds from the federal government beyond its restricted allocation. The amount that such states have to spend on cash assistance for needy families is not always enough to meet the needs of the poor within those states. In addition, under the act, states are required to place an increasing percentage of welfare recipients in work or job-training activities (or risk losing a portion of their federal funds), yet the act fails to provide the resources needed for increased childcare or job training or development. Job training and safe childcare are essential to parents seeking to get off—and stay off—welfare, and without investment in these crucial areas, welfare reform is not likely to be effective. Finally, the new act establishes a five-year lifetime limit on an individual's receipt of cash assistance and gives states the option to set a shorter time limit even if the welfare recipient has genuinely sought work opportunities. Individuals who reach their time limit will be unable to receive any financial assistance from the government no matter how desperate their needs and those of their families.

Take one example of what this means. Philadelphia sustained a net gain of 550 jobs in 1997 in the midst of one of the great economic booms in American history. In order to place all the welfare recipients who will need jobs over five years, it will need 50,000 new jobs!

Who is affected by these changes? Perhaps most telling is that prior to 1996, 20 percent of the discretionary budget (i.e., money that could be allocated yearly by Congress, such as trust funds like Social Security and required payments on the national debt) went to programs benefiting needy people. In the changes in 1996, twice that percentage, 40 percent, of the cuts made to balance the budget came from means-tested programs. Such sacrifices should not be made on the backs of those least equipped to sustain them.

Our tradition teaches that the moral test of public policy is what it does for the widow and the orphan, the elderly and the ill, and the children. Yet how does one square this vision with the policies enacted that *particularly* punish children?

- When a poor mother who genuinely seeks work and cannot find it has her children thrown off the welfare rolls in as little as two years in some states, it is her innocent children who are punished.
- When $23 billion is cut from the food stamp program over six years, on top of making $3 billion in cuts over the same time period to other vital child nutrition programs, it is needy children that will feel the greatest impact.
- When the families of 300,000 disabled children receiving Supplemental Security Income lose those benefits under new eligibility and funding rules, the children will fail to reach their full potential, and some lower-middle-class families will be forced to institutionalize children—a failure that will ultimately *increase* society's burden for their care.
- And when federal childcare funding (as projected by the Office of Management and Budget [OMB]) falls $2.4 billion short of what will be necessary to meet the increased need as parents enter the workforce, more and more poor children will suffer in unsafe day-care environments.

A nation that neglects its children, that allows children to go hungry, homeless, and unprotected, is a nation that shortchanges its future. Such neglect is unconscionable; it violates the most basic precepts of Jewish tradition and shuns our fundamental obligation to care for those who are less fortunate than we. Further, such policies punish others who genuinely want to be self-sufficient, who genuinely seek work but cannot find it and will, nonetheless, be hurt.

The Welfare Reform Act's cuts in food stamps—generally regarded as one of the nation's most effective social welfare programs—reduces benefits by up to 20 percent for approximately 25 million poor people (not including those categories of individuals—particularly legal immigrants—who were rendered entirely ineligible to receive them). In one of the harshest provisions in the act, approximately 1 million unemployed, childless individuals between the ages of eighteen and fifty are able to receive food stamp benefits for only three months out of each three-year period and after that point are denied vital nutrition assistance even if no employment is available to them. The Welfare Reform Act ends the federal guarantee of childcare to families receiving cash assistance. The president is seeking to soften these provisions.

LEGAL IMMIGRANTS AND REFUGEES

Legal immigrants were most deeply impacted by the Welfare Reform Act. The act denied all legal immigrants—current and future—from receiving *any* assistance through the SSI or food stamp programs until they become United States citizens. In all, 900,000 legal immigrants, many of whom work in minimum-wage jobs and pay taxes, lost their food stamps—50,000 children among them. SSI, in particular, serves as a lifeline to elderly and disabled immigrants and refugees, often providing the assistance crucial to helping them meet their rent payments, buy a winter coat, pay a heating bill, or put food on their tables. Moreover, all new legal immigrants will be barred from receiving Medicaid, cash assistance, childcare assistance, and most other nonemergency means-tested federal aid for their first five years in the United States, and states will have the option to extend the bar on eligibility for these programs until the immigrants become citizens. Refugees (who, as opposed to legal immigrants, are granted preferential immigration status because of their experience or well-founded fear of persecution) will remain eligible for SSI and food stamps for their first five years in the United States. After that, even refugees—a category that includes most Jews who came to America from the former Soviet Union—will be denied assistance if they fail to become citizens, with no exceptions granted refugees who lack the physical, emotional, or mental capabilities to take the steps required for naturalization.

In 1997, a coalition of religious and public interest groups led the successful effort to restore SSI funding to many disabled immigrants. In 1998, the same coalition restored some food stamps to elderly, disabled, and children immigrants and expanded the exemption for refugees from five to seven years.

Our tradition teaches us to protect the *ger*—the Hebrew word we erroneously translate in the Bible as the "stranger." The *ger* was not a person just passing through (albeit such a person, too, was entitled to some social benefits). The *ger* was the person who came to live in Israel, who was willing to abide by the rules of our society, to work and pay taxes whenever possible, to observe the nonritual laws of Israel—and to whom the Bible and Talmud grant all the social benefits of the society accorded to Jews. This is the exact situation of immigrants coming to our nation, yet the new Welfare Reform Act blindly denies most federal benefits to the vast majority of those immigrants whom the leaders of our nation have welcomed to our shores. Jewish values cannot be reconciled with a policy that makes legal immigrant parents of disabled children completely ineligible for SSI, denying their innocent children the essential resources they need to become contributing members of our society. Nor can we justify the teachings of our tradition with legislation that denies the family of a seven-year-old child, legally in the United States, from receiving any Food Stamp assistance, leaving him hungry and unable to concentrate on anything except his empty stomach. We are not fulfilling our fundamental moral obligation to provide for the stranger in our midst with a provision forcing an eighty-five-year-old legal immigrant woman, in spite of her age or lack of physical mobility, to learn English and pass a difficult citizenship exam in order to retain the Medicaid benefits she desperately needs to treat her heart condition. Such policies are anathema to the most fundamental teachings of our heritage.

Today, the gravest threats to our national security are internal rather than external. Surely the worsening quality of American life, the fate of our cities, the health of our children, the deterioration of our educational system, and the angry status of group relations are as much a measure of national security as is our military might.

We Jews have a profound stake in an America that is compassionate and whole. We are endangered by an America that is angry and torn apart. "The sword enters the world because of justice delayed and justice denied," states *Pirke Avot.*

JEWISH POVERTY IN THE UNITED STATES

Poverty affects Jews directly as well. Jewish poverty is far more extensive than most people imagine. Experts estimate that between 13 and 15 percent of the U.S. Jewish population, or 780,000 to 900,000 people, live in poverty or so narrowly above that even a temporary loss of a job, an illness, or an accident would immediately plunge them below the poverty line.

Moreover, the elderly are disproportionately hurt by poverty, and we Jews are the most elderly community in America. The median age of the American population in the 1990 census was about thirty-two, while the median age of the Jewish community is over thirty-six.

Exacerbating these problems is that we Jews are the only segment of the American populace that has been practicing zero population growth for a generation, with a shrinking number of working-age people supporting an ever-growing number of elderly in our community. The truth is, even if we dramatically increase our contributions to Jewish federations and charities, we cannot fully take care of our own. As Jews, we must stand together with that multiethnic coalition of decency that believes it should be a matter of national policy that those people who built our nation, fought our wars, and paid our taxes have an inalienable right to age with dignity.

JUDAISM AND POVERTY

America's concern for the poor is based, in part, on the legacy of the Judeo-Christian ethic derived originally from the Jewish Bible. Biblical ethics are permeated with laws assuring protection of the weak and the powerless. Our sages taught that poverty was the worst catastrophe that could happen to a person. "If all afflictions in the world were assembled on the side of a scale and poverty on the other, poverty would outweigh them all." (*Exodus Rabbah* 31:12) The tradition set about ameliorating the condition of poverty or when that was not possible, ameliorating the impact of poverty.

The Bible prescribes that when a field is harvested, the corners are to be left uncut and the gleanings reserved for the poor, the stranger, the orphan, and the widow. According to the Torah, every seventh year was a sabbatical year, during which the land was to lie fallow, and that which grew of itself belonged to all in order that "the poor of your people may eat." (Exodus 23:11) All debts were to be canceled. Every fiftieth year was a jubilee year, during which all lands were to be returned to the families to whom they were originally allocated. The law of the fiftieth year fell into disuse in Jewish history, but its spirit was preserved.

Our ancestors realized that an unrestricted pursuit of individual economic gain would result in massive concentrations of wealth for the few and oppressive poverty for the many. They sanctioned competition, but they rejected an "anything goes" mentality. The intent of the law was to restore the economic balance, to give those who had fallen an opportunity to lift themselves up again. Land was not the permanent possession of any human being. "The land shall not be sold in perpetuity; for the land is Mine; you are but strangers and settlers with Me." (Leviticus 25:23)

"If there is among you a needy person, you shall surely open your hand and lend him sufficient for whatever he needs." This verse from Deuteronomy (15:7–8) also became the basis for a highly developed system of loans. Throughout rabbinic literature, the loan is regarded as the finest form of charity. "Greater is one who lends than one who gives, and greater still is one who lends and, with the loan, helps the poor person to help himself." (Babylonian Talmud, *Shabbat* 63a) Almost a millennium after this was written, the medieval philosopher Maimonides defined the "eight degrees of charity," the highest of which is to enable a person to become self-supporting. Until modern times, every Jewish community had a *gemilut chesed* society, whose primary purpose was to grant loans to the needy without interest or security.

Jewish ethics clearly respect the institution of private property. Jewish tradition, however, never asserted that property rights take precedence over human rights, an assertion made by many in America today. Nor did Judaism accept the Puritan emphasis on the acquisition of property and worldly goods as a sign of virtue. On the contrary, for the Jew, human rights have priority over property rights. The tithe prescribed in biblical law was not a voluntary contribution but an obligation imposed on all in order that "the stranger and the fatherless and the widow shall come and shall eat and be satisfied." (Deuteronomy 14:29)

TZEDAKAH

There is no word in the Hebrew vocabulary for "charity" in the modern sense. The word used is *tzedakah*, which literally means "righteousness." *Tzedakah* is not an act of condescension by the affluent toward the needy; it is the fulfillment of a moral obligation. Injustice to humanity is desecration of God. "One who mocks the poor blasphemes one's Maker." (Proverbs 17:5) Refusal to give charity is considered by Jewish tradition to be idolatry.

Our sages taught that Abraham was more righteous than Job. According to rabbinic tradition, when great suffering befell Job, he attempted to justify himself by saying, "Ruler of the world, have I not fed the hungry and clothed the naked?" (Job 16:22) God conceded that Job had done much for the poor, but he had always waited until the poor came to him, whereas Abraham had gone out of his way to search out the poor. He not only brought them into his home but set up inns on the highway to give the poor and the wayfarer access to food and drink in time of need. True charity is to "run after the poor." (Babylonian Talmud, *Shabbat* 104a)

An act of *tzedakah* is the means by which we restore the image of God to every human being. The sensitivities of recipients are to be safeguarded at all times. "Better no giving at all than the giving that humiliates." (Babylonian Talmud, *Hagigah* 5a) "One who gives charity in secret is even greater than Moses." (Babylonian Talmud, *Baba Batra* 9b) In the Temple at Jerusalem, there was a "chamber of secrecy" where the pious placed their gifts and the poor drew for their needs, all in anonymity. In later times, a *tzedakah* box marked *matan baseter* ("secret almsgiving") was placed in synagogues.

The sages regarded *gemilut chasadim* ("acts of loving-kindness") as being on a higher moral plane than *tzedakah*: "One who gives a coin to a poor person is rewarded with six blessings, but one who encourages that person with words is rewarded with *seven blessings*." (Babylonian Talmud, *Baba Batra* 9b)

Jewish Welfare

In the talmudic period, the Jewish community supplemented the obligations of private charity with the first recorded system of public welfare.

The practices and theories of Jewish philanthropy that evolved in the second century C.E. anticipated many of the most advanced concepts of modern social work. Every Jewish community had four basic funds. The first was called *kuppah* ("box") and served only the local poor. The indigent were given funds to supply their needs for an entire week. The second fund was called *tamchui* ("bowl") and consisted of a daily distribution of food to both itinerants and residents. The funds' administrators, selected from among the leaders of the community, were expected to be persons of the highest integrity. The *kuppah* was administered by three trustees who acted as a *bet din* ("court"). They determined the merit of applicants and the amounts to be given. The fund was operated under the strictest regulations. To avoid suspicion, collections were always made by two or three persons. They were authorized to tax *all* members of the community, including *tzedakah* recipients, according to their capacity to pay—testimony to the principle that no individual was free from responsibility for the welfare of all. If necessary, they seized property until the assessed amount was paid. In most countries, clothing funds, burial funds, and schools to which everybody in the community could go—rich and poor alike—were also found.

By the Middle Ages, community responsibility encompassed every aspect of life. The Jewish community regulated market prices so that the poor could purchase food and other basic commodities at cost. Wayfarers were issued tickets, good for meals and lodging at homes of members of the community, who took turns offering hospitality. Both these practices anticipated "meal tickets" and modern food stamp plans. Some Jewish communities even established "rent control," directing that the poor be given housing at rates they could afford. In Lithuania, local trade barriers were relaxed for poor refugees. When poor young immigrants came from other places, the community would support them until they completed their education or learned a trade.

The organization of charity became so specialized that numerous societies were established to keep pace with all the needs. Each of the following functions was assumed by a different society on behalf of the community at large: visiting the sick, burying the dead, furnishing dowries for poor girls, providing clothing, ransoming captives, supplying maternity needs, and providing necessities for observing holidays. In addition, there were public inns for travelers, homes for the aged, orphanages, and free medical care. As early as the eleventh century, a *hekdesh* ("hospital") was established by the Jewish community of Cologne, primarily for poor and sick travelers. Many later medieval Jewish communities in Poland and Germany adopted this pattern. Spanish Jewish communities hired doctors to serve the entire community to ensure that health care was available to all.

APPLYING JEWISH TRADITIONS TO MODERN LIFE

If the values of the Jewish tradition generally coincide with the liberal agenda today and animate the attitudes of the Jewish community, what insights does the Jewish tradition offer on specific policy issues of today?

The Jewish concern for the dignity of the poor is violated by some of the more demeaning aspects of the social welfare system in America today. For example, in Jewish tradition, those who claimed they were poor were given relief immediately and investigation of the claim came later. The reverse is done in our society.

Even the poor who were the recipients of welfare funds were taxed. This helped each person fulfill the *mitzvah* of *tzedakah* and prevented the stratification of society into two classes. Every person was a giver. Each person helped the poor.

EDUCATION

The belief in the inherent ability of each person to progress if given the proper tools led the Jewish community to develop a comprehensive system of education for boys. Moreover, through much of Jewish history, girls also were taught to read and write. "Lack of learning results in poverty," the Midrash wisely observes. If a community grew to a certain size but failed to establish a school, its leaders were subject to punishment. Regardless of a family's economic status, each male child was guaranteed a decent education. "Be zealous with children of the poor, for from them learning will come forth," states the Talmud. (Babylonian Talmud, *Nedarim* 81a)

A lack of commitment to the funding of education is clearly a major factor in the bleak condition of inner-city public education in the United States. The Economic Policy Institute reported that the United States is fourteenth among industrialized countries in per capita spending on elementary and high school education.

The growing problem of poverty in America compounds the challenges faced by schools. Homeless, hungry, and ill students do not learn at the same pace as healthy, well-fed, happy children. Minority students suffer disproportionately. Illiteracy among minority students in some areas is as high as 56 percent. Nationwide, they earn lower test scores than white students and are overrepresented among dropouts and suspensions.

This disparity is exacerbated by the pattern of funding schools in accordance with the relative wealth of districts. In a Texas case, for example, the Supreme Court noted that the state's wealthiest districts were spending an average of $7,233 per student while the poorest were spending only $2,978. Such disparities lead to a self-perpetuating cycle in which less money and poorer facilities are assigned to the already disadvantaged while the more privileged children have built-in advantages in their school systems.

A well-educated citizenry is essential to democracy and to our economic health. A workforce that cannot read or write cannot compete in a global market. A commitment to education is a commitment to this country's future.

FULL EMPLOYMENT

According to Maimonides, the highest form of charity was achieved by preventing poverty "through a gift or loan; by teaching the person a trade; by putting the person in the way of business so that the person may earn an honest livelihood and not be forced to the alternative of holding out a hand for charity." (*Mishneh Torah*, "Laws of Gifts to the Poor," 10:7–12)

While this obligation of *tzedakah* applied to individuals, we know of at least one historical moment when a community, or government, undertook efforts to promote full employment. The historian Josephus recounts what may well have been one of the first public works projects ever undertaken to alleviate the debilitating impact of unemployment. "And now it was that the Temple was finished. So when the people saw that the workmen who were unemployed were about eighteen thousand and that they, receiving no wages, were in want because they had earned their bread by their labors about the Temple, they persuaded King Agrippa to rebuild the eastern cloisters." (Josephus Flavius, *The Jewish Antiquities*, XX, 9)

The New Deal and Great Society programs included public employment programs and job-training programs aimed at ensuring that the nation moved toward full employment. It is difficult to reconcile the values of that tradition with economic policies that in the early 1980s produced the highest unemployment rates since the Great Depression. Further, the Reagan and Bush administrations eliminated or sharply curtailed the public service employment and training programs; cut back unemployment insurance for the long-term unemployed; and implemented tax policies in 1981 that by disproportionately burdening the working poor actually created disincentives to work. The sweeping Welfare Reform Act that was passed in mid-1996, requiring those on welfare to work, likewise had no provisions for new funding for job training and creation. Such programs may help move some people to economic self-sufficiency, but many others will find themselves mired ever deeper in a cycle of poverty.

A Real Dilemma: Mazon

One of the most remarkable Jewish responses to hunger in America is an organization called Mazon: A Jewish Response to Hunger, which urges Jews to give 3 percent of the cost of a *simchah*, such as a wedding or a bar or bat mitzvah, to combat hunger. Mazon allocates funds to scores of local communities, mostly in America but also in Israel and countries worldwide. At the first meeting of the board of Mazon, someone asked, "Should these funds, which come from Jews, be limited to serving the Jewish poor, or should they be distributed ecumenically across the board?" This was the first—and one of the most delicate— policy dilemmas faced by Mazon. What do you think were the arguments on both sides? How would you have voted?

Response

The decision was that Mazon, being a Jewish antihunger agency, will make combating Jewish poverty a high priority, but allocations of funds will *not* be limited to Jewish beneficiaries. In contrast to some equally admirable Jewish groups that provide assistance only to Jews, Mazon gives to antipoverty interfaith and communal groups as well.

THE JEWISH COMMUNITY AND THE LABOR MOVEMENT

No ethnic group has been so closely associated with the development of the labor movement in the United States as American Jews. The labor movement played an indispensable role in allowing workers to organize to fight for decent wages, safer and fairer working conditions, effective job protections and pensions, and the right to strike if the employer treated workers unfairly. Once the leadership and membership of labor unions such as textile workers and the International Ladies Garment Workers were Jewish; then leadership but not membership became Jewish; and now some leadership, little membership, and declining support are characteristic of the Jewish community. Inevitably, as Jews moved in large numbers into professional fields (e.g., law and medicine) and moved up the economic ladder even to positions of ownership of companies, the once automatic pro-labor stance of Jewish organizations significantly dissipated. Moreover, instances of corruption and occasionally of racial discrimination within some labor unions generated further disenchantment and distancing on the part of many Jews.

This passion for the rights and dignity of labor is animated by the Jewish tradition. "Great is labor, for it honors the worker." (*Nedarim* 49b) Fair wages had to be paid in a timely manner. "In the same day, you shall give the worker his hire, for he is poor and sets his heart on it." (Deuteronomy 24:14, 15) An employee can break an employment contract, but the employer cannot. Employees who are laid off are entitled to severance pay, and they must have safe and fair work conditions. From talmudic times on, workers organized in worker federations and even the right to strike was known in certain communities. As Rabbi Uzziel, the late Ashkenazic Chief Rabbi of Israel observed: "The

Torah obligates [the employer] to make every effort to protect his workers from injury; failure to do so makes him liable to the moral crime of
'Thou shalt not spill blood in thy house.'"

A Real Dilemma: Permanent Replacement of Strikers

In 1938, in finding that an employer had unlawfully discriminated against several strikers when it refused to reinstate them
because of their leadership of a strike, the United States Supreme
Court observed, in a statement little noticed at the time, that

> it does not follow [from the right to strike] that an
> employer, guilty of no act denounced by the statute,
> has lost the right to protect and continue his business
> by supplying places left vacant by strikers. And he is
> not bound to discharge those hired to fill the places of
> strikers upon the election of the latter to resume their
> employment in order to create places for them.

For many years, in most major strikes, employers did not exercise
the right to replace strikers permanently, and the inability of
strikers to get their jobs back after a strike was not a major problem. But in the late 1980s, with a decline in the economy, with a
decrease in the unionized segment of the workforce, and with
the increased pressures on businesses from global competition,
more and more employers began to exercise the right to replace
their employees permanently when they went on strike.

Employers argued that without offering permanent employment they could not attract competent replacements to operate
their businesses during a strike and that without operating during
the strike, their businesses could not survive. Without permanent replacements, they claimed, the labor unions had them over
a barrel. Labor unions responded that while they did not challenge an employer's right to operate with replacements during
the strike itself, permanent replacement of strikers was the same
as firing them for going on strike, making a nullity of the right to
strike. And without a meaningful right to strike, unions lacked
any weapon with which to counterbalance the economic power
of employers.

In the 1990s, Senator Howard Metzenbaum (chair of the Commission on Social Action of Reform Judaism until he entered the U.S. Senate) introduced legislation to overturn the Supreme Court's 1938 pronouncement and ban the permanent replacement of strikers.

Labor sought the support of the Jewish community, pointing to the community's historic role in the labor movement and its traditional support of the fair treatment of workers and the right of workers to withhold their services. Furthermore, labor pointed out that national unions had worked with the Jewish community on common concerns (e.g., the civil rights and women's rights movements) as well as working vigorously for particular vital Jewish concerns such as the struggle for Soviet Jewry and numerous efforts on behalf of Israel. And they put their money where their mouths were, with many labor unions holding significant amounts of Israeli bonds in their pension portfolios. Reminding the Jewish community of the first tenet of coalitional politics— to have a friend you need to be a friend—the AFL-CIO turned to the Jewish community to stand with them on the permanent replacement issue.

The Commission on Social Action urged the two bodies to support Senator Metzenbaum's legislation. If you were on the UAHC or CCAR boards, what would you have done?

Response

For one of the few times in its history, the UAHC took a position, by a narrow margin, in opposition to labor's request. It decided to remain neutral (but not oppose) the legislation. Some of the board members recounted sour experiences with labor unions, not only as employers but as customers in health and service industries. The CCAR, on the other hand, voted by a substantial margin to oppose the legislation. The UAHC's position does not represent a sea change in attitudes, since the Jewish community and labor still agree on most labor issues, but rather reflects the gradual impact of a major shift in the social and economic status of American Jews.

A poignant illustration of the growing clash of Jewish views on labor occurred in 1997 when the National Yiddish Book Center was dedicated on the campus of Hampshire College in Massachusetts. The dedication of this center was seen as a major Jewish cultural event, but, remarkably, it became the occasion of a challenge by the Jewish Labor Committee (JLC) and thus an intra-Jewish controversy revolving around the question: Is the center "insulting" the values of Jewish culture by failing to use union labor in its project?

The Jewish *Forward* of July 11, 1997, described the episode:

> The dedication of the recently completed National Yiddish Book Center, on the campus of Hampshire College, was an event heralded throughout the Jewish world. But the JLC noted early on—after it was approached by the local carpenter's union—that the book center's benefactor, Aaron Lansky, was not using a union contractor for the construction. Last week, the JLC attacked Mr. Lansky in an open letter for insulting "the very people whose culture you wish to save" by having ignored their request to use a union builder. [*Note:* It was immigrants from Eastern Europe who spoke Yiddish who made up the Jewish labor union movement. The pro-labor ideology was integrally bound up with Yiddish culture.]
>
> "Shame on you," the letter reads. "Have you not read and learned the lessons in the books you collected? The books that deal with sweatshops, with awful working conditions, child labor, and long hours?...You recently discovered a cache of Yiddish protest songs that deal with the struggle of poor Jewish workers. You even offered them for sale to your members and supporters. How could you have been so coldhearted as to ignore our people's history?"
>
> Mr. Lansky, who had not seen the letter, said that he made a special effort to open the contracting to union companies. "In the end, we hired a company that paid its workers a dollar over the union rate." He said, "It wasn't like we violated labor standards."

If you had been consulted, how would you have responded? Who was right? Why? What's the Jewish issue?

Health Care

The Jewish tradition strongly affirms the obligation of humanity to use its God-given wisdom and abilities to cure diseases. (See the discussion "Medical Ethics" in chapter 3, "Bioethics.") The following *midrash* teaches that we should not regard sickness as the unfolding of God's plan; rather, we should intervene by fulfilling the commandment to heal:

> Once Rabbi Ishmael and Rabbi Akiva were strolling in the streets of Jerusalem along with another man. They met a sick person who said to them, "Masters, can you tell me how I can be healed?" They quickly advised him to take a certain medicine until he felt better.
>
> The man strolling with the two rabbis turned to them and said, "Who made this man sick?" "The Holy Blessed One," they replied. "And you presume to interfere in an area that is not yours?" the man remarked. "God has afflicted and you heal?" "What is your occupation?" they asked the man. "I'm a tiller of the soil," he answered, "as you can see from the sickle I carry." "Who created the land and the vineyard?" "The Holy Blessed One." "And you dare to move into an area that is not yours? God created these and you eat their fruit?" "Don't you see the sickle in my hand?" the man asked. "If I did not go out and plow the field, water it, fertilize it, weed it, no food would grow!"
>
> "Fool," the rabbis said, "the body is like a tree—the medicine is the fertilizer and the doctor is the farmer."
>
> (*Midrash Shmuel* 4)

Some of the greatest figures of Jewish history, including Maimonides and the great medieval Spanish poet Yehudah Halevi, made their living as physicians. It is no coincidence that Jews represented a disproportionate number of physicians and medieval researchers of renown. Nor is it a coincidence that an amazing percentage of Soviet Jews coming to Israel are doctors!

The obligation to provide medical care to all Jews in a community was a religious obligation accepted by Jews throughout history. It is no less binding upon us today. The community licensed and regulated doctors, as well as the cost of medicine. Moreover, citizens were instructed to live where medical care was available and, according to Maimonides, to take steps through diet and exercise to prevent illness. Many Jewish communities set up public health systems to be sure that everyone in the Jewish community—rich and poor alike—had access to decent health care. In many communities, public health systems were established. Thus in his authoritative *Jews in Spain*, A. A. Neuman wrote:

> The physician, on assuming the duties of his office to which he was generally appointed for a term of years, made a medical examination of every person in the territory under his jurisdiction and then gave everyone advice according to his findings, in the light of his knowledge of the science of medicine and as G-d inspired him. He treated the poor in the public hospital. He was obliged to visit every sick person three times a month.

While the United States spends more on health care than any other nation (the Congressional Budget Office estimates that as a nation, Americans spent $1.1 trillion in 1997, roughly 13.8 percent of the GDP), one out of every seven Americans (44 million in 1997) has no health insurance. More than a third of these are employed, and a quarter are children under the age of eighteen. Another 31 million Americans are underinsured as of 1997. The United States has one of the highest infant mortality rates in the developed world, higher than that of eighteen other nations. The immunization rate for Blacks in America would rank fifty-sixth among the world's nations, behind Albania and Botswana.

At its 1987 and 1993 biennial conventions, the UAHC urged that state and federal legislation be enacted to (1) ensure that all

Americans, whether or not they are able to provide for themselves, are guaranteed essential health-care coverage; (2) guarantee affordable health-care insurance covering catastrophic illness; and (3) provide for long-term health care, including adequate home health care, ambulatory day care, and health-regulated day care; assistance toward the cost of prescription drugs; changes in the deductible rule so that it is applied to each illness rather than each hospitalization, without requiring that one must be impoverished to receive governmental health-care assistance. While Congress derailed a 1993 attempt by President Clinton to enact a universal health-care system that guarantees coverage to all Americans, the UAHC remains committed to urging the federal government to create such a system in the future.

SOCIALLY RESPONSIBLE INVESTMENT: A NEW EXPRESSION OF JUSTICE

Do you think before you buy? What kinds of companies do you support? Can your money really make a difference? The concept of "socially responsible investment" is a method of applying the values of *tikkun olam* to the world of money and business.

Socially responsible investment (SRI) is founded on the concept that investments do make a difference and can be a way of creating positive social change. To practice SRI means to adopt a "double bottom line"—first, with regard to the rate of return and second, with regard to the consonance of the investing organization's values and the entities in which it invests. SRI reflects the concerns of Isaiah: "Why do you spend money for what is not bread,/ Your earnings for what does not satisfy?" (Isaiah 55:2)

Jeffrey Dekro and Lawrence Bush, in their book *Jews, Money, and Social Responsibility*, discuss the overriding Judaic concern with SRI, as framed by the Israeli scholar Meir Tamari:

> "(T)he achievement of economic wealth and the use thereof," writes Meir Tamari, "are very strictly limited and channeled by Judaism." All Jewish actions, "including those involved in the accumulation of material goods, are to be subjected to the ethical, moral, and religious demands of the Torah, so that the

> individual and society can attain a state of sanctity
> even while carrying out the most mundane acts...."

Socially responsible investment falls into three categories. First, the investor can consciously decide not to invest in corporations whose activities or policies she considers to be socially detrimental ("social screens"). Second, the investor as a stockholder in a corporation can seek to bring the corporation's policies into agreement with the investor's values. Finally, the investor can by carefully choosing her investments promote corporations and organizations whose activities and policies she approves of and/or whose agendas include socially responsible activities (for example, low-income housing projects or community development banks). In 1997, the Social Investment Forum reported that concerned investors, both individuals and institutions, took social considerations into account in their money-making decisions with $1.2 trillion. Seeds of this movement were planted as far back as the 1930s, but they took root in the early 1970s as concern about the business practices of some American corporations heightened. One of the first widespread national efforts embodying this concept was the campaign to encourage individuals and organizations to "divest" their investments in American corporations that conducted business in South Africa. This campaign played an important role in the success of the antiapartheid movement.

Today, potential investors may apply certain criteria or "social screens" in making their investment decisions. For example, they may first want assurances that the corporations in which they invest are not guilty of job discrimination or of polluting the environment. Rooted in the divestment tradition, this type of socially responsible investment is increasingly practiced. Scores of mutual funds focusing on such investments have sprung up to help investors.

A Real Dilemma: Should Synagogues Divest from Tobacco Companies?

A large congregation in Hartford, Connecticut, was challenged by its Social Action Committee to divest its portfolio of any stocks involving tobacco companies. Some members of the board questioned whether smoking is a moral issue; others, whether it is a Jewish issue. (The Social Action Committee argued that smoking was clearly a matter of life and death, a major health crisis, and an ethical challenge to the teachings of Judaism.) How would you have voted if you had been on the board?

Response

The congregation adopted the resolution to divest its portfolio of tobacco companies. This was the first Reform congregation to adopt such a resolution. Members of the board felt this position was consistent with the resolutions adopted by the delegates to the General Assembly of the UAHC. (See the discussion "Substance Abuse" in chapter 2, "Life-and-Death Issues: Policy on the Edge.")

Perhaps the greatest growth in socially responsible investment comes from community investment opportunities: community development banks, loan funds, and credit unions. These organizations have been established to repair the damage caused by investors when they withdraw from a deteriorating community and make it almost impossible for local residents to obtain funding for new businesses, new housing, and improvements to community facilities—schools, recreational areas, parks, etc. Without adequate funding, even the most determined community development coalitions are thwarted. Even modest funds devoted to community investing can have a significant impact, since they often help leverage substantial additional funds. Rates of return on community development investments may vary, depending on market circumstances. Increasingly, and almost always, this funding is made available through socially responsible community development banks and loan funds.

An example: In 1973, the South Shore Bank in Chicago, one of the nation's earliest community development banks, undertook a difficult, and some thought impossible, task. It sought to help revitalize one of Chicago's toughest, most downtrodden neighborhoods. By using targeted financing, which stimulated neighborhood reconstruction linked to education and employment programs, the bank has sparked the comeback of a neighborhood that most people had written off.

Today, the neighborhood boasts $160 million in new investments, 350 rehabilitated large apartment buildings, and property values that are rising 5 to 7 percent each year. The community is stable, crime is down, and emerging businesses are profitable—all testimony to the power and potential of socially responsible investment. This project has become a model for the community banks that have sprung up in cities across the country.

Delegates to the 1997 UAHC and CCAR conventions adopted similar resolutions committing their organizations to lead a new program: the Chai Investment Program (CHIP), with the goal of investing 1.8 percent of all invested funds (including endowment and pension funds) in community development and revitalization. The UAHC and CCAR challenged local synagogues and other national organizations to participate as well. The resolutions also encourage individuals in the Reform movement to follow similar investing practices.

A Real Dilemma: Making Good Money or Doing Good Deeds?

The investment committee of a synagogue is meeting to discuss its policies. A representative of the temple's social action committee proposes that in accordance with UAHC policy, 1.8 percent of the temple's investable funds should be invested in a local credit union that services an inner-city minority neighborhood. The rate of return on the funds invested in the credit union would be 1 percent less than the remainder of the synagogue's funds would receive.

Some members of the committee vehemently oppose the proposal. "Our fiscal responsibility is to our congregants," they say. "We must maximize the return on our investment. From that return, we fund important synagogue activities. If we want to be helpful to the inner city, we should do it directly, not through this backdoor device. We recognize that the amount we would give as a direct contribution is far less than we might invest, but investment and charity should be kept separate."

How would you vote if you were a member of the committee? Would your vote be different if the margin of return were 2 or 3 percent less?

Response

Increasingly, investment committees have been supporting the
UAHC's and CCAR's investing proposal. Most feel that
although investments are not charity, depositing funds in a credit
union, community bank, or other community development
financial institution is entirely appropriate, consistent with
Jewish traditions of responsible investing, and, potentially, a very
valuable method for advancing a more equitable society.

It might be an interesting exercise to work out the actual difference in return between an investment of, say, $50,000 at 9
percent and 6 percent—not unusual rates of return for the stock
market and a credit union, respectively. Consider, also, the aggre-
gate effect of more than 870 congregations, as well as a variety of
Reform movement entities such as the UAHC itself, investing
in community development.

··· 5 ···

The Environmental Crisis

The earth is *Adonai's* and the fullness thereof; the settled world, and all that inhabit it.

(Psalms 24:1)

Rabbi Judah said in the name of Rav: Everything that the Holy One, Blessed Be, created in God's world— God did not create a single thing in vain.

(*Shabbat* 77b)

These two compelling moral concepts remind us that the earth has been lent to us as a "trust" by God on the condition that we care for it, respect and protect it, and ensure that future generations will benefit from its bounty. As a Kashmiri proverb notes, "We have not inherited the world from our ancestors…we have borrowed it from our children."

The traditional Jewish view of our stewardship of the earth is conveyed in the following *midrash* on the story of creation:

When the Holy One, Blessed Be, created the first person, God took and led Adam around all the trees of the Garden of Eden. And God said to Adam: "Look at My works! How beautiful and praiseworthy they are! And everything I made, I created for you. Be careful [though] that you don't spoil or destroy My world— because if you spoil it, there's nobody after you to fix it.

(*Ecclesiastes Rabbah* 7:13)

All the evidence indicates that we are doing exactly what the tradition warned us not to do. As a result of the breakthroughs of the twentieth century, we are the first generation with the power to spoil and destroy God's world beyond repair.

ENVIRONMENTAL TRENDS: GOOD NEWS, BAD NEWS

When was the environmental movement born? Some say it was in the time of the Bible, which contains such novel ideas as the sabbatical year, crop rotation, and the first prohibitions against pollution and waste. Others see its origin in the works and writings of great activists-naturalists over the last century (John Muir, Marjory Stoneman Douglas, and Aldo Leopold). Most famously, Rachel Carson's 1962 *Silent Spring* helped to create what could truly be called a movement. Since then, even as environmental degradation continues all around us, great strides have been made toward ending and even reversing some of the damage.

In approaching environmental issues, a balance must be struck between the personal and the political. On the one hand, how can we ask the government to cleanup its act if we still harm the environment by our daily choices at work, school, and home? But on the other hand, why organize a "river cleanup" day if the paper mill upstream is discharging deadly dioxin? To avoid getting discouraged, we should always remember the power of just one individual. As Rabbi Tarfon said nearly two thousand years ago: "It is not upon you to complete the task—but neither are you free to desist from it." (*Avot* 2:21) Though none of us will single-handedly stitch up the hole in the ozone layer or end species extinction, we all have a Jewish obligation to do our part.

Environmental progress made over the last twenty years provides hope that we can, indeed, make a difference:

1. Threatened ecosystems are being restored. Florida's Everglades, a rich preserve hosting numerous endangered species, was polluted and strangled by urban growth, sugar plantations, and misguided flood management. Now the Army Corps of Engineers is undertaking the largest environmental restoration project ever, returning canals to their original river courses, paid for by a new tax on the local sugar industry that had long polluted the Everglades.

2. Some endangered species are bouncing back. The Endangered Species Act of 1973 has done such a good job helping the bald eagle and other species to recover that some have been "down-

listed" to "threatened." Reintroduction of wolves, sea lions, and other animals into their former native habitat has been fairly successful.

3. Our cities are generally cleaner. Cleveland's Cuyahoga River, which once was so polluted it caught on fire, now sports a popular new neighborhood on its banks. Pittsburgh's air, once dark in midday from coal smoke, now meets Environmental Protection Agency standards.

4. Industry is slowly "greening" itself. The Valdez Principles, which voluntarily commit companies to an open and progressive environmental policy, were signed by Sun Oil and other major corporations in the aftermath of the *Valdez* tragedy. The 3M chemical company saved $420 million a year by using fewer toxic chemicals and reusing as much waste as possible. Fast-food companies are using thinner straws, lighter plastics, and more recycled packaging materials.

5. Slowly, society is learning to think regionally. The San Diego area began a countywide protection program for endangered species and ecosystems. A nationwide effort is underway to create "wildlife corridors," allowing animals to migrate between parks, refuges, forests, and other safe havens.

6. People are making a difference. In the mid-1980s, one private citizen—Weston Birdsall of Osage, Iowa—inspired his town of 3,600 to make a concerted commitment to conservation. Through simple energy-saving mechanisms (like insulation and plugging leaky windows) and energy-conscious capital improvements, the town cut its natural gas consumption by 45 percent, saving an estimated $1.2 million.

7. Awareness is growing. From the first Earth Day in 1970, environmentalism has grown by leaps and bounds. Environmental organizations have influence; ecology is a respected science from elementary school to academia; environmental issues are politically "hot"; and religious people and institutions have made protecting God's creation a high priority.

Despite these remarkable advances, however, many trends point in the other direction. Quite literally, ours is the first generation that can imagine its "progress" leading our own species toward extinction. As Albert Einstein commented, "The unleashed power of the atom has changed everything, save our modes of thinking—and thus we drift toward unparalleled disaster."

How bad is bad? Consider:

1. A hole in the ozone layer over Antarctica has now grown larger than the United States; recently, another hole has opened in the Northern Hemisphere. Ozone protects us from ultraviolet rays that cause skin cancer in human beings and damage to plant and animal life.

2. Scientists estimate that every day we drive some one hundred species of living organisms to extinction. The current rate is significantly faster than at any other time in the last 65 million years.

3. Less than one-third of the forests that once covered the world remain intact. The contiguous forty-eight states contain less than 5 percent of their original, biologically rich "old growth" forests; of that, less than 30 percent is protected in national wilderness areas and parks. Rain forests across the world's tropics are being destroyed at the rate of two football fields every second—an area the size of New Mexico annually.

4. Coral reefs, among the world's most diverse ecosystems, are dying from a variety of factors: boat anchors, shrimp harvesting, sewage, tropical fish collectors, logging, agriculture, pollution, tourism, dynamite, and more.

5. Americans go through 2.5 million plastic bottles every hour—only a tiny percentage of which are now recycled—and we throw away enough glass bottles and jars to fill the 1,350-foot twin towers of New York's World Trade Center every two weeks.

6. Forty percent of the nation's surveyed waterways are still too polluted for fishing and swimming. Nearly 2,200 health advisories were issued in 1996 warning against consumption of fish, and beaches were closed or warnings were issued more than 2,500 times because of contaminated waters (EPA).

7. The world's population, which is a great contributor to the global ecological crisis, increases by some 90 million—an additional Mexico—every year. By the turn of the century, we will pass the 6 billion mark.

8. If the earth's temperature continues to rise at the current rate, every person on earth will be affected by the negative impacts of climate change. Rising sea levels from continued ocean heating and the melting of glaciers will lead to a sea-level rise of approximately half a meter by the year 2100, completely flooding over 10,000 square miles in the southeastern United States and whole Pacific island nations.

JUDAISM, ECOLOGY, AND THE ENVIRONMENT

The prophet Jeremiah, using God's words, could have been speaking to us when he warned his contemporaries: "And I brought you into a land of fruitful fields to eat the fruit thereof; but when you entered, you defiled My land and made My heritage an abomination." (2:7) Everyone who reads—or even looks around—can see how badly we, in our time, have defiled the land and ravaged God's earth.

Long ago in Jewish history, ecological ideals were translated into specific environmental regulations. Tanneries, which produced odor pollution, were sharply restricted in their proximity to residential centers. The location of threshing floors, which produced significant dust pollution, was likewise restricted, as were businesses that caused noise pollution. Communities were obliged to keep public streams and water supplies clean and roads in good repair.

Even wartime military camps were obliged to follow waste disposal procedures. Soldiers had to carry shovels and dispose of their human waste outside the camp so "the camp will be holy." (Deuteronomy 31:15) From this, our sages argued "how much more so" should care apply to our residential communities in times of peace.

The Levitical cities had to have a *migrash* (a pasture or green area) around them. Maimonides extended this requirement to all cities. The Jerusalem Talmud instructs: "It is forbidden to live in a city that does not have a green garden." (*Kiddushin* 4:12)

Concern for the perpetuation of animal species, represented by the story of Noah, is reflected in laws in the Torah (e.g., one should not kill a cow and its calf [Leviticus 22:28] or a bird and its young [Deuteronomy 22:6]). According to the medieval commentator Nachmanides, one who kills mother and children on the same day or takes them while they are free to fly away is considered as if that one destroyed the species (commentary on Deuteronomy 22:6).

This protection extends to less charismatic species as well. *Exodus Rabbah* 10:1 teaches that "even things you see as superfluous in this world—like flies, fleas, and mosquitoes—they are still part of the greater scheme of the creation of the world." In the classical Jewish view, everything has its place: Each stage of creation is "good." Moreover, the completed, interconnected whole is "very good." (Genesis 1:31) Indeed, our tradition recognizes that everything is connected: as the nineteenth-century Rabbi S. R. Hirsch wrote, "One glorious chain of love, of giving and receiving, unites all living beings."

Halachah also forbids cruelty to animals. Although an individual human life always comes before that of an animal, "animal rights" are very much a part of our tradition. Another environmental set of Jewish laws concerns Shabbat and the sabbatical year, the one day and one year in seven when both people and the land rest. Having a time not to produce or consume but simply to be is a needed corrective to our society's constant "growth" and acquisition.

The concept of *hamafkir nazakav hayav* (one who leaves a dangerous article in a public place is responsible for any damages that may result) could well apply to those who dispose of toxic waste in a manner that endangers the environment and human health. Similarly, the basic concept of liability for damages caused by the negligent control of an inherently dangerous condition (e.g., a pit or a fire) establishes the principle that one who owns something environmentally hazardous, for example a nuclear power plant or an oil tanker, bears responsibility for its elimination. If there is no alternative to engaging in hazardous activity, then all reasonable steps must be taken to mitigate the resulting risks to people and the environment.

Ecology poses profound religious, theological, and moral questions: Has God endowed us with dominion over nature? Is competition or cooperation the nature of our relationship to one another? Are human beings inherently greedy? What is our responsibility to the generations yet unborn?

Some say the despoiling of our world is rooted in the Hebrew Bible. They cite Genesis 1:28: "Be fruitful and multiply and populate the earth and conquer it. Rule over the fish of the sea and the birds of the heavens and over all living things on earth. I have given you all the grass and trees for you and all other living things to eat."

Jewish tradition, say its defenders, makes it clear that our "dominion" over nature does not include a license to slaughter indiscriminately or to abuse the environment. *Bal tashchit* ("do not destroy") is the basis of the talmudic and post-talmudic laws that prohibit willful destruction of natural resources or any kind of vandalism, even if the act is committed by the property owners themselves. One must not needlessly destroy or waste anything that may be useful to others. (See the discussion of *bal tashchit* in chapter 7, "Peace and International Affairs.") "The earth is *Adonai's* and the fullness thereof" (Psalms 24:1) implies that we are the stewards of nature, obligated to cherish and preserve it.

This view is eloquently expressed in the following passages from rabbinic literature:

> Of everything God created, nothing was created in vain, not even the things you may think unnecessary, such as spiders, frogs, or snakes.
>
> (*Genesis Rabbah* 10:7 and *Shabbat* 77b)

> Human beings were not created until the sixth day so that if their pride should govern them, it could be said to them, "Even the tiniest flea preceded you in creation."
>
> (*Sanhedrin* 38a)

> Why did God appear to Moses in the lowly bush? To teach us that nothing in creation is without God's holy Presence, not even the commonest bush....
>
> (*Exodus Rabbah* 2:5)

Or, as the authoritative nineteenth-century Orthodox scholar Rabbi Samson Raphael Hirsch, a strong proponent of the social justice essence of Judaism, wrote of *bal tashchit*:

> Yea, "Do not destroy anything" is the first and most general call of God.... If you should regard the beings beneath you as objects without rights, not perceiving God who created them, and therefore desire that they feel the might of your presumptuous mood, instead of using them only as the means of wise human activity— then God's call proclaims to you, "Do not destroy anything! Be a *mentsh*! Only if you use the things around you for wise human purposes, sanctified by the word of My teaching, only then are you a *mentsh* and have the right over them that I have given you as a human. However, if you destroy, if you ruin, at that moment you are not human but an animal and have no right to do the things around you. I lent them to you for wise use only; never forget that I lent them to you."

A Real Dilemma: Paper or Plastic (or Neither)?

Some time ago, a local NFTY (North American Federation of Temple Youth) group went to their temple board to ask them to ban Styrofoam in the synagogue. They pointed out that besides being wasteful, Styrofoam contained ozone-damaging chlorofluorocarbons (CFCs). Some board members felt that such an action would inconvenience the congregation, be "faddist," or have no significant impact. Others claimed that substitute materials, such as plastic or paper, could be destructive in other ways.

Response

Most board members took the debate about Styrofoam seriously; they launched a synagogue-wide environmental audit. Not only was Styrofoam banned, but the temple replaced all incandescent lights with compact fluorescent bulbs, and fully insulated the building. These actions proved to be both cost- and energy-efficient.

Though this is a success story, it also points to a difficulty: Styrofoam was replaced with other disposable products they thought were less problematic. In fact, the lifetime environmental impact of disposable Styrofoam, paper, and plastic goods are all comparably bad. Only reusable dishes, cups, and kitchenware are preferable, and even then it depends on the amount and temperature of the water one uses to wash them!

From this, we learn the importance of two things: knowing the issues well before making a decision and putting our energies into debates that truly matter. For instance, the other "paper vs. plastic" issue of shopping bags is quite clear—it takes little thought or energy to carry and use the same bags over and over again, thus saving many raw materials.

Below is a more detailed look at the question of where best to channel our energies.

CRISES IN CREATION—OUR BACKYARD

The human impact on the earth is already massive, and it is increasing. Just as it is important to learn about Jewish perspectives on the environmental crisis, so must we understand something of the political, social, economic, and scientific aspects of these issues. And while it may be tempting to point our fingers overseas to highlight the worst problems, many of them actually begin here in North America. Below is a brief question-and-answer section that wrestles with some of our real domestic environmental challenges, like hazardous waste and toxins, air and water pollution, transportation, and overconsumption:

1. *Are some waste products more dangerous than others? Dangerous enough to jeopardize our health?*
   Hazardous wastes are by-products of industries—some get reused or recycled, some get expensively treated or placed in special landfills, some are illegally dumped, and some are legally spewed into our air and water. There are two basic ways to lower the

amount of hazardous waste that is generated: lower our consumption levels of environmentally damaging goods or spend more money on research, prevention, treatment, and enforcement.

Pesticides are potentially hazardous products that are widely accepted for use on our crops. While certain pesticides are relatively safe and extremely effective, others kill birds and even people along with insects. Frighteningly, only a small percentage of the pesticides used on the food we eat have been thoroughly tested for their effects on human and environmental health. This is an even greater concern for farmworkers than for others, though we can all benefit from reducing use of such pesticides through steps like organic farming. (Organic methods include integrated pest management, which relies on insects' natural predators instead of toxic chemicals.)

One particular toxin, dioxin, is perhaps the most dangerous chemical we now face in our everyday lives. Dioxin enters the environment mostly through industry, from the chlorine used to bleach office paper and from incinerators. Besides being a carcinogen, dioxin affects our nervous, immune, and reproductive systems. And worst of all, recent EPA studies show that most children, women, and men in America have already approached the "safe" limit for dioxin exposure. Since it collects in fatty tissue, it stays in our own bodies and is passed on to future generations through mothers' milk. But alternatives do exist—besides advocating for a stronger and better-enforced Clean Water Act, our buying unbleached paper will help show the industry that saving the environment is good for business.

2. *Is it safe to drink our water and breathe our air?*
Water and air pollution—often thought of as entirely separate issues—are in fact closely related. Thus we breathe dioxins as well as drink them. Likewise, the smog we inhale in cities, along with background air pollutants called particulates, eventually drop onto land, where they are washed into rivers or groundwater, or directly into the sea. For this reason, we now speak of "acid deposition" rather than "acid rain," since airborne acidic pollutants fall as dust, rain, or snow before contaminating both American and Canadian waters.

More than half the population of the United States drinks groundwater, 40 percent of which comes from untreated, contaminated wells. Industrial wastes, erosion from logging, leakage from landfills, chemical wastes from mining and petroleum production, and pesticides and herbicides from agriculture are steadily accumulating in both ground and surface water. Such pollution has made freshwater fish and crustaceans among the most threatened types of animals in America, many of which have become extinct.

Air and water pollution threaten the lives of millions. Smog can quite literally be lethal—in the Los Angeles area alone, there are thousands of deaths a year caused or exacerbated by air pollution, and Mexico City is worse still. Air quality in America is contaminated by many pollutants, most notably the poisons that pour out of our automobile exhausts.

3. *Should we reexamine our love affair with the automobile?*
Though it provides an invaluably quick and easy way to get from place to place, the private automobile constitutes a major threat to the environment. Carbon dioxide in exhaust contributes to local smog as well as global warming; roads and highways destroy forests, wetlands, watersheds, and other natural systems; rubber and oil from cars wind up in the water supply. Cars and trucks emit the greatest part of carbon dioxide, hydrocarbon, and nitrogen oxide air pollution, resulting in as many as half of all cancer deaths linked to toxic emissions. Nearly all alternatives to the automobile—from better urban planning to trains to buses to bikes to feet—are more energy-efficient and emit less pollution than the private automobile.

Since over 40 percent of the oil that we use goes into our cars, fuel efficiency reduces our dependence on foreign oil even as it reduces global warming and helps the environment. The current Corporate Average Fuel Economy (CAFE) standards, passed in 1975, have gone a long way toward this end. These standards require that new cars average 27.5 miles per gallon. Raising the CAFE standards by another 40 percent, as many members of Congress have suggested, would save our country 2.5 million barrels of oil daily, along with hundreds of millions of tons of carbon dioxide. Each gallon of gasoline burned produces some thirty pounds of CO_2.

Critics say that such a CAFE standard increase would mean smaller and more dangerous cars. (Lighter and stronger newly developed materials used in building cars and swifter, more efficient engines make more efficient and safer cars possible.) While this is debatable, the overall public health implications of automobile use are rarely considered—many more people are killed by automobile-related pollution than by accidents in substandard cars. The "price at the pump" never reflects the real social cost of the automobile.

4. *Do we consume too much?*

The United States enjoys the highest standard of living in the world—and likewise has the highest per capita resource and energy use. While we might think that overpopulation in the developing world is the greatest environmental threat, the average American has an ecological impact equal to that of ten or even twenty people in Africa or Asia. Moreover, environmental problems in the Third World are the product of the industries, mining, and production of First World nations such as the U.S., Canada, England, Russia, Germany, France, and Japan.

With consumption comes disposal. The average American generates nearly a ton of trash annually, less than 11 percent of which gets recycled. Landfills, which often leach harmful runoff into our groundwater, are filling up, and incineration is costly and toxic. The most environmentally sound and cost-efficient way to alleviate the crisis is to reduce the amount of waste we generate in the first place. Waste education is far better than recycling, which is necessary but not always very effective. The challenge for both individuals and industries is to follow the famous 3 Rs in their proper order—reduce as much as possible, reuse as much as possible, and only then recycle the remainder.

CRISES IN CREATION—ACROSS THE GLOBE

The environments of particular regions work, grow, and maintain their health in connection with one another. Our country is not an island. American companies sell DDT they produce to Mexico (use in the United States is banned), whose farmers spray the chemical in fields that produce crops exported to the United States and elsewhere. The water and sewage drainage in turn affects U.S. border cities. Canada's Maritime Provinces are plagued by acidic pollutants from large U.S. cities, while eight Great Lakes states stand to suffer if Ontario Premier Mike Harris fulfills his 1996 pledge to downscale environmental regulations. The overdepletion of the fishing areas of Newfoundland destroyed the fish populations and profoundly affected Canadian and United States fisherman.

Nor is this interconnectedness limited to our continent. The news of the 1986 Chernobyl nuclear meltdown in Ukraine broke after Sweden reported high radioactivity; that radiation then spread around the world. In 1994, Spain and Canada nearly came to blows over fishing rights for the shrinking fish populations in the North Atlantic Ocean. The clear-cutting of the Amazon rain forest affects weather and rainfall in Africa. Japan's thirst for wood is devastating the rich rain forests of Indonesia and Malaysia. And even amphibians in the most remote swamps and fish in the deepest open seas are showing alarmingly high levels of human-made toxins.

A few critical international environmental issues—climate change, the ozone layer, overpopulation, and biodiversity—follow:

1. *Does global warming threaten our children's future?*
   Climate scientists from around the world agree that when humans burn gasoline, coal, and oil, carbon dioxide is released into the atmosphere, which traps heat near the earth's surface, much as glass windows trap heat inside a greenhouse. In fact, the burning of fossil fuels has increased the amount of carbon dioxide in the atmosphere by more than 30 percent—to levels unsurpassed in the past 160,000 years. Industrial and air-conditioner chemicals and methane—caused in part by cattle, mining, gas leaks, and rice paddies—are also significant contributors to climate change.
   Evidence shows that these "greenhouse gases" have con-

tributed to an increase in the planet's surface temperature by 1 degree Fahrenheit over the last 100 years. Without action to reduce the release of greenhouse gases, scientists predict that the earth's average temperature will rise between 2 and 6.5 degrees Fahrenheit by the year 2100.

If global temperatures rise significantly, sea levels will rise from the melting of polar ice caps, and fully one-half of the world's population could be affected. As sea levels begin to rise, poor residents of coastal areas and villagers in floodplains will be vulnerable to flooding and disease. Increased flooding, storms, and drought will also have devastating effects on agriculture and will contribute to famine in mostly impoverished areas.

Global warming also threatens human health and species extinction. Infectious diseases, such as malaria, are already spreading to new areas because mosquitoes and other disease vectors are increasing their range as temperatures rise across the world. Heat stress and air pollution will also increase human casualties, like the heat wave in 1995 that killed hundreds of people in Chicago. Plant and animal species will suffer due to the disruption of migration and ecosystems. Warming of the Antarctic is already disturbing the health of the ecosystem—threatening fish, birds, seals, and whales.

Only by attacking the root of the problem—radically cutting the use of fossil fuels, especially in high-consumption countries like the United States—can global warming be stopped. In late 1997, an international climate change treaty was negotiated in Kyoto, Japan. This historic accord calls on the United States to reduce carbon emissions by 7 percent below 1990 levels by the year 2012. (See chapter 7, "Peace and International Affairs," for more details.) The nations of the world are finally cooperating in reducing emissions of greenhouse gases and are slowly beginning to make the difficult commitments.

2. *How serious is the problem of ozone depletion? Can it really cause cancer?*

Many miles into the upper atmosphere, ozone screens much of the sun's hazardous ultraviolet radiation from reaching the earth. This layer of protective ozone is now being destroyed by the release of CFCs into the atmosphere, one molecule of which can dissolve 100,000 ozone molecules before it falls back to earth. Ozone is thinning everywhere, and actual holes in the ozone layer have been detected above Antarctica, Greenland, and the Arctic region.

If this depletion goes unchecked, the Environmental Protection Agency predicts the development of millions of skin cancer cases in the coming decades. Increases in ultraviolet radiation will compromise the immune systems of humans and many other animals. It could also cause the loss of billions of dollars worth of crops. Moreover, by affecting the surface-dwelling plankton that comprise the base of the oceans' food chain, its effects could be truly catastrophic.

CFCs are most commonly found in refrigerants, solvents, computer chip cleaners, and packing materials. They have been phased out of aerosol sprays and Styrofoam, and replacements are being tested in most industries, but many of these alternatives (like HCFCs and benzene) are still quite problematic. Hope comes from the Montreal Protocol, a 1987 international agreement to stop ozone depletion, though timetables for phase-outs vary. Scientific, political, and economic commitments are needed to turn this crisis around.

3. *Will the exploding populations of the world overwhelm our resources?*
Every day, the world population increases by some 250,000. That's a new Boston every two days, a new Israel every three weeks, a new India every decade. The bulk of this population growth is occurring in poorer countries, already ravaged by mass hunger and severe housing shortages. Consider this: The population of the earth doubled between the year 1 C.E. and 1200. Today, the population of the world will double in fifty years—and that reflects a recent slowdown in the rate because of three decades of intense population control efforts. Overpopulation causes huge social problems as well as environmental ones, since people will do what it takes to feed and shelter their families. And as developing nations try to attain a higher standard of living, more resources are being consumed by more people. Though no one knows the earth's maximum "carrying capacity," current trends are clearly not sustainable.

Economic development and the education and empowerment of women are two common responses to the challenge of controlling the population problem, since population growth falls with these developments. Yet economic growth often involves high environmental impact in addition to inequitable distribution. Additionally, family-planning programs in developing nations have met varying degrees of success, since they often run counter to traditional cultural and religious practices.

In any event, we must take quick and decisive action to lower the world's birthrate. In so doing, Americans face a tough choice: will we voluntarily allow our own standard of living to fall, or at least to not rise, in order to help out developing nations? And American Jews, with the mandate of "be fruitful and multiply" and memories of the Holocaust fresh in our minds, face a still tougher choice: are we somehow exempt, or should "zero population growth" become the norm in our community as well? (See chapter 13, "The Changing Jewish Family.")

4. *Why can't we see the forest for the trees? Are we destroying whole species of life?*
All across the world, God's unique creations are being wiped away forever. Though scientists believe that there is always a natural "background" extinction rate of perhaps 1 to 10 species a year, current annual estimates of extinctions are as high as 50,000. The human impact on earth is nowhere as striking, or as irreversible, as in the area of biodiversity.

Species diversity is important for countless reasons. More than anything, each species has an inherent right to exist; we *Homo sapiens*, after all, are but one among tens of millions of species. And theologically, how should God feel, watching us destroy what God called "good"? Yet we can also defend biodiversity from a purely human perspective.

The global gene pool may yet harbor cures for cancer, AIDS, and other diseases, since numerous medicines and other valuable goods have already come out of the rain forests and other reservoirs of biodiversity. Such places also help regulate the global climate and recharge our atmospheric oxygen. Furthermore, wild places and wild things have a spiritual and aesthetic value that we cannot calculate—and who are we to rob our children of these? Finally, species are often symbiotic with one another, so that if one goes, another goes; certain "keystone" species play critical roles in an ecosystem, much of which collapses following their absence.

The greatest tragedy—and our greatest hope—lies in the ease with which this situation could be reversed. Most of the millions of species in danger of extinction lie in what biologist E. O. Wilson has called "biodiversity hot spots," or fairly small and protectable areas holding numerous species. To protect these areas will take a worldwide commitment of money, cooperation with local and indigenous peoples, and lifestyle changes—for instance, just small reductions in the West's consumption of paper and meat would do wonders for the earth's rain forests.

A Real Dilemma: The Redwood Rabbis and the Redwood Forests

One of the last remaining unprotected ancient redwood forests is found in Northern California. Known as the Headwaters Forest ecosystem, it contains nearly 60,000 acres of trees, streams, and several endangered birds and fishes. Maxxam Corp., headed by a Jew who is a member of a Reform congregation, owned this land and began to log the area. Although he was in technical compliance with the law, protesters tried to prevent logging through civil disobedience, since many experts warned that even the legal logging would destroy many of these irreplaceable redwoods and would endanger species that dwell there, as well as the ecosystem they inhabit. Should Jews view the Headwaters as a Jewish issue, one in which we must speak out against the laws? Even if we do, do Jews have a special responsibility to try to influence the owner to refrain from destroying such a precious and valued piece of nature because he is Jewish?

Response

During the High Holidays of 1996, days before the Headwaters area was to be logged, two rabbis and one student rabbi from Northern California took out a full-page advertisement in the owner's hometown Jewish newspaper. The advertisement asked the owner to make a full *teshuvah* and protect the entire Headwaters region by creating a national park. Many other Jews and rabbis, including some who support protecting the Headwaters Forest, objected to the personalization of the issue and to the politicization of the High Holidays. The question remains: should the religious identity of the owner influence our response?

In California, a number of rabbis, mostly Reform, began to act more vigorously. The "Redwood Rabbis" protested logging in the Headwaters, spoke at rallies and press conferences, and organized a major Tu B'Shvat seder in 1997, where they engaged in civil disobedience—planting redwood seedlings on Maxxam property. Rabbis across America began to speak out, national media reported on the Redwood Rabbis' activities, and the Jewish community was widely seen as playing a leading role in efforts to preserve the redwoods. As of this writing, the outcome of the specific issue is unclear.

THE ENVIRONMENTAL JUSTICE MOVEMENT

While environmental problems affect us all, their immediate impact is far greater on the underprivileged. "Environmental justice" addresses the disproportionate environmental risks placed upon impoverished and minority communities. As its name implies, this growing move-ment-within-a-movement holds that environmental protection and social justice are inseparable—without one, the other cannot sustain itself. Consider these facts:

1. Black children in urban areas are at risk of lead poisoning at a rate four times that of white children. The lead comes from paint chips and from soil and dust contaminated by leaded fuel residues.

2. Nearly a third of a million U.S. farmworkers suffer from pesticide-related illnesses. Most of these cases are among ill-treated migrant workers, some 80 to 90 percent of whom are of Mexican descent.

3. Three out of five waste incinerators in the United States are located in poor or minority neighborhoods.

4. Industrial countries, with a fraction of the world's population, are responsible for more than 90 percent of the 360 million metric tons of hazardous waste produced globally each year.

5. In Brazil during the 1980s, more than 1,000 people were murdered over land-use issues; there were fewer than ten convictions. Nine environmental activists in Nigeria's Ogoni region, which has been poisoned by oil development, were executed by the military regime in 1995.

At the global level, is it fair for the industrialized world to demand that developing countries protect the environment while condemning the vast majority of the world's population to poverty and hunger? After all, Western nations achieved their power and wealth at the expense of both the environment and minority peoples. If we have to choose in developing nations to promote development or protect the environment, what should we choose and who shall make the choice? Justice ultimately demands that the people of those nations help shape those choices and that the changes should further both goals: ensuring that developing nations lift their peoples to a higher standard of living and protecting the earth by pursuing environmentally safe energy and industrialization processes. This may entail making tough choices about our own standard of living as well.

A Real Dilemma: West Dallas Community in Peril

Thirty years ago, residents in a neighborhood in the West Dallas area began noticing a variety of health problems. These started out as rashes, bleeding gums, and headaches, but soon there were unusual numbers of incidents of cancer, birth defects, learning disabilities, even limbs that required amputation. Led by the New Waverly Baptist Church and Rev. R. T. Conley, neighbors found out that a nearby lead-smelting plant was causing the health crisis. Initial efforts to regulate or shut down the smelter met with no response from either local officials or Texas state environmental agencies. Better-off residents began moving away, but that was not economically feasible for many poor families—predominantly African-American and Latino—in the area. What should the remaining residents have done?

Response

Reverend Conley organized educational meetings in the area, to raise both knowledge and concern. From this base, he helped church members build a coalition, the West Dallas Coalition for a Better Environment, with nearby homeowners and citizens associations. He also worked with national "environmental justice" and religious groups. The local coalition organized letter-writing and phone campaigns, protests, and public meetings. With the help of national groups, particularly the National Religious Partnership for the Environment (NRPE), national attention began to be focused on the plight of West Dallas. Facilitated by the NRPE, with help from the Religious Action Center, Reverend Conley and others from the WDCBE flew to Washington and met with then Housing and Urban Development Secretary Henry Cisneros. Secretary Cisneros and staff from the Environmental Protection Agency agreed to bring short-term clinic facilities to the area, to close the lead-smelting plant, to ensure financial settlements for people affected by the toxins, and to begin a major cleanup. While the cleanup is still underway, with the establishment of the clinic and the shutdown of the smelter, life is beginning to improve in West Dallas.

ISRAEL: A FRAGILE ENVIRONMENT

Though a small country, Israel contains such remarkably diverse types of ecosystems as coastal, wetland, desert, tropical, and mountain. Massive reforestation involving some 190 million trees, initiated and managed by the Jewish National Fund (JNF), has created green groves where land once lay barren.

As Israel has reclaimed deserts and swamps, often with problematic environmental consequences, its population has grown from 600,000 in 1948 to more than 5.5 million today. On the negative side, this massive infusion of immigrants has created such major environmental concerns as air and water quality (especially in Haifa Bay), toxic and solid waste disposal, and ecosystem and species preservation. This last concern arises most pointedly with the plans to build roads through what little wilderness remains on the coastal plain.

Despite these problems, one environmental concern eclipses all others: water. Israel currently uses 105 percent of its natural water capacity. Most of this comes from three major sources, and the extra 5 percent is from desalinization. Yet each of the three main sources is in peril. The coastal aquifer lies beneath Tel Aviv and the surrounding plain; it is becoming polluted by industrial wastes and infused with saltwater because of overpumping. The Yam Kinneret (the Sea of Galilee) and the Jordan River system are threatened by population growth and by the Jordan's headwaters lying in Syria, which has threatened to cut off the supply. And rights to the mountain aquifer, lying below Jerusalem and the West Bank, are among the most contentious items in Israeli-Palestinian negotiations.

The regional importance of water, and of the environment in general, cannot be overstated. The scarcity of water is among the factors that led Palestinians, Jordanians, and others to the peace table. It is widely assumed that water is replacing oil as the major resource affecting the politics and economics of the Middle East. The first Israeli diplomatic visit to an Arab country (besides Egypt) was for a regional environmental summit on water. And now there is even a fledgling regional grassroots environmental organization with members from Jordan, Israel, and Egypt.

In addition to the importance of water as an issue in the Middle East itself, global energy policy also affects the politics of the Middle East, since dependence on Arab oil provided the lever with which the Arab nations maneuvered numerous countries in Europe, Asia, and Africa into an anti-Israel posture at times over the past several decades.

A Real Dilemma: Alaskan Wilderness vs. Dependence on Arab Oil

A recent contentious environmental debate has centered on the opening of the vast Arctic National Wildlife Refuge (ANWR) for oil and gas development. Proponents argue that to minimize its dependence on foreign oil, including Arab oil, the United States must develop all of its resources; this region could offer a six-month supply. Opponents argue that this would devastate the nation's largest remaining wilderness area—home to 150,000 caribou and the Inuit people who live with and from them— much as oil development has done to other Alaskan regions.

This issue, with its Middle Eastern political implications, was clearly of concern to the Jewish community when it first came before Congress in 1992. Some Jewish leaders enlisted the assistance of the former director of the American-Israel Public Affairs Committee (AIPAC)—the key pro-Israel lobby in Washington D.C.—to lobby for the opening of the wilderness area. At the same time, environmental groups pressed the Jewish community to publicly oppose the opening.

Which side, if either, should the Jewish community have taken?

Response

While no Jewish organizations formally endorsed opening the ANWR, the UAHC was the only national Jewish organization to oppose the opening of the wilderness area. It believed that the modest gains in energy independence were not worth the huge environmental risks involved. It also thought that opening the ANWR would set a bad precedent for America and for the rest of the world and delay our developing a more comprehensive energy plan in which conservation and renewable energy sources would be major components.

This difficult issue, in which the UAHC joined with environmental groups against other Jewish organizations, will remain on the political landscape, for oil companies will continue their efforts to access Alaskan oil in the future.

ENERGY

Of all environmental issues, energy is among the most complex. The major choice before us is not whether but *when* we will replace the dangerous use of fossil fuels with clean, renewable energy sources.

There is a finite amount of fossil fuels on earth and we will run out within the next two centuries. Such a transition was a stated national priority following the oil embargo imposed in 1973 by Arab nations to protest United States support for Israel, but the political will has floundered in the decades since. Therefore gas, coal, and oil are an even larger component of our energy picture now than they were in 1975. Part of the issue is clearly political: the government now heavily subsidizes fossil fuel extraction and nuclear power, while funding for solar and other renewable energy research is minimal. As a society, we also need to take further steps in the conservation of energy—comprising less than 5 percent of the world's population, we use 27 percent of the energy consumed. But part of the issue reflects our personal behavior: How much do we bike or use mass transit? Do we use compact fluorescent bulbs, or even solar energy, in our homes? What kind of car do we drive?

As for nuclear power, it seems that the early environmental voices were correct. In America, the tide turned after the 1979 scare at Pennsylvania's Three Mile Island nuclear power plant. The world was and remains shocked by the scope of the 1986 Chernobyl explosion in Ukraine, which released massive amounts of radioactivity, killing thousands of people and making millions of acres uninhabitable indefinitely. Only Japan and France forged ahead with their ambitious nuclear power campaigns, and even these are in doubt following a 1991 accident in Japan that required the use of the emergency cooling system to prevent a meltdown.

A Real Dilemma: A Rabbi Tries to Stop a Nuclear Power Plant

Until the last decade, nuclear power was a popular alternative to foreign oil but environmentally problematic. A massive demonstration was once organized to oppose the construction of the Seabrook, New Hampshire, nuclear power plant, and Rabbi Arthur Starr of Manchester was asked to join other clergy in the protest as part of the interfaith contingent.

Should he accept? Whom would he represent? A Jewish voice? Himself? His congregation? Should he publicly oppose a project that promised to give the region an economic boost, provide for its energy needs, and reduce U.S. dependence on Arab oil?

Response

Rabbi Starr decided to attend the protest as part of the interfaith delegation. He participated as an individual, not formally representing his synagogue. Though he did not address the crowd of 20,000 who attended, he became a visible and active community voice against the Seabrook power plant. His leadership inspired others in the Jewish community to join the campaign.

Today, this is no longer such a dilemma. With wastes impossible to dispose of, escalating construction and operating costs, and dangerous operations, no new nuclear power plants have been planned since the early 1980s.

Finally, aside from the health and environmental threats of nuclear power plants themselves, radioactive wastes remain an intractable problem. Some remain toxic well beyond their half-lives of 250,000 years and more, while a nuclear power plant gives us electricity for a brief 40 years. Cleanup costs for defense installations alone, a legacy of the nuclear arms race, run well upward of $200 billion. And there is no safe repository for these wastes: the proposed locations are in the southwest, but it is not clear whether this is based on scientific site selection or on the low political clout of the largely poor Hispanic and Native American population in the areas proposed for such disposal.

A RELIGIOUS RESPONSE TO THE ECOLOGICAL CRISIS

Out of interfaith environmental work, there emerged in 1992 the aforementioned National Religious Partnership for the Environment, which joins together Catholics, Evangelicals, Jews, and Protestants in the name of protecting God's creation. The NRPE was formed to transform the environmental debate by bringing basic religious values into the scientific and political arenas. President Bill Clinton and Vice President Al Gore were instrumental in legitimizing these efforts by drawing on the environmental vision within mainstream religious thought.

The potential of an undertaking such as the NRPE is enormous, for churches and synagogues are more numerous—there are over 300,000 congregations—than any other public institution in American life; far more numerous than libraries, hospitals, schools, and firehouses combined. Think of what impact it could have if every one of them—starting with yours—engaged in a serious effort to conserve energy; to recycle goods and purchase recycled goods; to help clean up the neighborhoods and plant trees; to speak out on environmental policy for the 140 million congregants. What a transformation of the environmental issue we would see! Each of us can start in our own synagogue.

Each year, the four faith groups can educate approximately 120,000 congregations and other religious organizations about how environmental issues affect our communities, families, and, potentially, future generations. Through the Partnership, the religious community has also been vocal on federal environmental legislation. In 1995, the National Council of Churches of Christ, the Evangelical Environmental Network, and the Coalition on the Environment and Jewish Life came together and protested Congress's attempts to gut the Endangered Species Act. This joint effort marked a turning point in the fight to preserve endangered species legislation. Standing together, the religious community was successful in convincing our senators that the preservation of God's creation is a fundamental moral precept.

The Coalition on the Environment and Jewish Life (COEJL) is the Jewish umbrella organization in this undertaking. COEJL works to bring environmental values back into mainstream Jewish life and help environmentalists who are Jewish to see the connections with Jewish tradition, texts, and ritual. COEJL's educational materials, emphasizing the environmental significance of Jewish holidays (in particular, Tu B'Shvat environmental seders) and encouraging Torah study sessions that focus on environmental ethics, are used throughout the nation. The Religious Action Center of Reform Judaism, a coordinating agency of COEJL, is the locus of their legislative advocacy efforts.

WHICH REAL DILEMMAS TO DEAL WITH?

With all the pressing environmental issues out there and the awareness that radical changes are necessary, how should an individual, synagogue, or other group decide which to work on? Time and relevance are key considerations. The best issues hit close to home, such as knowing the safety of drinking water, protecting nearby natural areas, or fighting a proposed hazardous waste site in the area. The amount of time necessary for the project can also guide which one to choose. A riverbank cleanup raises awareness, connects people to a natural place, and takes only a few hours. However, influencing the vote of your representative to Congress on endangered species legislation can make a much larger impact. When deciding on which challenges to address by yourself or in a group, gauge the interests, time, and assets of participants and select accordingly. Always consider possible coalitions and the issues of environmental justice. Which population is most affected by this issue? Who should be working with us?

NEEDED: A RADICAL CHANGE

The need for huge changes in our environmental awareness and actions should be clear. Yet as of this writing, the American political scene was heading in precisely the wrong direction. Recent Congresses have waged an assault on the environment unparalleled in the thirty years since significant environmental legislation was first passed. Beginning in 1995, Congress reflected a new, antifederal, "me-first" sentiment, even though polls show that the vast majority of Americans believe in government regulation to safeguard the environment.

The attack on these essential laws concerned with endangered species, the Superfund, and clean air and water will likely continue in years to come. The extent to which these efforts will be thwarted depends on the environmental commitments of people of faith, including the Jewish community. Grassroots efforts and bipartisan cooperation are vital, as growing numbers of Republican members of Congress join Democrats in saying that protecting and preserving the environment is too important to be subject to partisan political competition. Most important, because the religious community transcends partisan politics, it can be indispensable in mobilizing the grassroots efforts and bipartisan cooperation that is so vital to success in pro-environmental advocacy. As David Saperstein said in testifying before Congress on behalf of those faith groups and denominations that are part of NRPE: "The Endangered Species Act has served as an ark, protecting and nurturing the remnants of God's creation until they, like the bald eagle, can soar on their own once again. If this ark needs repairs, then by all means patch it. But we cannot afford, spiritually or economically, to sink it."

The disasters at Bhopal, India (where thousands were killed by a poison gas leak from a chemical plant), at Chernobyl, and elsewhere are ominous storm warnings. They compel us to reexamine our divinities. We have made an idol of technology, believing it can solve all human problems. In doing so, we have forsaken God's call to serve and protect creation. And we must stop worshiping at the altar of consumption. Now, in order to survive, we must at last take seriously our role as *shomrei adamah*, guardians of creation.

··· 6 ···

Israel: The Path to Justice, Freedom, and Peace

We Jews may differ about God and religion, politics and education, but on the existence of Israel we are solidly united. So why include Israel in a book on Jewish dilemmas?

The answer is that Israel, now celebrating its fiftieth anniversary, is the paramount achievement of modern Jewish history, but deep beneath the surface are embedded the greatest dilemmas, the most elusive to grasp and the most painful to confront.

The nature of these dilemmas has changed dramatically over the past decade. The 1990s have seen the Middle East region transformed from an area of bitterness and bloody battle between ancient enemies to a hopeful part of the world struggling to break through to peaceful relations among its peoples. The bold vision of peace could be derailed by extremists on all sides, but powerful momentum has built up and drastically altered the map, the chemistry, the psychology, and the political landscape of the Middle East. Who could have foreseen the Rabin-Arafat handshake that mesmerized the world, the dramatic peace agreements between Jordan and Israel, and the serious possibilities of peace between Israel and Syria? The transformation of the area owes much to geopolitical factors, such as the Gulf War, the collapse of the Soviet Union, the emergent primacy of the United States, but it could not have happened without bold and visionary leadership in Israel—leadership determined to end the burden of occupation and to reach out to the Palestinian people and to its Arab neighbors. These mind-boggling changes helped strengthen Israel's position in the world community, end its isolation in the U.N., strengthen its economy, and potentially change the relationship between Israel and the Diaspora.

All these hopes have been severely strained, however, by the Rabin assassination, the inability of Arafat to contain terrorism or develop real democracy in the autonomous Palestinian area, and the stormy tenure of Netanyahu as prime minister of Israel.

THE CENTRALITY OF ISRAEL FOR THE JEWISH PEOPLE

It is often puzzling to Christians, and even to some Jews, to hear Jews spoken of as a people, a culture, or a nation. "Isn't Judaism a religion?" they ask. In doing so, they envision Judaism as a religious tradition akin to Methodism, Unitarianism, or Catholicism. But the civilization of Judaism long predated most of the religious traditions practiced today.

Judaism arose as one of the world's early civilizations. Were the other ancient civilizations—Babylonia, Persia, Greece, Rome, and Egypt—religions? Yes. Each civilization had its own religion. Were they cultures with their own language and literature? Yes, that too. Were they nation-states with a national consciousness? Each possessed a powerful nationalist identity. Were they peoples with a distinct sense of unity that remained with them when they traveled beyond the borders of their own country? That as well.

The main difference between Judaism and these other ancient cultures is that most of them died out long ago, while Judaism and the Jewish people endure. Jews today still reflect the characteristics that marked the Jewish people from their beginnings: a culture, a religion, a people, a nation.

Some Jews express their identity in nonreligious cultural terms (hence the existence of so-called "secular Jewish" organizations, another paradoxical idea for many Christians). Other Jews express their identity in Judaism's religious beliefs and synagogue observance. Still others do so by embracing the nationalistic Zionist aspirations of our people. Indeed, for some, that is the only component of their Jewishness. The majority of Israelis equate their Jewishness primarily with their living in the historic homeland rather than with the Jewish content of their lives.

All but a tiny minority of Jews affirm a central role of Israel in Jewish life. We are a proud people, and our peoplehood transcends our religious and racial differences. In moments of peril for Israel, as well as in moments of exaltation, we are not Reform, Conservative, Reconstructionist, Yiddishist, Zionist, Orthodox, or atheist. We are Jews, a united people sharing a common destiny, knowing in our bones that what happens to Israel will shape much of our future as Jews.

Jewish commitment to Israel is a powerful force, a fact recognized by the American people, our government, and the international community. But in calmer moments, that unity is very tenuous, and recent events demonstrate our vulnerability to splits and fractures both in Israel and the United States.

What is meant by the centrality of Israel for the Jewish people? Does it mean that American Jewry should subordinate its own needs to the overriding needs of the center, the State of Israel? As a practical matter, we have done this gladly since 1948 in response to the series of crises in Israel. But should we do it as a matter of *principle*, even if full peace, for example, came to Israel? Are we saying by "centrality" that the basic future of the Jewish people will be forged in Israel while in America and elsewhere Jews are doomed to assimilate and to live on the margins of the Jewish world?

These are not just idle questions. There is a haunting dilemma here. For what is the meaning of Israel's centrality if during many years, more Israelis go "down" (*yeridah*) to America than American Jews go "up" (*aliyah*) to Israel?

Some Jews regard Israel as primarily the *spiritual and religious* center of the Jewish world and Jerusalem as the focus of our historic faith and spiritual ideals. Others view Israel as the ultimate champion of the Jewish people, providing a haven for Jews in harm's way.

Still others argue that "centrality" is a misnomer. They contend that the Jews of the Diaspora are equal partners with the Jews of Israel, not senior or junior, central or marginal. Each of the great Jewries—and especially in America and in Israel—has a crucial role to play and a future to safeguard. Some even argue that Judaism as a *living religious civilization* has a better chance of creative fulfillment in America than in Israel. After all, the Jewish community in America is large, affluent, and powerful, enjoying the blessings of church-state separation and pluralism in the freest and wealthiest nation on earth.

In America, the synagogue community plays a large role, and American Jewry is free to build as vital, powerful, and affirming a Jewish life as we have the will to achieve. Here, as opposed to Israel, a wide spectrum of Jewish religious forms and ideas is encouraged and thrives. We are not hostage to external threats to our existence or limited by the meager resources of a small country. So why talk of "central"? Israel is part of the Jewish people, not the other way around.

This view is one of "affirmation of the Diaspora." In an influential paper, the late Dr. Gerson D. Cohen, former chancellor of the Jewish Theological Seminary of America (Conservative), challenged the concept of the centrality of Israel, countering with the theme of the *"centrality of the Jewish people."* He wrote that "Israel will have to send some of its best youths to the Diaspora to study...how to be Jews in the modern world."

A NORMAL STATE FOR A NORMAL PEOPLE?

What *kind* of state do we want Israel to be? There are those who say that since Zionism set out to cure the abnormal condition under which the Jewish people had previously lived, the Jewish state needs to aspire to be no more than a normal state, like any other state in the world. It is now a cliché that one early Zionist leader expressed satisfaction when he heard there was crime in the young Jewish state. "See," he said, "we have become a normal state. We have pickpockets and crooks and prostitutes like every other state."

But there is another view, which springs from the Jewish religious tradition. Israel is to be a *model* state, a *light unto the nations*, a messenger of peace, an example to the civilized world, an expression of God's covenant with the Jewish people. In this view, although Israel is a state with a Jewish majority, whether or not it is a truly *Jewish* state depends less on demographics than on the moral qualities of its citizenry.

Has Israel demonstrated moral leadership? In many ways, yes. No other small state has brought in millions of refugees, most recently over 20,000 black Ethiopian Jews and more than 800,000 former Soviet Jews, providing sanctuary to persecuted and poverty-stricken people from around the globe. No other small state has displayed the cultural vitality of Israel or provided such ambitious and selfless technical assistance to the poor nations of the world—especially those in Africa. No other small society has tapped the springs of science and technology for the common good as has Israel. No other developing nation has reclaimed the desert for agriculture and committed so much of its limited resources to social welfare. None has maintained such extensive democratic institutions—including free speech and free press—in the face of persistent warfare and terrorism.

But there is another side to the ledger, too. This side includes the failure to heal the "ethnic" rift between Ashkenazim and Sephardim; the second-class citizenship of Israeli Arabs, who are barred from the military and from a fair share of Israeli health, education, and housing benefits; the continued discrimination against non-Orthodox Jews; the infringements on the human rights of Palestinians living in the occupied territories; the failure to provide real equality for women; a variety of economic injustices, exacerbated by the floods of new immigrants seeking jobs and housing in the Jewish state; the inferior education that many Ethiopian children are receiving; and, above all, the failure to achieve a comprehensive peace with Israel's Arab neighbors. Will a dramatic improvement in this last area allow Israel to better address its domestic challenges, or will those problems be exacerbated once the outside threats, which allowed Israelis to put aside domestic differences, are alleviated?

CAN ISRAEL BE BOTH A JEWISH STATE AND A DEMOCRATIC STATE?

A Real Dilemma: The Issue of Israeli Arab Rights Tests the Jewish Character of Israel

In 1995, Adel Kaadan, an Arab Israeli citizen, saw an ad in the paper for an apartment near where he lived. He applied for membership in the Jewish cooperative village of Katsir, which had good infrastructure, low prices, and quality education facilities. Adel Kaadan is Hebrew-speaking and works in an Israeli military hospital; he is neither political nor radical and admittedly poses no threat to the safety of Katsir's Jewish inhabitants. Under no pretense, he and his family were denied admission to the cooperative, based simply on their Arab nationality. Kaadan was surprised and saddened by their decision, and in response, he filed a suit against the village with the Supreme Court. Kaadan said of the decision to prevent his membership, "They let me save their lives but to live next to them, no."

The legal basis for Kaadan's exclusion from the village is that Katsir is built on land leased to the Jewish Agency, which, by its own bylaws, is required to lease land only to Jews. The civil rights association arguing the case for Kaadan seeks a ruling from the

Supreme Court, which specifies that it is illegal for the state to lease lands to an agency that discriminates in its use of lands. Katsir's own residents, although politically left-leaning, say they are not ready for Arab-Jewish integration, do not want to weaken the Jewish identity of the community, and are already struggling to incorporate the recent influx of Jewish immigrants.

The Supreme Court chief justice, Aharon Barak, understood that this could be perhaps the most contentious court decision in Israel's history, perhaps even questioning the Law of Return (allowing Jews from everywhere to become citizens of Israel immediately) itself, and requested the parties to settle out of court. This case would force all of Israel to reconsider the principles upon which it was founded and how to preserve the integrity and the Jewish character of the state. Israel has always lived with this paradox, the unresolved conflict between being a Jewish state with a distinctly Jewish character and a democratic state that ensures equal rights to all its citizens. The late demagogue Meir Kahane argued that Israel could not be both Jewish and democratic. Should the Supreme Court decide that the principle of maintaining the Jewish character of the State of Israel, by allowing the existence of uniquely Jewish institutions, is more important than preserving the civil rights of minorities? Should the Court rule in favor of the forced integration of Jews and Arabs, knowing that such a decision would be profoundly destabilizing? Is the American situation parallel or different? How?

Response

The question before us presents an honest dilemma and forces us to examine some of the founding principles of the state of Israel. While this specific issue has not been considered by the Reform movement or its governing bodies, in keeping with Israel's Declaration of Independence that ensures "full social and political equality of all its citizens, without distinction of race, creed, or sex," no one's status as a citizen should depend on one's religious or ethnic identity.

On the one hand, the exclusion of anyone from a public institution or benefit, such as the right to live in a particular neighborhood, to hold a job, or to be admitted to a university, should not be determined by religion or ethnic identity. On the other hand, in a nation that is a Jewish state, the government has the right to discriminate on the basis of religion in its appointments of people to religious institutions, e.g., local religious councils. And certainly, Israel can strengthen the Jewish character and culture of Israel in many ways—by requiring the study of Jewish history in schools; by observing as national holidays the Jewish holidays; by asking the courts, as does the Jewish Heritage Law, to look to the values of "justice, equality, and compassion that are part of the Jewish heritage" in resolving legal disputes; and by asking the Knesset to seek policy guidance from Jewish law in shaping legislation for Israel.

Where does a secular (as opposed to a religious) kibbutz or moshav fall on the spectrum? A cornerstone of Israeli patriotism and strength, the kibbutz is an institution with a special Jewish character and a unique place in Israeli history. At the same time, can it really be distinguished from any historically Jewish neighborhood? Since Israel's survival depends in part on its ability to live in peace with its Arab neighbors and citizens, if Israel needs to err in these close calls, it should err in not sacrificing human rights and equality for minorities, even in the name of the Jewish character of the state. The Jewish identity of the state and its Jewish citizens will be little hurt by erring in these close calls; equality, democracy, and justice may be significantly tarnished if these calls go the wrong way.

REFORM JEWISH RIGHTS IN ISRAEL

For Reform Jews, there is a particularly nettlesome aspect to Israel's social justice agenda. After almost half a century, Israel still does not accord full religious liberty to non-Orthodox religious groups, denying Conservative and Reform rabbis the right to officiate at weddings, conversions, divorces, etc. It is a sad commentary that Israel has been wise enough to extend religious freedom to Christians and Muslims, indeed to all religions, but has not done so to all Jews. The result is the persistent danger of alienation of liberal Jews whose rabbis cannot serve as full rabbis in Israel.

That the vast majority of Jews in America are Reform and Conservative—Orthodox Jews represent less than 10 percent of American Jewry—sharpens the dilemma of Israel's policies on religious liberty.

In 1997, a profound threat to Israel-Diaspora relations exploded over the issue of conversions in Israel. The Israel Religious Action Center had brought a series of cases to the Israel Supreme Court, challenging the Orthodox monopoly on issues of personal status. When it became clear that the Court was beginning to question the monopoly and to press for equal justice, Orthodox parties went to the Knesset—the supreme authority in Israeli law—to overturn the prior decisions and to enshrine the continuation of the status quo regarding the issue at hand: only Orthodox rabbis can convert Jews in Israel. This decision touched the lives of hundreds of thousands of Russian immigrants and others who are not Jewish or whose Jewish status under Orthodox Jewish law is questioned (e.g., someone converted by a Reform or Conservative rabbi) and who might well want to be converted to Judaism and/or be married by a rabbi of their choice. As such, this issue transcends the Orthodox–non-Orthodox conflict. It will determine the nature of Israeli society, the role of freedom of religion in Israel, and the unity of the Jewish people. The furious reaction from American Jews strained the relations between Jews in Israel and the Diaspora. Protracted efforts were made in Israel to stitch together a compromise, but in the end, these foundered on the Orthodox Chief Rabbinate's unwillingness to accept any non-Orthodox Judaism as a valid expression of Jewish religious life.

In an effort to make Orthodox control of Jewish life permanent, Orthodox Israeli leaders have made many demands since Israel's founding: to amend the Law of Return so that only those converts who meet Orthodox halachic standards would be eligible for citizenship under the law; to register only such converts on national identity cards; to deny the right of Reform and Conservative Jews to be married by their own rabbis; to prevent non-Orthodox Jews from serving on the religious councils in Israel's cities that distribute funds to the municipal's religious institutions; and to allow only Orthodox Jewish prayer services to be held at the Western Wall. Clearly, all these demands divide the Jewish people, delegitimize Reform and Conservative Judaism and Reform and Conservative rabbis, and convey the impression that the government of Israel considers Reform and Conservative Jews as second-class Jews.

ISRAEL RELIGIOUS ACTION CENTER

The Reform Jewish movement has established an Israel Religious Action Center in Jerusalem to speak in the name of the Progressive movement (Reform) of Israel on such burning social justice issues as religious liberty, Reform rights, pluralism, women's rights, Arab-Jewish relations, the environment, and consumer rights. Inspired by the success of the RAC in Washington, this center has become a rallying point for Israelis from many backgrounds to lobby the Knesset, organize demonstrations, form coalitions, and seek redress of grievances.

A Real Dilemma: Is the Legal Struggle the Wrong Way to Go?

In the spring issue of 1996, the CCAR *Journal* published an article by Rabbi Stanley Ringler that challenged the priority the Reform Jewish movement in Israel gives to legal efforts to vindicate Reform rights under the laws of Israel. In Ringler's harsh critique, the Israel Religious Action Center is expending important resources to win small legal victories—such as the right of non-Orthodox Jews to serve on local religious councils and the right of non-Orthodox Jews to be buried in nondenominational cemeteries—which can then be thrown out by a majority in the Knesset. This is due to the fact that Israel does not have a constitution and decisions of the courts can be nullified by the Knesset, which is sovereign. Indeed, after the election of Mr. Netanyahu (along with a record twenty-seven members of Orthodox religious parties in the Knesset), one of the first demands of the religious leaders was the overturning of recent decisions of the Supreme Court because they upset the "status quo" of religious dominance in Israel. According to Ringler, the Reform community might have flourished in Israel if it had concentrated on building congregations and schools rather than on legal vindication and its short-lived victories.

The Reform leadership, in reply, pointed to the crisis of post-election Israel where pluralism was placed in severe jeopardy by the demands of a triumphal Orthodoxy. Both political and legal counteraction were imperative to prevent the delegitimization of non-Orthodox Judaism in Israel and the consequent shattering of Jewish unity in America, where more than 80 percent of Jews are Reform, Conservative, or Reconstructionist.

Response

In reality, there is a consensus that we need to do both. Reform Judaism will ultimately not succeed in Israel unless we create new Reform congregations, schools, community centers, kibbutzim, and other grassroots institutions that meet the needs of and appeal to a wide spectrum of Israelis; and we are at last making progress. By the end of the 1990s, polling data showed that most Israelis favored the rights of Reform and Conservative rabbis to officiate at marriages and other life-cycle ceremonies, and 45 percent said they would prefer Reform or Conservative rabbis to officiate or would be as comfortable with them as with an Orthodox rabbi. Nonetheless, the Orthodox are mobilizing to fight against the granting of religious equality to Reform and Conservative Jews. The Supreme Court, rather than the Knesset, has been our best protection since the Orthodox have the advantage of being organized in political parties that regularly win enough votes to make or break any ruling coalition. The fight in 1997 and 1998 over the rights of Reform and Conservative rabbis to officiate at conversions further heightened tensions. Secular Jews driving on Shabbat on streets in religious neighborhoods are often stoned. One of our kindergartens was burned to the ground. Death threats against our leaders are all-too-regular occurrences. Indeed, more Israelis now believe that there will be violence in Israel over religious issues than believe there will be strife with the Arabs. But so far, we have refused to emulate the Orthodox in creating political parties in Israel, believing that when religion enters electoral politics, both religion and politics are debased. Should this position be reexamined?

Ironically, the bitter controversy about conversion did have the unexpected by-product of familiarizing Israelis with the reality and prospects of non-Orthodox Judaism in Israel.

THE PALESTINIANS

Modern Zionism was founded by Theodor Herzl to end what he saw as the fundamental abnormality of Jewish life: our *homelessness*. Only a homeland, he argued, could reunite the Jewish soul and the Jewish body. Until we had a land of our own, we would be subject to persecution at the whim of every ruler in search of a scapegoat. Herzl was proved correct. The Nazi Holocaust revealed that virtually no country in the world, not even the United States, would provide a safe haven to the Jewish victims of persecution. The state of Israel was born out of the ashes of World War II and the destruction of the historic Jewish communities of Europe.

But ironically, in solving the problem of Jewish homelessness, another people was rendered homeless. In Israel's War of Independence (1948), almost 600,000 Arabs fled their homes in Jaffa, Haifa, and many towns that fell within the borders of the new Jewish state. (An equal number of Jews were forced to flee Arab nations to Israel, where they were immediately resettled.) According to Arab propaganda, those Arabs were forcibly driven out by Jews; the best evidence, however, indicates that most fled either in the panic of war or under the orders of Arab rulers who told them they could return after the Jews had been massacred. Recently, some Israeli scholars have suggested that Israel took advantage of this situation and through the use of psychological warfare orchestrated fear to prompt some Arabs to flee.

The refugees have never returned.

Kept in refugee camps as political pawns by the Arab states, raising their children on a propaganda diet rich in hatred for Israel, they yearn for the day of return to their former cities and villages. In their bitterness, many have joined Arab terrorist groups. Then, in the Six-Day War of 1967, Israel overwhelmed Arab aggression and occupied the West Bank and Gaza, bringing hundreds of thousands of stateless Palestinian Arabs under Israeli control.

In December of 1987, the Palestinians in the occupied territories began the *intifada*, a bloody rebellion that claimed hundreds of lives, mostly among Arab youths. The *intifada* demonstrated the seething fury of the Palestinians and the terrible price Israel had to pay for occupying territory that contained more than a million alien and hostile people.

What should be done about the Palestinians? It is sadly true that nothing was done for the Palestinians when Jordan and Egypt controlled the West Bank and Gaza. They were not even allowed to visit Egypt, much less create a Palestinian state. Under Israeli administration, Arabs from Jordan have been accorded the right to cross "open bridges" over the Jordan River, and Palestinians from the West Bank and Gaza have been allowed to visit and to work for relatively good wages in Israel.

But year after year, Israeli leaders refused to acknowledge that the Palestinians were anything more than refugees. "There are no Palestinians," former Prime Minister Golda Meir said. But Palestinian nationalism, inspired in part by the success of Zionism and stirred by Arab countries for their own purposes, spread among the Palestinians. As one of the most enterprising and best-educated segments of the Arab world, they began to demand their rights, *as a people, to a national homeland of their own.* Poetry, literature, music, art, and politics converged in a new sense of Palestinian peoplehood, creating a common cause, a common history, a common destiny.

How, then, do we determine which side has the more legitimate right to establish a country on a disputed territory? On the one hand, unlike the Kurds, Basques, Croatians, and Latvians, who can recall their own former independent national existence, there never was a country of Palestine. A distinctive Palestinian identity emerged only coextensive to modern Zionism. Over the centuries, the only people to think of the land we call Israel as its historic homeland has been the Jewish people, whose nationalistic dream has ancient roots.

On the other hand, whatever the history of the area, a generation of Palestinians has grown up believing deeply that they have a right to self-determination in their own land. They are willing to lay down their lives for that goal and have pursued it not only through means of violence and terrorism but by creating modalities of local autonomy wherever possible. Yet over the past fifteen years, a growing number of Palestinians seemed willing to give up the futile goal of destroying Israel and settle for a ministate in the West Bank and Gaza, living side by side, peacefully, with Israel. The example of Israeli democracy inspired a mirror-image vision of Palestinian nationalism—almost an Arab version of Zionism.

THE PEACE PROCESS

Then, in 1993, an extraordinary breakthrough for peace took place. Through negotiations in Oslo, Norway, Israeli and Palestinian representatives forged a peace treaty that was consummated at the White House when Prime Minister Rabin and Palestinian Authority leader Yassir Arafat signed the accord with President Clinton and shook hands in front of the world on September 13, 1993.

The agreement included mutual recognition of Israel and the Palestinian Authority and the return to Palestinian control of Palestinian population centers along with the entirety of the Gaza Strip (the densely populated narrow strip of land between Israel and Egypt). Conversely, the Palestinians pledged to control violent activity, including terrorism against Israel, to cooperate with Israeli security forces, and to eliminate provisions of its charter that called for Israel's destruction. Neither side has yet fully lived up to those agreements. For Israel, the failure of the Palestinian leadership to contain terrorist activity and to give up its sometimes harsh anti-Israel rhetoric is particularly vexing.

Finally, the Palestinians, the Israelis, and the international community agreed to cooperate on economic and environmental issues, which has led to significant international investment in the Palestinian area.

Indeed, in the first democratic election ever held by the Palestinian people, the voters turned out in astounding numbers and cast their votes overwhelmingly for a continuation of the peace process that had already resulted in the withdrawal of Israeli forces from the Gaza Strip and much of the West Bank. The election of Yassir Arafat in 1996 was a resounding endorsement of the peace process and a vote against the rejectionism and terrorism advocated by Hamas extremists. The election marked a historic rejection of mutual hostility of the bloody past. It reflected high hopes not only for mutual recognition but even a glimmer of reconciliation between two peoples joined by destiny, geography, and common fate.

These euphoric hopes subsequently suffered severe damage as a result of a series of terrorist massacres on the streets of Tel Aviv and Jerusalem, the assassination of Yitzhak Rabin by an Israeli fanatic, and the victory at the polls of a hard-line Netanyahu, who made clear his opposition to giving up much more land on the West Bank, to the sharing of Jerusalem, and to any suggestion of a Palestinian state.

THE UNITED STATES' ROLE

We in America cannot determine which political solutions will safeguard Israel's security while accommodating, at least minimally, the claims of the Palestinian people. Only the government and the people of Israel—in dialogue with the Palestinians—can decide this fateful question.

While our task as American Jews is, above all, to affirm the legitimacy and security of Israelis, it is also to accept the humanity of the Palestinians, to see them as *persons* and as a *people*, and to reject anti-Arab stereotypes and slogans. To think of all Palestinians as terrorists is as logical as equating all Jews with the Jewish Defense League or West Bank settlers. To understand Palestinians, we first have to speak with them, listen to them, and learn about their hopes and fears.

Several founders of Zionism believed that the ultimate moral test of Zionism was whether or not it could reconcile itself with its Arab neighbors. If the French and Germans could reconcile after two world wars, if Egypt and Israel could sign a peace treaty, if the United States and the USSR could end their enmity, why must Jews and Palestinians remain faceless enemies forever? And what of our religious tradition that demands that we *seek* peace and convert enemies to friends? Ultimately, only a political dialogue based on mutual recognition can resolve this seemingly intractable conflict.

A Real Dilemma: Middle East Peace Facilitation Act (MEPFA)

The underlying postulate of the peace process is that all the parties had to be convinced that peace would help improve their quality of life. For Israelis, this means enhanced security, partly through the effectiveness of the Palestinian Authority in taking steps to ensure Israeli security and particularly for combating terrorism. For the Palestinians, this would be manifested in political autonomy and improved economic quality of life made possible in part through the ability of the world community to provide economic aid.

When the Middle East Peace Facilitation Act was first passed providing such aid to the new Palestinian Authority, President Clinton was required to certify each year that the Palestinian

Authority is living up to the Oslo Peace Accords. Continued terrorist attacks and some inflammatory statements from Palestinian leaders, including Chairman Arafat, gave opponents of the peace accords ammunition to oppose aid to the Palestinians. While it is clear that the Palestinian Authority has made significant improvements in deterring anti-Israeli terrorism, pro-Israeli forces agree it could certainly do more. Each year, the American Jewish community faces a decision: should it support aid to the Palestinians or oppose it until the Palestinians do more to live up to Oslo? The Rabin-Peres leadership urged support for aid to the Palestinians. Prime Minister Netanyahu cannot conceal his aversion for Chairman Arafat and his coolness to the Palestine Liberation Organization (PLO) and the Palestinian Authority. Where should American Jews fit in? Should we continue to support U.S. aid to the Palestinians?

Response

The mainstream organizations in the Jewish community recognize that if the people living in Gaza, the West Bank, and Jordan do not feel that the quality of their lives has been improved by their participation in the peace process, there is no hope for the process to succeed. Compliance on both sides of the accords is a process, not an immediate step. Even the sharpest critics of the peace accords agree that on the most crucial issue—terrorism—the Palestinian Authority has improved its efforts to staunch such attacks. For these reasons, the Reform and Conservative movements, the Jewish defense organizations, and AIPAC (the key pro-Israel lobby organization) all generally supported passage of MEPFA in the 1990s. In 1997, however, the Congress and many in the Jewish community tired of the lack of progress in the peace process and the failure of the political leaders on both sides to take long-promised actions toward peace. Furthermore, the Palestinian Authority proved to be an inefficient and ineffective entity, wasting many of its resources. In August 1997, MEPFA expired and was not renewed by Congress. Although passage of MEPFA was not required for the United States to send aid to the Palestinian Authority, Representative Benjamin

Gilman (R-NY), chairman of the House International Relations Committee, held up other types of appropriations for the authority in FY 1998 and will most likely continue to do so in the future. Supporters of the peace process fear that hard-line American Jewish critics have greatly hurt peace efforts by pressuring the U.S. Congress to act in a way that undermines the spirit of partnership.

CAN JEWS DISSENT?

What do we American Jews do when we seriously differ with policies pursued by the government of Israel? The question is complicated by an additional problem: What American Jews say publicly frequently impacts on public opinion in the United States and sometimes even upon the policies followed by our government. The United States of America and America's Jews are Israel's most powerful and important allies. Their words and actions have a direct and crucial impact on the well-being and security of the Jewish state.

Since we do not live and die by the decisions that Israel makes, do we have the right to speak out? Furthermore, criticism issued out of love by American Jews can often be manipulated by Israel's enemies to validate their efforts to weaken Israel. So how should we act when our convictions differ from Israeli government policy in matters of conscience? For their part, Jews in Israel vigorously debate every major issue affecting their nation. Should American Jews be silent partners or, worse, predictable amen-sayers regardless of Israeli policies? Many American Jews were outspoken in opposition to their own government on the Vietnam War, disagreeing with those who demanded "My country right or wrong." Are we to be dissenters in America and silent spectators about events in Israel when our conscience or judgment tells us that something is wrong?

If we feel that new settlements in the West Bank and unilateral changes by Israel in Jerusalem seriously harm the prospects for peaceful negotiations and needlessly antagonize the Palestinians and the American government, should we say so? Privately to Israeli leaders? Publicly? Neither? Why?

Those who support free and open discussion say that Israel is the homeland of the Jewish people, of which we are equal partners, and that the character—especially the moral character—of the Jewish state *is* decidedly our business. Further, as we could not stand idly by if we saw brothers or sisters about to do harm, either to others or to themselves, so we must not stand idly by when we see Israel engage in policies or practices that we believe undermine its interests generally and, more particularly, its support in the United States. We can help Israel overcome its challenges only if we speak out frankly and involve ourselves in mobilizing support for solutions. The alternative is to create a falsely idyllic picture-postcard Israel, which encourages escape from reality rather than the necessary frank wrestling with the tough issues required of all Jews in Israel and the Diaspora.

The other side of the coin is that speaking out, for example, for our religious rights in Israel is quite a different matter from speaking out on matters of security and foreign policy for which the Israelis—and not we—must pay the ultimate price. They will live and die by the results of the decisions they make. They are in the trenches; we are on the sidelines. This consideration weighs heavily on every Jew committed to Israel and to the Jewish people.

A Real Dilemma: American Jews and U.S. Policy

Following the election of Benjamin Netanyahu and in the wake of terrorist attacks in Israel, the peace process virtually ground to a halt. Finally, in 1997, the U.S. government intensified efforts to break the stalemate. Under the vigorous leadership of Secretary of State Madeleine Albright, U.S. diplomats called on the Palestinians to strengthen their efforts against terrorism and urged Israel to take a "time-out" on the expansion of settlements and other unilateral steps that jeopardized mutual trust. To the Israeli government and some American Jews, this "pressure" on Israel by the United States represented a betrayal of the special relationship that has long existed between America and Israel. Should American Jewish groups support the Israeli government's position and speak out to protect Israel from "pressure"? Or should American Jews who believe that the peace process is indispensable to Israel's well-being communicate to the president and secretary of state our support for strong leadership, pressuring both sides to rescue the peace process? Should such

American Jews urge the Israeli government to change those policies that seem to impede the peace process? What about the argument that only the Israelis can decide the fundamental questions
of peace and that American Jews should bow out? Or the opposing argument that we have every right as Jews who have a stake
in Israel's security to express our views, especially if we believe
that only U.S. initiatives can save the peace?

Response

While acknowledging the sanctity of a democratic election and
giving the Israeli government the benefit of the doubt, the
Reform Jewish movement has long held that we have the right—
and the duty—to support the principles we believe to be indispensable to Israel's well-being, even urging the government of
Israel to change its policies. Over the past twenty years, when
many American Jews were critical of Likud hard-line policies on
settlements, Lebanon, and the *intifada,* we have convinced most
(albeit not all) American and Israeli Jews that such criticism was
healthy and proper. So, too, in the early days of the Oslo peace
process, we supported the rights of Jewish hard-liners to condemn
the peace process, no matter how much we disagreed with them.

In the late nineties, many Jewish organizations publicly
supported the Clinton administration's efforts to encourage Israel
to halt new settlements and refrain from any unilateral action
that might undermine the peace process. Prime Minister
Netanyahu's refusal to accede led to yet greater public differences. Many critics moderated their criticism, however, as a
means of encouraging the Netanyahu government to take the
difficult steps necessary to put the peace process back on track.

Talmudic sources highlight this discussion. In *Avodah Zara* 18a, it is
written that one who feels that protest in the face of injustice may be
effective and does not protest ought to be punished. With specific
regard to Israel, Rabbi Papa said, "And the princes of the exile
[exilarchs, or leaders of the Jewish community] are held accountable
for the transgressions of the whole household of Israel." (*Shabbat* 54b)

It is often said that if American Jews feel compelled to dissent, we should do so directly and privately with Israel's leadership. This may be good advice in most cases. But what if they spurn our counsel? Or what if, as in the question of the rights of Reform Jews or even the rights of Palestinian Arabs, the controversy rises to become an issue of profound moral and ethical principle? Is there any way to press our viewpoint short of speaking out publicly?

If we American Jews never engage in public criticism, thereby defining friendship for Israel by blind silence, will not America's non-Jewish friends feel they must choose between their convictions on specific policies and their general support of Israel? Do we not serve Israel better by setting an example for Americans that we can urge Israel to change specific policies we feel are wrong while continuing to support the Jewish state by advocating American foreign aid to Israel and working for closer United States–Israel relations?

And what happens to our credibility if we speak out on human rights violations and social injustice everywhere in the world except when such events occur in the Jewish state?

Every thoughtful American Jew will face this dilemma at one time or another. If one speaks out, one may risk attacks on one's Jewish loyalty and integrity. But a Jewish community sensitive to civil liberties must learn to respect internal dissent. Democracy, like charity, begins at home. And failure to resolve this dilemma could compromise Jewish security here and in Israel.

ZIONIST THOUGHT AND THE DILEMMA OF THE PALESTINIANS

The dilemmas we face today are not new. They commanded the attention of the seminal thinkers of modern Zionism. Foremost among them was Ahad Ha-Am, the architect of the vision of a Jewish state rooted in Jewish ideals and Jewish culture. He taught that a Jewish homeland must be reconciled with "consideration for the national rights of the Palestinian Arabs." He rejected the conventional wisdom of Zionist leaders who insisted that the Balfour Declaration was a mandate for a Jewish state in all of Palestine.

Ahad Ha-Am stressed what others chose to ignore: the British pledge in the Balfour Declaration was conditioned by the clause "that nothing shall be done that may prejudice the civil and religious rights of existing non-Jewish communities in Palestine." He was haunted by the moral compulsion that the development of a Jewish homeland should not displace or degrade those Arabs who also have "a genuine right to the land due to generations of residence and work upon it." To him, Palestine was a "common possession of two peoples."

Following Ahad Ha-Am's death, his disciple, Rabbi Judah L. Magnes, carried on this difficult struggle. Magnes was a Reform rabbi who made *aliyah* in 1922 and became a founder of the Hebrew University, which he served as president until his death in 1946. He brought Arabs and Jews together to work for a binational state in which the rights of both would be protected by constitutional safeguards. "One of the greatest cultural duties of the Jewish people," he said, "is the attempt to enter the Promised Land not by means of conquest like Joshua, but through peaceful and cultural means, through hard work, sacrifice, love, and with a decision not to do anything that cannot be justified before the world conscience."

The great religious philosopher Martin Buber believed that the moral challenge to Zionism was the question of its willingness to share the land with another people. He pleaded for the "harnessing of national-istic impulses and a solution based on compromise between two peoples." The binational state option, once part of the formal platform of the movement, fell victim to a half-century of ceaseless hostility between Arabs and Jews and the national Jewish trauma of the Holocaust.

Arabs and Jews generally see each other through a prism of stereo-types. Only powerful symbols like Sadat's visit to Jerusalem, the September 1993 handshake between Prime Minister Rabin and PLO Chairman Arafat, and the peace treaty with Jordan can break the "psychological impasse" that prevents Jews and Arabs from recognizing each other's humanity. But such occasions are all too rare. Abba Eban once said that the "Arabs never lose an opportunity to lose an oppor-tunity." But have we Jews in Israel and the Diaspora done all that we can to generate decent human relations between Arabs and Jews?

PEACE AND MILITARY REALITIES

Are the Israelis and Palestinians and Arab nations willing to make the necessary compromises for a settlement? Can peace be established without the creation of a Palestinian state and without an end to the mass hatred of Jews taught in Arab nations? Is there any chance for the acceptance of a Jewish state in the midst of a vast Arab sea or a Palestinian homeland alongside Israel? Can there be lasting peace without a solution to Jerusalem that both sides can live with?

Yitzhak Rabin, who had led Israel's military forces during the Six-Day War, was able to make some of the compromises for peace because the Israeli public trusted him to do nothing to harm Israel's security. Rabin made clear that he was doing this because his analysis of the military and political options offered no other choice. As he saw it, Israel is best equipped to take risks for peace against its potential enemies when it is strongest vis-à-vis those enemies—and it is likely that Israel will never be stronger than the Arabs than it is today.

Conversely, if the status quo remains, only disastrous options face Israel. Arab military power will grow stronger, making it more difficult to take risks for peace. And what will Israel do with the Palestinians in the West Bank? If Israel makes them Israeli citizens, their growing population and birthrate would lead to a non-Jewish majority in Israel in the next century, jeopardizing Israel as a Jewish state. If they continue to occupy the West Bank and Gaza, there would likely be increasing acts of terrorism and military resistance. (We saw this in the four years of the *intifada*, in which violent resistance—particularly from Palestinian youth—caused numerous Israeli deaths and began to demoralize the army.) These dangers would lead to growing support of extremist calls for Israel to engage in ethnic cleansing and to kick the .Palestinians out of their homes—something unthinkable to most Israelis and an action that would lead to international censure and isolation, even from Israel's best friends. Most Israelis believe Israel's security and political needs would best be met through peace based on an Israeli withdrawal from much of the West Bank and Gaza and the concurrent granting of Palestinian control over these relinquished areas. This could lead to a broader peace in the region, one that would marginalize the rogue states of Iraq and Iran and lessen the danger of proliferating chemical and nuclear weapons.

Coexistence with the Palestinians and also with Israel's Arab neighbors may be the only hope. The visions of Buber, Ahad Ha-Am, and Magnes may yet prove their value in a world of militarism and cynical power politics. This particular dilemma goes deep into the Jewish past

and the sources of our moral inspiration. In many ways, it will shape
the nature of our Jewish future.

A Real Dilemma: Weapons of Mass Destruction in Iraq and Israel

In 1997 and 1998, the United States threatened military action
against Iraq because it sabotaged the inspection system and
refused to comply with U.N. resolutions from the Gulf War
allowing open inspections of all sites that might be used to hide
or develop nonconventional weapons. Instead, Iraq continued to
harbor materials for chemical, biological, and nuclear weapons
and to develop the means to deliver them to Israel and other
nations. Although the U.N. is officially responsible for ensuring
that Iraq destroy its weapons of mass destruction, the United
States has been taking the primary leadership role in this
campaign. Instead of being appreciative of U.S. efforts to ameliorate the threat from an Arab nation that had several times made
war with its neighbors, the nightly newscasters brought images of
Arabs in several Middle Eastern countries protesting against
what they claimed was U.S. and Israel hegemony in the region,
leading to aggression against Iraq.

Some Arab nations questioned U.S. motives in calling for military action against Iraq, since in their eyes Israel is guilty of the
same crimes. So while the United States claims the role as police-
man of the world, it punishes only those whom it abhors ideo-
logically. Clearly, they believe, the United States has a double
standard. Israel had also long ignored some U.N. resolutions (e.g.,
refusing to withdraw from its occupation of southern Lebanon),
and it, too, has weapons of mass destruction. How is Israel's position different from Iraq's? How can the United States go to the
brink of war over Iraq's transgressions but defend and uphold the
actions of Israel? And is our support for strong U.S. action against
Iraq prompted by our concern for Israel's security or for U.S.
national interests?

Response

While on the surface this is a particularly nettlesome dilemma,
there are vast differences between Israel and Iraq that justify

different treatment. Iraq developed its nonconventional weapons to use offensively—against its own minority citizens and against other nations. Israel developed its nuclear capacity for defensive purposes, as a means of deterring attacks from vastly larger, hostile Arab neighbors calling for Israel's destruction. Israel has never used chemical, biological, or nuclear weapons against its own population or anyone else. Saddam Hussein is distinguished as the only world leader to use these weapons in cold blood not once but at least twice—against his Kurdish minority and then against Iranian soldiers.

Finally, the U.N. went through a long phase of rabid anti-Israel and anti-Semitic activity, churning out automatic Israel-bashing resolutions. Sorting out which of the U.N.'s anti-Israel resolutions should now apply and which should not is a difficult process. Even at its best, the U.N. has rarely been sensitive to Israel's military vulnerability and security needs. In contrast, there was universal agreement in the world community as to Iraq's violation of international norms.

The threat to Israel from Iraq is not merely an academic exercise; it is a blood-chilling reality. In 1995, testimony from Saddam Hussein's son-in-law, who was in charge of Iraq's biological program but then defected, confirmed that Iraq had a firm plan to send pilotless missiles to spray anthrax, a deadly chemical weapon, over the entire length of Israel shortly before the Gulf War began. One of the obvious reasons that Saddam did not carry out this plan was that Israel had the capacity to respond with overwhelming force. Israel has a moral right to develop weapons for self-defense when it is the primary, stated target of planned genocide. Paradoxically, however, Israel's possession of nuclear weapons capability gives it a status as a world military power that spurs the Arab nations to try and match it. Hopefully, a regional peace settlement might lead to new strategic realities that will allow a measure of disarmament. The Mideast and all other dangerous regions must, in the long run, become part of a world of law that universally bans weapons of mass destruction.

DOMESTIC CHALLENGES

Israel faces a number of pressing domestic challenges in the coming decades. In addition to the religious strains, Israel has been buffeted by tensions along the ethnic fault line, particularly between Ashkenazic Jews (European in origin) and Sephardic Jews (those from Arab, North African, and Spanish-speaking countries). Israel now has a 58 percent majority of Jews of Sephardic origin, and while it has made significant strides in the past two decades bridging the cultural and economic gap between Ashkenazic and Sephardic Jews, most top slots in economic and political spheres are still held by Ashkenazim. Despite Israel's productive economy in the 1990s, economic problems are mounting, with serious unemployment and inadequate housing, especially in the development towns; and those in poverty, particularly those from Arab countries, are in danger of being recycled into a second generation locked into a permanent underclass. In the 1950s, Sweden and Israel had the *smallest* gap between the rich and the poor. In the 1990s, Israel is second only to the United States in having the *largest* income gap between the rich and the poor. The resentment of the have-nots is intensified by the preferential housing and job opportunities accorded to 800,000 Soviet Jewish immigrants who have arrived since the collapse of the Soviet Union, as a means of enticing them to come and to stay—a pattern that further delays improvements for other needy Israelis. Diversion of limited resources into massive settlement building in the West Bank during much of the past twenty years also exacerbates all these strains.

As problematic as the tensions are between Jew and Jew, they are paralleled by the growing tensions between Israeli Jews and Israeli Arabs. Israeli Arabs feel themselves to be second-class citizens in Israel. With few exceptions, they are barred from serving in the military, and Arab communities receive less money per capita for the educational, health, and physical infrastructure than do predominantly Jewish communities. The government does little to promote Jewish-Arab harmony on the personal level. Prejudice and antagonism were intensified by the *intifada*, the Palestinian rebellion in the occupied West Bank and Gaza, and Israeli Arab citizens feel increasingly alienated from the majority Jewish population, which in turn fears a fifth-column threat. These trends are tearing apart the civility of Israeli society, polarizing Israeli Jews and Arabs who share citizenship in the same land.

The struggle for Israel's future depends as much on its ability to address its domestic challenges as on its capacity to deal with external threats. To those issues discussed above should be added the growing environmental threats, the issue of equality of women, and the need for electoral reform to further democratize the structure of the Israeli government.

In many ways, the vision of Israel's early *chalutzim* ("pioneers") of a society of economic equality and social justice has faded under the stress of austerity and the need to maintain a huge defense burden. As in other countries, a hunger for consumer goods has eclipsed much of the pioneering spirit of the early days, and a sense of national purpose wanes except in times of emergency.

Most Jews believe that only when and if Israel and its Arab enemies make peace and Israel can redirect segments of the 40 percent of its annual budget now allocated to defense can it fully address its domestic concerns.

That Israel in a mere half-century has done as much as it has for the cause of social justice is testimony to its abiding commitment to the age-old values of the Jewish people. That it has still much to achieve remains the goal—and obligation—of the people of Israel and the Jewish people around the globe. For all of us, the achievement of an Israel that becomes, once again, a light unto the nations will be the fulfillment of three thousand years of Zionist dreams.

SOVIET JEWRY

For twenty-five years, millions of Jews and non-Jews around the world campaigned for the freedom of the 3 million Soviet Jews who were persecuted by Soviet authorities. Synagogues around the world adopted Soviet Jewish prisoners of conscience like Anatoly (Natan) Sharansky and Yuli Edelstein (both now members of the Israeli Knesset). They twinned the b'nei mitzvah of their congregations with Soviet Jewish girls and boys who, on turning thirteen, could not hold their own. They rallied and protested and educated. Indeed, the great rally in 1987, in which a quarter of a million supporters came to the Mall in Washington to protest during Premier Gorbachev's visit, was coordinated by the

National Conference on Soviet Jewry and other Jewish organizations out of the Religious Action Center's conference room. With the collapse of the Soviet Union, their dreams were answered. In less than ten years, nearly a million Jews made *aliyah* to Israel.

Two million Jews remain, however, trying to rebuild Jewish life in the former Soviet republics.

A Real Dilemma: Should We Build Reform Institutions in the Former Soviet Union?

In 1990, the World Union for Progressive Judaism (WUPJ), the international arm of Reform Jewry, faced this dilemma: Should it invest part of its limited resources in assisting the development of a Reform congregation in Moscow? We faced bureaucratic obstacles from the state in obtaining a building for the synagogue; we faced opposition from Orthodox, particularly chasidic, groups, who saw us as undermining the traditional Jewish community; and we faced the criticisms of those who maintained that the only way to secure the lives of Soviet Jews was to get them out as soon as possible. What should the WUPJ have done?

Response

After much deliberation, a firm decision was made to move ahead vigorously in the establishment of a liberal Jewish community in Moscow. Whether we liked it or not, there were Jews who were going to stay. These Jews had rights as well. Moreover, the democratic reforms in the former Soviet Union have a fighting chance to make it, and Jews who join in that fight deserve our support. Members of the Moscow congregation were heavily involved in the liberal democratic movements, and many stayed up for three days and nights to face down the forces of repression during the 1991 coup attempt. Today there are over 40 Reform congregations and groups in the former Soviet republics.

ETHIOPIAN JEWRY

In May 1991, almost overnight, in one of the most efficient and dramatic airlifts in history, an entire community, the black Jews of Ethiopia, were swept out of the Middle Ages and transported to a modern Jewish state. In that one stunning event, the very meaning of Zionism, Israel as a sanctuary for Jews in jeopardy anywhere in the world, was vindicated. An American journalist observed that this rescue was the first time in history that black people had been taken from one continent to another "in love, not in chains."

While Arabs were slaughtering their fellow Arabs in Iraq and Kuwait, Jews gave the world a glowing demonstration of the humanity and unity of the Jewish people. Strapped for resources, already drained by the Soviet Jewish *aliyah*, the people of Israel embraced their Ethiopian brothers and sisters, many of them ill or elderly, all of them needy. What other society would do this?

The miracle was made possible by the generous intervention of the United States. President Bush had personally signaled to the rebel leaders in Ethiopia that he wanted to see a safe harbor for the Jews. The U.S. Congress, especially the late heroic black Congressman Mickey Leland, had kept the plight of Ethiopian Jews alive in the consciousness of the world. American Jews also played a strong role in ministering to the Ethiopian Jews during the long years of their waiting for redemption.

Organizations like the American Association for Ethiopian Jewry; the North American Conference on Ethiopian Jewry; the Joint Distribution Committee; and the Reform movement's own Project REAP (Reform Movement's Ethiopian Jewry Assistance Program), which helped to provide medical care to the Jews of Ethiopia, made the difference between life and death for thousands of Ethiopian Jews awaiting rescue. Many Israeli leaders, too, refused to turn their backs on this ancient community. And the Ethiopians themselves kept their Jewish faith alive through centuries of travail, going back perhaps to biblical days.

The absorption of these Jews into Israeli life has been bittersweet. They absorbed Israeli culture and modern life with amazing rapidity. Conversely, Israelis have accepted them with open arms and little prejudice compared to other Western nations.

On the other hand, the Chief Rabbinate of Israel has questioned their status as Jews and now requires symbolic conversions. Israel's economic limitations and the massive immigration of Soviet Jews has depleted job, housing, and economic opportunities that otherwise would have been open to the Ethiopians. At the same time, the Ethiopian Jews are caught between their desire to be accepted and assimilated into Israeli society and their wish to preserve their distinctive religious and cultural customs and identity. By 1994, much progress had been made in absorption efforts, but some systemic problems had evolved. Forty percent of Ethiopian Jews were still in temporary mobile home caravans, many others had been forced by economic limitations to buy housing in the poorer urban areas, unemployment among those living at caravan sites remained at 13 percent, and only a small minority of students were integrated into college-track educational programs. Project REAP was reactivated in 1994 to assist in the absorption efforts.

In 1995, the Israeli government formally acknowledged many of the problems facing Ethiopian immigrants. Significant steps were taken and in the areas of housing and employment, there has been significant progress. For example, the policy of affirmative action that was implemented in every facet of the absorption process of Ethiopian immigrants has assisted in the moving of 90 percent of the residents from temporary sites to permanent housing.

One major problem remains: for a variety of circumstances, and in spite of the best intentions, the vast majority of Ethiopian high school students receive mostly vocational, nonacademic education and have little or no opportunity to progress to a university. As a result, a growing number of Ethiopian youths are feeling isolated, alienated, and locked out of mainstream Israeli society. Hundreds of Ethiopian *olim* (immigrants) between the ages of thirteen and eighteen have dropped out of school and now work at odd jobs, loiter on the streets, drink, and engage in violence and juvenile delinquency. Hundreds more Ethiopian youngsters could soon join them, forming the nucleus of a permanent underclass. The possibility that racism, from which Israelis have largely been spared, might raise its ugly head was illuminated in 1995 when the press revealed that because of the high rate of HIV infection in Africa and fear of the spread of AIDS, Israeli hospitals had segregated out the Ethiopian blood from that of other Israelis giving to blood banks and had later thrown it all out. The result was a near riot by Ethiopian Jews and a profound reexamination by Israelis of the emergence of racial stereotypes and prejudices surrounding the absorption of Ethiopians.

Project REAP, the Israel Religious Action Center, the Israeli Association for Ethiopian Jews, and a new coalition of national Jewish offices in the United States and Israel have urged key Israeli and American Jewish officials to take immediate steps to solve these issues. Finally, in 1997, the Israeli government joined these coalitions in leading a broad-based effort to end the inadequate education of Ethiopian Jewry as a means of assuring equal justice in Israel's distinctly multiethnic society.

... 7 ...

Peace and International Affairs

*A Real Dilemma: Does Commitment to Israel Mean Supporting
High United States Defense Budgets?*

Ever since the Vietnam War, one of the central arguments of
Jewish neoconservatives was that mainstream Jewish organizations particularly, and Jews in general, made a major mistake by
consistently taking dovish antimilitary budget stances. A dovish
position might have reflected Jewish values and interests during
the Vietnam War, they admitted, but after the Yom Kippur War
(1973), in which Israel was almost wiped out in a surprise assault
by its Arab neighbors, Israel's very survival was clearly seen to
depend upon a strong American military. Jewish neoconservatives argued that support for a strong U.S. military was vital to
serve as a deterrent to Soviet and Arab aggressive intentions in
the Middle East, including threats to Israel. Even today, Israel's
ability to take risks for peace depends on its confidence that the
U.S. military is strong enough to help Israel deter military threats
to its security.

Neoconservatives said that support for efforts to cut the United
States military budget, opposition to new weapons systems, as
well as alliances with antiwar groups whom the Pentagon
regarded virtually as political enemies would weaken the
American military and would engender the resentment of the
Pentagon. The United States government and its Department of
Defense would thereby be less inclined to be supportive of Israel.

Despite the collapse of the Soviet threat, these arguments
continue today, especially in the aftermath of the Gulf War. The
debate over the Strategic Defense Initiative (SDI; the so-called
"Star Wars" plan intended to allow us to shoot down attacking
missiles) illustrates these dilemmas. We have strongly opposed

those efforts to develop a satellite capacity—the most criticized part of the plan—as extraordinarily expensive and technologically infeasible. However, military and scientific experts believe a ground-based capacity such as the U.S. Patriot and the Israeli Arrow missiles could work. How can we ask for American funding for Israel to develop the Arrow missile, the portion of SDI that most benefits Israel, if we oppose most other funding for Star Wars as being wasteful and unjustified? Do we endanger Israel if we continue to push for deep cuts in Pentagon spending?

What should the Jewish community have done? What should it do now?

Response

Almost none of the mainstream Jewish organizations adopted the policies of the neoconservatives. Public opinion and voting-data analyses indicate that the Jewish community has remained as liberal as ever on both domestic and international issues. In the early eighties, the support of sixteen national Jewish organizations for the nuclear freeze campaign, aimed at reversing the nuclear arms race, confirmed that conclusion. Most Jews believed that a strong military did not depend on bloated budgets as much as on sensible priorities. They believed that the stress on nuclear weapons systems not only brought the world closer to a global catastrophe but drained money from the kind of conventional weaponry that both the United States and Israel needed.

Moreover, the backlash predicted by the neoconservatives never occurred. Despite the assertive liberal character of the Jewish community, much of the past three decades has seen unprecedented military alliances between Israel and the United States. And while Congress, including most Jewish senators and representatives, never gave Presidents Reagan and Bush the funding they requested for Star Wars—generally because they believe space-based weapons would not work and would only lead us closer to war—there has been overwhelming congressional support for the Arrow missile (a land-based defense against shorter-range missiles). That support grew after the uneven performance of the more primitive Patriot missiles used during

the Gulf War. The Arrow is expected to compensate for many of
the deficiencies of the Patriot and would likely be widely used by
both the United States and Israel.

IS JUDAISM TRADITIONALLY PACIFIST?

In the winter of 1998, Washington, D.C., was awash with rumors and
speculation about a sex scandal which, some believed, would threaten
the presidency itself. But urgent world affairs did not wait for the scandal to reach its legal and political denouement. Iraq's Saddam Hussein
defied the United Nations and threw out the international inspectors
who, according to the cease-fire terms reached after the Gulf War in
1991, are charged with the responsibility of inspecting, monitoring,
and destroying that nation's arsenal of weapons of mass destruction,
including biological, chemical, and nuclear devices. Lacking the international coalition that was able to evict Saddam from Kuwait the last
time and weakened by his domestic crisis, President Clinton sought to
rally American public opinion. Should the Jewish community support
the projected air war? If so, on what grounds? Or should we have joined
those voices demanding a negotiated settlement? Or should we have
kept silent, and why?

It has been argued that the above dilemma is really a no-brainer, that
the value of peace has the highest priority in the Jewish value system,
and that therefore Jews should be peacemakers on issues of foreign
policy. This would be a valid argument if we conclude that Judaism is a
pacifist faith and therefore we Jews, like Quakers, would automatically
line up against the use of force or violence.

Jewish tradition does not glorify war or extol the war-maker. In Jewish
history, the heroes are sages and saints, rarely warriors. Rabbi Yochanan
ben Zakkai, for example, is revered for his nonviolent triumph over
Roman might. The historian Josephus reminds us of Jewish nonviolent
resistance to the bloody Caligula. King David himself was not permitted to build the Temple because his hands had spilled blood in battle.
A talmudic story depicts God rebuking the angels of heaven for burst-
ing into songs of joy when the Red Sea closed on the drowning
Egyptian pursuers: "My creatures are perishing and you want to sing
praises!" (Babylonian Talmud, *Megillah* 10b).

Likewise, Chanukah, because it originally celebrated a military victory, was virtually ignored by Jews until it was transformed into a holiday commemorating the rededication of the Temple. It is no accident that on the Sabbath during Chanukah, Jews recite the passage "Not by might, nor by power, but by My spirit, says *Adonai*." (Zechariah 4:6) The Book of Proverbs declares, "If your enemy is hungry, give him bread to eat; and if he is thirsty, give him water to drink." (Proverbs 25:21) And in the same spirit we are taught, "Rejoice not when your enemy falls." (Proverbs 24:17)

With the destruction of the Jewish state in 70 c.e., the prophetic vision of peace became the dream of the Jewish people. Whether by ideology or by external circumstances, military action by the Jewish community almost completely ceases from the end of the Bar Kochba revolt in 135 c.e. until the eighteenth-century Enlightenment allowed Jews to participate as citizens of the nations in which they lived. Only in the twentieth century, in their struggle for Israel and resisting the Nazis, did Jewish communities go to "war." The ideal of universal peace had become the hope and at times the mission of the people of Israel.

The Apocrypha, the Midrash, and the Talmud place a high priority on the ideal of peace. Indeed, no subject of morality is accorded such depth of feeling and passion of conviction as the value of world peace. Jews are taught not merely to love peace but to "pursue it." Israel's majestic contribution to civilization was the inspired vision of a *universal* peace, not only for Israel but for all peoples. Micah's prophecy casts a ray of hope across the millennia:

> And God shall judge between many peoples,
> And shall decide concerning mighty nations afar off;
> And they shall beat their swords into plowshares,
> And their spears into pruning hooks;
> Nation shall not lift up sword against nation; neither
>   shall they learn war any more.
>
> (Micah 4:3)

This attitude, so basic to Judaism, was strikingly reaffirmed in the classical rabbinic period:

> Great is peace, for all blessings are contained in it, as it is written...*Seek peace and pursue it.* (Psalms 34:15)

> Great is peace, for God's name is peace. (*Leviticus Rabbah, Tzav*, 19:9) The Law does not command you to run after or pursue the other commandments but only to fulfill them upon the appropriate occasion. But peace you must seek in your own place and pursue it even to another place as well.
>
> (*Numbers Rabbah, Hukkat*, 19:27)

But the tradition did not rest content with generalities; it was very specific about applying these ideals to daily life. Thus, for example, while Judaism does recognize the duty of a person to preserve his or her own life and defend others, it is very specific in *prohibiting the shedding of innocent blood.*

Judaism further insists that even in the most clear-cut case of self-defense against a precisely identified assailant, the use of *excessive* violence is not to be sanctioned:

> It has been taught by Rabbi Jonathan b. Saul: If one was pursuing his fellow to slay him, and the pursued could have saved himself by maiming a limb of the pursuer but instead killed his pursuer, the pursued is subject to execution on that account.
>
> (*Sanhedrin* 74a)

However, while the limitation of violence is one of the most basic of all Jewish ethical teachings, the recent deployment of weapons of indiscriminate mass destruction makes it increasingly difficult to justify war from a traditional Jewish perspective. Even in a war that would be considered justified by the Jewish tradition, Jewish law considers killing another person an offense before God, and a sin offering was made by all soldiers.

During the agony of the Vietnam War, which split Americans like no issue since the Civil War, many Jewish young men invoked the Jewish teachings cited above to win conscientious objector status. The UAHC and the CCAR opposed the war as a violation of both Jewish and American principles, and we tried to establish the principle of selective conscientious objection for young Jewish men who were not pacifists in general but were deeply opposed to that particular war.

But if the Vietnam War was immoral and almost destroyed two countries—Vietnam and America—did that mean that every war was wrong, that force was never justified, that the spilling of blood was never necessary to avert an even greater evil?

In our paradoxical history, in which Jews dreamed of peace but frequently fought wars, how are these two realities reconciled? An evaluation of the 1991 Gulf War, Operation Desert Storm, provides an insight into the substance and the relevancy of the Jewish balance struck through its creation of rules regulating when wars could be fought and how they must be fought.

The Gulf War and the Jewish Community

A Real Dilemma: Should the UAHC Support War in the Gulf?

In December 1990, the Union of American Hebrew Congregations Board of Trustees met to consider whether or not to support President Bush in his threat to use force to expel Iraq from Kuwait. Seeking peace, organizations like the UAHC and other Jewish bodies vigorously opposed the Vietnam War in the 1960s and '70s, strongly criticized the escalating defense budgets of the 1980s, and called for arms control agreements to reduce the number of nuclear and conventional armaments proliferating throughout the world.

Could these same Jewish organizations, long identified with antiwar positions, justify a position in 1991 as enthusiastic supporters of President Bush in his military campaign to reverse Iraqi aggression against Kuwait? Was it simply that unlike in the Vietnam War, in which Israel was not directly involved, Israel's very survival was seen to be at stake in the Gulf War? And if that was the reason for passionate Jewish support, weren't columnists like Pat Buchanan basically correct in asserting that American Jews were for the Gulf War because of their commitment to Israel?

If you had been a UAHC board member, how would you have voted? Why?

Response

The board voted overwhelmingly to support the United Nations vote and the leadership of President Bush in resisting Saddam Hussein's aggression. In fact, most American Jews were unashamedly concerned about Israel's survival in a region dominated by a dangerous tyrant brandishing an arsenal of conventional, biological, chemical, and possibly nuclear weapons and proudly affirming his plan to "incinerate half of Israel." But Jews and non-Jews alike also believed that fundamental American interests were at stake in the Gulf. Saddam Hussein was viewed as a threat to all the nations in the region and therefore to the peace of the world. Also, America had a duty to protect the oil supplies vital to the free world and to America.

Did the Gulf War make Israel safer? Obviously yes, by weakening Saddam Hussein. Did it, as President Bush predicted, open a window of opportunity for peace in the Middle East? The enhanced credibility of the United States with the Arab countries was certainly responsible in large measure for their willingness to engage in the peace process.

History, as always, will be the final judge of the efficacy and morality of the Gulf War. Will it be seen as the start of a new world order or just business as usual? On the one hand, we had believed that our war was not against the Iraqi people but only against its leader and armed forces. Now it turns out that in some ways it was the other way around. The tyrant is still in power, defying the United Nations, stonewalling its resolutions, negotiating with world leaders, spewing venom against Israel, threatening the Kurdish minority, playing hide-and-seek with his nuclear, chemical, and biological weapons, and maintaining its extended-range-missile capacity. At the same time, the impact of the war and the subsequent international sanctions on the Iraqi people was and is savage. How many hundreds of thousands were killed? How many children died from hunger and disease?

On the other hand, Iraq's biological and chemical arsenal, which it obviously had no qualms about using against its neighbors, Arab or Jewish, was at least partially destroyed. And while Saddam concealed some of his nuclear materials, many of his facilities were damaged. The United Nations was revived as a force for world peace and international law, and the allies intervened to provide some protection, albeit short-lived, for the Kurds in the north against the Iraqi army. Saddam's position was clearly weakened, particularly in the face of continuing economic restrictions from the international community.

THE JEWISH TRADITION AND THE GULF WAR

Looking back at the Gulf War provides a fascinating case study of how the rules of the Jewish tradition on warfare can be applied to contemporary warfare. Jewish rules and regulations of war fall into two categories: first, the different kinds of war and the justification and authority to wage them; second, the rules of how warfare should be fought. Together, these two categories of rules comprise what in Christian and secular terms is called just-war theory.

One of the most fascinating aspects of the Gulf War was how often the just-war theory was invoked in discussing the war. Unlike earlier wars in this century, in which international norms were generally discussed only after the war was over, the prosecution of the Gulf War repeatedly involved politicians justifying their actions on the basis of the just-war theory, including the moral rightness of using force instead of sanctions and the appropriate amount of force necessary to achieve various goals of the war.

In light of the widespread opposition of mainstream Protestant and Catholic communities to the war, at the same time that there was decisive Jewish community approval of the war, it is interesting to note both the similarities and contrasts between Christian and Jewish just-war theory.

As indicated above, just-war theory involves (1) moral justification for *beginning* the war and (2) moral means in *fighting* the war. As to the question of a moral justification for fighting wars, both the Jewish and Christian traditions say that the underlying cause for the war must be just. Self-defense in general or defense of an innocent bystander (i.e., Kuwait) would be a valid criterion in both traditions. But one relevant contrast between the two traditions does emerge: the issue of who is qualified to declare war. Christianity presumes that competent authority to declare war can vest in the executive (king, president, prime minister, etc.) of the polity alone. Judaism requires that in an offensive war, there must be some check on the prerogative of the military or executive authority to wage war. In ancient times, that check came through the approval of the Sanhedrin, much as the U.S. Constitution requires the approval of Congress. In this instance, such approval was forthcoming in the "use of force" debate and vote of Congress in December 1990.

There are also several interesting contrasts between the various traditions on when and how to wage war. First, the Christian tradition advocates the use of force only as a last resort. By such a standard, the argument for giving sanctions against Iraq more time to work would have been compelling. Judaism maintains only that a good-faith effort must be made to avoid war. Some strands of the *halachah* interpret this as requiring an effort for a peaceful resolution of at least three days before an attack; others maintain a requirement to sue for peace on three consecutive days. On this basis, repeated and much-publicized American efforts to avoid war in the Gulf clearly would appear to have met the Jewish tradition's requirements even while they failed the Christian standards.

Second, both traditions have a preeminent concern to protect civilian life. The Jewish tradition says that a city should not be surrounded on all sides so that those who wish to flee might do so. When a city is conquered, the noncombatants, particularly women and children, are given stringent protection. By this standard, the stated concern of the allied troops to protect civilian lives was in vivid moral contrast to brutal and intentional Iraqi SCUD missile attacks on the civilian center of cities in Israel and Saudi Arabia as well as the conquest of Kuwait itself.

Third, Christianity requires a test of proportionality (i.e., the force necessary to achieve a military objective is permissible). Although some strands of Jewish thought seem congenial to this idea, the Jewish tradition is less concerned about proportion than it is with deciding which categories of targets are subject to attack and which are not. No force could be used against certain targets (such as innocent civilians and fruit-bearing trees) except in specified exceptional circumstances. Conversely, no limitation on force is set for appropriate targets. In this sense, the saturation bombings of military targets that some Christian thinkers described as disproportionately excessive might well be permitted by the *halachah*.

Fourth, Judaism is unique in its concern for nonhuman targets. In

Deuteronomy 20:19, we are told to spare the enemy city's fruit trees for "are trees of the field human to withdraw before you into the beseiged city?" This important law is called *bal tashchit,* or "do not destroy." The Talmud extends *bal tashchit* to a wide range of activities in civilian life, reasoning that if we can't destroy in war, how much more should we not destroy in peacetime.

In the military context, *bal tashchit* forbids destroying anything indispensable to the renewal of civilian life. In the late 1960s, Jewish peace activists cited this law as they decried "deforestation," the destruction of Vietnam's wilderness along with its people. *Bal tashchit* can also be applied to the Gulf War: Saddam Hussein's wanton destruction of the environment through oil spills and fires was a gross and flagrant violation of Jewish law. The pulverizing allied bombing of civilian targets aimed at crippling the economic, health, housing, electrical, and water infrastructure of Iraqi society is also inconsistent with Jewish tradition.

THE POST–COLD WAR ERA: UNITED STATES POLICIES AND JEWISH INTERESTS

Even before the Gulf War, the post–Cold War era presented dynamic and far-reaching changes in global affairs. The Soviet bloc had shattered; communism was disintegrating as a viable economic system in the modern world, collapsing under the weight of its own stagnation; tenuous democratic reforms swept Eastern Europe and transformed the Soviet Union into a shaky commonwealth of independent republics. Around the world new, fragile democracies took hold, many endangered by internal economic, ethnic, and/or religious tensions.

As the Iron Curtain becomes a faint memory, some remember the simplicity and clarity of the Cold War with nostalgia. At that time, American foreign policy could be accurately predicted by weighing options on the "balance of power" scale; today the plethora of opportunities and challenges does not lend itself to obvious equations.

In a world without either serious military threats to the survival of the United States and diminishing ideological threats to our democratic values, what is the need or justification for American intervention around the world? Is it possible to set objective standards that will determine how, in what manner, and with whom the United States should intervene to protect its interests?

During the Cold War, it was common for the superpowers to back rulers, many unsavory, in various nations whose presence served as a surrogate for superpower forces. With superpower backing, these rulers were often able to dominate the political scene in their nations. Ironically, in the aftermath of the Cold War, as the United States and the USSR withdrew active military and financial support for these local leaders, internal strife often broke out. In some cases, this resulted in healthy democratic competition. Too often, however, it resulted in tragic civil wars. In such cases the United States, NATO and/or the United Nations had to make difficult decisions as to whether to intervene or not.

Every conflict seems tantalizingly easy for the United States to solve, if we only had the "will" to do so. Yet, as we have seen in Bosnia and other places, the solutions are more elusive than they might at first appear.

What, then, is the proper role of the United States in this post–Cold War world? Shall we retreat into an isolationist cocoon, ignoring the horrors of genocide, starvation, and totalitarianism if these evils do not immediately seem to affect us? Shall we act as the world's police force, forever sending our sons and daughters to solve the conflicts of other nations? Is there some course in between?

Any hopes that the breakup of the USSR would lead to a new world order in which the need for military intervention would be minimal and only economic competition would mark the relations between nations were eroded in the 1990s by a series of wrenching decisions regarding American intervention: Somalia, Rwanda, Haiti, and, most keenly, Bosnia.

The first such case occurred in Somalia when rival forces in its civil war intentionally created a famine in large areas of the country. With hundreds of thousands of lives at stake, the U.N., with direct U.S. involvement, sent in forces to stop the war and protect the flow of relief supplies. Initially, the operation was an enormous success: the fighting was stifled, relief supplies flowed, and the planting and harvests resumed. But in a disastrous twist of events, one of the clans stepped up its military operations against the U.N. forces. After a fiasco in which eighteen U.S. Marines were killed and one of the dead bodies was dragged through the streets, the United States withdrew its forces. The U.N. force followed the American lead in withdrawing from Somalia.

Critics of the U.S. and U.N. intervention argued that the Somalia catastrophe is a fitting example of the futility of getting entangled in local civil wars. Proponents responded that on the whole, the intervention was successful. Hundreds of thousands facing starvation were saved, and even with the renewed strife after the U.N. evacuation, starvation never reached the levels that existed beforehand and none of the forces resumed the use of starvation as a military weapon. Nonetheless, the scars were deep enough that when, in 1994, Hutu Rwandans rose up against the governing Tutsi minority and massacred hundreds of thousands of men, women, and children, the world basically stood by, providing only humanitarian relief to those refugees who managed to flee Rwanda to neighboring countries. In the space of three months, between 500,000 and 1,000,000 Tutsis were slaughtered—often at a rate of killing that reached the highest levels of extermination in World War II. These tribal hatreds continued, resulting in calls for ethnic cleansing and the use of force by both government armies and opposition militias. Zaire, Burundi, and Rwanda all exploded in 1996. Again, the world stood by and watched, ignoring emphatic warnings, and by the time it was prepared to act, the disaster had occurred. Would the world react faster if violence were to erupt again, either in Kosovo or elsewhere, or would we all sit waiting for the situation to resolve itself?

A more successful intervention took place in Haiti in 1994 when the United States sent troops in to support the reestablishment of democratic government and the return to power of democratically elected President Jean-Bertrand Aristide, who had been overthrown in 1991 by a military coup led by General Raoul Cédras. Under the threat of American intervention, a negotiated resolution forcing out the military coup leaders was arranged, and American troops oversaw a peaceful transition back to democracy that held for the year following the intervention. In Haiti, a nation with little democratic tradition, it will be difficult to sustain the success of these efforts, but it is overwhelmingly believed that U.S. intervention made a profound difference in avoiding civil war and at least temporarily restoring democracy.

BOSNIA

Nowhere has the pain of inaction been felt more acutely than in the former Yugoslavian state of Bosnia. We see the price of such failure in our shameful response to the savagery and injustice of the war of "ethnic cleansing" in Bosnia: scores of thousands of civilians dead; hundreds of thousands driven from their homes; whole towns destroyed; the appalling use of rape as organized military policy and enforced impregnation as social policy.

Jewish voices—especially leaders of the Reform movement, including UAHC Presidents Alexander Schindler and Eric Yoffie, as well as Leonard Fein, director of the Commission on Social Action of Reform Judaism—were among the most vocal in calling for international intervention to stop the killing and ethnic cleansing. Jewish newspaper columnists, liberal and conservative, from William Safire to Leon Wieseltier to Anthony Lewis, led editorial calls for stronger action. The Religious Action Center organized the first public demonstration on behalf of Bosnia during Chanukah 1993 in front of the soon-to-be-opened U.S. Holocaust Memorial Museum in Washington, D.C.

When should America intervene? On the one hand, we cannot police the world, stop every civil war, right every wrong. On the other hand, we must never let the argument that we cannot do everything, everywhere, prevent us from doing anything, anywhere. There are times the civilized world must try to draw the line. And there was more that we could have done in Bosnia even without deploying ground forces. Can you imagine our response if it were Jews involved and the world had said, "We won't lift the arms embargo and send arms so they can defend themselves; it will only make things worse"? Stronger economic sanctions, effective international war crimes tribunals, enforcing the no-fly zone, and early targeted bombing of Serbian military sites might well have led the Serbian military to back off the genocidal activity earlier.

And even if it did not succeed fully, we could look our children and Bosnia's children in the eye and say, "We tried; we really tried." And at least we would have sent a powerful signal to other tyrants: "Even if we cannot in every case stop you, there are costs—very real costs—for genocidal activity."

Finally, in the summer of 1995, after a spring of more ethnic cleans-

ing—primarily from the Serbs, who attacked U.N.-protected zones and
drove out Bosnians, and the neighboring Croatians, who attacked Serb-
held areas taken in the early 1990s and forced the withdrawal of
Serbians—the international community signaled its willingness to
become more actively involved. Massive bombing campaigns against
Serbian military targets brought the parties back to the bargaining table
with the hope that a diplomatic solution might soon be found. The
Dayton Accord followed.

What have we learned from these tragedies of war and ethnic
violence?

When should the international community intervene in civil strife
or in wars against neighboring nations? Should it do so whenever it can
win? Or should the international community do so only in extraordinary situations, such as when genocidal activity has taken place? When
nuclear, chemical, or biological weapons are used or are about to be
used? When human-created starvation is used as an instrument of war?

A Real Dilemma: When Is It "Genocide"?

Throughout the period between 1991 and 1995, there was a
debate in the Jewish community as to whether or not the activity in Bosnia constituted genocide. Critics of such language
maintained that to refer to ethnic cleansing as "genocide" was to
demean and diminish the concept of genocide and was therefore
demeaning to the Holocaust. Those who supported referring to
the Bosnian conflagration as genocide acknowledge that the
Holocaust was unique but argue that the primary purpose of
adopting a treaty against genocide in the wake of the Holocaust
was to ensure that a *genocide like* the Holocaust would never
happen again. This could be accomplished by punishing actions
that marked the beginning of genocidal activity. Political leaders
and opinion-makers looked to the Jewish community to decide
how to handle this difficult question. What should the response
of the Jewish community have been?

Response

While some in the Jewish community were not in accord, there
was a surprising consensus on this issue: genocidal activity

covered a range of actions, and the best way to stop genocide was to do so as early as possible. For this reason, the Jewish community strongly supported international war crimes tribunals in the Netherlands that indicted Serbian leaders. (The tribunals were headed by an extraordinary Jewish jurist, Richard Goldstone, who had been the head of the South African Supreme Court during the transition stages from apartheid to democracy.) Even today, the Jewish community is at the forefront of urging the peacekeeping forces to be more vigorous in apprehending indicted war criminals In Bosnia and Serbia. And during the pivotal point in mobilizing more assertive American action to stop the war, the Jewish community was arguably the most active segment of the American public in calling for the lifting of the international arms embargo of Bosnia and for a more robust U.S. military involvement in responding to Serb aggression. The Religious Action Center was the key lobbying coordinator on both votes regarding lifting the arms embargo.

MODERNIZING THE ARMS RACE

The extraordinary events of the early 1990s that culminated in the dissolution of the USSR raised many problems of vital concern to the United States and to the Jewish community. Will democracy be the norm in these new republics, or will new tyrannies of the left or right emerge? Will ethnic strife tear these republics apart in civil war? Will the Jewish communities of those republics survive in such an atmosphere of ethnic tension or war?

And what of the United States? With whom does it negotiate new economic treaties and arms control agreements? In early 1992, the Russian Republic attempted to consolidate all of the former Soviet strategic nuclear weapons under its exclusive control. Not all republics agreed, and regardless of the strategic weapons, there will still be smaller tactical battlefield nuclear weapons in many of the republics. Should the United States provide significant foreign aid? Will a large foreign-aid package to the republics reduce the amount of United States foreign aid available to other countries, such as Israel? And will a restive American public, increasingly hostile to foreign aid, support such efforts?

The disintegration of the Soviet Union has reduced but not eliminated the threat of nuclear weapons. Between 1980 and 1994, the United States and the now former Soviet Union signed only two major arms control treaties: the Intermediate Nuclear Forces Treaty (INF), signed in December 1987, and the Strategic Arms Reduction Treaty (START), signed in July 1991.

The START Treaty, signed by President George Bush and Soviet Prime Minister Mikhail Gorbachev, marked the first actual reduction in long-range nuclear weapons. By the end of the century, over 4,000 nuclear warheads would be destroyed on both sides as a result of this treaty, marking the first real steps toward disarmament.

One positive aspect of START is the reductions it mandates in intercontinental ballistic missiles (ICBMs). After seven years, Russia will reduce its ICBM arsenal by roughly 50 percent and the United States will reduce its arsenal by 35 percent. This means that each side will be less dependent on nuclear warheads that can span oceans in under an hour to reach their destination. Instead, both sides will rely more on bombers and submarines to deploy their warheads, giving more crucial time for countermeasures, hot lines, and possible emergency diplomatic solutions in case of a cataclysmic accident or mistake.

At the same time, however, START places almost no constraints on the modernization of nuclear weapons, allowing the United States and the republics to develop and deploy newer and increasingly more destructive weapons systems.

Thus today, the United States and the independent republics of the former Soviet Union still have between them some 46,000 warheads, almost all of which are more powerful than the bomb that devastated Hiroshima. A single one of these bombs could destroy Los Angeles; the detonation of a handful could alter, at least temporarily, the climate of the earth. We must not forget that the weapons plants, labs, and scientists that existed in the USSR before the breakup of the Soviet Union are, for the most part, still there. With the Soviet Union broken into independent republics, several with their own nuclear arsenals, the world could be left in a far more dangerous and volatile situation than during the Cold War, especially since many Russian nuclear scientists are unemployed, unpaid, or otherwise alienated.

Furthermore, as long as these dangerous arms remain the "weapons of choice" for the United States and the former Soviet Union, there is always the danger of an accidental war erupting. In the late 1980s, both the Soviet Union and the United States accidentally shot down civilian airliners, believing that they were military planes. A study in the early 1980s indicated that on a number of occasions, U.S. Defense Department computers falsely indicated that we were under attack by USSR missiles, bringing the United States to the brink of war.

The United States and the Soviet Union had for many years indicated that they were willing to live within the constraints of deterrence. Since we currently have over ten times the number of weapons necessary to destroy the other side, we could, theoretically, drastically cut the number of weapons without undermining our strategic position. Economic pressures have greatly increased the desire to cut deeply into the military budgets on both sides, leading to the most serious consideration of drastic reductions that we have seen in more than forty years.

In September 1996—in a move certain to aid in the restructuring of the world's moral compass—President Clinton and the four other nuclear weapon states signed the Comprehensive Test Ban Treaty, which the United Nations subsequently passed. The CTBT would effectively ban all nuclear test explosions; it would help stop the deployment of new, sophisticated nuclear weapons; and it would also make it far more difficult for other nations to obtain advanced nuclear weapons. In September 1997, President Clinton sent the treaty to the Senate for ratification, where it is now awaiting consideration by several committees. The CTBT received public support from the top echelons of the U.S. military, as well as from four former Joint Chiefs of Staff chairmen. By 1998, the primary obstacle to U.S. ratification of the CTBT was not ideological or strategic opposition, but rather a procedural morass. Senator Jesse Helms (R-NC), the Senate Foreign Relations Committee chairman, long stated that he would hold up consideration of the CTBT until NATO expansion (achieved in 1998) and the Kyoto treaty (on global climate change) were submitted by the Clinton administration and voted upon by the Senate, which could stall the process for several more years. The danger of nuclear proliferation multiplied in 1998 when India and Pakistan announced nuclear tests, defying U.S. and world opinion.

A Real Dilemma: The Morality of Making Nuclear Weapons

A few years ago, a Roman Catholic bishop called upon his parishioners who worked in nuclear weapons plants to quit their jobs because the building of nuclear weapons was "contrary to Roman Catholic teaching" and because weapons of mass destruction are incompatible with moral conscience. There was deep division in the aftermath of the bishop's plea, with controversy spreading well beyond the church.

A Jewish scientist from the Northeast wrote to the Commission on Social Action: "I am a Jew, not a Roman Catholic, but I believe Catholic teachings on war and peace really derive from the Jewish biblical tradition. The bishop's statement has stirred some doubts and conflicts in my conscience—doubts that festered for years but that I allowed to be dormant in my mind until now. Can a Jew like me, who cares about Jewish beliefs and human life, continue to devote my scientific abilities…to the development of weapons that if used would lead to mass slaughter of innocent lives? Have I been deluding myself all these years by saying that nuclear weapons on both sides have kept the peace for half a century? Even if I could justify this work during the cold war with a Stalinist Soviet enemy, can I justify it now? Should I put an end to my participation in this work and make my living in more constructive pursuits? What does the Lord require of me?"

How should the commission have replied? What would you say?

Response

In response to the Jewish scientist's inquiry about Jewish teachings, the commission explained what is outlined in this chapter. In particular, use of nuclear weapons would per se violate the extensive laws of civilian protection and environmental concerns aimed at ensuring the postwar resumption of normal civilian life. In addition to the enormous destruction, the desecration of land and property would result in precisely the inability of life to resume—something Jewish tradition seeks to prevent.

However, can the possession of nuclear weapons for the sake of deterrence and maintaining a balance of power be justified? It is particularly difficult to find a halachic resolution to this question. Former British Chief Rabbi Immanuel Jackobovits, who in 1962 wrote that the possession of nuclear weapons could not be justified according to Jewish law, wrote in a letter to one of this book's authors in 1982 that the very success of the balance of terror for three decades had changed his halachic evaluation of this issue.

With regard to what the Jewish scientist should specifically do, the commission said that Judaism is not structured like the Church: we do not issue encyclicals, and we put a premium on individual autonomy and individual choice. Only an individual can resolve so personal a dilemma. But his wrestling with conscience is very Jewish indeed, and the question of how Jewish tradition views nuclear weapons, particularly the inevitable slaughter of innocent civilians if the bomb is used, is not settled. Israel is believed to possess nuclear weapons to protect itself by deterring aggression from the likes of Iraq, Iran, and Syria. Is such possession immoral? Can use of such a weapon be morally justified? Under what circumstances?

Nuclear Weapons: A Lesson from Jewish History

One of the most powerful speeches ever given on the dangers of nuclear war came from Samuel Pisar. A noted French lawyer and author and a Holocaust survivor, Pisar was asked to address the Israeli Knesset on this subject during the second gathering of the International Holocaust Survivors Conference in 1981. He observed:

> To us, the Holocaust is not only an indelible memory of horror; it is a permanent warning.
> For we have seen the end of creation. In the shadow of permanently flaming gas chambers, where Eichmann's reality eclipsed Dante's vision of hell, we have witnessed a pilot project for the destruction of humanity, the death rattle of the entire species on the eve of the atomic age, of thermonuclear proliferation—the final solution....

Here, with the authority of the numbers engraved on our arms, we cry out the commandment of six million innocent souls, including one and a half million children, of whom I used to be one: never again!

From where, if not from us, will come the warning that a new combination of technology and brutality can transform the planet into a crematorium? From where, if not from the bloodiest killing ground of all time, will come the hope that coexistence between so-called "hereditary enemies" is possible—between Germans and Frenchmen, Chinese and Japanese, Americans and Russians; above all, coexistence between Arabs and Jews?

Despite these very genuine fears, perhaps the greatest threat of nuclear war comes not from the superpowers, present and former, but from "horizontal proliferation," the spreading of weapons of mass destruction to other countries.

In 1991, there were five countries in the world known to possess nuclear weapons: the United States, the Soviet Union, France, England, and China. Four others—Israel, South Africa, Pakistan, and India—are widely believed to have nuclear weapons deployed or the components that can be assembled in a short period of time.

Most international experts believe that within the next fifteen years there will be as many as thirty-five nations with the capability to build or purchase nuclear military technology. The Soviet republics of Kazakhstan, Ukraine, and Belorussia held nuclear weapons and although they turned their nuclear weapons over to Russia after the breakup of the USSR, they maintain the capacity to develop components of nuclear weapons today. According to the Central Intelligence Agency and the Nobel Peace Prize-winning Stockholm International Peace Research Institute (SIPRI), among the likely new members of the nuclear "club" will be Argentina, Brazil, Taiwan, Iran, North Korea, Libya, Iraq, and Iran.

As Jews, we have a particular stake in this burgeoning crisis. The image of a madman like Saddam Hussein with his finger on a chemical or biological bomb is no longer the stuff of overheated imaginations.

Will the next round of missiles Saddam Hussein purchases be new and improved nuclear SCUDs capable of destroying Israeli civilian centers like the missiles that Iraq fired during the Gulf War? What nation will Libya blackmail with its nuclear capability other than Israel? Even the *prospect* of the use of such weapons would likely compel Israel to launch a preemptive strike, raising the possibility of another and deadlier Arab-Israeli war.

What can we do?

It is impossible to stop the flow of technology. The technological capability to build nuclear weapons will become increasingly cheaper, simpler, and more accessible as time goes on. The best we can do is act decisively to slow it down and control it. The United States is the largest purveyor of nuclear technologies in the world, followed by Germany, Italy, Sweden, England, and France. That means that most of the nuclear technology in the world is sold by the United States and its closest allies and friends.

The current international nuclear nonproliferation treaty is inadequate and ineffective—underscored by the ironic fact that Saddam Hussein's Iraq was and is a *signatory* to it. North Korea, too, signed it and flouted the treaty and the entire international community. The United States should lead the world in demanding substantially tighter regulations on the sale of such technologies. It should insist that stiff international sanctions be brought against anyone who violates nonproliferation treaties.

The United States must also end its own obsession with nuclear weapons and continue to reduce the role of nuclear power plants as a primary energy source.

In addition to the approximately twenty countries that are believed to be developing nuclear arms, ten are said to be developing biological weapons and thirty are developing chemical weapons. Among them are Iran, Cuba, South Africa, Ethiopia, Iraq, and Libya. It is not easy to control the spread of such weapons because the ingredients are inexpensive, relatively easy to obtain, and often also used for nonmilitary purposes.

There are, however, legislative steps that can be taken. In 1991, the Religious Action Center helped draft legislation addressing (and mobilized a bipartisan coalition of senators and representatives committed to) the proposition that countries using weapons of mass destruction be outlawed by the community of nations and that governments and corporations assisting in the development of such weapons be exposed and subject to economic sanctions.

President Bush vetoed this legislation in October 1990, but after both houses of Congress again passed the legislation by overwhelming margins in late October 1991, the president signed a bill containing very strong sanctions. Since the Religious Action Center's inception over three decades ago, there has been no piece of legislation in which it has played a role that has more potential signficance for humankind than the passage of this historic legislation.

Another approach culminated in October 1996, when after two decades of negotiations in Geneva, Hungary became the sixty-fifth nation to ratify the Chemical Weapons Convention, which triggered the CWC's entry into force. The United States was slow in ratifying the treaty but gained Senate approval just days before the April 29, 1997, deadline. Although there were criticisms that the CWC is not verifiable or enforceable, U.S. leaders from Reagan to Bush to Clinton determined that ratifying the treaty was in America's national security interest.

The CWC is the most ambitious arms control treaty ever implemented. The CWC bans an entire category of weapons of mass destruction—including the production, acquisition, and stockpiling of chemical weapons. Out of the twenty-five nations the United States believes to have chemical weapons, nearly three-quarters of them have signed the CWC. Participation in the CWC decreases the threat to our own soldiers by reducing the number of countries with chemical weapons arsenals.

A Real Dilemma: Land Mines—An Explosive Problem

Not only nonconventional but conventional weapons also pose significant dilemmas. While there are many who believe that land mines are an effective, inexpensive way to deter the movement of tanks, heavy weapons, and troops on battlefields, few would hold that the innocent civilians who die from them long after the conflict has ended are necessary casualties. However, the debate between those who believe the United States should sign a comprehensive ban on land mines and those who believe a ban would compromise the security of U.S. troops is a heated one. Should the United States sign the treaty to ban all antipersonnel land mines? Should the UAHC support the international effort to ban land mines?

Since 1996, President Clinton publicly stated several times his commitment to sign a treaty that would ban both "smart" land mines (those that self-destruct after a certain period of time) and "dumb" land mines (those that must be taken out of the ground and deactivated). Over 125 nations signed such a treaty in December 1997 in Ottawa and pledged to abolish all types of land mines. The United States did not sign the land mines treaty, seeking special exceptions related to protecting its troops in places like Korea. The treaty remains open, and advocacy groups will continue to push for the United States to sign it at a future date.

Those supporting the ban have horrifying numbers to back them up—land mines kill nearly 26,000 people each year, nearly 80 percent of them civilians. A person is killed or injured by a mine every twenty-two minutes. But should we endanger our own soldiers by withdrawing an important line of defense against the enemy in places like Korea? The use of mines across the demilitarized zone (an area where there are no civilian residents) helps prevent a surprise attack. Without them, far more U.S. soldiers and tanks would need to be deployed. However, reports have shown that more American deaths were caused during the Persian Gulf War from our own land mines than from any other cause. Will an international ban really solve the problem of innocent people dying from land mines? The Pentagon and military strategists argue no: first of all, most of those who are participating already do not use land mines; second, some of the largest producers of land mines—Russia, China, India, North Korea, and Iraq—are not participating in the negotiations and will not be signing the treaty. The other side argues that the United States should be a role model and a moral leader to the rest of the world. If we continue to produce and lay even "smart" land mines for our security needs, how can we expect other nations to cease their activities?

Jewish discussions about land mines raise another important

point: the use of mines by Israel. Israel, along with the United States, is one of the top fifteen producers and exporters of antipersonnel land mines and also will not be signing the treaty. Does Israel, because of its vulnerable security situation, have extenuating circumstances that necessitate the use of land mines or justify its selling land mines to other nations whose needs may not be as legitimate? Or do the moral implications of the use of land mines weigh more heavily on Israel because it is a Jewish state?

Response

In 1994, the Commission on Social Action passed a resolution that encouraged an international ban on the use, production, stockpiling, sale, transfer, or export of "long-lived" antipersonnel land mines. As the international and American community became more knowledgeable about and sensitive to the issue of land mines, it became clear that "long-lived" mines were only one aspect of the problem. In 1996, the CSA reevaluated its position to encourage a ban on all types of land mines, including "short-lived" mines that self-destruct within a prescribed time period but are equally lethal because they cannot distinguish between the footfall of a soldier and that of a child.

With this broader position, the Religious Action Center became increasingly involved through advocacy and grassroots work with the International Campaign to Ban Land Mines, which received the Nobel Peace Prize in 1997. At rallies, conferences, and congressional meetings, we tried to provide a moral perspective from Jewish just-war theories about the protection of civilians. In this effort, our voices were strengthened by the increasing roster of distinguished retired military leaders demanding a total ban on land mines.

DEMOCRACY AND HUMAN RIGHTS

The democratic revolutions in Eastern Europe were among the most astonishing changes in the 1980s. They were anticipated by the unexpected victory of the Aquino democratic forces in the Philippines and the restoration of democracy in Chile, Nicaragua, Pakistan, Panama,

Argentina, and elsewhere. But in each of these countries, as in the Eastern European countries, there is no guarantee that democracy will be sustained.

Unlike in the United States or Western Europe, there is precious little democratic tradition in Eastern Europe or elsewhere in the world; experiments in democracy and pluralism were either short-lived or nonexistent before 1989.

Furthermore, wherever nations are wracked with serious economic crises or ethnic strife, antidemocratic demagogues and extremists strive for power on platforms that foster scapegoating and anti-Semitism. No example is more virulent than the early 1930s high unemployment and runaway inflation in the Weimar Republic of Germany, which helped breed the frustration and despair that Hitler's Nazis exploited in their rise to power.

There are, of course, particular Jewish stakes in the changing face of the Eastern bloc. Most of those nations have long been servile and virulent Soviet-bloc enemies of Israel. Within a few months of overthrowing their Communist regimes, all reestablished diplomatic relations with Israel. Most joined the United States in voting in the United Nations to reverse the odious resolution equating Zionism with racism.

Furthermore, each of these countries has small and sometimes beleaguered Jewish communities whose well-being depends in large measure on the development of democratic, pluralistic systems. The Jews remaining in former Soviet-bloc countries occasionally face new threats from nationalistic, anti-Semitic elements that had been kept in check by authoritarian Communist regimes.

The Jewish communities of Eastern Europe find themselves in a paradoxical situation. Formal restrictions have been lifted, Hebrew schools begun, synagogues reopened, communities reorganized; at the same time, grassroots anti-Semitic incidents have heightened the sense of unease among Jews.

Clearly, the interests of the Jewish community can best be served by Western policies that strengthen the embryonic democratic regimes of these nations and challenge the governments to repudiate the hate groups in their midst.

The United States must also balance its support for the new global free market and its commitment to human rights. Nowhere has this dilemma been more difficult than in our relations with Communist

China, the nation with a fifth of the world's population and a vast market for American goods. After bold promises made as a presidential candidate, assuring the American people he would withhold trade benefits until China met international standards of human rights, President Clinton actually delinked our trade with China from the issue of human rights. This, despite the repellent role of modern China in brutalizing Tibet, suppressing dissent within its own borders, and dispensing nuclear assistance to rogue nations in all parts of the world. The administration argues that positive engagement in mutual economic contacts offers the best possibility of influencing the Chinese to reform their practices. If we impose tougher sanctions, the Chinese will shut us out of their growing economy and turn to other nations, costing Americans jobs and minimizing our influence on Chinese human rights behavior. Critics of this policy contend that while we embargo and boycott little nations like Cuba, we are willing to pander to an economic colossus and that we have caved in to greedy corporations, thus supporting a regime that uses torture, gulags, exploitation of prisoners, and persecution of such religions as Christianity and Buddhism. Should the Jewish community get into this fight? On which side? Why? What arguments from Judaism and recent history would you draw? Would it be relevant to know the nature of Israel's relationship with China?

THE CUTTING EDGE: ENERGY AND THE GLOBAL CLIMATE

After five years of intensive diplomacy, 150 nations gathered in Kyoto, Japan, in December 1997 to negotiate the first binding agreement to reduce global greenhouse gas emissions. The agreement, known as the Kyoto Protocol, commits the industrialized nations to reducing, by an average of 5.2 percent, their emissions of six gases believed to be contributing to the warming of the earth. The United States agreed to bring its emissions 7 percent below 1990 levels by the year 2012. The European Union, which pressed for an even more aggressive target, agreed to an 8 percent reduction, and Japan agreed to a 6 percent reduction. While many Third World nations did not sign on, the developed nations believed they needed to lead the way. The agreement marks an important first step in our work to reduce the threat of climate change on future generations.

In responding to both environmental and nuclear proliferation threats, our number-one technological priority for the next century should be the development *of environmentally safe, low-cost, renewable sources of energy: sun, wind, water, and geothermal.* This commitment could positively affect the state of our world's climate and international peace. It is the absence of such effective energy sources, together with the high cost and political volatility of oil, that encourages many Third World countries to demand nuclear technology as a means of meeting their growing energy needs. These demands will increase as they seek to bring their people into the developed world. Since there is no clear line between "nonmilitary" nuclear technology and "military" nuclear technology, once a country has the technology, it can eventually learn to adapt it to military uses if it chooses to do so.

This problem will become magnified by the growing threat of nuclear terrorism. Plutonium waste dumped into the water reservoirs of New York City could do as much human damage to the population as a nuclear bomb dropped on the Empire State Building. As technologies improve to allow for smaller explosive devices, a suitcase in the trunk of a car can be as effective a delivery system as a ballistic missile or submarine.

WHAT SHOULD AMERICA DO?

One obvious answer is foreign aid. The taxpayers of the United States spent hundreds of billions of dollars to fight Communist expansion. Can we not now allocate even a fraction of that amount to increase our foreign aid from its twelve-year-low level of $12 billion to seal our "victory," thus mitigating the chances that we will ever need to engage in a cold war again? Until the 1998 budget, foreign aid expenditures had fallen for fifteen years. Of the world's twenty-four developed nations, we are now dead last in the amount of developmental and humanitarian foreign aid we give as a percentage of GNP (or per person).

In 1995, congressional leaders announced that they wanted to cut out almost all foreign aid. Can we afford this shortsightedness as Jews or Americans? If the democratic experiments in Eastern Europe and the republics of the former Soviet Union do not survive and they return to the economic security of Communism on the one hand and the only alternative to Communism that many of these nations have ever known—the militaristic, ultranationalist, anti-Semitic forces of the right—it will be a disaster for their Jewish communities. If we do not invest in the forty fragile new democratic experiments worldwide that have arisen since 1984 and in peaceful reconciliation of long-term struggles that have also occurred since then—in the former Soviet republics, Eastern Europe, Cambodia, El Salvador, the Middle East, sub-Saharan Africa, and South Africa—we shall see nation after nation descend into violence, warfare, and tyranny. And we shall, eventually, just as surely be engulfed in these conflicts as we were in two world wars and the Cold War and at *far* greater cost in money and people than support for democracy and human rights entails now. And we will have betrayed the people of those nations, our values, and our strategic interests. Future generations will look back upon this moment as one of the great failures in all of human history.

THE UNITED NATIONS

American Jews were among the most passionate champions of the United Nations at its inception in 1945 and through the early decades, climaxing with the famous U.N. partition vote establishing the state of Israel. But over the past two decades, the United Nations has frequently been utilized as a weapon for one-sided and even anti-Semitic resolutions assaulting Israel and its policies. These unjust attacks culminated in passage of the infamous resolution of the U.N. General Assembly equating Zionism with racism, one of the ugliest slanders ever visited upon the Jewish people. Fortunately, under the leadership of the United States, that obscene equation was finally expunged and with the end of the Cold War and the beginning of a peace process in the Middle East, the United Nations finally began to treat Israel with some respect and with a measure of fairness. This made it easier to refocus on the U.N.'s role in pursuing *tikkun olam* on the international scene: its endless commitment to children, to ending disease and illiteracy and discrimination, to preserving the environment, to responding to natural disasters, and to the values of justice and freedom and peace.

Real Dilemma: Should the United States Pay Its Past Dues to the United Nations?

For many years, the U.S. Congress refused to pay America's dues to the United Nations or its arrears for peacemaking forces in various parts of the world. The Congress argued that the U.N. must be reformed, that it is inefficient, that the peacemaking missions in Somalia and elsewhere went awry, and that we can therefore use our dues as a lever to force necessary change. Critics of the Congress, including the president, said we have a moral and legal obligation to pay our fair share; we are using the U.N. more in the past decade and we need it desperately to deal with such world issues as global warming, international development, the proliferation of weapons of mass destruction, and coping with the threat of rogue states like Iraq.

Is this a Jewish issue? Why? What should the UAHC and CCAR do about this dilemma?

Response

For Reform Judaism, it was not a dilemma. It was a moral and political outrage. The vision of international cooperation in pursuing the goal of peace and justice represents the most powerful vision of the biblical prophets, and the U.N., with all its problems, represents a modern expression of those values. We demanded that the Congress pay America's bills and end the disgraceful spectacle of the largest and richest nation seeking to impose its will on the international community while refusing to pay its dues to the world body.

INTERNATIONAL ECONOMIC JUSTICE

The economic inequity between the world's haves and have-nots constitutes one of the most explosive ethical challenges and long-range political dangers to the world in the post–Cold War era. If there is one area in which United States foreign policy has failed most abysmally in the past fifty years, it has been in the area of economic justice. Tragically, today this situation is getting worse, not better.

More than half a billion people suffer from serious malnutrition and related diseases, and millions of children under the age of five will die of malnutition or related causes this year. For example, 39 percent of Africans live in "absolute poverty," with daily incomes below $1. The number of undernourished people in Africa has more than doubled, from around 100 million in the late 1960s to 215 million today and is projected to increase to 265 million by the year 2010.

Father Theodore Hesburgh, the distinguished former president of Notre Dame University, argues that this "systematic geographical discrimination" threatens the stability and security of "Spaceship Earth." We unthinkingly accept this global inequity and discontinuity every day. To paraphrase Father Hesburgh: If you are an American, you look forward to an ever-lengthening life characterized by improving health, education, economic and social well-being. If born in Africa, you will live a short life of illness, malnutrition, illiteracy, and hopelessness. Our children confront the frightening prospect of a glutted market of Ph.D.s; Southeast Asian children too often never step foot into a schoolroom. We are overfed and overweight; in South America, from the time of birth, too many suffer from systemic malnutrition that prevents their brains from developing fully. We decide where to purchase our second homes; they live in huts of cardboard or mud. We travel supersonically across this globe, even venture out into the universe; they grow up to bitter frustration and despair, trapped in urban ghettos and rural slums whose poverty curtails their lives. We spend trillions on weapons that, if used, would destroy all of God's creation; they pray for enough resources to sustain their meager quality of life. President Clinton's visit to Africa in 1998—the first visit to Africa by a U.S. president in over twenty years—highlighted these tragic realities and raised expectations. He promised more aid and more trade. The United States is morally bound to follow through on these promises.

PEACE DIVIDEND

The startling changes that have swept the former Soviet Union and Eastern Europe offer the United States the opportunity to reshape our nation's priorities in a way not possible since the end of World War II.

If we are going to increase our economic competitiveness, move to the cutting edge of the world's technological development, house the homeless, revitalize our educational system, address the acute situation of inadequate and costly health care in the United States, protect the environment, and rebuild the infrastructure of our cities, a higher proportion of military funds must be reallocated to civilian needs.

Plans to redistribute our resources were sidetracked by the Gulf War and by the political constraints on the Clinton administration, long criticized for its lack of support for a strong military.

According to the General Accounting Office, up to 50 percent of the $300 billion annual military budget continues to be devoted to NATO for defending Western Europe. Nearly $35 billion, which is 14 percent of the Pentagon budget, is spent on strategic nuclear programs, also designed primarily to counter yesterday's Soviet menace. We do not need the massive military structure and excessive budget designed to confront a superpower enemy that no longer exists.

Regardless of the extent to which the peace dividend is postponed and whittled down, the necessity of concentration on this country's real needs only increases. The Clinton administration has tried to focus on the needs of America, our unfinished agenda, but has often been sidetracked by the need to address international and other crises.

However the president balances out our domestic needs and international interests, we must recognize that our security depends more on the state of our cities and the status of intergroup relations than it does on B-2 bombers; more on the health of our children and the educational standards of our schools than it does on cruise missiles and chemical weapons; more on the sense of purpose and the morale of our citizenry than on ever-escalating military budgets. This decade provides a unique opportunity to reassess America's priorities for the twenty-first century and, to put it bluntly, choose life over death. Abba Eban, the venerable Israeli statesman, once wrote:

> In each of us and in every nation and every faith, there are arsenals of destructive rage, but there are also powerful armies of moral strength. The choice is ours, even as it has been since these words were addressed to our people: "See, I have set before you this day the blessing and the curse, life and death; therefore, choose life that you may live, you and your seed after you."

As we look out on the human condition, our

consciences cannot be clean. If they are clean, then it is because we do not use them enough. It is not inevitable that we march in hostile and separate hosts into the common abyss. There is another possibility— of an ordered world, illuminated by reason, governed by law. If we cannot touch it with our hands, let us at least grasp it with our vision.

That is the vision to which we are called. May we have the courage to grasp it. For it is indeed the new dimension needed for the social justice challenges of a new century.

··· *8* ···

Civil Rights and Race Relations in America

A HISTORY OF CIVIL RIGHTS

In 1997, President Clinton called on the American people to begin a searching and honest dialogue on the subject of race relations. This struck a chord with American Jews because few values have been as central to their value system as those of equal justice under the law, mutual respect among groups, and the innate dignity of every human being. These values underlay the enormous advancements in civil rights and race relations that have transformed American identity throughout two generations.

It is not surprising, given the persistence of racial inequities, that younger people today do not realize how far America has come since the so-called civil rights revolution in the 1960s and '70s.

HOW FAR WE'VE COME: SOME PERSONAL REFLECTIONS

Some early memories of the authors dramatize recent American history. In the life of the older of the coauthors of this book, this was the harsh reality: The Twin Cities of Minnesota, in which he was born and raised before World War II, were together known as "the capital of anti-Semitism," and entire areas of the cities were *judenrein* (no Jews could live there). There was massive discrimination against Jews in virtually every corporation and business; Jewish quotas existed in colleges and universities; there was a virtual ban on holding any political office; and Jews were excluded from clubs, service organizations, and every community institution of significance. And Blacks, of course, were even more marginalized than Jews! But St. Paul and Minneapolis were not that different from other cities throughout America in the prewar era.

In his lifetime, one of the coauthors of this book (Al Vorspan) served as a gunnery officer in World War II and vigorously objected to the fact that black sailors on his ship were not permitted to staff the guns, even in battle, but could only serve the meals in the officers wardroom. As late as 1963, he was arrested and jailed for the crime of sitting down for lunch with Rev. Martin Luther King, Jr., and other clergymen in St. Augustine, Florida. Visiting our congregations in Mississippi in the fifties and sixties, the state where Andrew Goodman, Michael Schwerner, and James Earl Chaney were ambushed and killed for their civil rights work, he found that only a handful of Blacks were permitted to vote in elections in all of Forrest County. American apartheid oppressed the southern Black in all facets of life, but, in more subtle ways, it also tormented and diminished minorities in the North.

The other coauthor (David Saperstein) grew up in the fifties and sixties in a New York suburb. One-third of his community was African-American, yet every single black student went to just one of the three elementary schools. His mother helped lead the integration effort that by the early sixties succeeded in integrating each of the schools. In 1965, his parents led clergy in a two-month voting-registration effort in one of the most intransigently racist areas of Alabama. Threatened and bitterly harassed, in the end one of their team was murdered in cold blood, shot down trying to go to a restaurant to eat; another was badly wounded.

When civil rights and religious groups finally mobilized the conscience of America against racial evil, changes came at last. Thanks to the landmark civil rights laws, the back of legal segregation was broken. The walls of legal discrimination were smashed and Blacks, Hispanics, Jews, and others began to breathe the air of an open, free society. Racism and anti-Semitism still exist in ample measure, but open discrimination in the armed forces, housing, and employment is illegal and unrespectable. A distinguished black American like Colin Powell, who, according to the polls, was considered by many to be the most respected person in America, would be a formidable presidential candidate if he chose to run. There are many serious racial challenges yet to be overcome in our America, but the distance between the days of yesteryear and today represents a sea change.

As discussed in the next chapter, few segments of the American community have invested themselves as deeply as the Jewish community in the struggle for civil rights. Not only because of the demands of faith but because of enlightened self-interest as well, Jews served in the forefront of the fight to end racial segregation in education and public accommodations and to assure equal access to voting in all parts of the United States. Jews hurled themselves into the dramatic events that transformed the South—Selma, Birmingham, Mississippi, and St. Augustine. Young Jews were martyred in Mississippi. Reform rabbis went to jail in Alabama, Mississippi, Florida, Georgia, and throughout the South, working for the Student Nonviolent Coordinating Committee (SNCC), contributing funds, and working to support historic civil rights moves.

Indeed, the Leadership Conference on Civil Rights, housed at our Religious Action Center in Washington, D.C., framed the landmark civil rights laws. The Reform Jewish movement spearheaded efforts to rally the Jewish community for the cause of civil rights.

That movement has not fulfilled all of its goals. Indeed, large segments of the black community still suffer from poverty, joblessness, and family breakdown. The federal government has cut social spending for affordable housing, job retraining, welfare, and virtually every social program. The condition of the poor—especially the black poor—has receded from the political radar; it is a nonstarter in political campaigns that focus on the "middle class." Many civil rights laws, including those setting up affirmative action programs, have been eroded by court decisions, state referenda, and congressional assault.

Further complicating the issue, the era of the traditional Black-Jewish-Christian-labor partnership—the backbone of the civil rights coalition from 1930 to 1970—is giving way to a broader coalition of decency that embraces Hispanics, Asians, Blacks, immigrants, religious groups including Jews, Muslims, Hindus, Buddhists, and Sikhs, homosexuals, women, people with disabilities, and responsible segments of the business community. Such a coalition will shift with every issue—abortion, immigration, church and state—but may be broad enough to represent a center of conscience in a multiethnic society.

A Real Dilemma: Race Relations—Black-White or Multiracial?

Just prior to announcing his national dialogue on race, President Clinton invited twenty national civil rights leaders, including one of the book's authors, to his office to seek advice on several vexing questions. Key among them was whether the dialogue and the President's Commission on Race should focus on black-white relations or on multiracial relations encompassing Latinos, Asian-Americans, Native Americans, and others. The group was divided on this issue. What would you have advised the president?

Response

One of the authors, David Saperstein, shared these views with the president: If we are as a nation to deal with the realities of race in America, we cannot afford to be distracted into a debate between the two approaches, as if we had to choose either one or the other. Clearly, we must address both issues. On the one hand, the history and content of the intense cultural, religious, political, and economic racism that has scarred America's relationship with its black population makes it distinct from the discrimination that plagues other groups. Furthermore, the moral and human horror of slavery has left wounds that still mar black-white relations, and we can never resolve the tensions of race relations in America without coming to grips with this immense tragedy. On the other hand, it is also true that there is persistent deprivation and discrimination affecting many racial minorities. (See chapter 9, "Jews, Blacks, and America's Multiracial Society.") And by the middle of the next century, nonwhites will comprise the majority of Americans; Latinos will surpass Blacks as America's largest minority.

The bottom line is that if any effort at improving racial relations is serious, it must address both aspects of race relations. The president attempted this in the choice of his commission members, its staff, and its agenda. It reflected and addressed most of the major racial groups and their concerns. Several, however, including Native Americans, complained bitterly that their concerns were ignored in both the failure to appoint a Native American to the commission and the failure to address their concerns adequately, despite the appointment of Native American staff and placement of their issues on the agenda.

CIVIL RIGHTS AND THE JEWISH TRADITION

From slavery to segregation, racism has been the most vexing moral issue American society has faced. And as events in the 1990s remind us, we are not free of its tensions: the fiery riots in Los Angeles in 1992, after the police in the Rodney King trial were acquitted at their first trial; the startlingly different reaction of blacks and whites to O. J. Simpson's acquittal; and the wave of church burnings in the mid-nineties mostly targeting black churches in the South. All these sent moral shock waves through America, vividly illuminating the state of race relations, the condition of the inner cities, and the priorities of the nation.

Of all the great issues of our time, perhaps none evokes a stronger resonance from Jewish teaching than the search for human rights. Judaism contributed profoundly to the concept of the sanctity and dignity of the individual. Respect for the fundamental rights of others is each person's duty to God. "What is hateful to you, do not do to your neighbor." (Babylonian Talmud, *Shabbat* 31a)

Equality in the Jewish tradition is based on the concept that all of God's children are "created in the image of God." (Genesis 1:27) From that flows the biblical injunction "You shall have one law for the stranger and the citizen alike: for I *Adonai* am your God." (Leviticus 24:22)

This is not to say that the Jewish tradition is free from racist attitudes. There are, of course, some powerful ethnocentric strands in the Bible (e.g., the idea that somehow the surrounding nations are inherently not as good as Israel). These ideas have persisted through the centuries: some of the philosophical writings of the medieval poet Yehudah Halevi, many medieval Kabbalists, some nineteenth-century chasidic writers, and some modern Israeli champions of a Greater Israel—all of whom believed that somehow the Jewish soul is distinct and superior to that of others.

But this ethnocentricity was never allowed to run unchecked. Permeating the tradition is the understanding that God is the God of all people. The radical message of Jonah's prophecy to Nineveh (coincidentally, Nineveh was located in what is today modern Iraq) is the belief that God's concern extends equally to all people, not only to the children of Israel. It is also one message of the prophet Malachi's query:

"Have we not all one parent? Has not one God created us? Why do we deal treacherously everyone against their siblings, profaning the covenant of our ancestors?" (Malachi 2:10) It is likewise the vision of Amos: "'Are you not as the children of the Ethiopians to Me, O children of Israel?' asks God. 'Have I not brought up Israel from the land of Egypt and the Philistines from Caphtor and the Arameans [Syrians] from Kir?'" (Amos 9:7) If God could equate the Israelites with the most exotic peoples known to the Jews, even Israel's hated enemies, then truly all of God's children must be equal.

In the Talmud (*Mishnah Sanhedrin* 4:5), it is asked: "Why did God create only one person, Adam?" The answer is illuminating. "All people are descended from a single human being, Adam, so that no one can say, 'My ancestor is worthier than yours.'" Even more applicable to the issue of race is the version found in *Yalkut Shimoni* 1:13: God formed Adam from the dust of all the corners of the earth—yellow [clay] and white [sand], black [loam] and red [soil]. Therefore, the earth can declare to no race or color of humankind that it does not belong here, that this soil is not its home.

These ideas were not abstract moralisms of people who, as the quintessential victims of history, set forth standards they hoped others would follow for the protection of the Jews. These ideas were translated into laws when Jews had power. Thus throughout the Torah, the Jews are reminded that they should treat equally and with compassion the stranger (i.e., the resident alien who is willing to accept their laws and values) in their midst.

And in the Jerusalem Talmud, the *halachah* sets a standard by which Jewish communities should treat the minorities within them, a standard called *mipnei darchei shalom*, "for the sake of the ways of peace." When Jews and non-Jews live together in a community, they collect *tzedakah* together, they administer it together, and they give to Jew and non-Jew alike, for the sake of peace in their community. (Jerusalem Talmud, *Demai* 24a) Those Jews knew that without sharing the social and economic benefits that Jewish social law provided, they would generate bitterness and anger that would undermine the good communal relations indispensable to Jewish values and Jewish self-interest.

For decades, a priority concern of synagogue social action and of Jewish community relations has been the protection and enhancement of equal rights and equal opportunities for all persons and the creation of conditions that contribute to vital Jewish living. The security of the Jewish group, as of all groups, rests on the foundation of full equality, individual rights, and personal liberties for all, without regard to race, religion, gender, or sexual orientation. If any group can be subject to discrimination and persecution, then Jews, too, can be victimized. Only in a society that accepts those biblical values as their norm, only in a society that abjures prejudice against any group will Jews be safe and secure.

THE JEWISH ROLE IN THE CIVIL RIGHTS STRUGGLE

Jews have been in the forefront of the struggle to achieve equality of opportunity for African-Americans, Latinos, Asians, and members of all groups suffering from discrimination. Jews recognize that discrimination against any racial or religious group in American life threatens the ultimate security of the Jew. More important for our purposes is the view that Judaism, to fulfill itself, must exert the full weight of its moral prestige toward the achievement of equal rights and opportunities for all persons, regardless of race, national origin, gender, or sexual orientation. This principle is the essence of our religious faith, as it is the essence of democracy itself.

The term "civil rights" as used in this book refers to the inherent right of every citizen to equality of opportunity. The term "civil liberties," used to designate freedoms of speech, assembly, press, religion, and others, will be taken up in a later chapter. While these two areas are related, each has had a markedly different development in recent years.

It is not surprising that Jews responded powerfully to the fight against racial segregation and discrimination in America. After all, no group in history has been so frequently the victim of racial hatred.

Jews more than any other segment of the white population played an active role in the dramatic civil rights struggles of the fifties and sixties when the Black-Jewish alliance was at the heart of the civil rights movement.

- When the Mississippi Summer of 1964 was organized to break the back of legal segregation in the then most stubbornly resistant state of the Union, half of the young people who volunteered from all parts of the United States were Jews. In that struggle, two of the three martyrs killed by white extremists in Philadelphia, Mississippi, Andrew Goodman and Michael Schwerner, were Jewish; the third, James Earl Chaney, was black.

- Jews helped found and/or contributed substantially to the funds raised by such organizations as the National Association for the Advancement of Colored People, the Southern Christian Leadership Conference, and the Student Nonviolent Coordinating Committee.

- For many years, Kivie Kaplan (a vice chair of the Reform Jewish movement) was the national president of the NAACP; Arnie Aronson and Joe Rauh, Jr., served as secretary and general counsel, respectively, to the Leadership Conference on Civil Rights (LCCR); Jack Greenberg was the executive director of the NAACP Legal Defense Fund—all of them Jews; just a few of the many Jews who played key roles in the civil rights movement. Fittingly, in 1998, President Clinton presented the Presidential Medal of Freedom to Arnie Aronson, an American Jewish leader who with the legendary A. Philip Randolph and Roy Wilkins founded the LCCR. For decades, Arnie led Jewish and Black civil rights leaders in mapping strategies to pass more than thirty far-reaching civil rights laws.

- From 1910 to 1940, over 2,000 primary and secondary schools and 20 black colleges (including Howard, Dillard, and Fisk universities) were erected in whole or in part by contributions from Jewish philanthropist Julius Rosenwald. At the height of the so-called Rosenwald schools, nearly 40 percent of southern Blacks were educated at one of these institutions.

- Rabbis marched with Martin Luther King, Jr., throughout the South; many were jailed, some were beaten. Prominent among these was Rabbi Abraham Joshua Heschel, who was a spiritual partner to King in the struggle against racism. Many of the leaders of the UAHC and CCAR were arrested with Martin Luther King, Jr., in St. Augustine, Florida, in 1964 after a challenge to racial segregation in public accommodations. (See "A Statement from St. Augustine," below.)

- Jewish political leverage contributed to passage of landmark civil rights laws, nationally and locally.

Indeed, the Civil Rights Act of 1964 and the Voting Rights Act of 1965 were drafted in the conference room of Reform Judaism's Emily and Kivie Kaplan Religious Action Center building in Washington, under the aegis of the Leadership Conference on Civil Rights, which for decades was housed in the Center. Over the next decades, the Jewish community continued as avid supporters of over a score of the most far-reaching civil rights laws in the nation's history, addressing persistent discrimination in voting, housing, and employment against not only women and racial minorities but the disabled as well. The Reform movement has been particularly looked to as various of its leaders have, throughout the 1990s, represented the Jewish community on the executive committees of the LCCR and the national board of the NAACP (in fact, David Saperstein is the only non–African-American on the NAACP board).

For most of the Jews involved in this struggle, the ideals of Judaism played an important part in inspiring their participation. Few documents speak more vividly of this connection or more powerfully recapture the passions of the time than the following statement from prison in St. Augustine, Florida, by sixteen rabbis and one of this book's authors (Al Vorspan), who were arrested in connection with civil rights activities on June 18, 1964.

Why We Went: A Statement from St. Augustine

St. Augustine is the oldest city in the United States. It was here on St. Augustine's Day, August 28, 1565, that Pedro Menéndez de Avilés first sighted land. In 1965 it will celebrate its 400th anniversary—indeed, it has requested federal funds to enhance this historic observance. St. Augustine has other distinguishing characteristics. In American history books yet to be written, this small, neatly kept Florida community will long be remembered as a symbol of a harsh, rigidly segregated, Klan-dominated, backward-looking city which mocked the spirit of the doughty African-born, dark-pigmented priest for whom it was named.

St. Augustine is a tourist town. By far the highest percentage of its income comes from the visitors who walk through its quaint streets staring at "excavations" from the eighteenth century only now being restored. Most visitors stop at the Slave Market, supposedly only a relic of bygone days. True, they no longer sell slaves… on [the] trading blocks. [But] the spirit of racial arrogance persists and is reinforced by the sway of terror long exerted by hooded and unhooded mobsters.

We went to St. Augustine in response to the appeal of Martin Luther King addressed to the CCAR Conference, in which he asked us to join with him in a creative witness to our joint convictions of equality and racial justice.

We came because we realized that injustice in St. Augustine, as anywhere else, diminishes the humanity of each of us. If St. Augustine is to be not only an ancient city but also a greathearted city, it will not happen until the raw hate, the ignorant prejudices, the unrecognized fears which now grip so many of its citizens are exorcised from its soul. We came then, not as tourists, but as ones who, perhaps quixotically, thought we could add a bit to the healing process of America.

We were arrested on Thursday, June 18, 1964. Fifteen of us were arrested while praying in an integrated group in front of Monson's Restaurant. Two of us were arrested for sitting down at a table with three Negro youngsters in the Chimes Restaurant. We pleaded not guilty to the charges against us.

Shortly after our confinement in the St. John's County Jail, we shared with one another our real, inner motives. They are, as might be expected, mixed. We have tried to be honest with one another about the wrong, as well as the right, motives which have prompted us. These hours have been filled with a sense of surprise and discovery, of fear and affirmation, of self-doubt and belief in God.

We came to St. Augustine mainly because we could not stay away. We could not say no to Martin Luther King, whom we always respected and admired and whose loyal friends we hope we shall be in the days to come. We could not pass by the opportunity to achieve a moral goal by moral means, a rare modern privilege that has been the glory of the nonviolent struggle for civil rights.

We came because we could not stand silently by our brother's blood. We had done that too many times before. We have been vocal in our exhortation of others but the idleness of our hands too often revealed an inner silence; silence at a time when silence has become the unpardonable sin of our time. We came in the hope that the God of us all would accept our small involvement as partial atonement for the many things we wish we had done before and often.

We came as Jews who remember the millions of face-less people who stood quietly, watching the smoke rise from Hitler's crematoria. We came because we know that second only to silence, the greatest danger to man is loss of faith in man's capacity to act.

Here in St. Augustine we have seen the depths of anger, resentment, and fury; we have seen faces that expressed a deep implacable hatred. What disturbs us more deeply is the large number of decent citizens who have stood aside, unable to bring themselves to act, yet knowing in their hearts that this cause is right and that it must inevitably triumph.

We believe, though we could not count on it in advance, that our presence and actions here have been of practical effect. They have reminded the embattled Negroes here that they are not isolated and alone. The conscience of the wicked has been troubled, while that of the righteous has gained new strength. We are more certain than before that this cause is invincible, but we also have a sharpened awareness of the great effort and sacrifice which will be required. We pray that what we have done may lead us on to further actions and persuade others who still stand hesitantly to take the stand they know is just.

We came from different backgrounds and with different degrees of involvement. Some of us have had intimate experience with the struggle of minority groups to achieve full and equal rights in our widely scattered home communities. Others of us have had less direct contact with the underprivileged and the socially oppressed. And yet for all of us these brief, tension-packed hours of openness and communication turned an abstract social issue into something personal and immediate. We shall not forget the people with whom we drove, prayed, marched, slept, ate, demonstrated, and were arrested. How little we know of these people and their struggle. What we have learned has changed us and our attitudes. We are grateful for the rare experience of sharing with this courageous community in their life, their suffering, their effort. We pray that we may remain more sensitive and more alive as a result.

We shall not soon forget the stirring and heartfelt excitement with which the Negro community greeted us with full-throated hymns and hallelujahs, which pulsated and resounded through the church; nor the bond of affectionate solidarity which joined us hand in hand during our marches through town; nor the common purpose which transcended our fears as well as all the boundaries of race, geography, and circumstance. We hope we have strengthened the morale of St. Augustine Negroes as they strive to claim their dignity and humanity; we know they have strengthened ours.

Each of us has in this experience become a little more the person, a bit more the rabbi he always hoped to be (but has not yet been able to become).

We believe in man's ability to fulfill God's commands with God's help. We make no messianic estimate of man's power and certainly not of what we did here. But it has reaffirmed our faith in the significance of the deed. So we must confess in all humility that we did this as much in fulfillment of our faith and in response to inner need as in service to our Negro brothers. We came to stand with our brothers and in the process have learned more about ourselves and our God. In obeying Him, we become ourselves; in following His will, we fulfill ourselves. He has guided, sustained, and strengthened us in a way we could not manage on our own.

We are deeply grateful to the good influences which have sustained us in our moments of trial and friendship. Often we thought of parents, wives, children, congregants, particularly our teenage youth, and of our teachers and our students. How many a Torah reading, Passover celebration, prayer book text, and sermonic effort has come to mind in these hours. And how meaningful has been our worship, morning and evening, as we recited the ancient texts in this new, yet Jewishly familiar, setting. We are particularly grateful for what we have received from our comrades in this visit. We have been sustained by the understanding, thoughtfulness, consideration, and good humor we have received from one another. Never have the bonds of Judaism and the fellowship of the rabbinate been more clearly expressed to us all or more deeply felt by each of us.

These words were first written at 3:00 A.M. in the sweltering heat of a sleepless night, by the light of the one naked bulb hanging in the corridor outside our small cell. They were, ironically, scratched on the back of the pages of a mimeographed report of the bloody assaults of the Ku Klux Klan in St. Augustine. At daybreak we revised the contents of the letter and prayed together for a new dawn of justice and mercy for all the children of God.

We do not underestimate what yet remains to be done, in the North as well as the South. In the battle against racism, we have participated here in only a skirmish. But the total effect of all such demonstrations has created a revolution; and the conscience of the nation has been aroused as never before. The Civil Rights Bill will become law and much more progress will be attained because this national conscience has been touched in this and other places in the struggle.

We praise and bless God for His mighty acts on our behalf.

Baruch Atah Adonai matir asurim. Blessed art Thou, O Lord, who freest the captives.

A Real Dilemma: Opposing Jews Who Would Rather Jews Be Silent

A constant dilemma for those involved in social justice is how to balance the obligation to speak out in the face of injustice when Jewish brothers and sisters more directly affected by these issues say to us: don't do it; you don't understand the issue as well as we; your actions will be counterproductive; you may even jeopardize our well-being.

In the civil rights movement, there were Southern Jews who were deeply resentful of Northern Jews who came down and "stirred up trouble." There were Southern Jews who courageously opposed segregation; many others were simply silent. But there were others who openly supported segregation and were angrily and publicly critical of Jewish civil rights workers.

How should the Jewish civil rights activists have responded to public attacks by their coreligionists?

Response

Occasionally, a public response was needed. More often, a private response was chosen. But whenever possible, Jewish acquiescence or support for segregation was challenged by the civil rights activists. The following letter was written by Rabbi Eugene J.

Lipman, founding director of the Commission on Social Action of Reform Judaism and one of the sixteen rabbis in jail, in response to a visit by a member of the local Jewish community.

June 21, 1964

Dear [Sir]:

We have met, though my name means nothing to you. We met in St. John's County Jail the other evening, when you slavishly responded to the call of your masters and came to teach manners to sixteen teachers of your religion.[...]

My purpose in life is to teach and to exemplify Judaism. There is much room within our religious system for disagreements—but not on basic moral principles. Your espousal of human inequality is a basic violation of Judaism. Your acceptance upon yourself arrogantly of the right to represent yourself as a Jewish leader and to flank yourself with Klansmen as you spoke with complete lack of *derech eretz* to your teachers—this, too, was a violation of Judaism.

How I wished you had the courage to say to our jailers that you, as a Jew, have too much self-respect to wallow in Hoss Manucy's* manure pile! How I wished that you had come to us—whether or not you agree with our actions—to ask if you, as president of a *shul*, could be of help to us![...]

There is a hierarchy of law in the world. When the laws of your state are morally wrong, as they are, we as Jews are expected to oppose them and to work to change them in the direction of moral rightness. This is your duty, as it is mine.

I wish you well, in the direction of the right.

Sincerely,

Rabbi Eugene J. Lipman

---

* Manucy was the sheriff and the leader of the local Klan.

AFFIRMATIVE ACTION

In the last three decades of the twentieth century, the Jewish and black communities diverged and clashed in an intense debate on one particular issue in the realm of race relations—affirmative action. As major civil rights laws were passed in the sixties, it became clear that it was not enough to prohibit discrimination against Blacks. Society had to do something positive to redress the lasting impact of centuries of past injury to racial minorities and women. Federal courts, executive branch agencies, and Congress mandated "affirmative action," requiring colleges, employers, and government agencies to reach out in positive steps to bring long-deprived members of minority groups into the mainstream of American life.

Implicit in this effort was the idea that it is not enough for a professional school, for example, to say that from now on they will accept anybody without discrimination when millions of black Americans are already handicapped by generations of poor schooling, unfair treatment, and blatant inequality. Moreover, lingering racist attitudes can find ever more subtle ways to prevent qualified members of minority groups from breaking through the barriers of job and education discrimination. Affirmative steps were seen as necessary to break the cycle of discrimination.

Thus affirmative action programs mushroomed in all phases of life. Such programs opened opportunities for millions of qualified women and minorities. But it pitted the principle that "each person should be evaluated on his/her own merits, without regard to race, sex, religion, or natural origin," against the principle that "a society that systematically discriminates against particular groups has the moral obligation to act affirmatively to offset the impact of that discrimination by targeting remedies, if necessary, at those groups." Inevitably, tension about this conflict simmered, then exploded.

At first glance, it would seem that reconciling affirmative action with Jewish tradition might prove difficult, as suggested by the following statement that says the rich and poor should not be treated differently by judges: "You shall do no unrighteousness in judgment; you shall not respect the person of the poor nor favor the person of the mighty, but in righteousness shall you judge your neighbor." (Leviticus 19:15) Yet even this clear position was bent to the realities of creating justice. In a well-known talmudic story about a dispute between brothers, the rules of evidence were changed to put an excessive burden on the rich and powerful brother when witnesses for the weaker brother were fearful of testifying. "Thus do we do for all who are powerful," says the text. (Babylonian Talmud, *Baba Metzia* 39b) The promise of equality is not sufficient if there are obstacles that make the reality of equality impossible.

In the 1990s, affirmative action again became a hot-button issue in American politics. In 1996, California became the first state in the nation to ban consideration of race, ethnic heritage, and gender in public programs. The result of this ban was a dramatic drop in admissions of Blacks and Latinos to the state's most competitive public universities. At the University of California at Berkeley, for example, the most selective public university in the country, African-Americans, Hispanic-Americans, and American Indians together made up 10.4 percent of the admitted freshmen for 1998; in 1997, they made up 23.1 percent. At UCLA, representation by these groups fell to 12.7 percent, from 19.8 percent in 1997.

AFFIRMATIVE ACTION AND ISRAEL

Modern Israel has comfortably and systematically used affirmative action—even quotas—with great social effectiveness. In its early pioneering period, in the 1920s, the *Yishuv*—the nascent Jewish community in Palestine—invoked a doctrine known as *kibbush avodah*, the conquest of labor. Jewish landowners were importuned to hire Jewish workers to do manual labor. This was not because Jews were better at this type of work than their Arab neighbors; instead, it was because the leaders of the *Yishuv* understood that there needed to be a Jewish working class if there was to be a productive and successful Jewish society. Israel's legendary first prime minister, David Ben-Gurion, once told Leonard Fein, director of the Commission on Social Action of Reform Judaism, that in his opinion *kibbush avodah* was "the single most important element in preparing the way for a Jewish state." This is a compelling example of why, in some situations, society needs, at least temporarily, to base decisions on more than mere "merit" (i.e., the talents of candidates) alone.

Since its founding, Israel has faced an imbalance between Sephardic

Jews (many of them having been educationally and economically deprived) and Ashkenazic Jews. The nation took forceful steps in mandating affirmative action programs for the Sephardim in education and employment. Over many years, special remedial programs were set up to assist them to become competitive. On basic high school standardized examinations, all Sephardic Jews were given an extra point over Ashkenazic Jews—a process similar to "race norming" (which in the United States has been so harshly criticized) in which minority students are measured against others in the same minority group rather than against all those who take the standardized exams.

Qualified Sephardim received a number of guaranteed university placements. As a result, anti-Sephardic discrimination was reduced faster than even the most optimistic sociologists and politicians of the 1960s and 1970s had predicted. While serious problems still linger, particularly the development of a Sephardic underclass, large-scale overt discrimination has been significantly phased out of Israeli society.

In Israel today, affirmative action programs are also being utilized to bring Ethiopian Jews into the mainstream. Special employment and housing programs have helped significantly to integrate Ethiopian Jews into Israeli society. But a major challenge remains. Like an earlier generation of Sephardim, Ethiopian children are falling behind their Israeli peers in school and university despite the fact that they are just as intelligent and motivated. Until recently, the educational inequalities were largely ignored, allowing for segregated classes of Ethiopian children and unnecessary tracking of Ethiopian students into vocational rather than college preparatory programs. Presently, there is an effort to eradicate these differences by creating programs that provide invaluable enrichment for Ethiopian students from preschool through high school. Without such affirmative action programs, which would attempt to compensate for past deprivation or discrimination, Israel will be faced with a far greater and more difficult problem: the polarization of Israeli society into two groups, black and white, grossly unequal.

The words of the late Israeli Prime Minister Yitzhak Rabin illuminate the moral questions that affirmative action raises:

> ...years ago we thought that an equal opportunity
> would solve the problem of the gap between the vari-

ous communities. If we have learned anything in these last years, it is that equal opportunity is not sufficient. Preferential treatment is necessary if we are to bridge the gap and catch up with the 50 percent of our population who, through no fault of their own but because of centuries of cultural and educational discrimination, could not compete.

REVERSE DISCRIMINATION?

Many white Americans feel that special treatment for qualified minorities amounts to reverse discrimination against themselves and their children. During the 1970s, '80s, and '90s, protest and anger swelled into legal challenges, with the courts increasingly tilting against affirmative action. Public opinion has become conflicted. On the one hand, in 1996, a statewide referendum in California to end affirmative action in public employment, education, and contracting at the state level passed after a bitter battle. On the other, one year later a referendum in the city of Houston upheld affirmative action programs by a similar margin. Nonetheless, these new political and judicial challenges mark a severe setback for affirmative action programs across the country, all of which will now face strict scrutiny and the possibility of being repealed. The Clinton administration sought to hold back the flood by maintaining federal affirmative action programs, saying, "Mend it, don't end it." Polls show that the American people are divided on this issue. A majority continue to support "affirmative action" for minorities and women but oppose it when it's described as "preferential treatment."

Because of the growing popularity of anti-affirmative action measures, many Blacks feel betrayed and cheated by an America that seems to be turning its back on the goal of full equality. When in the 1980s unemployment reached Depression-era levels within the black community, particularly among young Blacks (almost 40 percent of whom were jobless in some cities), fuel was added to the fires of resentment. Such discrimination continues to persist today, not only against Blacks but also against other minorities and women. In March 1995, for example, the U.S. Department of Labor's Glass Ceiling Commission reported that there is indeed an employment barrier only rarely penetrated by women and minorities. Consider: 97 percent of the senior managers of Fortune 500 companies are white; 95 to 97 percent are male. In Fortune 2000 industrial and service companies, 5 percent of senior managers are women—and of that 5 percent, virtually all are white. And where there are women and minorities in high places, their compensation is lower. For example, black men with professional degrees earn 79 percent of the amount earned by white males who hold the same degrees and are in the same job categories. This is harmful to women and minorities, to businesses, and to our nation.

Yet the concept of affirmative action does indeed contain an inherent moral contradiction. On the one hand, equality promises that every person will be judged on the basis of merit without regard to race, sex, creed, age, handicap, sexual orientation, or national origin. On the other hand, when a society systematically discriminates for generations against a segment of that society, it has a responsibility to act affirmatively to lessen the impact of that discrimination for specific minorities. How can these two valid principles be reconciled? And for how long?

To insist that abstract equality be used as the only standard of allocating job opportunities is to keep millions of minorities and women from having a fair chance to shape their destinies. On the other hand, if we assign opportunity on the basis of group identity only, we destroy the principle of individual merit.

And where is it written that a person is automatically deprived merely because he or she is black? Today, one-third of Blacks are in the middle class. The child of a prosperous black lawyer or surgeon may be no more deprived than is the white next-door neighbor. This scenario has led opponents of traditional affirmative action to argue that the measure be applied not to groups per se but to *individuals*, regardless of color, religion, or ancestry, who have suffered actual deprivation and who are, therefore, entitled to a special hand—a position taken by the Supreme Court in the 1995 *Adarand* decision as far as government-run (but not private) affirmative action programs are concerned. But in treating people generally, the state and the school and the employer must be "color-blind"; otherwise, racial injustice will be replaced by reverse discrimination. Moreover, if we rely too heavily on proportional representation, what does this mean for Jews, who comprise only 2.2 percent of the United States population?

Affirmative action advocates respond that Blacks *as a race* were enslaved, mistreated, and cheated by society; women *as a class* were disadvantaged. Blacks, women, and other disadvantaged groups suffered deprivation as groups, and society must redress these past grievances by introducing genuine affirmative action using group remedies. It is in the public interest to overcome the ugly heritage of the past, to bring the disadvantaged into the mainstream of American life, and to ameliorate the impact of the racism that still persists in our society.

Racism against Blacks is a particularly invidious, deeply entrenched aspect of Western civilization, and no one can measure how three hundred years of slavery, segregation, and deprivation have damaged each individual. Without a special effort to guarantee qualified Blacks entrance to higher education and corporate opportunities, there might never be adequate minority representation in the nation's colleges, graduate schools, and corporations. Deep-seated racial prejudice may limit the ability of Blacks to compete no matter what their background or qualifications.

The persistence of racism was dramatized in a controversy involving Texaco Inc., in 1996. Blacks and other minorities had long accused the corporation of discriminatory hiring and promotion practices and of being clever enough to hide the kind of evidence of discriminatory intent that the *Adarand* decision would have called for if applied to the private sector. The controversy surfaced when a high-ranking official released secret tapes of high-level meetings in which the palpable racism of the corporate leadership was exposed. Under normal circumstances, however, such proof is nearly impossible to find. In the absence of a "smoking gun," what recourse do minorities and women have without affirmative action programs? Further, how do we define "qualified"? Universities, in practice, have always given preferences to children of alumni, to athletes, to veterans, and to achieve geographical distribution. Why not to ensure racial and gender diversity?

Even with affirmative action programs, the percentage of black students at professional schools has generally fallen in the past twenty years. As colleges in California, Texas, and other areas restricted or abandoned affirmative action, minority admissions plummeted—to the consternation of even some critics of affirmative action who understood the value of diversity in the campus setting. Equality is not served by bringing everyone to the starting gate to compete in a race in which minority youngsters are crippled by a history of inferior schooling, bad housing, demoralizing treatment, and lingering racist attitudes.

The controversy surrounding affirmative action reached its peak during a series of landmark legal cases in the 1970s and 1980s. In the *DeFunis, Bakke, Webster,* and *Fullivove* cases, the policy arguments over affirmative action were sharpened in legal briefs.

> ### A Real Dilemma: The DeFunis Case—Should We Oppose a Fellow Jew Who Claims to Be Harmed by Affirmative Action?
>
> In 1973, the Commission on Social Action faced one of its thorniest dilemmas: whether to join with a coalition of civil rights organizations in supporting an affirmative action program at the University of Washington Law School. Through affirmative action, the university was attempting to diversify its essentially white male student body by reaching out to qualified women and members of racial minorities.
>
> Several Jewish organizations publicly opposed the University of Washington program, contending it was basically a quota. They supported the plaintiff, Marco DeFunis, a Jewish student who alleged he was the victim of reverse discrimination. The Commission on Social Action (CSA), after examining the facts in depth, concluded that the university's affirmative action program did not resort to a fixed percentage—a quota—but relied only on good-faith general goals and timetables. Should the fact that DeFunis was a Jew have affected the CSA's decision on whether to support the university's position against Marco DeFunis's legal challenge?
>
> #### Response
>
> The Commission on Social Action joined an *amicus* (friend of the court) brief in support of the university, believing its affirmative action program was a flexible, good-faith effort to bring into the mainstream of the law school members of groups long discriminated against. They made this judgment even in the face of the information that DeFunis's family was a member of a Reform synagogue in Seattle, Washington.

As this and other affirmative action cases worked their way to the Supreme Court, they gradually caused severe strains in the old Black-Jewish civil rights coalition that had helped forge the landmark civil rights legislation of the 1960s.

GOALS AND TIMETABLES VS. QUOTAS

Almost all Jewish organizations support affirmative action programs that use goals and timetables to measure whether progress is being made in eliminating discrimination but oppose quotas under any other circumstances. Only the Orthodox Jewish agencies and the Anti-Defamation League of B'nai B'rith (ADL) oppose the use of goals and timetables, arguing they would inevitably lead to quotas. Two other agencies, the American Jewish Congress and the Women's American ORT, support the use of temporary quotas after court findings of discrimination.

But the nuances and splits in the Jewish community were lost on much of the Black community when, during the major affirmative action cases of the seventies and eighties, some of the most high-profile opponents turned out to be those few Jewish groups who rejected affirmative action. In the minds of many Blacks, these groups spoke for all Jews, despite repeated public opinion polls showing that Jews support affirmative action with goals and even quotas at significantly higher percentages than does any other segment of the white community of America.

While the courts were upholding affirmative action programs well into the 1980s, the Reagan administration was vigorously trying to destroy these programs and to stop other civil rights legislation. In the late eighties, the Supreme Court began to join in efforts to limit the scope of civil rights laws generally. In response, at the very height of President Reagan's popularity, a regalvanized civil rights coalition, including Blacks and Jews, achieved a series of twenty-four major legislative victories that continued through the Bush presidency, expanding the scope of civil rights coverage. The victories include: the extension of the Voting Rights Act, the Fair Housing Act of 1990, the Japanese Reparations Act (compensating Japanese-Americans for having been unfairly incarcerated during World War II), the Americans with Disabilities Act, and the Civil Rights Act of 1991 (overturning the effect of six Supreme Court decisions that sharply narrowed the protection against discrimination in the workplace).

VOTING RIGHTS

The 1965 Voting Rights Act, one of the United States' most important civil rights laws, guaranteed that no American would be deprived of the right to vote because of his or her race, sex, creed, national origin, or religion. It helped shatter legal segregation in the South. Between 1960 and 1996, the number of Blacks in Congress jumped from six to thirty-nine, including one senator (Carol Moseley Braun of Illinois). The number of black local and state officials has also risen.

The problem was that opponents of integration became much more clever in limiting the impact of the voting rights law. If, for example, the population of a given community was 40 percent black, they might do away with geographical representation for the city council and make all city council members "at large." That is, every city council member would be elected by the entire population of the city. If the election had been along geographic lines, the predominantly black neighborhoods would ensure that someone from their neighborhood would be elected. But if all the members were elected at large, then the 60 percent white majority might vote in a manner that ensured that no representative who lived in the predominantly black neighborhoods would ever be elected. Similarly, in elections to the U.S. Congress, white-controlled state legislatures would often draw congressional district lines that split up black communities and ensured that Blacks would never total a large enough base of voters to have anyone from their neighborhoods elected to Congress.

Solving these problems was difficult. On the one hand, every person's vote should count the same as another's; no group of people, such as African-Americans, should be subject to rules that make it impossible for them to ensure that someone sensitive to their interests would be elected. On the other hand, no group (Blacks, Jews, Latinos, etc.) has a *right* to have one of its members elected to Congress. That would be a quota system, which is strongly opposed by the Jewish community. Indeed, over the past twenty-five years, the Jewish community has been the most outspoken critic of any system that would guarantee any particular group specific representation, believing that merit should be the principal qualification to elected office, not race or religion. A system based on merit helps explain why Jews, who comprise 2.2 percent of the population, make up approximately 8 percent of the Congress. President Clinton agreed with the Jewish community on this issue.

A Real Dilemma: Lani Guinier

One of President Clinton's first nominations to the Justice Department was a brilliant black woman law professor, Lani Guinier. After the Reagan and Bush administrations' restrictive interpretation of civil rights legislation, President Clinton promised to appoint a forceful assistant attorney general for civil rights who would take a broad and expansive approach to these laws. His choice, Professor Guinier (whose mother, incidentally, was Jewish), had long ties with the Jewish community—but some deep intellectual differences with the community on voting rights issues.

With the exception of Reconstruction after the Civil War, Blacks were denied the right to vote in many areas until the civil rights movement. Even after the right to vote was theoretically won, practical obstacles like "literacy tests" and "poll taxes" were used in the South to prevent Blacks from exercising that right. The Voting Rights Act of 1965 was aimed at removing those obstacles.

Professor Guinier had written extensively on the problems with the Voting Rights Act and was understood by many to have recommended changes in the system that would have guaranteed that Blacks and other minorities would have representation approximately the same as their percentage of the population. This position was strongly opposed by Jews.

So here was the dilemma. President Clinton had nominated a very talented, popular black law professor whom our community appreciated because we knew she would enforce civil rights law vigorously. She was passionately supported by our key allies in the black community. But she held views on one of the most contentious issues of our time that ran contrary to the Jewish community's consensus positions. If we opposed her nomination, it would cause immediate severe strains in Black-Jewish relations. If she were confirmed, it would likely lead to strains down the road over the voting rights issue and possibly changes in the law that run counter to Jewish positions and interests. For that matter, if she had been confirmed, should she have attempted to implement her own views or should she have implemented the views of the administration even if they disagreed with her own? Should the Jewish community have supported Professor Guinier's nomination? Opposed it? Or remained neutral?

Response

Most Jewish organizations decided to postpone taking a position on Professor Guinier's nomination until they heard how she explained her positions in her Senate confirmation hearings. In particular, they wanted to see if she would be willing to implement the positions taken by the administration, even if they differed with her own. The only Jewish organization that did take a position early on, the National Council of Jewish Women, endorsed Professor Guinier's nomination. The media then caught hold of the controversy over Guinier's writings and in the ensuing public debate, President Clinton withdrew the nomination. The UAHC worked closely with black organizations to persuade Jewish organizations not to take a stance until they heard Professor Guinier explain her positions in full—which never happened.

The use of quotas poses a major problem for Jews, who historically have been excluded from schools and professions in Europe and in the United States because of anti-Semitic quota systems.

A small but vociferous group of black conservatives also has challenged affirmative action, saying that if most Blacks achieved their advancement as a result of affirmative action, how could one be sure that they were truly qualified? Even the most qualified Blacks would be shadowed by suspicions engendered by programs to help less able people. Furthermore, what incentive would Blacks have to stand on their own feet if society is willing indefinitely to give them special benefits? Supreme Court Justice Clarence Thomas is among those

Blacks who have opposed racial preferences as harmful to the self-reliance, independence, and pride of Blacks. This view is rejected by the substantial majority of black and Jewish organizations.

THE CURRENT STATUS OF BLACKS IN AMERICA

Discussions about affirmative action should not blind us to the dire condition of many American Blacks today. On the one hand, in the past thirty years significant gains have been made among some Blacks, with the development of a black middle class. On the other hand, despite general improvement in employment rates in the late 1990s, among black adults the rate of unemployment is 2 times higher than among white workers. For black teenagers, the rates are more alarming. For young black men, ages sixteen to twenty-four, the rate is 2.3 times higher than for young white men (37 percent to 16 percent). Blacks are approximately 13 percent of our total population, but they comprise only 2.3 percent of lawyers and judges, 3.3 percent of physicians, 1.9 percent of dentists, 3.8 percent of engineers, and 4.0 percent of college and university professors. As former Supreme Court Justice Thurgood Marshall said in his angry dissent in the *Bakke* case, "At every point, from birth to death, the impact of the past is reflected in the still disfavored position of the Negro." Even in the growing job market of the 1990s, the chances of the average poor black person working his or her way out of poverty and despair remain bleak. Only in 1998 did the average black person with a college degree begin to earn as much as the average white person with a high school diploma.

Many in Black America are mired in a crisis marked by the disintegration of the family; the dominance of single-parent, female-headed families (65 percent of black children are born out of wedlock); children bearing children; the catastrophic drug epidemic; AIDS; and the startling reality that *a black male in Harlem has the same life expectancy as a peasant in Bangladesh.*

Indeed, in the inner cities, the problems are even more acute. The epidemic of crime and drugs and the breakdown of inner-city families have taken a terrible toll, particularly on young black males. Many inner-city black youths find little or no future in America. They are trapped in decaying slums and failing schools, permanently unemployed. To survive, they are dependent on an inhumane welfare system and/or street crime. Many end up hustling on the street, the training ground for serious crime and the dead end of the drug world. Today, a black urban male has a 30 percent chance of dying before reaching the age of twenty. *One out of three black males is in jail, on parole, or on probation.*

Even the most far-reaching affirmative action programs would not solve our most serious racial problems. Half a century ago, Gunnar Myrdal, in his classic *An American Dilemma*, put the challenge squarely: "You are cutting off an underclass that is not needed, not employable. You must create out of this underclass, or their children at least, human beings who fit into modern America, who are needed, who are productive, who have a value." The state of black America demonstrates that we have not yet heeded Myrdal's warning.

This waste of a generation is not only a human disaster, but it creates a society in which no one is safe. History shows that Jews have most to fear in an angry and polarized society. Recent events prove again that in an atmosphere of tension and hopelessness, Blacks, like other groups, seek easy scapegoats to blame for their misfortunes (e.g., Koreans in the Los Angeles riots), and Jews are often the target.

The United States Supreme Court, once the champion of minority rights, seems to have abandoned its defense of the vulnerable in our society. Reinforced by the appointments made by Presidents Reagan and Bush, the Supreme Court has embraced a conservative interpretation of the Constitution, whittling away the right of women to have an abortion and making it significantly more difficult for a victim of discrimination to get redress from the courts. The underlying problems will only grow more acute as America becomes over the next decades a nation in which the majority of its population is comprised of its combined minority populations. Yet there is a growing understanding that America has much to learn from diversity. Businesses understand that they will be strong only if they embody the diversity of the communities they serve. That is one key reason why so many corporate leaders are strong proponents of affirmative action programs. Governments increasingly recognize that if they are to serve all components of our society, those components must be heard and have real opportunities to be represented.

INTEGRATION: SUCCESSES AND FAILURES; THE BREAKDOWN OF PUBLIC EDUCATION

In the 1950s and 1960s, racial integration in public education was not only seen as a national goal but as a moral imperative. Protestants, Catholics, and Jews played prominent roles in the massive effort to end segregated schooling in America, recognizing the truth of the Supreme Court's seminal school desegregation decision, *Brown v. Board of Education*, that "separate but equal is inherently unequal."

Today, new questions arise, perturbing even traditional civil rights groups like the NAACP. Do minority students really learn better in desegregated schools? Does desegregation cause "white flight" (whites who move out of integrated school districts)? Does integration lessen or increase racial conflict? Can integration really be achieved without combining city and suburb? Is busing an effective or fair way to achieve integration? Have Blacks begun to give up on integration?

These questions must be seen in the context of the declining quality of public education, particularly in the inner cities. For three generations, the public school system was the great leveler of American life. Rich and poor, immigrants and longtime residents, Christians and Jews, blacks and whites met for what was the only close interaction of their lives. For three generations, the public schools educated America's youths, raising the level of literacy, resulting in a more technically proficient, competitive, humane, and tolerant society.

In the past generation, that pattern has reversed itself. White flight left urban schools the squalid, underfunded province of minorities and poor whites. In the face of declining tax revenues, facilities deteriorated, the general quality of education fell, and rates of literacy sank alarmingly. In this context, hopes of breaking the cycle of deprivation and victimization appear bleaker than ever.

Jewish attitudes toward public education often reflect the same dilemmas. The system helped convert a poor Jewish immigrant community into one of the most upwardly mobile and successful minority groups in the history of America. But increasingly, Jews who remain in the city feel compelled to put their children in private schools. Indeed, the rising Jewish interest in Jewish day schools stems, at least in part, from a desire to escape the impact of busing and integration on the quality and safety of public schools.

The overwhelming majority of Jewish youngsters still attend public schools. Most attend suburban schools where the public schools still do an excellent job. But where public schools have declined in quality and are swept by violence or tension, can Jewish parents be expected to sacrifice their child's education on the altar of high principle?

What, then, is the future of urban public education? Perhaps public education is to become a dumping ground for poor nonwhites—a school for children left behind in the mass exodus to suburbia or to the sanctuaries of private schools. The move toward vouchers, diverting government funding for private schools, including parochial religious schools, would accelerate this move. In the long run, is such a prospect good for America? Is it good for Jews? Is it good for anybody?

For Jews, the breakdown of the public school system poses other particular concerns. Studies indicate that those with higher levels of education are less likely to hold racist and anti-Semitic attitudes. But over the past two decades, educational levels have leveled off or fallen. Will this result in increased anti-Semitism? Quite likely. The despair that those confined to the worst schools feel as they are increasingly locked out of the better jobs in a technological world requiring good education can only breed the kind of anger that helped fuel the violent conflicts in Los Angeles and in Crown Heights, Brooklyn, in the 1990s.

JEWISH DAY SCHOOLS, INTEGRATION, AND THE PUBLIC SCHOOLS

Today, the Jewish community remains largely committed to public education, but increasingly disquieting doubts disturb our traditional support for the institution that equipped our immigrant forebears with the tools to live in a pluralistic and free society. The condition and the quality of some of the nations' public schools have worsened. The historic Jewish honeymoon with public education has begun to fade; Jews, like others, have begun to examine alternative educational systems, including private Jewish day schools. At the same time, a growing number of Jewishly motivated parents, increasingly frustrated by the obvious limitations of the usual "weekend/after-school" Jewish education programs offered by most Reform and Conservative synagogues, enrolled their children in a full-time education program providing the best of both worlds: a first-rate Jewish education and a first-rate general education. Long the domain of Orthodox Jewry, day schools are booming within Conservative Judaism, and the Reform movement—which had once bitterly opposed day schools as a threat to public education—now has twenty day schools.

How should the Jewish community, which has so benefited from the public school system in America and which recognizes that the future strength of this nation depends on the quality of public education, balance these concerns against its commitment to Jewish continuity?

A Real Dilemma: The UAHC and Jewish Day Schools

At its biennial convention in 1985, the UAHC considered a resolution on whether to encourage full-time Reform Jewish day schools. Some delegates argued that to do so was an abandonment of the public school system; indeed, they argued that the breakdown of public schools has been exacerbated by the expansion of Jewish day schools. Others argued that it was a necessary affirmation of an intensive Jewish educational option. If you had been a delegate, how would you have voted?

Response

The UAHC held that its commitment to public schools should not preclude its support for legitimate efforts to strengthen Jewish education through the option of day school. Such support, however, was predicated on two conditions: first, that synagogues undertake efforts to strengthen the public schools in their communities and second, that the movement reaffirm its commitment to separation of church and state, including opposition to federal aid to full-time religious education.

The result: By 1998, the Reform Jewish day school movement had, as noted above, grown to a score of schools, with more virtually every year. In many other communities, Reform synagogues actively support community day schools. The UAHC has strongly maintained its opposition to aid to parochial schools (although pressure to reevaluate this position has come from some Reform day schools). However, as to the second part of the resolution, too few congregations have been able to do anything substantial to assist the public schools in their communities. In the late 1990s, however, there has been a surge of volunteers for tutoring and mentoring efforts aimed at helping public school students, and a growing number of interfaith coalitions have begun to develop programs to support public education in their communities.

The many questions that arise from the desegregation process require constant and candid examination. All this should not obscure the fundamental truth that America, despite a history of racial arrogance and slavery, has broken the back of legal segregation and paved the way for a truly open, free, and multiracial society. We still have much to do to achieve this goal, but we have already come a long way.

··· 9 ···

Jews, Blacks, and America's Multiracial Society

A s a religious tradition, Judaism clearly rejects racism; but as individuals, Jews are as prone to racial bigotry as other people. Many Jews are sensitive to the impact of discrimination from their own history; but Jews can also be found among the slum landlords and merchants who exploit the poor. Jews rarely resort to violence when African-Americans or Hispanics move into the neighborhood; instead, Jews leave the cities. Indeed, in pursuit of a better life for their families, Jews joined the massive post–World War II exodus, moving from the cities to the all-white suburbs, one unintended effect of which was to abandon poor Blacks to virtual urban ghettos.

A Real Dilemma: When Synagogues Join White Flight

Until the 1950s, the vast majority of Jews belonged to synagogues in urban centers, enriching the lives of all who lived in the community through cultural, educational, and communal activity.

In the past two generations, a radical shift in living patterns sent most Jews to the suburbs. Those Jews who were mobile enough to flee the problems of the cities and live out the "American dream" literally moved their synagogues with them to the suburbs.

But what happened to those left behind: the older and poorer Jews who could not leave or those who preferred urban life? Without the synagogue, the Jewish support system that sustained them eroded. The public schools and other communal institutions in the area deteriorated as Jews withdrew from the political and civic leadership they had long provided.

Was it wrong for congregations to have moved? How would you have voted if you had been a board member of an urban synagogue considering relocation to the suburbs?

Response

Scores, if not hundreds of congregations, had to deal with this problem. For many, the feasibility of staying downtown simply did not exist. The distance between the old facility and the new center of Jewish population was too great. Moreover, the deterioration of the quality of life in the old neighborhood was so severe that many members were afraid or unwilling to attend Friday evening Shabbat or holiday services. To have remained behind would have ill served the members of the congregation and, as new synagogues were founded in the suburbs, might have spelled the death knell of the synagogues that failed to adapt.

Nevertheless, a surprising number of congregations made a conscientious effort to remain downtown or at least to maintain a presence in the city. In a few communities, where the distances were not great, congregations decided to stay, drawing suburban members downtown. Some congregants had always remained downtown, enriching the community and now benefiting from urban renewal as a new generation of families returned to the city from the suburbs. In many other communities, the congregation kept the old facility and then built a suburban annex and/or religious school to meet the needs of both the urban and suburban segments of the Jewish community. In all these cases, it was the continuing Jewish commitment to the well-being of the general society and to the cause of civil rights and Black-Jewish relations that kept them in the cities.

In the fifties and sixties, Jews, more than any other segment of the white population, played an active role in the struggle for civil rights. Despite the close cooperation between African-Americans and Jews in the civil rights movement, it is probably correct to say that Black-Jewish relations were never as good, even in the old days, as we romanticize them to have been. They were inherently unequal, not peer-to-peer. Jews once provided much of the expertise, the legal assistance and financial resources, often creating a subordinate role for those we sought to help. The black community, determined to take control of its own destiny, ultimately rejected the former relationship as patronizing. Many Jews felt betrayed. While the revolt against condescension was healthy and overdue, it often led to excesses of black separatism, further estranging Blacks from Jews.

Many Jews abandoned or were pushed out of the civil rights movement at exactly the time of heightened consciousness of Jewish ethnic identity and the particularistic agenda of the Jewish people. Many activists plunged into the battle for Soviet Jewry and Israel. Ethnic assertiveness became the new battle cry in America, and the sense of national cohesiveness began to falter. After the traumas of civil rights, the Vietnam War, and Watergate, no single issue united all groups. With each group going its own way, fighting its own battles, civil rights lost its sense of coherence as a definable movement.

In this new mood of group separatism, Jews and African-Americans have largely drifted apart. Given the suburban middle-class character of Jewish life, most Jews do not know members of other minority groups on a personal basis. Employing a black or Hispanic domestic rarely contributes to relationships of equality. Jews and Blacks have too little human contact, exacerbating negative stereotyping. Too often, Blacks think of Jews as whites who are rich, powerful, and racist; Jews regard Blacks as welfare clients, violent, anti-Semitic, and anti-Israel.

The reality is that there has been overall improvement in the situation of the black community with the growth of a substantial middle class. Despite persistent images, most Blacks do not live in the inner city, and most people on welfare are white. As to Israel, most Blacks and even higher percentages of black political and organizational leaders have been stalwart supporters of Israel. To the average black person, however, Israel is as remote as Nigeria is to the average Jew.

CROWN HEIGHTS

Tragically, one inner-city community where Jews chose to stay erupted into violence in 1991. On the evening of August 19, 1991, seven-year-old Gavin Cato was riding his bicycle on the sidewalk in front of his home at the corner of Utica Avenue and President Street in Crown Heights, Brooklyn. He was with his cousin Angela.

At eight-twenty that evening, the late Lubavitcher Grand Rebbe Menachem Schneerson was being driven home in a three-car motorcade, following his weekly visit to the cemetery where his wife is buried. The motorcade was escorted by police. Twenty-two-year-old Joseph

Lifsh, one of the motorcade drivers, reportedly ran a red light, collided with another car, and veered onto the sidewalk. His car struck Gavin and his cousin Angela. Gavin was dragged underneath the car. Twelve of Gavin's neighbors lifted the car off the dying child. Angela, seriously injured, was pinned against the wall of the apartment house.

Rumors spread through the community that a private Jewish ambulance had arrived at the scene first and attended to Joseph Lifsh rather than to the young black victims. In fact, the private ambulance and the city ambulance arrived at the same time, and the police ordered the private ambulance to rescue the injured Lifsh, who was being beaten by the crowd. Gavin Cato died at the hospital.

The grand jury testimony later revealed that Lifsh had tried desperately to avoid hitting the children. He was not indicted, thus generating a firestorm of controversy in the community, which is 85 percent black and 15 percent Jewish, mostly chasidic.

With wild rumors sweeping the community, violence erupted throughout Crown Heights. Three hours after the incident, Yankel Rosenbaum, an Australian chasidic scholar visiting Brooklyn, was stopped in his car by a gang of twenty young hoodlums, assaulted, stabbed, and left bleeding on the hood of his car. He subsequently died in the hospital, a victim of what Mayor David Dinkins later called "a lynching." This was the first physical confrontation between Blacks and Jews in the twentieth century that resulted in fatalities or casualties.

Several days of anti-Jewish rioting and rampaging ensued. Jews were attacked at random by black youths, shouting "Heil Hitler" and "Kill all the Jews." The violence was triggered by the incendiary statements made at the Cato funeral and elsewhere by such community leaders as Sonny Carson, Al Sharpton, and C. Vernon Mason. The Chasidim and other Jews likened the attacks to a pogrom and denounced them as a modern reenactment of Kristallnacht.

More than 65 civilians and 158 police officers were wounded over three days of rioting. The Reverend Al Sharpton, an outspoken black leader, equated the accidental death of Cato with the slaying of Rosenbaum, demanding that Lifsh be arrested for murder, thus inflaming group relations and inciting violence. So acute and lasting were the tensions surrounding Crown Heights that Mayor David Dinkins, New York's first black mayor, elected in good measure with

Jewish support, saw his base of support in the Jewish community melt away, dooming his chance for reelection. Eventually, in 1997 some of those who had murdered Yankel Rosenbaum were finally brought to justice and found guilty—in large measure because of the persistent pressure of many in the Jewish community. On April 1, 1998, a federal judge imposed a 19½ year sentence on Lemrick Nelson, Jr., who was convicted of the murder. New York Mayor Rudolph Giuliani apologized for the city's handling of the riots as part of a legal settlement with chasidic residents of the neighborhood.

MINISTER FARRAKHAN AND THE NATION OF ISLAM

For more than a decade, the bone in the throat of Jewish Americans has been Minister Louis Farrakhan, the head of the small but influential Nation of Islam, whose relentless and vicious Jew-bashing outraged Jewish sensibilities. Calling Judaism a "gutter religion" and accusing Jews of prime responsibility for slavery, of exploiting Blacks and controlling America, Minister Farrakhan aroused incredible pain and fury among American Jews. Making matters worse, in 1993 his disciple, Khalid Abdul Muhammad, touched off a virtual firestorm by delivering an anti-Semitic tirade reeking with such violence and ugliness against Jews, Catholics, women, and homosexuals that it evoked echoes of Nazism itself. Instead of repudiating his disciple, Minister Farrakhan gently admonished him for the style of his attack but defended the "truth" of his charges. While this episode derailed Farrakhan's efforts to forge a formal relation with mainstream black organizations and with the Congressional Black Caucus, the fact that both Farrakhan and Khalid Muhammad became sensations at public appearances, especially at standing-room-only events at college campuses, winning thunderous ovations from black audiences, deepened the hurt of American Jews.

On the other hand, because Farrakhan's rhetoric of personal and family responsibility strikes a chord in contemporary culture, because his unremitting message of black pride has captured the imagination of many young Blacks, and because his organization has, in a handful of inner cities, been one of the few organizations to go into the streets to address, head-on, problems of crime and drugs, it has been very difficult for other black leaders to publicly criticize or isolate Minister Farrakhan.

Indeed, his peaceful Million Man March, in October 1995, which brought many hundreds of thousands of black men to the nation's capital, both to oppose the conservative Congress's dismantling of the civil rights agenda and to call African-American men to reclaim their families and communities, further strengthened Minister Farrakhan's role in the African-American community.

How should the Jewish community deal with the relentless challenge of Minister Farrakhan and his Nation of Islam? For years, the policy consensus was clear: condemn him and his vicious anti-Semitic record, urge black leadership to repudiate him, and reject calls for dialogue unless and until Minister Farrakhan acknowledges and apologizes for the hurts he has inflicted on Jews. At the same time, Farrakhan's influence—resulting from the Million Man March—has grown so that he is a major force within the black community *leadership*. He is far harder to marginalize and is increasingly accepted on the national scene and in local communities as a legitimate player in coalitions of religious, civic, and communal groups. If Jews refuse to involve themselves in coalitions in which the Nation of Islam participates, they may find themselves increasingly isolated. On the other hand, if Jewish organizations remain in those coalitions, they grant a measure of legitimacy to the Nation of Islam. Do these changed circumstances require the Jewish community to reexamine our policy and strategy?

This dilemma was dramatized by the events in Philadelphia, Pennsylvania, in 1997. The following statement concerning this situation is drawn from deliberations of the largest national coalition of Jewish community relations organizations—NJCRAC (formerly National Jewish Community Relations Advisory Council, now called the Jewish Council for Public Affairs):

> Burt Siegel, executive director of the Philadelphia Jewish Community Relations Council (JCRC), discussed recent developments and decisions facing the Jewish community following an invitation by Mayor Rendell to Louis Farrakhan to participate with other civic and religious leaders in a city-organized unity rally. Concerns expressed by Philadelphia Jewish organizations and their refusal to participate in the rally

was, in turn, publicly criticized by the mayor, and a number of sharp exchanges ensued. Given the likelihood that future city initiatives involving the civic and religious communities may include the local Nation of Islam mosque and that Minister Farrakhan's success in Philadelphia may lead to similar appearances in other cities, Siegel suggested it was important for CRCs to review policies regarding constructive options for response. While he noted the special circumstances in Philadelphia that prompted the mayor's actions—urgent concern about an ugly racial issue that had occurred and potential for rioting at a time when the President's Summit on Community Service was scheduled to convene in Philadelphia; as well as investment by the city in hopes of winning one of the presidential conventions in the next election—what was important, he said, were implications for how we deal with events including Louis Farrakhan within an effective community relations strategy.

Mayor Rendell, who is Jewish, had been close to the Jewish community, Siegel observed, and the city had officially kept Louis Farrakhan at arm's length. However, the special circumstances underlying the mayor's decision prompted other groups, including coalition partners, to support the mayor and to puzzle over the Jewish community's refusal to do so. Almost no one, no politician, no coalition partner, took exception to Rendell's move, Siegel reported. As a result, the Jewish community found itself isolated. Indeed, the observation was made that if the community was not represented this time, some people would miss them. After a while, however, no one would remember they were ever there. Moreover, if the Jewish community continued to stay away, after a while no one would remember that the Jewish community was *ever* at the table. This creates a difficult issue that must be addressed, Siegel continued. Do we refuse to come to the table? If we are not there, have we allowed those

we wish to marginalize to, instead, set the agenda and
marginalize the Jewish community? Siegel noted that
the Philadelphia Jewish community is now in the
process of reevaluating how the community should
respond to these situations.

If you had been a member of the JCRC, how would you have voted?
What would your conclusion have been regarding the best policy for
the national Jewish community? Why?

*A Real Dilemma: Responding to the Nation of Islam's Effort to Be
Part of the Mainstream*

In the summer of 1994, the oldest and largest civil rights organization, the NAACP, facilitated a black leadership summit to
address the grave challenges facing the black community. Invited
to the summit was a broad range of leadership, including a
number of separationist advocates who disavow the traditional
integrationist stance of mainstream agencies like the NAACP.
Included in that group was Minister Farrakhan. Taking place six
months after the controversy involving Nation of Islam
spokesperson Khalid Muhammad's hate-filled speech at Kean
College in which Muhammad attacked not only Jews, gays, and
Catholics but moderate black leadership, many were concerned
about Minister Farrakhan's invitation.

The Jewish community had to decide what to say about the
summit, in particular whether to protest publicly Minister
Farrakhan's involvement. The summit raised a broader question
as well. Was the willingness of mainstream black groups to participate in public events with, and work with, such extremist anti-
Semitic leaders and organizations cause to reevaluate the Jewish
community's relationship with its longtime allies in the black
community? Critics argued that the NAACP and other groups
were abandoning their traditional course of intergroup relations
and legitimizing Minister Farrakhan's hate speech and anti-
Semitism by including him in such a forum. Supporters of the
NAACP responded that inviting someone to a summit of the
black community no more reflects legitimizing or agreeing with

their views than did Prime Minister Rabin's meeting with PLO Chairman Yassir Arafat in the early 1990s reflect agreement with the PLO's views. Further, they argued, at a time of crisis in the black community, they could not turn away any resources that might help, and the Nation of Islam had done good work in a number of inner cities in addressing the problems of crime, violence, and drug abuse. They didn't need to agree with them on everything to work with them on some things.

Response

While the summit meetings were protested by a small group of Jewish activists, mainstream Jewish organizations remained restrained for several reasons. First, it was felt by most that Blacks have the right to invite whomever they wish to a black summit and neither Jews nor any other nonblack group had a right to determine the invitation list. We might express our concerns and regrets but must recognize that ultimately only Blacks can make these decisions. Second, the community was far more concerned with what came out of the meetings than who was invited in, i.e., whose agenda would prevail at the summit: that of the mainstream integrationists or the separationists; that of the inheritors of Dr. King's message of love and tolerance or the hatemongers. Third, there was also a recognition that publicly protesting this invitation would only play into the hands of the extremist elements of the black community by turning this event into a Black-Jewish issue, by putting those who disagree with Minister Farrakhan into a posture of defending his presence on procedural grounds, and by giving significantly more national publicity to Minister Farrakhan.

As to the NAACP generally, while there was widespread concern and confusion regarding whether the distinguished agency was in fact charting a new course in the mid-nineties away from its traditional integrationist, coalitional values, the president and chairman who had presided over the summit were voted out of office (albeit on other grounds) and new leaders, committed to continuing the NAACP's traditional intergroup cooperative strategy, were voted into office. The NAACP remains an organization of over 2,000 chapters that day in and day out do the nitty-gritty work of civil rights and do so in far closer cooperation with the Jewish community than with groups like the Nation of Islam. It was generally felt at the time of the summit (and then again at the time of the Million Man march in 1995, when Jews generally did not criticize the march for Minister Farrakhan's leadership) that the real crisis will come if the NAACP or any of the other mainstream coalition partners of the Jewish community attempts to bring Minister Farrakhan into any of the intergroup coalitions of which we are a part. That would be intolerable for many of the coalition partners whom he has attacked and would precipitate a major crisis in the traditional civil rights coalition.

Looking Ahead

Can Black-Jewish relations be salvaged? Tensions over Minister Farrakhan and the bloody Crown Heights confrontation certainly brought the two groups to a historical low point. But there are still substantial grounds for hope. Many Blacks and Jews continue to share a vision of a just, generous, and open society. Despite our dramatic economic differences, public opinion polls show that our attitudes and values are remarkably alike: we both recoil against bigotry and advocate for a primary role for government in solving social inequity; and we are essential partners in virtually every successful coalition for social justice.

In presidential, congressional, and local elections, Jews and Blacks vote more alike than any other identifiable groups. Approximately 70 percent of Jews and 90 percent of Blacks opposed the 1984 Reagan and the 1988 Bush candidacies; no other groups gave the Democratic candidates a majority. Even higher percentages of Jews and similar percentages of Blacks supported Bill Clinton in 1992 and 1996—85 percent and 83 percent, respectively, for the Jewish vote and 80 percent and 84 percent, respectively, for the black vote.

In fact, in communities across America, Blacks and Jews are working together daily to address their common concerns. The Religious Action Center of Reform Judaism, through its Marjorie Kovler Institute for Black-Jewish Relations, published a manual on cooperative programming in black churches and Jewish synagogues, based on existing successful programs from across the country. Over 250 such programs are described at length. Consider the following:

- In Los Angeles, black and Jewish doctors, nurses, and congregants sponsor an annual health fair that serves over three hundred people with basic checkups, blood work, referrals to city agencies, and follow-ups with local clinics.

- In Hamden, Connecticut, a black church and a Jewish synagogue have founded an interfaith AIDS network that provides financial and emotional support for people living with AIDS.

- In Plainfield, New Jersey, a black Episcopal church and a Reform synagogue jointly bought a dilapidated building and members of both congregations rehabilitated it to house low-income families.

- In Manhasset and Great Neck, Long Island, the black and Jewish communities created a summer employment workshop to teach teens job-hunting skills. The same coalition also closed down a crack house that threatened the safety of a local housing project.

In October 1996, the Religious Action Center of Reform Judaism, in conjunction with the United Negro College Fund (UNCF), the National Association for the Advancement of Colored People (NAACP), and Hillel, the Foundation for Jewish Life on Campus, cosponsored a conference that gathered black and Jewish students, faculty, and administration from diverse colleges and universities across the nation to review and analyze successful models of cooperative programming, dialogue, and study between Blacks and Jews. The conference focused on identifying the common elements of effective programs that build and strengthen Black-Jewish relations on college campuses. The participants left with a renewed pledge to continue and strengthen their efforts to work together and to foster close ties between the communities.

Such mutual efforts promote better Black-Jewish relations. But lasting improvement will require Blacks and Jews to change their perceptions of each other. This generation of Blacks—especially young people—has little awareness of past Jewish contributions to human equality. And even those who are aware want to know "What have you done for me lately?" This attitude often infuriates Jews, who want to feel some appreciation for sacrifices they have made to achieve equal rights for Blacks and other minorities.

Black youths will have to understand recent history, including the Holocaust and its profound impact on the Jewish psyche, if any new relationship is to be forged.

And Jews, too, in addition to learning about African-American history, will have to modulate injured feelings and stop expecting constant gratitude. Jews must understand that Blacks see us as people who block their hopes for progress as often as we advance them—in affirmative action, in minority housing, as well as in Jewish support for the death penalty, which many Blacks see as code words for "get tough with Blacks."

Can this drift be arrested? While at times it is difficult to look ahead with confidence, we must try because both Jews and Blacks have a common stake in an open and compassionate society.

When Jews and Blacks square off against each other, we elate our common enemies—Nazis, the KKK, and other foes of equality in America. Whether we like it or not, Blacks and Jews are joined together in a common destiny. It is time to renew that special relationship and to unite in the struggle against poverty, ignorance, bigotry, crime, and an ineffective welfare system. But the old Black-Jewish paradigm is gone. What is emerging is a new and much broader coalition of decency, of which both Blacks and Jews are important members.

LATINO- AND ASIAN-AMERICANS: TWO EMERGING POWERS IN AMERICAN SOCIETY

By the year 2015, Latinos are expected to exceed Blacks as the largest ethnic minority in America. In the Twin Cities of St. Paul and Minneapolis, for example, Latinos already have replaced Blacks as the largest minority group. In Los Angeles, nearly one-third of public school students are now of Latino origin, but the percentage in kindergarten is almost 50 percent. In Seattle, the Hispanic population is growing almost twice as fast as that of non-Latino whites. High levels of immigration, larger than any since the turn of the century, together with a high birthrate have made Latinos the fastest-growing minority group in American life.

Latino power can grow significantly if Spanish-speaking communities think of themselves as a coherent and unified group rather than as Puerto Ricans, Cubans, Hondurans, or Mexican-Americans. The tide of Latinos who come, legally or illegally, to escape poverty and unpopular regimes in Latin America has become a flood. The Latino population is markedly young, urban, and spread across the entire United States. There are profound differences among various Latino groups, including their relative assimilation into American life and their readiness to reach out to other ethnic and minority groups in common cause.

There is a broad range of issues in which the Jewish and Latino communities have common concerns, including issues of civil rights, immigration, social justice, health, welfare, and education. Jews and Latinos have been allied in the past, most notably in support of union leader Cesar Chávez defending the rights of American farmworkers. And Jews remain concerned about the high rate of joblessness among Latinos, which cuts off avenues of hope and improvement—a problem compounded by the fact that 47 percent have had less than a high school education as compared with 27 percent of Blacks and 15 percent of whites.

But there are serious limitations to our relationship. The recent arrival of many Latinos to the United States means that we have little shared history. They know little of Jewish concerns, Israel, Soviet Jewry, and church-state separation. We are often limited in communication because of language differences. And the voting patterns of Latinos are far more diverse than those of Blacks and Jews.

The Jewish community has even less contact with the various Asian-American communities. Many of them, particularly from Southeast Asia, are also recent arrivals. We do not share a common history, common language, or even the common Judeo-Christian religious roots we share with Latinos and Blacks. Asian-Americans have traditionally been conservative politically; a significant majority have voted Republican until the late 1990s.

Yet we have much in common with Asian-Americans: strong family and community structures, ancient historical and cultural traditions, a tendency to place great emphasis on academics. All of these offer opportunities for coalitional activity that we need to explore.

As both Latinos and Asian-Americans become more potent political forces in America, Jewish self-interest will mandate that we make a conscientious effort to reach out to these communities and strengthen our coalitional activities with them.

A Real Dilemma: Latino-Jewish Relations in New York City

In New York City's Washington Heights section, a community of politically powerful Orthodox Jews lives side by side with a politically underrepresented Dominican majority. Having lived in that part of the city since the 1930s, Jews have formed their own schools and cultivated a strong internal sense of community. The Dominicans, by and large recent immigrants, are working to establish themselves, as have many other immigrant groups before them.

In recognition of serious overcrowding, the New York City school board decided to build a number of schools in the surrounding area. One of the schools was to be located directly behind a yeshiva. The Orthodox community opposed the location, claiming that traffic patterns and construction obstacles made it an inappropriate site. Despite Orthodox protests, the school board maintained that this location was the best choice to serve the needs of the community.

For the area's Reform Jews, the situation was also problematic. As the children and grandchildren of immigrants whose families achieved success through public education, they understood and empathized with the Dominican community's desire to improve public education. But as Jews, they felt themselves a part of *Klal Yisrael* and though they disagreed with the Orthodox position, they did not want to take issue with it openly. Ultimately, the Reform Jews accepted the school board's assessment that the site was appropriate. In fact, many were convinced that the Orthodox concerns shielded an underlying fear that the new school would bring minority crime to the neighborhood, endangering Orthodox youths attending the yeshiva.

Nevertheless, many Reform Jews worried about creating a rift in the Jewish community, believing that the damage to intra-Jewish relations might outweigh the benefits of taking a public stand on the underlying ethical issue.

Should the Reform synagogue in the area have taken a public stand on this important community issue?

Response

Temple Beth Am in Washington Heights decided that the most constructive approach for the entire community required their public support for the construction of the new school.

In addition to supporting the school's construction, Temple Beth Am initiated several programs that would build bridges between local Jews and Dominicans. The congregation stimulated efforts in both communities to increase enrollment in the public schools and to develop a multicultural curriculum. In addition, such interfaith activities as joint worship services provided an opportunity for the two communities to work to increase understanding.

NATIVE AMERICANS

While Blacks and Latinos suffer conditions of great deprivation, arguably their status is better than that of Native Americans.

> As we near the beginning of the twenty-first century, American Indians (Native Americans) remain largely trapped by nineteenth-century poverty: 16 percent of reservation homes lack electricity, 21 percent an indoor toilet, and 56 percent a telephone. And for the most part, federal policy makers and administrators are still held captive by the ghosts of paternalism and dependency.... This has created a federal bureaucracy ensnared in red tape and riddled with fraud, mismanagement, and waste.

The above comes from a 1990 congressional report—the forty-third such study since 1792—on the disastrous consequences of United States policies on Native American affairs. In 1990, 45 percent of all reservation-based Native Americans lived below the poverty line. Roughly half of all adult Native Americans are unemployed; of those working, a majority make less than $7,000 a year. By law, Native American–owned businesses are entitled to preferential treatment where federal contracts are concerned. In practice, however, the Bureau of Indian Affairs, much despised by Native Americans, has virtually ignored enforcement, often offering such contracts to phony front companies run by non–Native Americans.

The 1990 report also found widespread child abuse by teachers at bureau schools and charged the BIA with failure to protect the health of Native Americans. On reservations, three out of eight people die before they reach the age of forty-five (in contrast with one out of eight in the general population). Housing is mostly substandard and much is uninhabitable. It will take more than a momentary spasm of national sympathy, such as Kevin Costner evoked with his award-winning movie *Dances with Wolves*, for America to come to grips with the tragic plight of its indigenous people.

While some effort has been made to build relations between Native Americans and Jews, these two communities rarely cross paths. Jews live mostly in urban or suburban middle-class neighborhoods. Native Americans, the poorest single group in America, live mostly in isolated rural areas. Yet Jews and Native Americans have much in common.

Both Jews and Native Americans share the legacy of oral traditions and historical memories of exile from their homelands. Many of their religious rituals are grounded in the cycles of life, in agriculture, and in connection to the land. We have both suffered at the hands of majority communities frightened by our "strangeness," eager to force "outsiders" to fit their perception of the world. Unable to fit, Jews and Native Americans have undergone the trials of ghettoization and persecution. Ironically, Native Americans and Jews both consider 1492 a turning point in their history of persecution.

Contemporary Native Americans and Jews share certain common concerns as well. In the face of powerful assimilating cultural forces, both seek ways to preserve their heritage. However, Native Americans face the additional burdens of widespread poverty, unemployment, and illiteracy in their heroic efforts to recapture and reinvigorate nearly extinguished cultures.

Cross-cultural understanding is the key to Native American–Jewish cooperation. A good example of this type of positive interaction is illustrated by a youth group from Central Synagogue in New York, led by Rabbi Tom Weiner, that journeyed to the Rosebud Reservation in South Dakota. During their three-week visit, the students participated in various Lakota ceremonies and experienced a number of customs: most memorably, preparation for the summer Sun Dance.

The Native Americans found inspiration in the Hebrew songs sung every night and in the Shabbat services conducted by the group. Recalling the experience, Rabbi Weiner stated, "We, in the end, helped them in the practice of their newly rediscovered tradition, just as our students became more knowledgeable and proud of being Jews."

All this points to the possibility for a rich Jewish–Native American dialogue if we can create opportunities for such encounters. Visits to reservations are but one example. Some Jews live near reservations, providing greater opportunity for common activity, and some Jews have played and continue to play an active role in protecting the religious rights of Native Americans. Additionally, Native Americans face the task of developing their own agriculture and small industry. Several exchanges have taken place between kibbutzim and reservations, and Israeli drip irrigation technology, for example, has greatly increased the agricultural yields among the Navajo. This type of creative approach to Jewish–Native American relations holds open the hope for additional constructive exchanges in the future.

A Real Dilemma: Gambling on Reservations

In the 1990s, improvement in the plight of certain Native American tribes resulted from the explosion of gambling casinos on Indian reservations. Limited sovereignty frees the tribes to negotiate with states to create and maintain gambling endeavors if the state already sanctions gaming. Although many tribes decided not to sanction or participate in gaming efforts, over 120 tribes have created over 131 such casinos in twenty-three different states. With no less than 60 percent of all profits going to the tribes for government and social services, the millions in new revenues have provided for improvements in education, health care, reservation infrastructure, and employment for thousands of Indians, as well as spurring economic growth in the surrounding areas.

The UAHC and the CCAR, although staunch supporters of

Native American sovereignty, have long had qualms about legalized gambling, believing such organized activities prey disproportionately on the poor and result in widespread gambling addiction. Despite this objection, does the benefit to the Indians and respect for their unique rights justify these casinos or should the UAHC and the CCAR oppose them?

Response

Caught on the horns of this moral dilemma, as of early 1998, no Jewish organization has formally endorsed or opposed Indian reservation gambling, although the CCAR did decide on formal opposition to legalized gambling generally. Increasingly, however, national religious groups are looking more carefully at the issues of both legalized gambling and Indian gaming as the states, in part spurred by the success of the casinos, are legalizing casinos across the nation and expanding state lotteries. With the increasing momentum of the antigaming effort, this issue cannot be avoided much longer.

MULTICULTURALISM

In the 1990s, a new debate facing the civil rights movement pitted identity on one side and the problematic ideal of America as a "melting pot" on the other. The debate has focused on what is known as "multiculturalism": programs and curricula to promote racial and ethnic diversity and respect for differing backgrounds.

The issues raised in this debate go to the heart of America's understanding of itself. This nation has traditionally been uncommonly hospitable to people of diverse backgrounds. But for most of our history, the working assumption has been that the diversity would, in time, diminish, that each new cohort of immigrants would, in a generation or two, adapt to the American environment and become "American."

But what does "American" mean? By the year 2020, most Americans will be of non-European background. Is diversity really something to overcome, or is it actually a source of strength? And how can we ask or expect that people will assimilate as long as bigotry and discrimination remain so conspicuous a part of the American way?

On the other hand, if we choose to celebrate America's diversity, do we not run the risk that we will fragment, that we will end up with a mosaic with no grout to hold the stones together or connect them to one another?

The arena where these issues are most frequently and contentiously played out today is the college campus. It is one thing to move beyond Western tradition by insisting that the curriculum be opened up to include the history and literature of diverse groups. It is another to claim that only members of particular groups are competent to teach the history and literature of their group or that the Western tradition should be regarded as "just another" tradition rather than as the tradition that has most powerfully shaped this country, its institutions, and its patterns. How in fact can we ensure that a mature recognition and acceptance of America's diversity will become a source of strength rather than of fragmentation? And where in all this do the Jews—with our own history and our own literature—fit?

The Jewish community recognizes that the goal of multicultural education is fully compatible, in theory, with the diversity and pluralism it advocates. We are mindful of the benefits that we and others will derive from the exposure to the range of human experience and to the range of the Jewish experience. But we are concerned when under the banner of diversity, inept and even fraudulent scholarship is endorsed, racialism is encouraged, and walls rather than bridges are erected.

··· 10 ···

Safeguarding Our Civil Liberties

A Real Dilemma: Anti-Semitic Rock Lyrics

In the early 1990s, the rap group Public Enemy—already embroiled in a controversy ignited by the anti-Semitic statements of one of its members—released a song entitled "Welcome to the Terrordome," which included the following lyrics:

> Crucifixion ain't no fiction
> So-called chosen, frozen
> Apology made to whoever pleases
> till they got me like Jesus.

These words smack of anti-Semitism. They revisit the repulsive and discredited charge that the Jews killed Jesus. Most Jews would agree that these offensive and inciting lyrics do not belong on the airwaves or in music stores. The wide circulation that the recording industry affords its products would seem to justify such concern. Similar concern about anti-women, anti-gay, anti-police, pro-drug, pro-violence, and pro-promiscuity lyrics have been growing throughout the 1990s.

But would banning these lyrics violate the First Amendment to the Constitution? Are Public Enemy's lyrics a form of free speech, protected by the very same Constitution that allows every citizen to speak his or her conscience free from the censorship of government and of society? Does not the rap group have a legal right to sing its lyrics, Anti-Semitic or not, just as other groups or individuals have the legal right to criticize them? Or does the right of free speech end when incitement to bigotry begins? What about the lyrics of rap artist Ice Cube, who in "Death Certificate" called for the assassination of a Jewish music group manager and threatened Koreans with death? Do such threats make a difference?

This dilemma is particularly acute for the Jewish community. We are, of course, committed to the fight against anti-Semitism. At the same time, we have remained vociferous critics of any attempt to curtail free speech. In the Public Enemy dilemma, these two agendas are pitted against each other. Danny Goldberg, former chair of the American Civil Liberties Union (ACLU) Foundation of Southern California and now president of Mercury Records, summed up the conflict when he wrote that "the real issue here lies in the conflict between the need for free expression and the desire to fight bigotry."

Should Jewish organizations have supported efforts to ban such expressions of hate?

Response

The debate involving Public Enemy's lyrics illustrates that Jews are found on both sides. Universally, Jewish groups denounced the lyrics as an overt and offensive attack on the Jewish community. A few Jews demanded that the song be removed from the airwaves.

Others, including the UAHC, feared that government censorship would diminish our freedoms, stifle artistic expression, and lead us down a path on which there would eventually be restriction of unpopular expression of all kinds, including that of minority groups such as Jews. While vigorously opposing censorship, some argued that the best way to deal with offensive speech is not to ban it but to condemn it and continually delegitimize it.

If American Jews have attained an unprecedented measure of security and success in America, one major reason is the majestic sweep of the Constitution and its Bill of Rights. Indeed, the Constitution protects every American but especially those who are, by definition, different (i.e., minorities). For Jews, the Bill of Rights is the very sanctuary of our liberties. It keeps us from being what we have been virtually everywhere else in all the centuries of our wanderings: strangers at the gates, subject to the vagaries of popular opinion and prejudice.

Here in America, as nowhere else in our long history, Jews as individual citizens enjoy equal justice. Here, too, we are free to live Jewish lives and to speak out as a community on great public issues in accordance with the ethical insights of our tradition.

If the Bill of Rights is our primary protection, it is nonetheless true that tension sometimes exists between the rights of free expression and our sense of dignity and security. Every year seems to generate new examples of such dilemmas:

- A university invites Minister Louis Farrakhan, considered a blatant anti-Semite by most Jews, to address the student body.

- A gang of neofascist skinheads seeks to recruit students at a local junior high school.

- A former high official of the Ku Klux Klan runs for the United States Senate.

- A racist organization runs newspaper advertisements inviting open debate on whether the Holocaust really happened.

- Chat rooms on the Internet expose children to pornography and sexual predators.

AMERICA'S REVOLUTIONARY CONTRIBUTION TO THE CONCEPT OF RIGHTS

What makes America so special? What makes this so special and unique a place in the Jewish Diaspora? To put it simply: The American Revolution turned history upside down. Or rather, it turned the understanding of the relationship between the state and the people upside down.

Prior to the creation of America, government granted rights according to an individual's membership in some group or class. These rights were "derivative" or "subsidiary." Government gained its authority from God, and monarchs ruled as instruments of God. Wherever Jews lived, the leaders of their communities negotiated the rights their members were accorded. What government could give, it could just as easily—

and often did—take away. The American Revolution changed all that by building government on the concept of inalienable rights.

The true revolutionary genius of America was to reverse the relationship between the group and the individual, declaring that human beings possessed certain inalienable rights granted to them by God, not by governments. Expressed loosely in the Declaration of Independence, then later written into law in the Bill of Rights, these rights included freedom of speech, the press, worship, and assembly. Rather than drawing authority from God and ladling out rights, government drew its power only from those being governed and existed to protect the inalienable rights God had granted *them*.

Thus America became the first country in the world in which one's basic rights were not subject to arbitrary limitation by the government or the whims of the majority.

In America, it does not matter whether all 260 million Americans believe that what you say is absurd; it does not matter whether the 535 members of the Congress, the nine justices of the Supreme Court, and the president of the United States agree that the way you worship is wrong. So long as your exercise of your rights does not interfere with the exercise of the rights of anyone else or does not endanger the nation that secures your rights, you have the inalienable right to say what you want and to worship the way you please.

Since the late 1970s, a growing force of religious conservatives loosely known as the Religious Right have begun to challenge this fundamental concept of American democracy. They would now flip American history on its head and create a nation based on certain fundamental and unalterable *Christian* values, in which rights and power would flow from religious beliefs. The threat to Jews, to religious and other minorities, and to mainstream Christians is clear: our rights would once again be subject to the benevolence of others. (A more detailed discussion of the Religious Right and its impact on religious liberties follows in the next chapter.)

Throughout the 1980s, the Religious Right and its secular allies again and again tried to rein in what it saw as a far-too-permissive society. It tried to control what we read in libraries and schools (censorship), how we pray (school prayer), what we learn in biology class (scientific creationism), and what we see in our art galleries or on our televisions. It organized politically, meeting at the grassroots level, and gained a growing following in state and local governments. This led to more and more members of Congress also coming from the Religious Right; but it has not yet prevailed in its efforts to reshape national policy, usually losing on key congressional votes. On the other hand, these radically different visions of America fought it out on the political battleground of the 1980s. As with Senator McCarthy in the 1950s, the Jerry Falwells and Pat Robertsons of the Religious Right represented those who were afraid of the great American experiment of democracy, afraid to test their beliefs and policies in the robust clash of ideas that is at the center of the "free marketplace of ideas," so central to democracy. That they are willing to jeopardize the First Amendment and our basic rights to impose their goals on our society alarmed all who cherish freedom. Their argument that the focus on "rights" had gone too far resonates for many Americans who believe America is slipping into a social and moral morass. Many Americans express the belief that rights need to be better balanced against responsibilities.

Are there times when our rights should be restrained, and how do we determine when those times are? Contrary to what many in the religious and radical secular Right assert, the courts have long found an appropriate way to balance the rights of the individual against the needs of society.

COMPELLING STATE INTEREST AND FUNDAMENTAL RIGHTS

We know that the Constitution and the Declaration of Independence hold that fundamental rights are ours by dint of our humanity. But what happens when a fundamental right comes face-to-face with a conflicting societal interest? How do we decide when the societal interest must give way and when the fundamental right must give way? How do we avoid creating an anarchic society in which murder may be defended as a ritual sacrifice without creating a fascist society in which every individual is subservient to the state? In most areas of constitutional law, the United States Supreme Court has answered this question by ruling that fundamental rights could be abridged by the state only when the state could prove a *compelling* interest in doing so and only if the state pursued that interest in a manner that abridged that right as *narrowly as possible*.

The most famous illustration of this is the restriction against yelling "fire" in a crowded theater when there is no fire. An individual's right to free speech must give way to the state's "compelling interest" in public safety. And while the state can narrowly prevent one from saying something that endangers public safety, the state cannot prevent a person from otherwise talking in theaters.

This concept of compelling state interest has worked as an elegant mechanism for balancing one's individual's rights against one's responsibilities to the state and the community. But events since 1990 have begun to seriously erode the concept of compelling state interest, endangering all our rights.

In 1990, in *Employment Division of Oregon* v. *Smith* (a fuller discussion can be found in the following chapter, "Religious Liberty: Will the Wall Come Tumbling Down?"), the Supreme Court entirely discarded the "compelling state interest" in cases where a generally applicable law happened to bar an individual from his or her "free exercise of religion." The Court ruled that as long as a law did not single out a religious practice, it could be applied in a way that *in its effect* barred specific religious practices. (So, for example, a Catholic priest could theoretically be charged with contributing to the delinquency of a minor for serving communion wine to a minor as long as the law in question applied to anyone serving wine to a minor in any context.) Now, to prevent religious rituals from being affected by general state laws, we must lobby state legislatures for religious exemptions rather than having these rights protected by the courts. This turns the two-centuries-old American understanding of fundamental rights on its head, suggesting now that these rights no longer proceed from our own humanity but must be granted by elected legislatures and subjected to the whims of the majority. If the Court applies the same analysis to our other fundamental rights, then we will be saying *Kaddish* for our basic liberties in this decade of the two hundredth anniversary of the Bill of Rights.

When Free Speech and Jewish Security Collide

In the American experience, Jews have tended to be strong supporters of civil liberties. It is no accident that Jews constitute a significant proportion of the membership of the American Civil Liberties Union (ACLU), the principal nongovernmental agency in America dedicated to safeguarding the First Amendment of the Constitution. To the ACLU, the right to a free press and to free expression is virtually absolute for everyone, including Nazis and Communist party members. To begin to make exceptions, even in a good cause, is to begin to whittle away at the force of the American Constitution. To its critics, the ACLU is rigid, unrealistic, and extremist.

For the past fifty years, American Jews have tended to identify Jewish security with the maintenance of the very constitutional freedoms the ACLU seeks to protect.

Nothing dramatized these tensions more vividly than the gut-wrenching conflict over the right of Nazis to march in Skokie, Illinois.

A Real Dilemma: Should Nazis March in Skokie?

Skokie, Illinois, is a suburb of Chicago that in 1978 had a population of approximately 60,000 persons, including some 40,000 Jews (of whom 7,000 are survivors of Nazi concentration camps). To America—and perhaps to much of the world—Skokie is remembered as the place where American Nazis sought to organize a protest march in 1978 "to combat Jewish control of America." City officials refused to grant a license for such a demonstration. The Nazis went to court, asserting that their First Amendment right to march publicly in Nazi uniform and to express their ideas had been violated.

The American Civil Liberties Union went to court in *support* of the right of the Nazis to march. Opponents argued that just as one cannot yell "fire" falsely in a crowded theater because of the harm it would do, American Nazis displaying swastikas and yelling anti-Jewish obscenities should not be allowed to inflict emotional harm on concentration camp survivors. Leaders of the Jewish Defense League (JDL), a militant right-wing Jewish group that advocated using force to protect Jewish interests, announced that whatever the courts held, the JDL would forcibly prevent the Nazis from marching. Mainstream Jewish organizations had to respond both to the Nazis and to the JDL. What should they have done?

Response

While most Jewish organizations agreed that Nazis have freedom of speech, even for their repellent message, the Jewish community split on the substantive issue: do the Nazis have the right to bring that noxious message to a specific neighborhood where it would cause pain to a particular group (e.g., the Holocaust survivors of Skokie)? The UAHC, while continuing efforts to have the location switched, decided not to express formal opposition to the march for substantive and tactical reasons. First, in our view, the effort to block them had given this tiny crew of misfits millions of dollars worth of publicity. Second, most decent Americans oppose Nazi ideology, and this should not be Jews vs. Nazis but Americans vs. Nazis. Finally, because we were doomed to lose in the courts, we decided that it would be better to get the march over with and off the network news.

In the end, as the danger of violent confrontation reached a fever pitch, the Nazi march was relocated from Skokie to Marquette Park in Chicago, where it passed with only minor disturpbances.

The Skokie dilemma raised many disturbing questions among America's Jews. How secure are we really? Can we rely for our safety on the abstractions of constitutional safeguards? Should we support Canada's approach, where speech advocating group hatred is a crime? Have we become so liberal we have bartered away our particular Jewish interests for a vague universalism? Or, on the other hand, have we become so intimidated by extremists that we would sacrifice long-term protections (preservation of the fundamental freedoms enshrined in the First Amendment) for short-term gains (banning anti-Semitic displays)? Has the Jewish community abandoned its faith in civil liberties now that the issue has come home to roost for us, just as some Jews gave up on racial integration when it came to *our* schools and *our* neighborhoods?

A Real Dilemma: Jews for Jesus

A branch of Jews for Jesus reserved space for a conference in a local hotel. The town's rabbi criticized the hotel for allowing its premises to be used by an organization that misleads the public by pretending to be a movement of Judaism but is repudiated by all branches of Judaism because its central tenets violate the central beliefs of Judaism. The area ACLU defended the hotel's right to rent to Jews for Jesus, however repugnant the group may have been to other Jews. What would you have advised? Should the Jewish community have sought to persuade the hotel to cancel the meeting? Should other, less restrictive options have been employed, such as organizing a counter meeting to educate the public about the "false advertising of Jews for Jesus"? Does the right of free speech extend to those who advertise falsely?

Response

Many Jewish groups did try to get the meeting canceled, and they succeeded, arguing this was not a free speech issue but one of false advertising. The Supreme Court has held that there is a "compelling state interest" in preventing false advertising, even if it means limiting free speech. In this situation, the Jewish community pressured the hotel into canceling the meeting. Jews for Jesus went to court, claiming invasion of its First Amendment rights. The court did not sustain their claim. But was it censorship?

CENSORSHIP

Censorship can be defined as any action by an individual, a group of individuals, or the government that results in the removal, alteration, or repression of a particular item because that item is deemed objectionable, preventing other individuals or groups of individuals from gaining access to that item. The "item" may be a book, a piece of art, a theater performance, a school curriculum, or anything else that can be defined as a form of expression.

Since censorship can be both direct (through governmental sanction) and indirect (through the withdrawing of otherwise approved funding), the consequences are more important than the motivations. For example, an attempt to prevent the American Nazi party from distributing its literature, however well intentioned, is still censorship because it results in preventing the Nazis from arguing their point of view and preventing those who wish to be exposed to the Nazis' message from doing so. Attempts to restrict public funding of the arts on the grounds that tax dollars should not be used to support what many might consider obscene can be another manifestation of censorship. While it is true that the government isn't constitutionally required to fund the arts, once it decides to do so, should it be required to provide funding solely on the basis of artistic merit, as opposed to the *message* of the art? Is it censorship when the government refuses funding to admittedly good art on the grounds that the allocations committee finds the art's message offensive? Opponents of government funding for art they deem offensive argue that while the government can't ban the offensive art, the Constitution doesn't require that the government use our tax dollars to support it.

Both nationally and locally, Jews have been outspoken opponents of censorship, believing that the First Amendment becomes an empty, meaningless promise when applied selectively. When Jews have espoused ideologies or have been members of political groups considered to be offensive by many (a few as members of the Communist party in the 1930s; many more as members of civil rights organizations and as anti–Vietnam War protesters in the sixties and early seventies), we have been quick to condemn the selective application of the First Amendment. We have asserted that even those who advocate the overthrow of the United States government should not be prosecuted as long as their words are not translated into illegal acts. Jews, in our commitment to free speech both as Jews and as members of a democratic society, must not falter when it is now *our* ox that is being gored.

A Real Dilemma: Protecting the Flag

In 1989, the U.S. Supreme Court, in a unanimous decision, decided that flag burning was a form of political expression protected by the First Amendment's free speech clause. Many conservative groups responded to the Court's controversial decision in fury, calling for a constitutional amendment to protect the flag. Such an amendment would essentially exempt flag desecration from the protections of the First Amendment, allowing state and local governments to outlaw desecration of the American flag. The amendment would for the first time in American history alter and limit the First Amendment and would allow state and local governments to imprison individuals for engaging in what is now a constitutionally protected form of political expression. Throughout the 1990s, members of Congress have tried several times, and failed, to add such an amendment to the Constitution, but the efforts will continue.

Proponents of the amendment argue that our founders gave the people the right to amend the Constitution if and when they saw fit and that amending the Constitution is a just exercise of that right. They also argue that the flag should be viewed as a uniquely revered national object and not used as a vehicle of politicized speech. Because it is unique, they assert, this amendment will not be a precedent for future amendments. Further, some proponents seek to make this vote a test of patriotism, suggesting that those who support the right of flag desecration are betraying America.

Opponents believe that liberty requires protecting all forms of expression, even speech that is offensive. They acknowledge that when the Supreme Court ruled on flag burning, it applied the *principle* of freedom of speech in a way that many people found offensive. But they assert that First Amendment law often involves highly controversial, deeply offensive forms of speech. It is inevitable that the Supreme Court will protect some forms of speech that many believe are wrong—indeed, this protection of unpopular, minority views is precisely what the First Amendment's free speech clause is all about. If we amend the principle of free speech because we do not like one particular application of that principle (in this case, flag desecration), then we open the door to altering the principle every time the Supreme Court protects an offensive and unpopular form of speech or expression. It would not be long before the First Amendment would be rendered largely meaningless by various amendments and exemptions. What should the Jewish community do?

Response

Most in the Jewish community oppose the flag desecration amendment. Opposition to the flag desecration amendment does not, in any way, shape, or form, denote support for flag desecration. They assert that opposition to the flag desecration amendment is a statement in support of the sanctity of our very first freedoms—freedoms the Jewish community has experienced nowhere else in the Diaspora.

While the founders did envision amending the Constitution to enable it to change with the times, they made it especially difficult precisely because they did not wish to see the document amended frivolously. This amendment strikes at the core of our constitutional and civil rights, proposing to change forever a set of rights that lie at the core of American freedom. We need to think long and hard about whether or not we want to tinker with the First Amendment, and a review of the amendment suggests it is a very bad idea.

Since the ratification of the Bill of Rights, most amendments to the Constitution have been procedural in nature (limiting the term of the president, changing the method of electing senators, clarifying the order of succession in the event of the death or disability of the president), and those that have substantively dealt with individual rights have always *expanded* those rights and/or extended existing rights to additional groups (such as the amendments granting voting rights to women and lowering the federal voting age to eighteen). We have never amended the Constitution explicitly to restrict previously enumerated individual rights—something this amendment undeniably would do.

Ironically, the strongest evidence that the Supreme Court was correct comes from those who strenuously oppose the decision. Opponents of the decision argue that the flag is an unmistakable symbol of the United States of America. They are right, and that is precisely why the Supreme Court was right. Since the flag is an unmistakable political symbol, desecrating it is undeniably a form of political expression. Unlike pornographic, commercial, and violently provocative speech (so-called "fighting words"), all of which the Supreme Court has seen fit to restrict in the past and all of which arguably lie on the periphery of the First Amendment, political expression lies at the very heart of our freedom of speech. Offensive as flag burning is—indeed, precisely because it is such a *politically* powerful form of expression— banning flag burning would be the beginning of the end of the First Amendment.

Those who suggest that America is endangered by flag desecration have mistaken symbol for substance. It is precisely by protecting the most offensive forms of political expression—and it is hard to imagine anything more politically offensive and uncivil than the burning of the flag—that we display confidence in and strengthen the very core values of American democracy that the flag represents.

Censorship and the Jewish Tradition

Judaism was, arguably, the first legal tradition in history to enshrine the concept of majority and minority views. If one reads the classic texts of the rabbinic era, the *Mishnah* and the *Gemara*, every page brims with the arguments both of the majority and of those who dissented from them, recognizing that each reflected aspects of God's truth. "These *and* these are the words of God," the Talmud observes about these disputes. (*Eruvin* 13b) Implicit in such an approach was the realization that today's minority could become tomorrow's majority.

Our almost automatic opposition to censorship, wherever it occurs, reflects a long Jewish history in which learning and the cultivation of the mind have been seen as deeply pious acts. In medieval Europe, when most of their Christian neighbors were illiterate, Jews undertook to teach every Jewish child how to read. That tradition lives on. The population of Israel reads more books per capita than the population of any other nation in the world. And that tradition drives our defense of academic freedom in America.

Jewish tradition cherishes free speech. "When a person refrains from speech, the ideas die, the soul stops, and the senses deteriorate," said Moses ibn Ezra, insisting on respect for honest differences of opinion. (*Shirat Yisrael* 12c) The assertion of unpopular opinions permeates the Bible: the prophet Nathan denouncing King David for having stolen Bathsheba from her husband; Elijah excoriating King Ahab for his evil doings; prophets chastising neighbors and ruling powers alike; Job asserting his innocence; Abraham arguing with God—these are but a few of the many examples of fiercely unpopular opinions freely and openly expressed.

This tradition continued over the centuries. The schools of Hillel and Shammai differed sharply in most of their interpretations of the law; so the Talmud included both positions and an ocean of opinions, majority and minority. Studies of the *shtetl*, a small Jewish town in Eastern Europe, confirm the long tradition of respect for differing views that animated these tightly knit Jewish communities. This regard for free expression and this sensitive respect for differences have left their mark upon modern Jews.

This is not to pretend that Jewish history was 100 percent libertarian. Even when there was diversity of views, the debate took place within the limits of the fundamental tenets of the covenental relationship between God and the Jewish people. And even that diversity of opinion was sometimes marred by efforts at censorship: Jeremiah was sentenced to die as a traitor because of his criticisms of the government; Amos was denounced; Elisha ben Abuyah was thrown out of the Sanhedrin for heresy; the writings of Maimonides were put under a ban by some scholars and were burnt in some communities; Spinoza was excommunicated for his views; Orthodox rabbis have excommunicated Chasidic and Reform Jewish leaders at different times in history; and, certainly, most of the Orthodox rabbinate in Israel today is no friend of civil liberties. But these failures to implement the ideal have not destroyed the ideal itself.

Moreover, because Jews had an almost universal capacity to read, these censorship efforts usually failed. In the end, the Jewish love of learning proved to be irreconcilable with efforts to control the mind.

EIGHT INCIDENTS OF CENSORSHIP IN THE 1990s

What do the following books have in common: *Of Mice and Men*; *Catcher in the Rye*; *The Adventures of Huckleberry Finn*; *The Joy Luck Club*; *Flowers for Algernon*; Anne Frank's *Diary of a Young Girl*; *The Grapes of Wrath*; *The Chocolate War*; *Slaughterhouse-Five*; *The Color Purple*; *Black Boy*; *1984*; *To Kill a Mockingbird*; *I Know Why the Caged Bird Sings*; *One Day in the Life of Ivan Denisovic*; and *Ryan White: My Own Story*? In the 1980s and 1990s, they all were targets of censorship by local communities across America. Below are examples of censorship campaigns in the mid-nineties conducted by right-wing groups, as documented by People for the American Way and the National Coalition against Censorship:

1. In Rockford, Illinois, Luis Rodriguez's acclaimed *Always Running* was removed from library shelves after a complaint about "sexually explicit scenes and use of profanity." Members of the local right-wing Citizens for Excellence in Education (CEE) group claimed that the book "promotes youthful sex, drug use, and unfair criticism of our great teachers" and that it is "irreligious, anti-family, left wing, anti-American and radical." Since then, seventeen other books have been restricted.

2. Maya Angelou's *I Know Why the Caged Bird Sings* was removed from the curriculum at the Unified School in Gilbert, Arizona, and at Lakota High School in Cincinnati, Ohio. Parents complained that the book "does not represent traditional values" and that it is "too graphic."

3. The Lindale, Texas, school board eliminated the entire reading list for the district's advanced placement English program and established a new one "reflecting the board's idea of Lindale's Christian values." Among the books removed from the reading list were Amy Tan's *The Joy Luck Club* ("profane"); Harper Lee's *To Kill a Mockingbird*; Mark Twain's *The Adventures of Huckleberry Finn*; Herman Melville's *Moby Dick*; and Nathaniel Hawthorne's *The Scarlet Letter* ("conflict with the values of the community"); and Rudolfo Anaya's *Bless Me, Ultima* ("full of weird spirituality").

4. In Greenville, South Carolina, a middle school principal ordered the removal of *Warriors Don't Cry* by Melba Beals from an eighth-grade English class, saying the book, which describes the desegregation of Central High School during the civil rights movement, portrays the town of Little Rock, Arkansas, in a negative light.

5. In Ouachita Parish, Louisiana, more than two hundred books, including *Everything You Need to Know about Sexual Abstinence* and *Everything You Need to Know about Incest*, were removed from a high school library after the principal ordered the librarians to remove anything having to do with sex, whether pro or con!

6. Jane Smiley's Pulitzer Prize–winning novel *A Thousand Acres* was pulled from a college prep English class in Lynden, Washington, after a complaint by parents (of a student not in the class) that "no normal sixteen- to eighteen-year-old boy could read this material and not be affected." The novel was further condemned by Cathy Mickels of Washington's Alliance of Families in a press release and on her radio show.

7. Laura Ingalls Wilder's *Little House in the Big Woods* was removed from classrooms amid accusations that it "promotes racial epithets and is fueling the fire of racism." The book was later reinstated, but complainants also want the book removed from the library.

8. Because of a policy that bans any instruction that has "the effect of encouraging or supporting homosexuality as a positive lifestyle alternative," William Shakespeare's *Twelfth Night* was removed from a Merrimack, New Hampshire, high school English class.

People for the American Way (PFAW) documented 338 cases of censorship nationwide in 1994–1995. Censorship cases have been steadily increasing. In 1995–1996, PFAW documented 475 incidents of censorship or other attacks on public education—300 book censorships and 175 "broad-based" censorships. For every censorship case it documents, PFAW estimates another ten are not documented. If these figures are correct, thousands of books and other materials are removed yearly from school libraries and curricula. As a result, tens of thousands of public school students are denied access to certain ideas and materials because somebody else thinks these ideas are "inappropriate." Is this the way a democratic society, interested in equipping its citizens to deal comfortably with complex and controversial issues, should educate its citizens?

CENSORSHIP FROM THE LEFT

Recent attempts at censorship have come from left-wing and liberal groups as well. Motivated by genuine concerns about the rise of racist and anti-Semitic incidents over the past decade and the alarming rise in violence against women and children, certain liberal groups have called for the censorship of art and literature they regard as racist, anti-Semitic, misogynist (anti-women), or pornographic.

While one may certainly question the ways in which publications like *Penthouse* and *Hustler* depict women, censorship is not the answer. Preventing the local newsstand from selling pornographic magazines will do little to defeat sexism. Nor will their removal from the marketplace encourage men who view women solely as sex objects to regard them differently. It will, however, erode valuable freedoms.

Similarly, preventing the American Nazi party and the Ku Klux Klan from distributing their literature will not wipe out anti-Semitism, racism, homophobia, intolerance, or bigotry. Nor will banning *The Adventures of Huckleberry Finn* (as some Blacks urge because of what they see as a negative depiction of Jim) or *The Merchant of Venice* (as some Jews urge because they believe Shakespeare's depiction of Shylock feeds anti-Semitic stereotyping). Indeed, both of these works can be seen as eloquent commentaries on the evils of racism and anti-Semitism in their immediate societies. Permitting only "politically correct" language on college campuses would stifle expression in precisely the place where free thought and discourse ought to be nurtured. While one can respect the motivations behind efforts to stop potentially inflammatory and offensive material—material that is undeniably racist, misogynist, pornographic, or anti-Semitic in nature—censorship is a blatant assault on our cherished right to freedom of speech.

Censorship in the Schools

> I hope I live to see the day when, as in the early days
> of our country, we won't have any public schools. The
> churches will have taken them over again and
> Christians will be running them.
>
> (Rev. Jerry Falwell)

The following scenario has become increasingly familiar: a small band of parents, disturbed that their children are being taught what they consider "secular humanism" and/or "situation ethics," protests the inclusion of a book in the school curriculum. One school system, while refusing to strike the book from the curriculum, did eliminate several offensive passages. What was the book? *Composition and Applied Grammar: The Writing Process*, a widely used grammar textbook.

While opposition to a grammar book may seem comical, those who ban books take themselves very seriously and approach their mission with a religious fervor. Often, they seek to impose a strict fundamentalist interpretation of the Bible on every subject from science to English, denouncing opposing views as "godless" and "valueless."

The object of their wrath is so-called "secular humanism," which they say pervades the educational establishment, impairs traditional Christian values, and undermines parental authority.

Groups such as Citizens for Excellence in Education (CEE), Concerned Women for America (CWA), the Eagle Forum, the National Legal Foundation (NLF), and Education Research Analysts (ERA) all have one goal in mind: to erode the secular nature of public education and infuse public schools with fundamentalist Christian values. To achieve this goal, they carefully set up parents' committees in local communities to harass public school officials; elect like-minded individuals to local school boards; and create an atmosphere of intimidation and fear, intimidating textbook publishers from covering controversial subjects.

Dr. Robert Simmonds, founder of CEE, the activist component of the National Association of Christian Educators, has stated: "There are 15,700 school districts in America. When we can get an active Christian parents' committee (CEE) in operation in all districts, we can take complete control of all local school boards. This would allow us to determine all local policy: *select good textbooks, good curriculum programs, superintendents, and principals. Our time has come!"*

Supplementing its censorship campaigns, the Christian Right is attacking public education with its latest battlefront tactic—"parental rights" legislation. Such legislation would enable parents to set broad limits to the state's ability to "interfere with" parents' upbringing of their children. The parental rights movement would accomplish this goal in part by transferring to parents jurisdiction over public school curricula. Proponents of parental rights legislation claim it is meant to be a vehicle by which control over public schools can be returned to the local level. While the language of the parental rights movement appears innocuous, opponents warn that the movement is one of deception and is replete with dangerous consequences—for instance, it would undercut efforts to ensure academic standards in public education as set by professional educators and would make it difficult both to enforce child abuse laws and to remove children from abusive homes.

THE GABLERS: ESTABLISHING A LINK BETWEEN MATHEMATICS AND DRUG ABUSE

Mel and Norma Gabler, self-appointed saviors of morality in Texas, have a mission as they see it: a mission from God. In the worldview of the Gablers, nothing is as it seems. Every topic of discussion in the classroom reflects the struggle between the forces of good and evil, between the forces of the Christian God and the "secular humanist" anti-Christ. The Gablers have targeted a variety of standard textbooks as the demonic instruments by which atheists and secular humanists are converting impressionable young minds to their faith. "Until textbooks are changed," they have declared, "there is no possibility that crime, violence, venereal disease, and abortion rates will decrease." Their views on countless academic topics reveal this paranoid view of academic inquiry and exploration. Consider the following example concerning the teaching of math:

> When a student reads in a math book that there are no absolutes, suddenly every value he's been taught has been destroyed. And the next thing you know, the student turns to crime and drugs.
>
> (Donna Hulsizer, *Protecting the Freedom to Learn*)

If the Gablers were merely a kooky couple who spent their time complaining about the state of the world, their primitive views would be nothing more than a curious amusement. But they are not, and their efforts amount to much more than curious amusement. They are, in fact, founders of Educational Research Analysts (ERA), a Texas-based group that appoints itself to "monitor" textbooks for offensive material. They "document such discrepancies as indisputable factual errors and the presentation of moral relativism while censoring Judeo-Christian values." They believe that "many texts today do not teach early American values but are substituting Marxist propaganda, belittling the American family unit, equating the Bible with myths, denying absolute values, and destroying the fabric of this nation." If the examples of the Gablers' wisdom (or lack thereof) quoted above left you chuckling, don't laugh too loud: chances are that some, if not all, of your children's textbooks have been modified to mollify the Gablers.

Since founding Educational Research Analysts in 1973, the Gablers have had a powerful influence on which textbooks are approved for use in Texas public schools and which are not. As Texas and California are the largest textbook markets in the country, publishers have traditionally geared their textbooks to sell well in these two states. In 1991, the two states announced their intention to begin purchasing the same textbooks—a decision that could give them extraordinary control over which textbooks survive financially in America.

With the Gablers' impressive influence in Texas, this means that for the past twenty-four years, textbook publishers have been reluctant to include anything in their textbooks that the Gablers—and others of their ilk—would find offensive. The results have been devastating. If your biology textbook made little or no mention of evolution or presented creationism as a valid scientific theory, thank the Gablers. If your American history textbook skipped over the Vietnam War, the problems faced by Native Americans, or slavery, thank the Gablers. If your world history textbook ignored the Crusades, the Spanish Inquisition, or the Holocaust, the Gablers may be responsible.

Privacy and the Jewish Tradition

Justice Louis D. Brandeis, the great Jewish Supreme Court justice, once wrote: "Privacy is the most comprehensive of rights and the right most valued by civilized men." The right to privacy has ancient Jewish antecedents. In commenting on the story of Balaam's refusal to curse the children of Israel, the Talmud tells us that "he saw that the entrances to their tents were not directly opposite each other, so that one family did not visually intrude on the privacy of the other." (Babylonian Talmud, *Baba Batra* 60a) This legend presaged the ruling that houses in Jewish communities had to be built so that residents of one house could not look into the homes of their neighbors. If the builder failed to abide by this rule, he was required to erect at his own expense a wall that protected the privacy of the neighbors. (*Baba Batra* 6b)

Today perhaps more than ever before, personal privacy is at risk. Wiretaps and electronic bugging, particularly with new technologies that can see in the dark, tape conversations through windows, and record at very long distances, as well as computerized filing systems all based on our Social Security numbers, can yield vast amounts of information to parties from secret government intelligence agencies to credit rating corporations to private individuals.

The late Supreme Court Justice William O. Douglas warned a generation ago that personal privacy "has almost vanished in the United States." He added that Americans "may, in time, rebel against its loss."

The Fourth Amendment to the Constitution reads:

> The right of the people to be secure in their persons, houses, papers, and effects, against unreasonable searches and seizures, shall not be violated, and no warrants shall issue but upon probable cause, supported by oath or affirmation, and particularly describing the place to be searched and the persons or things to be seized.

Jewish law went beyond even the modern Fourth Amendment in securing a person's right to privacy, as illustrated in Exodus 22:25–26 and quoted in Deuteronomy 24:10–11: "When you lend your neighbor any manner of loan, you shall not go into his house to fetch your pledge. You shall stand outside, and the person to whom you made the loan shall bring the pledge to you."

Eavesdropping, gossipmongering, and slander are strongly condemned in Jewish teaching. Unauthorized disclosure of information was strictly prohibited. In the Talmud, we read that Rabbi Ami expelled a scholar from the academy because he disclosed a report he had received confidentially *twenty-two* years earlier. By the eleventh century, the privacy of mail was absolutely safeguarded by Rabbenu Gershom.

In Judaism, privacy is seen as an aspect of one's sanctity as a child of God and as a shield for human personality. Without this protection, one is stripped of individuality and selfhood and is effectively dehumanized. Jewish sensitivity to civil liberties—and to the precious right to be left alone—has much relevance to our current struggle to resist the onslaught of brainwashing, subliminal advertising, bugging, wiretapping, and other technological intrusions.

A Real Dilemma: A Friend Contemplates Suicide

Josh is a camper at a UAHC camp. His father taught him about the growing plague of youth suicide and gave him a copy of Sol Gordon's wonderfully helpful book *When Living Hurts* (New York: UAHC Press, 1985), which lists some of the danger signals of youngsters contemplating suicide. The book urges personal intervention if one sees a friend or a classmate showing these telltale signs. Josh became painfully aware that one of his bunkmates, Sam, was acting strangely and saying things that fit the description of a person at risk. Sam confided in Josh: "Nobody loves me.... Nobody will care if I die.... What's the use of going on like this?" Josh went to his counselor and told him about Sam. Sam was called in and later lashed out at Josh for invading his privacy. Did Josh do the right thing? What would you have done?

Response

Josh felt terrible at first, but he may have saved Sam's life. In the Jewish tradition, the principle of *pikuach nefesh* requires that to save a life almost any Jewish law can and should be broken, including the obligation to keep secrets. Sam was crying out for help; Josh heard him and took responsibility. He did the right thing.

Privacy and Random Testing for Drugs

In the United States, the right to privacy has faced widespread challenge in the recent trend toward drug testing in the workplace. Many companies and some federal agencies have instituted random urine tests for drug use for all employees. While employers and the public have a clear interest in maintaining a drug-free workplace, the right of a person to be left alone is flagrantly violated by a mandatory urine test, which is degrading, sometimes inaccurate, and unrestricted by the rule of law.

Only when there is a "compelling state interest" in limiting our privacy, such as when there is "probable cause" to suspect a crime or when the workers are responsible for public safety (e.g., airline pilots, nuclear plant operators, subway conductors, and school bus drivers), should such testing be mandated. While this standard applies in theory to the government and not to private employers, our basic freedoms will be sharply jeopardized if private parties feel free to use modern technology to invade our privacy and find out information about us we wish to keep to ourselves. Workplace drug testing opens a Pandora's box.

Furthermore, such invasions of the privacy of employees can reveal extensive information unrelated to the drug issue. Urinalysis can disclose not only drug use but also whether an employee or job applicant is being treated for a heart condition, depression, epilepsy, diabetes; or it can reveal if a woman is pregnant. To allow employers in the public or private sector to have indiscriminate access to such information is to rip away the right to privacy.

In 1989, the Supreme Court upheld the right of federal agencies to test employees for drug use without reasonable suspicion. The Court ruled that the employees' right to privacy was outweighed by the government's interest in ensuring a drug-free workplace. Lower courts and state legislation have been more restrictive in the use of drug testing, allowing it only in individual cases where there is sufficient suspicion of criminal use of drugs or in jobs involving public safety. Usually such legislation also requires confirmatory tests and confidential handling of the results.

AIDS TESTING AND CIVIL LIBERTIES

The ability to test for the AIDS virus has introduced new ethical and legal dilemmas over how to balance public health concerns with the right to privacy.

AIDS tests have the potential to save lives when their results are used responsibly to help prevent the spread of the virus. However, when the test results are made public, the person who has tested positive for HIV antibodies often faces severe discrimination by the fearful general public, by employers, and by health insurance companies.

One set of questions revolves around whether or not doctors and test centers should be required to report positive HIV tests to public health authorities, who would treat the virus like a sexually transmitted disease, contacting all former partners and suggesting they be tested. While this might well help alert people who do not suspect they are HIV positive, AIDS public interest groups and civil liberties advocates such as the ACLU emphasize the importance of privacy in AIDS testing.

They argue that although people should act responsibly to take precautions against spreading the virus, there should be no law requiring the mandatory reporting of test results to health authorities. Some health-care experts point out that such mandatory reporting would, in fact, scare people away from voluntary testing programs, making it more difficult to curb the spread of the virus and thereby undermining community-based prevention efforts.

Most testing programs are aimed at individuals at high risk for HIV infection—individuals who are in minority groups, often distrustful of government and fearful of further discrimination should they be discovered to be HIV positive. In states that have instituted mandatory name-reporting legislation, there were drop-offs in the number of people being tested. The ACLU also argues that once the government has a list of the names, addresses, and sexual orientation of people who test positive for HIV, the list would be an irresistible target for insurers, school systems, or any state agency that might gain future access to the list.

The reverse side of this argument concerns people's "right to know" information that would allow them to make educated decisions about protecting their health. Further, public health officials argue that as the hysteria about AIDS has subsided, as the virus has been increasingly controlled, and as it has spread slowly into heterosexual, nondrug-using components of this society, the fears of discrimination and being shunned are no longer as valid. The failure to treat the AIDS epidemic as the public health community would treat any other contagious disease unnecessarily endangers people. By not tracing the sexual contacts of those with the virus, former sexual partners of infected patients may unknowingly be transmitting the virus to others, including their own spouses.

One particularly controversial aspect of this debate relates to health-care workers who test positive for HIV. Of the more than 600,000 AIDS cases known in the United States, there has thus far been only one documented report of a health-care worker passing on the AIDS virus. This occurred when a Florida dentist seemed to have infected five of his patients. One, the late Kimberly Bergalis, publicly demanded a law forcing health-care workers to divulge to their patients their HIV status.

A Real Dilemma: Testing Health-Care Workers for HIV

Is it a patient's right to be informed if his or her doctor has tested HIV positive? If so, is this information relevant only if the doctor will be performing operations in which bodily fluids might be exchanged, or should this right apply to all health-care professionals?

Although the Centers for Disease Control released guidelines on the subject, which did not recommend mandatory testing legislation or mandatory reporting of results, Congress considered legislation in the early 1990s that would have imposed maximum criminal penalties of ten years in prison and a $10,000 fine for health-care workers with the AIDS virus who do not inform their patients of their condition. The legislation would have required all surgeons and dentists who perform certain high-risk operations to be tested for the AIDS virus and if found positive, to stop performing them. It was strongly opposed by the medical profession as well as civil liberties groups and eventually dropped in a House-Senate conference.

Should the UAHC have supported or opposed passage of such legislation?

Response

The UAHC joined with the medical profession and civil liberties groups opposing this legislation for the reasons stated above. Also, if a doctor must divulge, why not a patient? And what would be the effect on both doctor and patient? Instead, the UAHC supported increased safety measures by doctors, nurses, and dentists to reduce the possibility of transmitting the virus. These precautions are now routine, and the passage of time, with very few instances of transmission from medical personnel, has quelled the hysteria on this issue that existed early in the 1990s.

YOU CAN MAKE A DIFFERENCE

As the Supreme Court tends to withdraw from its historic role as the primary guarantor of our fundamental rights and as it increasingly turns decisions regarding those rights back to the states and localities, the role of individual activists takes on greater significance. An individual, by taking a stand, can make a difference in the ongoing battle for freedom and civil liberties.

Sometimes that difference can make itself felt right in your own community. The Gablers, for example, appointed themselves arbiters of what could be read and taught in public schools. If this Texas couple could make a difference, so can you. Students and parents must let teachers, administrators, and school board members know that the vast majority of Americans support academic freedom as the surest road to educational excellence. Parents need to be very careful when electing school board members: look very carefully at the views of candidates, ask for definitions of vague references to "traditional" and "family" values, and demand that candidates for the school board be committed to academic freedom.

Lastly, where necessary, create a local coalition of concerned groups to monitor censorship efforts in your schools and local libraries, and be ready to take a stand against censorship attempts. Where such groups exist, their track record in defeating Christian Right extremists is excellent.

A Real Dilemma: Standing Up for Free Speech

In the winter of 1975, when the Jewish world was reeling from the shock of a United Nations resolution equating Zionism with racism, protests and demonstrations were mounted everywhere. In Dallas, 2,000 delegates to the General Assembly of the UAHC, led by the youth delegation of the North American Federation of Temple Youth (NFTY), joined in passionate song and prayer against this international anti-Semitic outrage. Similarly, in thousands of local communities, Jews called upon their Christian neighbors to rally with them to protest the United Nations resolution.

In San Jose, California, Jewish youngsters from the Reform Temple Emanu-El gathered at a nearby shopping center to collect signatures on a petition opposing the United Nations resolution. Leading the temple youth were Michael Robins and David Marcus. The managers of the Pruneyard Shopping Center came out and accused the petitioners of "trespassing on private property" and demanded they leave the shopping center. Michael and David refused, contending that they had a right to reach the public and that a petition is a fundamental expression of free speech. The boys were outraged by what they regarded as a denial of their civil rights. They shared their concern with their families and others in the congregation. What should they and the Jewish community have done about it?

Response

An attorney, who was a past president of the temple (Philip Hammer), agreed to take their case without charge. In court, they asserted the right of free speech at privately owned shopping centers, arguing that such premises are public forums. Viewing this case as a threat to their property rights, the shopping center owners spent more than $250,000 before the United

States Supreme Court finally resolved the case.

Step-by-step, Michael and David pushed their case through the legal system, losing in the superior court, appealing to the next higher court. Finally, after five years, the Supreme Court, in June of 1980, handed down its landmark decision (*Pruneyard Shopping Center* v. *Robins et al.*), unanimously upholding the right of Michael and David—and therefore all citizens—to freedom of speech and assembly on the premises of a privately owned shopping center that is open to the public. Michael and David had struck a blow not only for their own rights; they had enlarged the definition of civil liberties for all Americans.

"Some people thought it was an absurd attempt," said Michael after the victory. "They didn't think we could take on big business and win. But in this case, the democratic process worked; financial resources were not an issue." Added David: "It proves that the individual can still make a difference. Two people can still make their mark on society." David celebrated by having lunch with his father, a Jewish educator who had come to America to escape Nazi persecution. He had taught David that free speech is always worth fighting for.

··· 11 ···

Religious Liberty: Will the Wall Come Tumbling Down?

DOUBLE JEOPARDY: THE TWIN THREATS TO FREEDOM OF AND FREEDOM FROM RELIGION

The religious freedom provisions in the First Amendment of the Constitution are embodied in two key clauses: the establishment clause and the free exercise clause. Together, these two laws prevent government from controlling, manipulating, or interfering with religion. They ensure that no one's standing as a citizen and no one's rights will ever depend on one's religious practices or beliefs. These two clauses that begin the Bill of Rights read: "Congress shall make no law respecting an establishment of religion, or prohibiting the free exercise thereof...." Using the Fourteenth Amendment, the Court has extended these prohibitions to state and local governments. Now, as we enter the third century of the Constitution and its Bill of Rights, these twin pillars of religious liberty are under severe attack from a conservative Supreme Court anxious to limit the Court's role as guarantor of rights and insensitive to the concerns of religious minorities and a Republican-dominated Congress willing to eviscerate the Constitution's establishment clause.

In 1990, the Supreme Court issued a decision that was perhaps the most revolutionary decision regarding religious rights in American history. The damage done to the free exercise clause—which guarantees free exercise of religion—was staggering.

The case was *Employment Division of Oregon* v. *Smith*. The main issue in *Smith* was the right of Native Americans to use peyote in religious ceremonies as they have done for centuries. The Court, however, virtually ignored this specific issue and, instead, rewrote the entirety of free exercise First Amendment protections.

Until this case, the Court always had held that First Amendment rights were "fundamental" or "inalienable" rights that came from our being God-created human beings. No Congress or legislature could arbitrarily take such rights away; they had to be given special protection. As discussed in chapter 10, "Safeguarding Our Civil Liberties," over the past several decades, the Court translated this idea into the "compelling state interest" test. In the realm of religious liberty, this meant that the state could not interfere with religious activity and had to exempt religious groups from general laws unless it could prove a compelling reason not to.

Two examples: although the Court ruled, in *Wisconsin* v. *Yoder*, that the state of Wisconsin could not prove a compelling state interest in forcing Amish children (in violation of their religious beliefs) to attend school beyond the eighth grade (reasoning the children had a basic general education), the Court later ruled, in *United States* v. *Lee*, that the federal government's compelling interest in ensuring the solvency of Social Security is enhanced by all employers paying into the system, thus justifying a requirement that an Amish employer (against religious objections) withhold Social Security taxes from his predominantly Amish employees' wages.

Although the "compelling state interest" standard had allowed the court to strike a balance in difficult cases in which the needs of government conflicted with religious liberty, in *Employment Division of Oregon* v. *Smith*, the Supreme Court threw the "compelling state interest" criterion into the dustbin. The Court ruled that government would no longer need a compelling state interest to limit religious liberty. The Court's surprisingly sweeping decision greatly weakened the religious freedom protections guaranteed by the Constitution, casting a pall over a two-hundred-year-old tradition of religious liberty in America.

In the aftermath of *Smith*, when facing laws restricting free exercise, religious constituents must now appeal to their state legislature to grant legislative protection of religious practices that previously had been considered constitutionally protected. Justice Antonin Scalia, writing for the majority in *Smith*, sent an ominous message to all religious groups when he stated that the traditional protection of religious freedom is a "luxury" that America can no longer afford and explicitly acknowledged that minority religions would be particularly hurt by his new approach.

The implications of this ruling were profound. Armed with *Smith*-shaped jurisprudence, legislatures conceivably could ban the use of sacramental wine by Christian and Jewish minors, deny the right of students to wear religious garments like yarmulkes (head coverings), and forbid public school students from taking time off for religious holidays. Through the doorway opened by the *Smith* decision, government-sponsored restrictions on religion already have found their way into American life.

Indeed, within a few years, lower courts responding to *Smith* handed down rulings in favor of the state and against minority religious practices in over sixty cases. For example:

- *Minnesota* v. *Hershberger*, where the Amish objection to putting large orange reflecting triangles on the back of their buggies was rejected.

- *Montgomery* v. *County of Clinton*, where a Jewish woman's objection to an autopsy on her son (because it violated Jewish law) was spurned.

- *Hunafa* v. *Murphy*, where a Muslim prisoner's objection to being served pork in violation of his religious practices was brushed aside.

In these and scores of similar decisions, courts indicated the result would have been different before *Smith*.

This incursion into the most fundamental of our civil liberties—freedom of religion—is disconcerting evidence that this cornerstone of the great American experiment must be given determined protection, lest it be dismantled brick by brick. So long as the Court does not function as the guarantor of our basic rights, it will fall to Congress to preserve these rights. It took three years to reverse the effect of the Supreme Court's *Smith* ruling. The Reform movement's Religious Action Center played a key role in mobilizing and coordinating the efforts of an extraordinary coalition of over sixty national religious denominations and faith groups from the Catholics to the Sikhs; from the fundamentalist Christians to the Unitarians; from the ultra-Orthodox Agudas Israel to the Reform Jewish movement. Together, they successfully fought for the passage of the Religious Freedom Restoration Act (RFRA), one of the most important bills for religious freedom in the history of America, which legislatively restored the compelling-interest test in all free exercise cases.

Then, in 1997, the Supreme Court, in a case called *Flores v. Boerne*, struck down RFRA. The Court rejected Congress's view that RFRA was merely giving legislative protection to a right for which the Court had held there was no constitutional protection (as the Congress had done with civil, women's, and disability rights) and ruled that RFRA was an impermissible effort of the Congress to tell the courts how to interpret the First Amendment. Further, the Court held that RFRA embodied too broad an effort of the federal government to tell states what they could and could not do in the arena of religious liberty protections. Bitterly disappointed, national religious groups have begun to introduce and work toward the passage of state RFRAs and a more limited federal RFRA (known as the Religious Liberty Protection Act of 1998), an approach that might well pass the Supreme Court's review.

A Real Dilemma: Are Prisoners Entitled to Protections of Their Religious Liberties?

Although RFRA enjoyed near-unanimous support on Capitol Hill—it passed the House without a dissenting vote, and only three senators voted against RFRA—its application has been more complicated, particularly in the development of an appropriate standard for evaluating the religious liberty claims of prisoners.

The religious liberty rights of prisoners are at once a source of optimism for those who work to help rehabilitate prisoners and a source of concern for those charged with prison administration. A number of religious organizations run special fellowships geared toward the incarcerated; they claim that religion has played a uniquely transformative role in the lives of many behind bars. On the other hand, prisoners have the time and often the inclination to litigate every grievance, and some state correction directors and attorneys general argue that prisoners might use RFRA to initiate endless litigation and to demand special privileges. It may be unsafe or inconvenient for prison officials to accommodate even common religious observances (e.g., religious dietary requirements, Sikhs wearing ceremonial knives or turbans, Jews requesting wine for a seder, etc.), let alone unusual religious practices that they invent, such as the prisoner who went to court to assert that his religion required that he be served filet mignon and champagne daily.

In the battles leading up to the passage of RFRA in 1993, efforts to include a prisoner exemption were beaten back by the coalition supporting the bill. Thus RFRA enacted a uniform standard of religious liberties protections—for prisoners and nonprisoners alike. At the same time, it responded to the correction officials' concerns by asking the courts to give due respect to the prison officials' description of what constitutes the compelling interest of maintaining safety and discipline in the prison.

Now on the state level, however, law enforcement personnel are far stronger politically than they were at the national level, and in several cases they have made it impossible to pass a state RFRA without a prisoner exemption.

Should RFRA supporters accept state RFRAs that include prison exemptions, reasoning that without the federal RFRA, something is far better than nothing; or should they insist on an all-or-nothing approach and allow the RFRAs to fail in such states?

Response

The RFRA coalition has stood firm in supporting only legislation that contains one standard of religious liberty for all, including prisoners, despite indications that such a staunch position may be blocking the passage of RFRA legislation in a number of states.

In defense of their position, members of the coalition note that the fears of prison officials notwithstanding, while the national RFRA was alive, RFRA claims from prisoners did not, in fact, clog the court system. (The Justice Department reports that prisoners' RFRA claims account for less than 1 percent of cases brought by prisoners in U.S. courts.) Proponents of an all-or-nothing approach also note that under RFRA, prison authorities continued to have broad discretion to regulate problematic conduct.

THE JEWISH COMMUNITY'S ROLE IN THE STRUGGLE FOR SEPARATION OF CHURCH AND STATE

There are many students of American Jewish life who believe that the struggle to expand separation of church and state in America is one of the greatest contributions Jews have rendered to the enlargement of American freedom.

Bear in mind that the United States is the first country in the history of the world to build its society on the foundation of the separation between church and state. This is one of America's unique gifts to civilization and the chief guarantor of our religious liberty.

But have we been too strict, too absolute in our defense of the First Amendment? Has our position run counter to our own Jewish interests? For example, has our belief that the government should not fund sectarian educational institutions undermined our efforts to maintain Jewish day schools? If public education is failing to maintain the quality of education that Jews cherish, should we not reassess our long-held stand? Or does strict separation of church and state remain the best policy for Jews because it is best for America?

To answer these questions, a brief history of the Jewish community's role in the struggle for church-state separation is instructive. In the twentieth century, when Jews became secure and organized as a community, they fought openly to eliminate government support for religious activity in the public schools, stop federal aid to parochial schools, and remove religious symbols from public property. We have taken this position not out of prejudice against other religious groups but as a consequence of our own long historical experience, which demonstrates that whenever the state is controlled by any church, or vice versa, Jews—and freedom—suffer.

Only in America have Jews been free to pursue our faith and to organize our communal lives, equal under law and in practice, without government interference. Thus America—through its Constitution—created a system of religious liberty that has proved to be generally fair and effective, one that Jews wish to preserve. Jews have learned, through history, that both religion and the state flourish best when they are separate.

Jewish organizations frequently have gone to court to challenge violations of the First Amendment's prohibition against establishment of religion. They played a crucial role in supporting the *McCollum* case in 1948, in which an atheist non-Jew challenged a program that required children to be released for an hour of religious instruction inside the public school building. The Supreme Court declared in *McCollum* that released time on public school premises is unconstitutional.

Later, Jewish groups joined in legal challenges against such practices as Bible reading and reciting the Lord's Prayer in the public schools, arguing that religion belongs in the church, synagogue, and home, not in the public school where every child is entitled to be free from any religious compulsion or coercion, however subtle. The Supreme Court, until recently, has sustained these challenges, effectively eliminating these practices from the public schools. The essential doctrine of the Supreme Court is articulated in *Everson v. Board of Education* (1947):

> The establishment of religion clause of the First Amendment means at least this: neither a state nor the federal government can set up a church. Neither can pass laws that aid one religion, aid all religions, or prefer one religion over another. Neither can force nor influence a person to go to or to remain away from church against his will or force him to profess a belief or disbelief in any religion. No person can be punished for entertaining or professing religious beliefs or disbeliefs, for church attendance or nonattendance. No tax in any amount, large or small, can be levied to support any religious activities or institutions, whatever they may be called, or whatever form they may adopt to teach or practice religion. Neither a state nor the federal government can, openly or secretly, participate in the affairs of any religious organization or groups and vice versa. In the words of Jefferson, the clause against establishment of religion by law was intended to erect a wall of separation between church and state.

Supreme Court decisions such as this have not been universally popular with the American public.

A Real Dilemma: Prayer at Graduation Ceremonies

In 1989, Daniel Weisman's daughter, Deborah, graduated from the Nathan Bishop Middle School in Providence, Rhode Island. Like many across the country, this graduation ceremony began with an opening prayer, delivered in this instance by a Reform rabbi. Believing that this religious presence at a public, federally funded school violated the separation-of-church-and-state provisions of the First Amendment, Daniel Weisman brought the case, known as *Lee* v. *Weisman*, to court.

Lower federal courts ruled in favor of Weisman, stating that graduation prayers amounted to an official endorsement of religion in violation of the establishment clause of the First Amendment. At the urging of the Bush administration, which supported school prayer, the United States Supreme Court agreed to review the case.

Actually, the case began the previous year when a Christian clergyman gave the prayer at the graduation ceremony "in the name of the Father, the Son, and the Holy Ghost." When school officials were challenged on this, Rabbi Leslie Gutterman was asked to deliver the prayer the following year. Even though this constituted a "religious" prayer in a state instrumentality (a public school), the intent was to provide a prayer that would be universal instead of sectarian and divisive. If you had been the rabbi, would you have accepted the invitation or not? Why? If you had been the CCAR and the UAHC, would you have supported or opposed Weisman's position in the Supreme Court?

Response

Rabbi Gutterman agreed to conduct the opening prayer. The rabbi, who believes strongly in church-state separation, felt that a general and universal mention of God in such a ceremonial setting was not itself a violation of church-state separation. In addition, he believed it would avoid the discomfort that a Christian sectarian prayer had caused for Jewish youngsters in the past.

Rabbi Gutterman was startled to find that forces hostile to

church-state separation were using his words to their benefit and
that the case was going to the Supreme Court as a landmark test
of religious liberty. When the Department of Justice asked the
Supreme Court to use the case to redefine the traditional separation of church and state, both Rabbi Gutterman and the Reform
movement became deeply concerned that his invocation might
be used to redefine the First Amendment through a Supreme
Court *endorsement* of prayer in the public school classroom. The
UAHC and the CCAR supported the Weismans, arguing that
even a nondenominational prayer is a violation of the First
Amendment. In the end, the Supreme Court, by a narrow 5-to-4
vote, rejected the government's attempt to mandate prayer, arguing that such attempts violated the First Amendment.

The battle over graduation prayer is far from over. One of the more
contentious church-state issues to come through the courts in the 1990s
is the question of whether there can be student-initiated prayer at grad-
uations and other school-sponsored events (e.g., assemblies and athletic
events) rather than school-initiated prayer as in the *Weisman* case.
Proponents argue that preventing students from having prayer where
and when they want it, if they write and give it, is a violation of their
free exercise of religion. Opponents maintain that such an option will
lead to the abuses about which the court in the *Weisman* decision was
most concerned. Some school officials will actively encourage students
to ask for such a prayer. Students will be less sensitive about inclusive
prayer, forcing school officials to monitor and censor inappropriate
prayers. Finally, student peer pressure to attend and participate in such
prayer can be even more socially coercive than the pressure from teachers that was involved in *Weisman*. A better suggestion would be for
churches and synagogues, either together or separately, to organize their
own "baccalaureate services" before or after the actual graduation.

Propaganda campaigns by right-wing and fundamentalist groups have
sought to depict these decisions as "antireligious" and as "eliminating
God from the public schools." The Republican party made overturning
these decisions a priority of its national platform in 1992. Throughout
the 1980s and 1990s, the Congress repeatedly considered constitutional
amendments that would have radically reworked the entire relationship of government entities with religious faiths by allowing for govern-

ment-endorsed religion in public forums, including public schools and government-subsidized parochial schools and religious ministries. Yet, though the Religious Right armed itself with congressional allies, such attempts have thus far failed; the good sense of the American people has recognized the folly of tampering with the Bill of Rights.

But as the Supreme Court tilts to the right, many of the battles won in the past will have to be refought, this time against a judiciary less committed to strict separation and religious freedom, as evidenced by the *Smith* peyote case discussed earlier.

THE SUPREME COURT VS. THE FOUNDERS: CHANGING VIEWS OF THE ESTABLISHMENT CLAUSE

What made the *Lee v. Weisman* case so important was that the Bush administration played an aggressive role in urging the High Court to use the case to reinterpret the Court's existing understanding of the establishment clause. For years, the courts have decided cases involving governmental establishment of religion according to the strict guidelines of the "*Lemon* test," named for the Supreme Court's 1971 decision in *Lemon v. Kurtzman*. Under the *Lemon* test, to be constitutional, a law or other act of government (1) must have a secular purpose; (2) must not have a primary effect that either advances or inhibits religion; and (3) must not foster "excessive entanglement" between religion and government.

In *Lee v. Weisman*, the Bush administration asked the Court to adopt a more lenient standard that would weaken the wall separating church and state. By a narrow 5-to-4 vote, the Court refused to change the existing law. But Justice Anthony Kennedy did not rely on the *Lemon* test to strike down prayers at high school graduation ceremonies. Instead, he crafted a new "coercion" standard, arguing that the prayers violated the Constitution by coercing attendees into religious activity. While proponents of church-state separation cheered the Court's decision, Kennedy's new "coercion" standard gave them pause. Did Kennedy and the Court intend eventually to replace the *Lemon* test, or merely supplement *Lemon*? Kennedy's coercion standard is far more limited than *Lemon*. While *Lemon* recognizes—and prohibits—subtle ways in which the state can begin establishing religion (e.g., funding parochial schools), the coercion standard guards against only the most egregious, *coercive* forms of establishment. If the coercion test replaced the *Lemon* test, the Court might well allow religious displays on public property, state support for religious schools, state regulation of religious institutions, and even the declaration of an official "state religion" in individual states. None of these involves actually coercing anyone into any particular religious activity, but all have long been held to violate at least one of *Lemon*'s three prongs.

A Real Dilemma: Drawing School Districts—The Case of Kiryas Joel

Following the *Weisman* case, the Supreme Court exhibited a mixed record in considering other efforts to lower the wall separating church and state. It allowed, for example, private groups to erect freestanding crucifixes and other religious symbols on public property and allowed government funding to pay for religious publications on college campuses. The most interesting case for the Jewish community, however, involved chasidic disabled children from Kiryas Joel, a town in New York. These children had attended the area public schools but often were teased by non-Jewish students for their customs and appearances and felt uncomfortable with celebrations of Christmas and secularized non-Jewish holidays such as Halloween and St. Valentine's Day.

In 1989, the residents of Kiryas Joel convinced the state legislature to draw a public school district to include only the chasidic Jews. The only public school in this district was one used to educate children with disabilities (all the other children attend yeshivas). This meant that tax dollars supported a public school attended by chasidic disabled children only, a school that in practice accommodated many Orthodox religious practices that in a mixed school would clearly have violated the establishment clause.

Almost immediately, the New York School Boards Association (NYSBA) filed a lawsuit challenging the legislature's action and charging that the legislature had violated the bounds of church-state separation by intentionally creating a school district under the control of a religious group. Three district courts in New York agreed with the NYSBA that the legislature's move was unconstitutional. Yet the district officials of Kiryas Joel persisted in defense of the new school district and brought the case to the Supreme Court.

The broader American-Jewish community, including the Reform movement, faced the challenge of whether to side with the Chasidim of Kiryas Joel or support the decisions of the New York courts. How would you have voted?

Response

Despite the fact that this district helped Jewish children, most national Jewish organizations, including the Reform Jewish movement, took the position the Supreme Court eventually adopted: drawing school district boundaries along religious lines was "establishment of religion" and would destroy our public school system. Further, if this had been upheld, all across America, religious groups would have redrawn village lines and school boundaries to create Baptist, Mormon, Jewish or other schools, thus dividing America along religious lines at a time when we needed to draw Americans together.

These issues must be viewed as part of the wider war over the First Amendment's establishment clause. What do the words of the First Amendment really mean? What do they allow; what don't they allow? And what purpose did the Founding Fathers intend for them? Was the establishment clause meant only to prevent the state from expressing a preference for one religion over another (as Supreme Court Chief Justice Rehnquist argues), or was it really meant to build a "wall of separation" between church—all religions—and state? In contrast to many other controversies regarding the original intent of the Bill of Rights, at least part of the specific intent of the Framers on this question is clear—and it directly repudiates the "nonpreferential" school of thought. The Founders did indeed mean to construct a wall of separation.

During the course of the original debates over the wording of the relevant section of the First Amendment—"Congress shall make no law respecting an establishment of religion, or prohibiting the free exercise thereof"—several alternative formulations were proposed.

1. One motion would have deleted the words "religion, or prohibiting the free exercise thereof," inserting in their stead, "one religious sect or society in preference to others." This is exactly the position asserted by Chief Justice Rehnquist. Yet this motion was defeated.
2. A second motion would have stricken the entire amendment. It, too, was defeated.
3. A third would have substituted the following for the language that was ultimately approved: "Congress shall not make any law infringing the rights of conscience, or establishing any religious sect or society." This motion, too, was defeated.
4. A fourth and final proposed wording read, "Congress shall make no law establishing any particular denomination of religion in preference to another, or prohibiting the free exercise thereof, nor shall the rights of conscience be infringed." This was likewise defeated.

The Framers drafted their language in such explicit terms precisely because of the important distinction between "preference" on the one hand and "establishment" on the other. This language speaks across the gulf of 210 years to affirm the establishment clause as a wall separating church and state, requiring the government to remain neutral on religious matters, neither supporting, endorsing, nor inhibiting religion. Far from being hostile to religion—as some would suggest—this policy of neutrality has allowed religion to flourish and grow with a strength and diversity unmatched anywhere in the Western world today. Indeed, polls indicate that in the United States, church and synagogue attendance, the importance of religious beliefs in the lives of citizens, and the numbers believing in God are substantially higher than in any other Western country, including all those with established, preferred, or state-sponsored religions.

How tragic that Chief Justice Rehnquist and others have lost sight of the fundamental connection between church-state separation and religious vitality. When religious activities—any religious activities—carry the overtones of coercive government sponsorship, these symbols of faith that lift the spirit and enliven the mind become rote rituals of uniformity that dull the spirit and stifle the mind.

FEDERAL AID TO EDUCATION

Federal aid to religion, particularly in the realm of parochial education, has always been a divisive issue in the sphere of church-state relations. The fundamental question concerns equal justice and religious freedom: does the government have a right to give my tax money to support the religious activities of a church whose religious teachings may violate my deepest religious conscience? Until the 1960s, the United States had never given public funds to private and parochial schools. In 1965, the Elementary and Secondary Education Act opened the doors for private schools (and to an extent, parochial schools) to participate in a limited way in public programs that included provisions for textbooks, teacher training, and remedial educational services.

In recent years, the Jewish community has been split on the key issue of federal aid to parochial schools. Most Jewish groups, including the Reform and Conservative movements, oppose federal aid to nonpublic schools for two reasons: first, because they believe government support for religious education undermines the separation of church and state; and second, because Jewish agencies are committed to the preservation of the public school as perhaps the most important training ground for democratic values in our society. Public aid to nonpublic schools diverts the nation's limited educational resources from, and thereby weakens, public education. It inevitably encourages the growth of separate networks of parochial schools, which reduces interaction of children from varied backgrounds and leads to conflict among religious groups to secure public funds. In the Netherlands, for example, state aid to church schools in the fifties and sixties resulted in an 80 percent decline in public education. Furthermore, because private schools can select among applicants while public schools are open to all, publicly aided private schools likely would become the schools of the white middle class, abandoning poor whites and most nonwhites to public schools.

On the other side, the Orthodox community, which maintains a large system of day schools, believes that federal aid to religious schools is not a violation of separation of church and state. Orthodox leaders have argued that the United States government must take responsibility for the education of every American child, no matter what kind of school he or she may attend. In response, the Conservative and Reform movements assert that while a person has every right to send a child to a nonpublic school that teaches religious dogma, he or she has no right to ask the government to pay for it. No one should be forced, through the tax system, to sponsor the promulgation of religious beliefs and practices with which he or she may profoundly disagree. (See the discussion "Jewish Day Schools, Integration, and the Public Schools" in chapter 8, "Civil Rights and Race Relations in America.")

THE SURVIVAL OF PUBLIC EDUCATION

A key consideration in evolving Jewish opinion about the importance of church-state separation concerns the deteriorating condition of public education in America. (See the discussion in chapter 8, "Civil Rights and Race Relations in America.")

On the whole, the U.S. public school system is an extraordinary success for most students. The schools educate approximately 90 percent of the nation's K through 12 students, a higher percentage than any other nation on earth, providing the majority of our youth with a solid basic education and a strong grounding in the meaning of American citizenship. Since the public schools operate under strict compliance with antidiscrimination laws, the schools ensure that all our children receive an education and that no student is discriminated against because of his or her race, creed, gender, or physical capabilities. A higher percentage of public school budgets than private school budgets is spent on the cost of education for disabled students. Moreover, studies show that America's youth are taking more rigorous courses than ever before, so that between 1982 and 1996, the number of advanced placement examinations taken in a given year tripled. In addition, the National Assessment of Educational Progress (NAEP) reports that average performance in mathematics and science has improved over the past twenty-five years.

Despite its successes, American public education is in serious trouble in the inner cities, and general achievement levels have flattened out for many years. On the Third International Mathematics and Science Study (results released in March 1998), for example, American high school seniors placed nineteenth among seniors in twenty-one nations in general knowledge of math and science. Further, between 1967 and 1997, national scores on the Scholastic Aptitude Test (SAT) fell 38 points in verbal aptitude and 5 points in mathematical aptitude, although both sets reflect a recovery from still lower scores in 1980—an encouraging development. Clearly, our public schools still graduate many students who are functional illiterates. For instance, each year, nearly half of the students at the University of California are required to complete a course in remedial English. A Carnegie Foundation report concluded that "general education is now a disaster area, which instead of being shaped by a coherent educational philosophy is often determined by a number of internal and external forces—faculty interests, student concerns with the job market, 'relevance,' social fads, and the like."

These failures are particularly acute in some urban centers and for minorities. Average SAT scores of most minority students are 40 to 80 points below the national average, although the verbal and math scores for all minorities have improved significantly since 1987.

The Carnegie Foundation's report found that SAT scores are directly proportional to family income: Students from families with income under $10,000 score an average of 768 (combined verbal and math scores) out of a possible 1,600. The average for students with family incomes in the $30,000 to $40,000 range was 884, compared to the 997 average of students from families with incomes over $70,000. The epidemic of guns and drugs that spread in our schools in the 1980s and '90s further exacerbated these problems.

This deterioration of urban public education can be fatal to democracy. Illiterates are not likely to know or care about their rights. Some 47 percent of a sample of seventeen-year-olds did not know that every state elects two senators. One out of two of these youngsters believed that the president appoints members of Congress. What does this mean for the great hope of universal public education that was to cultivate a community of informed and civilized citizens as the very bedrock of democracy? How can democracy survive the intellectual wasteland of a television age and a collapsing school system? Can public education be rescued from swift decline? How? Jews—along with all other concerned persons—must confront such questions and help find answers.

VOUCHERS AND EDUCATIONAL CHOICE

In recent years, a new attempt at government support for parochial schools has arisen under the guise of "educational choice" as a response to the deteriorating condition of the public school system. Essentially, "educational choice" allows parents to choose among the public schools in a district and, in many proposals, between public and private schools. Government funds for education are given to parents in the form of tax credits or vouchers, which are then applied to tuition. Proponents argue that this approach treats all Americans equally: it gives tax credits or vouchers to the parents, and they can then choose the school where they want to use the money. Because the benefits go to people and not directly to the schools, proponents argue that these benefits do not violate church-state separation requirements. Furthermore, they argue that the plan would create healthy competition for students (and thereby for money) among schools, giving better schools rewards for performance and encouraging poor schools to measure up.

Critics of "educational choice," including most in the Jewish community (except the Orthodox community), argue that such "voucher" proposals are grave violations of the church-state separation enshrined in the Constitution's establishment clause. Both the intent of the proposal and its end result are to provide federal funds to parochial schools. Critics also point out that public schools would be severely crippled by the loss of funding that a choice plan including parochial schools would entail, as taxes are diverted from public school expenditures. Public school programs for economically disadvantaged children would suffer enormously, and those children, whose parents lack the resources to send them across town or to pay private school tuition, would be left behind without the means to make a true choice for better education.

THE CHILD CARE DEBATE

A Real Dilemma: Child Care

In 1990, the United States Congress, after years of delay and posturing, finally began to move on comprehensive child care legislation. Designed to help the millions of families with working parents, the bill would have put $2.5 billion into child care programs, would have greatly expanded child care slots, and would have set safety and quality standards nationwide. The Reform Jewish movement, long a supporter of some sort of national child care program, supported the bill from the start, as did most of the Jewish community.

Yet changes in the church-state provisions of the bill, made just weeks before a final vote, forced the Reform movement and civil liberties groups to question their support of the bill. The original version of the bill would have allowed federal funds to go to churches and synagogues conducting child care programs, as long as those programs were nonsectarian and did not discriminate against pupils and employees on the basis of religion. Some civil libertarians felt that even this support of religious institutions violated the First Amendment; most religious groups, however, including mainstream Jewish organizations, supported the compromise.

At the last minute, however, an amendment was added to strike the limitation, allowing for federal support for child care programs that included explicit sectarian religious activity and teaching.

Some of the bill's supporters said that the child care bill was too important to let die over such an issue: pass the bill, then fight these particular provisions in court. Others said that to support such a flagrant church-state violation, particularly when we could no longer count on the courts, would set a precedent that would lead to widespread destruction of First Amendment guarantees and increased governmental regulation of the religious institutions that accept these funds.

What should the Reform movement have done?

Response

As desperately as this country needs child care, the Union of American Hebrew Congregations and other Jewish groups felt that to allow the child care bill to blast a hole in the wall separating church and state would ultimately do more harm than good and to accept it would betray our own integrity. Most alarmingly, it would encourage governments and states to fund a wide range of overtly religious social service programs.

As with many national groups, we remain passionately committed to increasing the quality and quantity of child care.

> But we knew that no one else would care about a Jewish couple
> in a small midwestern town who, although armed with federal
> child care vouchers, would not be able to find a program in which
> their three-year-old daughter would not be expected to say the
> Lord's Prayer or be taught that Jesus was the son of God.
>
> Despite the Jewish community's opposition, the bill passed.
> The UAHC is looking for an opportunity to contest the church-
> state provisions of the bill by bringing our case to the courts, but
> when we consider the changing complexion of the judiciary, we
> are not optimistic.

In the late 1990s, similar dilemmas arose over various welfare reform
and social welfare proposals whereby conservatives forced through
provisions allowing government funding to go to religious organizations providing social services with religious content. In addition to
allowing overt religious proselytization, such a provision would also
permit religious discrimination in the hiring of those who run
programs. Unfortunately, a variety of these provisions continue to arise
within different legislative vehicles.

RELIGIOUS SYMBOLS: PUBLIC LANDS AND PUBLIC FUNDS

Every December a host of church-state controversies make headlines:
most notably, the intrusion of religious symbols on public lands and in
government buildings. The debate over the Chanukah menorah or the
nativity scene (crèche) displayed on public property has become so
common that Marc Stern, an attorney for the American Jewish
Congress, has called Chanukah the "Festival of Litigation."

By displaying a religious symbol in a public place and/or by using
government funds to pay for such symbols, the government would seem
to be offering sponsorship to beliefs that, the Constitution tells us,
belong to the private sector of the church and not to the public arena
of the state. The menorah on the steps of city hall or the Christian
nativity scene in its lobby appear to violate the First Amendment's
prohibition against established religion. And while many argue that
these displays are merely a recognition by the government of holidays
celebrated by its citizenry, the fact remains that when they are allowed

on public land or paid for with public funds, the state appears to accept and endorse their religious content.

As convincing as this argument might seem, recent Supreme Court decisions permit such displays under certain circumstances. In its 1985 decision *Lynch* v. *Donnelly*, the Court ruled by a 5-to-4 majority that Pawtucket, Rhode Island, could use state funds to pay for its nativity scene even on private property. The Court arrived at this decision by rationalizing that if secular objects such as Santa Claus and his reindeer, a wishing well, and a dancing bear were closely and inseparably linked with the nativity scene, the religious content of the scene would be adequately subsumed by the larger display of secular items. Thus the whole scene, including the crèche, would become a secular seasonal display of American culture. But do secular items effectively cancel out the religious symbolism of a crèche or a menorah? Has the Supreme Court the authority to divest Christian (and Jewish) symbols of their religious significance? Furthermore, even if secular items could negate religious symbols, how many secular items are needed to neutralize the display?

The Supreme Court affirmed its puzzling interpretation of the religious symbol issue in a 1989 decision, *County of Allegheny v. American Civil Liberties Union*. In this case, the Court decided that a crèche standing in a courthouse lobby was a religious symbol inappropriate for display on public property. At the same time, however, the Court upheld the constitutionality of a menorah on display on the plaza outside the county courthouse. Moreover, in two 1995 decisions the Supreme Court further lowered the wall of separation itself, permitting government funding of an overtly religious magazine in the *Rosenberger* case and the erection of an unattended religious symbol on public property (in the case of the Ku Klux Klan cross) in the *Capitol Square* case.

Why the menorah and not the crèche? The Court reasoned that the menorah was a religiously neutral symbol because it stood next to a Christmas tree and a sign proclaiming the blessings of freedom. In contrast, the crèche stood alone inside the courthouse, fully maintaining its religious symbolism. How curious! Does a menorah lose its religious significance when in proximity to a Christmas tree? On the outcomes of such tortured logic rests the fragile future of church-state separation.

A Real Dilemma: Menorahs on Public Property

The Lubavitch chasidic group in your community announces that it will place a ten-foot menorah in a public park to balance the nativity scene annually displayed there. The local Jewish Community Relations Council calls an emergency meeting to consider whether to oppose in court the chasidic display. You are a member of the committee. How would you vote?

Response

In several Jewish communities, local Jewish Community Relations Councils, joined by organizations like the American Jewish Congress and the UAHC and CCAR, have taken legal action to stop the Lubavitch project, arguing that on public property, *Jewish* religious symbols are just as inappropriate as are *Christian* symbols. These Jewish groups believe that the Lubavitchers are weakening the protections of religious liberty that the establishment clause helps secure.

In Burlington, Vermont, Rabbi James Glazer opposed the Lubavitchers and won an important federal appeals court case, relying on the Pawtucket case (*Lynch v. Donnelly*), ruling that menorahs cannot stand alone on public property.

THE RELIGIOUS RIGHT: WHAT DOES IT WANT?

In the past two decades, two major factors have caused religious fundamentalists to move more aggressively into the political arena. The first was unhappiness with the decisions of the Supreme Court and other federal courts that asserted the rights of women and the rights of minorities (including Blacks, Latinos, the handicapped, Jews, Catholics, and atheists) in opposition to those who would deny those rights. The fundamentalists became increasingly alarmed as these court decisions radically affected the communal institutions they saw as theirs, particularly in taking religion out of the public schools that trained their children. They found themselves held to a standard that in their view weakened the religious underpinnings of the value system that had long anchored the public school curriculum.

The second factor making for the politicization of the Religious Right was the intrusion of radio, movies, television, and rock-and-roll records that flooded their children's world with abhorrent images and values. All efforts to persuade their children to shun those intrusions were futile. In justifying his call for kids to destroy their rock records, TV evangelist Jimmy Swaggart told one of the authors of this book, "You know, if only Norman Lear had not put *All in the Family* into our homes, we would not be facing the problems our nation faces today."

Gradually, the reality began to sink in: if fundamentalists could not protect their children from the negative political, social, and cultural environment out there, then it was time for them to go out and change that environment.

Interestingly, one of the techniques adopted by the Religious Right to achieve its goal was to co-opt the very same technologies and public tactics it had so vehemently opposed. It remains to be seen whether in the long run such tactics as televangelism, Christian rock music, fellowships for athletes and beauty queens, and pro-Christian political organizations will empower or subvert the fundamentalists. The moral and legal scandals that disgraced TV figures like Jim Bakker and Jimmy Swaggart have weakened the credibility of the Religious Right. But at the 1992 Republican convention, the likes of Pat Robertson and Pat Buchanan were alive, well, and brimming with calls for a "religious war" to control the culture of America.

Through the 1990s, the Christian Coalition, the largest Religious Right political organization, has been among the most powerful and influential political forces in the nation. In areas with large Religious Right populations, the Christian Coalition has helped elect local, state, and congressional candidates to office. In areas with more diverse populations, however, the Christian Coalition has been far less successful, only rarely getting its candidates elected. In addition to its electoral efforts, the Christian Coalition is using its clout across America to try to reshape the nation, once and for all, by changing the Constitution.

CHANGING THE BILL OF RIGHTS

For a number of years, the Religious Right's number-one legislative priority has been to pass a constitutional amendment tearing down the wall separating church and state. In 1998, a constitutional amendment on school prayer was voted on by the House for the first time since 1971. This version would allow government-sponsored sectarian prayer, proselytization, and other religious activity to take place not only in public schools but in any government setting; religious symbols associated with the history of a particular community could be erected on city halls, courthouses, and schools; finally, there could be government funding for overtly sectarian religious activity. Because of the organized opposition of much of the religious community, it was defeated as it was in 1971, this time by 41 additional votes. All of the millions of dollars spent by the Religious Right, all of its political organizing and election of candidates beholden to them did not change the good sense of the Congress and the American people. The notion that someone's tax dollars could be sent out by the government to religious groups to be used to convert the taxpayer's children represents exactly the kind of activity that led Jefferson and Madison to write their religious freedom laws. Given a choice between Pat Robertson/Newt Gingrich and Thomas Jefferson/James Madison, the Congress opted for the vision of our founders.

If these amendments had been passed, America would be a very different nation than the one we have known, with America's 2,000 faith groups, denominations, and sects locked in bitter competition over whose prayer will be said, whose symbols will be placed where, who will get how much of the limited government funding available for their activities. Minority religions will be the losers; religious freedom will suffer; and America will be involved in exactly the sectarian strife it has been spared by the grandeur of the First Amendment—strife that has torn so many other nations apart.

The Religious Right argues that a reintroduction of religion into public schools will benefit America, reasoning that if schools include public prayer and religious traditions in their curricula and daily schedules, children will return to their moral and religious moorings, and society's problems will be ameliorated. To the contrary! It is demeaning to religion to suggest that something significant religiously will happen in an enforced moment of prayer. Even more, a fight over school prayer distracts America from real solutions to real problems.

It is a measure of the American people's repugnance for the agenda of the Religious Right that despite its all-out support, such attempts have heretofore failed; the good sense of the American people and the

Congress has recognized the folly of tampering with the Bill of Rights.

In response to the efforts of the Religious Right to have a constitutional amendment passed, President Clinton, opposing the amendment, took steps to address some of the valid concerns the Religious Right cited to justify the amendment. He sent a set of guidelines on the proper protection of religious speech in our schools to every public school district in the nation, providing a clear explanation of the broad range of religious expression already permitted under the Constitution. These expressions include the right of students to pray when they want so long as it does not interfere with other children's rights and is not organized by school officials, as well as the right to wear religious symbols, to read the Bible on their own time in school, to gather in religious clubs in secondary schools before or after school when other clubs meet, to study "about" religion, and to engage in character and values education. All these things are currently protected by the First Amendment.

Soon after, President Clinton issued another set of guidelines protecting the religious rights of workers in the federal workforce. Taken together, these steps demonstrate that within the existing First Amendment, it is possible to respect and protect religious expression in an environment of tolerance.

PRESSURE ON THE STATES AND LOCAL COMMUNITIES

Having learned from its failure to have its agenda implemented in Congress, the Religious Right has retrenched and begun organizing from the grass roots up. It has taken over school boards and library boards, town and county councils, and zoning commissions. In particular, the Religious Right has targeted Republican party caucuses and state conventions, having gained a controlling influence in twelve to twenty Republican state parties by the mid-1990s. The values and the vision of the Religious Right remain a threat to America and to the Jewish community.

This tactical shift is very important and requires a significant shift in the tactics of liberal activism—from the national to the local, with less emphasis on court victories and more on state and local electoral and legislative victories—if we are to preserve our religious freedom.

Such a shift has already occurred in the pro-choice movement as pro-choice activists, once secure in the knowledge that *Roe v. Wade* protected a woman's right to terminate her pregnancy, mobilize to ensure that the right to choose is not restricted at the local level and to replace anti-choice state and local officials with pro-choice challengers. In some states, these efforts have been enormously successful (e.g., California, Florida, and Virginia). In a growing number of states and territories, however, the right to choose is being dramatically impaired (e.g., Pennsylvania, Louisiana, and Guam).

If the current geography of the abortion debate is an indication of things to come in other areas where the Supreme Court is relinquishing its role, the nature of religious liberty in the United States will soon be determined state by state, locality by locality.

In states where we, as Jews, constitute a formidable political force (New York, for example), we can be fairly sure that our rights will be protected and respected. But what about midwestern and southern states in which Jews do not constitute a significant force?

To succeed in such states, we must rejuvenate the traditional Christian-Jewish coalition for decency. Whenever possible, it is important that non-Jewish leaders be involved in these efforts. Allowing such disputes to be perceived as Jewish-Christian conflict can only distract people from the important issues involved and can spell harsh intergroup conflict. And what of other religious minorities—Muslims, Hindus, Native American church members, and many others—whose rights are also threatened by the Religious Right? If we are to protect their rights and ours, we must be prepared to fight as effectively on the local level as we have on the national level.

A Real Dilemma: Cooperating with the Religious Right

During the late 1990s, forces favoring the separation of church and state faced a decision on whether to dilute some of the energy of the Religious Right by seeking to work with them in identifying those areas in which there is agreement on what is allowed by current law in terms of religious authority in the public schools and what accommodations the law requires for the religious beliefs and practices of federal government employees. If we worked with the Religious Right, we would legitimize them. Further, these projects ran the risk of identifying exactly those areas of religious activity that the government *cannot* engage in, thereby sharpening the focus on those areas that a constitutional amendment would address. On the other hand, we might weaken the Religious Right's arguments by clarifying the many areas of individual religious activity that are permitted and by showing how many of the infringements of rights so often cited by the Religious Right as justifying a constitutional amendment (e.g., a teacher telling a student she cannot wear a religious symbol or read a Bible in her spare time) could be solved by simply applying the First Amendment as it is written. Should we have worked cooperatively with the Religious Right groups?

Response

The Reform movement and most proponents of the separation of church and state decided to work with the Religious Right groups to delineate the current law and produce a set of guidelines for the schools and for workers in the federal workplace. (A precedent for such interaction had been set already in the early 1990s when these same groups coalesced to work on the Religious Freedom Restoration Act.) When the president disseminated these guidelines to all school districts and federal workplaces, there was immediately a sharp reduction in the number of lawsuits over religious issues in the schools. The use of the guidelines seems to have strengthened the political arguments of the pro-separationists rather than those of the Religious Right by ending the rare infringement of religious freedom that takes place in the schools—the kind of incidents that the Religious Right cites in justifying why we need a constitutional amendment allowing government sponsorship of religion. At the same time, these efforts instigated a cooperative dialogue with the Religious Right that has begun to change the attitudes of some of its leaders. These developments are one hopeful sign in this ongoing conflict.

A QUESTION OF PRIORITIES

In past decades, the maintenance of separation of church and state has been one of the highest priorities of the American Jewish community. Today we are divided, reducing Jewish influence and impact. The Orthodox community stands with the Roman Catholic community and the more fundamentalist segments of Protestantism on the key issue of public funds for parochial schools. And some Jewish observers now feel that American society is sufficiently tolerant that local violations of church-state separation are not worth opposing for fear of antagonizing our Christian neighbors.

They say the Jewish leadership has been too rigid, too absolute, unwisely challenging seemingly innocuous programs. They say we have risked serious community and interfaith conflicts in many cities and suburbs by challenging such insignificant Christian practices as silent prayer. And they say we have eroded our position as a faith group by lining up with atheist and secular groups in court tests and public controversy. What do you think?

··· 12 ···

Facing Anti-Semitism

In the decades following World War II, American Jewry experienced a glorious chapter of religious renewal, creativity, and cultural acceptance, becoming the freest, most affluent, and most secure Jewish community in the history of the Diaspora. Anti-Semitism declined significantly during this golden age, and most Jews no longer thought of themselves as guests in somebody else's home but as equal partners in a pluralistic America. With discrimination against Jews at a low ebb, many American Jews became somewhat complacent about the danger of anti-Semitism, leaving the matter to such groups as the Anti-Defamation League, which specializes in preventing, monitoring, and containing bigotry.

The 1995 bombing of the Alfred P. Murrah Federal Building in Oklahoma City shattered the complacency of most Americans regarding the strength and danger of extremism in America. The exposure of a widespread network of right-wing militias that were virulently racist and anti-Semitic raised alarms throughout the nation, especially among minority groups like the Jewish community.

In the 1980s and 1990s, David Duke had triggered some initial unease because he made significant advances into mainstream America. A former grand dragon of the Ku Klux Klan, one who regularly celebrated Adolf Hitler's birthday and whose entire career has consisted of exploiting racial fears and hatred, Duke pretended to have moderated his extreme views as he entered electoral politics. During his campaign, he cleverly pressed the hot buttons of affirmative action, welfare spending, and increased taxes. At a time of economic distress, he played on racial fears, blaming "them" for all the ills of society (e.g., crime, drugs, AIDS, welfare, and unemployment).

Armed with these buzzwords, Duke surprised everybody by winning a seat in the Louisiana state legislature. As a representative, he passed no bills in the legislature but helped to shift the agenda to target Blacks.

In 1990, Duke ran for the United States Senate and almost won, losing to Senator J. Bennett Johnston but winning 40 percent of the total vote and more than *60 percent of the white vote.* In 1991, Duke collected a war chest from all over the United States and ran for governor of Louisiana, losing to Edwin Edwards but gaining 39 percent of the vote and *more than 55 percent of the white vote in the state.* In 1992, he ran for United States president but was eclipsed by another right-wing candidate, Patrick Buchanan, whose own bigoted views on Jews, Blacks, women, and gays did not prevent him from attracting a large number of protest votes in many state primaries.

That a majority of white Christians in an American state would bestow their votes on Duke, a racist figure with such a bigoted background, is cause for distress and alarm. That Buchanan's bigotry did not seem to hurt him with a significant part of the electorate at large added to our anxiety. In light of these phenomena, plus events such as the attack on Jews in Crown Heights and ominous race-baiting and anti-Semitism on college campuses, and considering widespread economic insecurities, it seems that anti-Semitism in the United States is not merely a horror of the past. This evil needs watching; it compels a higher priority; and it is everybody's business.

SKINHEADS

The ADL first learned of skinheads when a small gang of neo-Nazis from Chicago, calling themselves Romantic Violence, surfaced at a 1985 conclave of hate groups in Michigan.

The skinheads originated in Great Britain and now have a following of some 8,000 to 10,000 there. They have counterparts in all of Europe, Canada, Australia, New Zealand, South Africa, and several Latin American countries. In 1990, several hundred rowdy skinheads demonstrated in Leipzig, Germany, screaming "To hell with Jews." The ADL has reported that while some skinhead groups continue to menace communities across America, their overall national membership seems to have stagnated at 3,000 to 5,000. One of the reasons for this decline is vigorous law enforcement by both federal and local authorities, who have responded to the call for vigilance made by Jewish and other organizations.

Skinhead violence is directed generally against competing gangs, but it would be a mistake to discount their lethal threat to racial and religious minorities. In 1988, a group of skinheads in Portland, Oregon, brutally assaulted three Ethiopians, killing one of the victims with a baseball bat. The skinheads responsible for the attack, who call themselves East Side White Pride, were sentenced to lengthy jail terms.

MILITIAS

The emergence of terrorist bombings in the United States—especially the bombing of the World Trade Center in New York and the Murrah Federal Building in Oklahoma City—represented a profound reality check for the American people. In the aftermath of these agonizing shocks, there was a rush to pass anti-terrorism laws, which would strengthen law enforcement. In addition, there was heightened concern about the dark, subterranean underground of hatred, despair, and antigovernment paranoia that has fueled white supremacists, home-grown Aryan and Nazi groups, as well as armed militia units in most states of the Union. What threat do these militias represent? How serious is that threat? What can be done legally to disarm militias and put an end to their harassment and intimidation of local officials? What public policies should be pursued to reduce the prospects of another Oklahoma City?

These questions have not been answered. They cry out for full-scale congressional hearings to focus the brightest light on the network of "wanna-be" terrorists, hate-crazed misfits, and psychopaths operating in the shadows of American life and spinning plans of violence and terror.

LEGAL STEPS AGAINST ANTI-SEMITISM

While one cannot change anti-Semitic attitudes or restrict anti-Semitic speech by passing laws, one *can* use the legal system to help check anti-Semitic activity. A step in that direction was passage of the Hate Crime Statistics Act in 1990, mandating the FBI to document every "hate crime": crimes based on race, religion, ethnicity, and sexual orientation.

In early December 1991, a case challenging a Minnesota hate crime ordinance, *R.A.V. v. St. Paul*, came before the United States Supreme Court. The case involved a teenager who was accused of burning a cross outside the home of a black family. Under a St. Paul ordinance, it is a misdemeanor to display symbols that arouse "anger, alarm, or resentment in others." In the 1942 Supreme Court case *Chaplinsky* v. *New Hampshire*, the Court ruled that one could be prosecuted for using language considered to be "fighting words," which "by their very utterance inflict injury or tend to incite an immediate breach of peace." There has been much debate over the implications of the *Chaplinsky* decision for the cross-burning case. *R.A.V.* v. *St. Paul* raises serious questions about where we draw the line between hate-crime violations and infringements on First Amendments rights. In 1992, the Supreme Court threw out the St. Paul ordinance as too broad and thus violative of the constitutional guarantee of free speech.

Consider the following composite situation based on actual situations that erupted in a number of congregations nationwide.

A Real Dilemma: A Synagogue Vandalized

Your synagogue is vandalized in the middle of the night. Ugly anti-Jewish graffiti, including swastikas, are spray-painted on the outer walls of the building. The rabbi calls you and other members of the board of the temple to an emergency meeting in his or her study at 7 A.M. What should we do?

The rabbi, of course, has already called the police and reported the attack. But questions remain: Should we go public as a means of warning the community that anti-Semitic activity is taking place in its midst? Would that just blow the incident out of proportion and run the risk of copycat crimes taking place at other Jewish targets? Should we quickly have the paint and graffiti removed so as not to disturb our members? Should we call upon the neighboring churches and other faith groups to speak out on this incident as an affront to us all? Should we organize and publicize an intergroup cleanup of the synagogue? Should we play this up, as a challenge to the conscience of the community, or play it down, as an act of vandalism, and leave it for law enforcement to handle?

Response

Some congregations have chosen to downplay such incidents, but all have notified the police. Most have released the facts to the press. When the synagogues have reason to believe that this is the work of an organized anti-Semitic group, as opposed to an act of individual vandalism, they are more likely to publicize the incident to rouse the awareness and concern of the community. In most cases, the general community responds quickly and visibly. In particular, churches are usually very quick to join Jewish organizations in denouncing the attack and participating in an interfaith cleanup of the graffiti. In communities like Mamaroneck, New York, such occurrences in the 1990s resulted in major, community-wide gatherings that denounced the anti-Semitic acts and offered the community's commitment to tolerance and pluralism.

Perhaps the most remarkable occurrence of this nature took place in an overwhelmingly non-Jewish community, Billings, Montana. When an outbreak of hate crimes struck Billings in 1993 (Ku Klux Klan flyers were distributed, a synagogue received bomb threats, tombstones in the Jewish cemetery were overturned, and a Native American family had swastikas painted on its home), Tammie Schnitzer helped rally her community in response. A convert to Judaism, Schnitzer gained firsthand knowledge of the terror of hate crimes when a brick was thrown through her son's window where he had a Chanukah menorah on display. Refusing to be intimidated by these acts, the people of Billings rose in opposition to the hate and ignorance that had been displayed in their town. The local newspaper printed full-page menorahs, which were displayed in homes and businesses throughout town. The PBS documentary *Not in Our Town* retells the Billings story and has been used as an educational tool on public television as well as at hundreds of universities, schools, churches, synagogues, and union halls. The story is also told in a song entitled "Not in Our Town" by Fred Small:

> When the Klan came to Montana, they made no
>   grand parade
> No hooded knights on horseback, no banners boldly
>   raised.
> Hate mail and bomb threats, midnight telephone calls
> "White Power," swastikas spray-painted on the wall.

Five-year-old Isaac woke screaming in the gloom
"Mommy, there's a man at my window, looking into
    my room!"
"Son, there's nothing out there but the shadows the
    branches make."
The little boy went back to sleep, his parents lay
    awake.

For Isaac's bedroom window showed their faith for all
    to see
The candles of the menorah stood for hope and
    memory
The next night out of the darkness a cinder block was
    hurled
It shattered Isaac's window and the boundaries of his
    world.

Chorus:
One moment of conviction, one voice quiet and clear
One act of compassion—it all begins here.
No safety now in silence, we've got to stand our
    ground
No hate, no violence—not in our town.

The cop was not unfriendly—he said, "Ma'am, if I
    were you,
I'd take down that menorah, that Star of David, too."
Isaac's mother, Tammie, said, "I'm sure that's good
    advice.
But how then could I ever look my children in the
    eye?"

Then at the doorway a little girl did stand
A gift for her schoolmate in her outstretched hand.
A menorah drawn in crayon, from a Gentile to a Jew
It read, "To Isaac from Rebecca, I'm sorry this
    happened to you."

Chorus:
"Have you seen the paper? Did you hear the news?
What kind of people are we? We thought we knew.
Can children primed in prejudice in peace together
    dwell?
If we look out through this shattered glass, do we see
    ourselves?"

Margaret MacDonald called her pastor on the phone
"This time the Jews will not face their foes alone.
We'll make paper menorahs, display them from our
    homes.
We'll show the bigots there are more of us than they
    have stones."

Shopkeepers handed out menorahs by the score
Children in their Sunday schools colored dozens more
Though in the town of Billings live not one hundred
    Jews
Menorahs now were everywhere on every avenue.

Through the drifting snow Tammie drove her chil-
    dren 'round
Menorahs by the thousands in the windows of the
    town
"Are all those people Jewish?" asked Isaac as they
    went
"No," his mother answered, "they are your friends."

Chorus

(Words and music by Fred Small.
Copyright 1994 Pine Barrens Music
[BMI]. Used by permission.)

Are Jews Responsible for Anti-Semitism?

Jewish behavior does not cause anti-Semitism. It was not Jewish behavior but Nazi genocidal policy that condemned 6 million Jews to slaughter. Hitler claimed it was the actions of Jews that made their elimination necessary: they were capitalists; they were Communists; they owned all the wealth; they were an inferior breed; they were anti-Christian. If the bloody chronicle of anti-Semitism proves anything, it is that "good behavior" does not shield Jews from blood libel accusations, religious persecution, or mass murder.

Yet such rationalizations linger. In 1992, a poll of Germans by the prominent magazine *Der Spiegel* found that 32 percent of the Germans believed that Jews themselves are at least partly responsible for being persecuted and hated by others. This finding reflects a growing trend of anti-Semitic attitudes and incidents throughout Europe.

Perhaps this is due to the passing of firsthand memories of the Holocaust, or maybe it is because of the pervasive economic problems of many of those countries. The "scapegoating" manifestation of anti-Semitism has been the most prevalent. Leaders faced with difficult political or economic problems have often sought to distract the masses by blaming the Jewish minority for the nation's ills. The dictator of Malaysia in 1997 blamed "Jewish speculators" for the collapse of his nation's economy. One might ask, "Why the Jews?" It is not always the Jews, but we are singled out often enough to keep us vigilant against anti-Semitic or racist attacks.

The early teachings of Christianity ignited anti-Semitism and reinforced it through the long centuries of our painful history. Christian scripture blamed "the Jews" for the crucifixion of Jesus, and early Christian thinkers began to speak of the crime of deicide: the killing of Jesus Christ.

Christian teaching asserted that the Jewish covenant created at Sinai was replaced by God sending "His son, Jesus, to redeem the world." As there was no longer a role for the old covenant, the continued role of those Jews who held to it became open to question. The refusal of Jews to accept fundamental articles of Christian faith was threatening to Christians. Jews believe in one God who is a unity; Christians believe that God is at the same time three (the Father, Son, and Holy Spirit) and one. Jews believe that redemption comes from remaining loyal to

God's covenant and following God's commandments; Christians believe that redemption comes from belief in Jesus. Jews believe that the Messiah could not have come because the world is still filled with persecution and bloodshed; Christians believe the Messiah once came to bring a purely spiritual redemption and will return to bring the messianic world.

When someone challenges the fundamental building blocks of your worldview, vigorous responses are common. The classic responses of Christians to Jews were attempts to convert them; to make sure that their inferior status would serve as a constant reminder of the error of their ways; to isolate them in ghettos; or to expel them from the Christian realm. This remained the norm until the so-called Age of Reason, beginning in the eighteenth century, when science, logic, and reason became the fundamental assertions of a new worldview—assertions Jews could embrace as easily as Christians. The ghetto gates opened, and most Jews moved into the mainstream of Western civilization.

The record of church authorities in Jewish persecution over nineteen hundred years is far more mixed than Jews commonly believe. While all too often the clergy participated in anti-Jewish activities or turned a blind eye to them, over the centuries, many Christian leaders intervened to save Jews and to stifle overt anti-Semitic activity. The Jewish community needs to revise its teaching of this aspect of our history to provide a more balanced and accurate picture of Jewish-Christian relations. Nonetheless, the traditional doctrine that the Jewish religion has been superseded may have led Christians to draw the conclusion that the Jew is therefore expendable and may have indirectly paved the way toward the Nazi Holocaust.

REFORM IN THE CHURCH

In the wake of the Holocaust, many Christian leaders began a soul-searching reexamination of the link between Christian teaching and the darkest chapter of human evil in history.

In recent decades, interfaith relations have undergone sweeping changes, especially within the Roman Catholic Church, which has formally reinterpreted some of its fundamental teachings to eliminate the anti-Semitic bias derived from historic interpretations of Christian

Scripture. Moreover, after Vatican Council II, convened by Pope John XXIII in 1963, the Roman Catholic Church—which had spurned interfaith contact for centuries—began to establish friendly relations with Protestants as well as with Jews.

Priests and rabbis exchanged pulpits. Roman Catholics became increasingly active in interreligious coalitions to address communal problems. Textbooks in Catholic religious schools were examined to eliminate or at least soften passages offensive to Jewish sensibilities. The Roman Catholic Church in the United States established an office for the improvement of Catholic-Jewish relations to stimulate dialogue, joint action, and mutual respect.

At a historic meeting in Prague in 1990, Catholic leaders for the first time accepted responsibility for the role Catholic teachings played in the bitter history of anti-Semitism, climaxing in the Holocaust. Repentance was the theme of the meeting, which was later echoed by the pope at a historic meeting with world Jewish leaders. Subsequently, the Church established formal relations with Israel and exchanged official representatives. And in 1999, in a document entitled "Shoah," the Church acknowledged its failures to respond adequately to the extermination policies of the Nazis.

Many Protestant scholars had similarly challenged their churches to cast off the sin of anti-Semitism, arguing that the false charge of "Christ-killer" was historically inaccurate and a cause of bloodshed and hatred throughout the centuries. The National Council of Churches, representing most Protestant denominations, has long maintained a liaison office to strengthen Protestant-Jewish relations.

HOW SECURE ARE JEWS IN THE UNITED STATES?

For the past fifty years, sociologists and demographers have been engaged in fairly detailed studies of anti-Semitic attitudes and behavior. They show that the number of people holding anti-Semitic attitudes has fallen steadily since the end of World War II. While this is a significant improvement, tens of millions of Americans maintain negative attitudes toward Jews. When it comes to acting out those attitudes, the number of overt anti-Semitic incidents has fluctuated over that time period but within fairly predictable limits—around 6,000 reported each year. In 1996, 8,734 hate crimes were reported, and 16 percent of all reported were motivated by a religious bias. Anti-Jewish incidents in particular accounted for 13 percent (according to material published by the ADL).

Three conclusions can be drawn from these statistics. First, all the surveys indicate that the more educated a person, the less likely he or she is to hold racist, including anti-Semitic, attitudes. As educational standards, driven by the success of our public school system in America, improved in the twentieth century, anti-Semitic attitudes declined. The stagnant standards of American public education, as seen over the past fifteen years, may cause a reversal of this trend.

Second, the post–World War II culture of America has deemed overt racist behavior as unacceptable. In addition, an array of legislation counters discrimination. Respect for the pluralistic character of America has encouraged tolerance in our intergroup relations. Hence the relatively small number of anti-Semitic incidents.

Third, anti-Jewish incidents often reflect more general problems in our society. Most anti-Semitic vandalism is *not* committed by members of organized hate groups but by young people out of school or out of work, looking for trouble. (Sadly, there have even been incidents perpetrated by emotionally disturbed *Jewish* young people.)

Most anti-Jewish incidents parallel hate crimes against Catholic churches or against Blacks, gays, immigrants, and other minority groups. When the economy is sound and people are confident about America, such crimes generally decrease. When unemployment increases and people despair, such hate crimes proliferate. It should also be noted that the police, the FBI, and other authorities are now more alert to hate crimes and more efficient in listing them.

The one group that does not correspond entirely to these norms is the African-American community, among which the percentage holding anti-Semitic attitudes has been 10 to 14 percent higher than among whites. This is a source of great concern to Jews. If we are to confront it, however, we must recognize that there are two different expressions of anti-Semitism among Blacks, including one that is different from that measured by most studies. The classic form of anti-Semitism is grounded in stereotypes: Jews are greedier than others, more powerful, and less loyal citizens. Such caricatures are generally rejected with increased education. Concerning this type of prejudice, anti-Semitic attitudes have fallen among educated Blacks as well.

The anti-Semitism that emerges among certain African-American intellectuals is a more political anti-Semitism: i.e., Jews are representatives of the white community, are economically exploiting people of color at home, and are supporters of Israel, a Western colonial outpost oppressing native populations abroad. This strain of anti-Semitism finds ample expression on many of the nation's college campuses, where Third World ideologies are commonly heard. This strand of politicized anti-Semitism is more resistant to the techniques employed in combating the more traditional variants of anti-Semitism.

On the other hand, the ADL surveys have also reflected two encouraging trends. First, the overall percentage of Blacks holding anti-Semitic attitudes has fallen at the same rate over the past fifty years as has the rate for whites. Second, while there was a common myth among Jews that anti-Semitic attitudes among Blacks actually increased with their level of education, ADL studies indicated that it is not so. Anti-Semitic attitudes fall with higher levels of education for all people.

In many ways, America offered protections against anti-Semitism unknown to the experience of the Jews in Europe. Because of the Christian roots of life in Europe and of the distortion of science to offer pseudoscientific justification for anti-Semitism, there was a tradition of government, religiously, academically, and institutionally sanctioned persecution of Jews. It was in this tradition that Nazi persecution of the Jews found fertile soil.

America, on the other hand, was a nation based on the enlightened humanistic beliefs of the Age of Reason. Democracy was a political system that in theory embodied those beliefs, particularly that of the equality of God's children. There was no widespread tradition of state-, church-, or university-approved anti-Semitism. The First Amendment served as sanctuary and security for every group, especially those most different.

In America, theories that deny the legitimacy of the Jewish people or the truthfulness of the Holocaust are normally regarded as loony and illegitimate. While there have always been religious extremists who targeted Jews, mainstream religious leaders and organizations have long accepted Jews as the third of the tripartite mainstream religious categories of American life (Protestant, Catholic, and Jew), a paradigm now being enlarged for Muslims. And while there were instances of state restriction of Jewish rights well into the nineteenth century, the more common experience was the legal protection afforded by the First Amendment's promise of religious freedom and separation of church and state.

Although even the legal and political advances of America could not eradicate the legacy of centuries of popular, folk anti-Semitic attitudes, the underlying beliefs of America have offered the Jew protection and opportunities unmatched anywhere in our history. Could it happen here? Could there emerge a serious anti-Semitic movement in America? Yes. There could, but it would be far more difficult than in Europe for this to become a mainstream trend precisely because of our different ideological history and our constitutional safeguards, and it would take a major economic collapse.

Alan Dershowitz, a professor at Harvard Law School and author of the best-selling book *Chutzpah*, believes that anti-Semitism is a growing problem in America. Moreover, he believes that American Jews have allowed themselves to become second-class citizens by acting like guests in a gentile home. Indeed, Dershowitz believes our leaders are afraid to condemn anti-Semitism and to confront those who are insensitive to it mainly because we are afraid of rocking the boat. We are afraid of being accused of dual loyalty—to the United States and to Israel.

Is Dershowitz right or wrong about anti-Semitism in America today? Right or wrong about the failures of Jewish leaders to speak out? The authors think Dershowitz is wrong on both counts.

A Real Dilemma: Jonathan Pollard

In 1991, Alan Dershowitz appeared before a committee of the National Jewish Community Relations Advisory Council (now the Jewish Council on Public Affairs—JCPA), the largest coordinating body representing major national and local Jewish organizations. He was then a leading advocate for Jonathan Pollard, an American Jew convicted of committing espionage on behalf of Israel. An intelligence agent for the United States Navy, Pollard admitted to stealing a large number of top secret documents and transmitting them to Israel, arguing that he did so as a committed Zionist to protect Israel. He was convinced that secret data (i.e., information about Iraq's nuclear, biological, and chemical capabilities) had to be shared with Israel for its own safety and security. He pleaded guilty and was sentenced to life imprisonment.

Dershowitz argued that no American spy in recent years, even those who provided enemies with classified information vital to our security, was given so harsh a sentence. Israel, he pointed out, is an ally, not an enemy. Dershowitz alleged that Pollard provided only information that had been promised to Israel by the United States but had been wrongly held back. The cruel sentence, he contended, was a reflection of the anti-Israeli, even anti-Semitic, attitudes of some people involved in the case.

At the same meeting, the United States attorney who prose- cuted the case argued that it was not the United States that had wronged Pollard, but Israel and Pollard who had betrayed the United States; that the stolen information was highly significant and compromised American intelligence agents; that he had sold (not given) the information to Israel; that this was not a Jewish issue but one of American law; and that Pollard was not Alfred Dreyfus and Dershowitz was not Émile Zola.

Dershowitz asked the Jewish organizations to speak out publicly for a commutation of Pollard's sentence on the grounds that the punishment was excessive. Jewish self-respect required no less, he concluded. What should those Jewish organizations have done?

Response

In the beginning, most Jewish groups refused to become involved, arguing that there was no evidence of anti-Semitism and that if the sentence was excessive, it could be appealed properly under American law and justice. While a number of groups, including the UAHC, were willing to join in a call for rehearing the sentence, they were not prepared at that time to advocate a reduction in the sentence or to agree that Pollard had been victimized by anti-Semitism.

Several Jewish organizations, however, including the Central Conference of American Rabbis (the Reform rabbinical associa- tion), decided that the extreme nature of the Pollard sentence suggested an anti-Israeli or anti-Semitic bias. The CCAR signed a brief asking for commutation of the sentence. In fact, a judicial review of the sentence was held in 1992 and by a 2-to-1 margin, a federal court of appeals upheld the sentence. (Ironically, both majority judges were Jewish; the dissenting judge, who called the sentence a travesty, was not Jewish.)

An underlying theme of the Pollard case was the so-called dual-loyalty allegation, falsely suggesting that Jews are more loyal to Israel than to the United States. By acting *for* Israel and *against* the United States, no matter how well intentioned his action may have been, Pollard has added credence to this anti-Semitic canard. For Jewish organizations to rally to Pollard's support without clear evidence of an anti-Israeli or anti-Jewish intent on the part of the American government might have the appearance of legitimizing these accusations. On the other hand, this does not mean that pleas for fairness in sentencing and for mercy—parole after serving the minimum ten years—would be inappropriate. Thus in 1993, the UAHC Biennial delegates passed a resolution calling for the president to commute Mr. Pollard's sentence, and the UAHC has urged the president to do so since then. Rabbi Alexander Schindler has visited Pollard in jail and has eloquently advocated his release. However, as of 1998, the president has chosen not to commute Pollard's sentence.

OPTIMISM OR PESSIMISM?

The expression of bigotry and meanness has indeed become more acceptable in America today—with more *overt* bigotry being expressed against Jews, Blacks, women, gays and lesbians, Koreans, and other Asians—than in the past several decades. The widespread burning of black churches in the mid-1990s was particularly alarming. Yet it would also be wrong to panic and exaggerate. Most American Jewish teenagers have not experienced anti-Semitism firsthand. Discrimination is illegal in employment, housing, medical care, and virtually every area of public life. On the whole, Jews at the end of the twentieth century are not disabled by anti-Semitism but instead enjoy unprecedented acceptance in American society. Jews make up 2.5 percent of the population but 10 percent of the U.S. Senate (in 1997, both of California's senators were Jewish as were five of its representatives in Congress, and both senators from Wisconsin, a state with a small Jewish population, were Jewish). In the 1990s, there were more Jews in Congress than ever before (in 1991, thirty-three in the House, ten in the Senate), and some were elected from districts or states with negligible Jewish populations. And where once the State Department was the bastion of white, Protestant culture, in 1998 numerous high-ranking officials, including the deputy secretary of state and several assistant secretaries of state, are Jewish. The secretary of state, Madeleine Albright, affirmed her Jewish roots, and it was a nonissue in American life except among Jews. Moreover, two of seven Supreme Court justices in 1998 are Jewish. Ironically, even in the trial of Terry Nichols for the Oklahoma City bombing, the jury selected as the forewoman a Jewish woman who was a convert to Judaism, a Reform Jew, who had lived in Israel for six months (and who opposed the death penalty, based partly on her reading of Jewish tradition).

Few barriers remain that keep Jews out of the best universities, the most desirable neighborhoods, the elite boardrooms of corporate America, or even the most exclusive country clubs. Jews have become presidents of the very Ivy League universities that once maintained anti-Jewish quotas, and the faculties and student bodies have strong Jewish representation.

All surveys confirm that Jews are widely accepted. An overwhelming majority of Americans do not object to living next door to a Jew, voting for a Jew, working with a Jew, and—more and more—even marrying a Jew. It could be argued that assimilation, not anti-Semitism, is the real threat to Jewish survival in America. Indeed, it has been argued that ironically, anti-Semitism keeps the Jewish people viable as a distinct group.

A Real Dilemma: JAP Anti-Semitism

The term "Jewish American Princess" or "JAP" has become a hateful stereotype of Jewish women as rich and self-indulgent. In recent years, the phrase has been used by Jews and non-Jews alike as a catch-all term to denigrate Jewish women. As the slurs depict her, the new "princess" has an insatiable greed for material things but little appetite for love, sex, or intellectual ideas. At Syracuse

University, students established "anti-JAP zones," which were out of bounds to any woman who displayed behavior construed as "JAPpy." At basketball games, women labeled as JAPs were publicly humiliated. Was this behavior anti-Semitic? Should the university have responded? How should the Jewish community have reacted to these incidents? If you had been a student at Syracuse, what would you have done?

This issue became more complex at the University of Michigan when members of a *Jewish* fraternity printed and sold "JAP-Buster" T-shirts around campus. How should the Jewish community have responded when Jews legitimize a self-hating sexist stereotype? By speaking out publicly against the JAP stereotype, does the Jewish community turn a crude craze into a cause célèbre?

Response

In both cases, the Jewish community felt that it was necessary to respond to the Jew-baiting incidents. Increasingly, national Jewish organizations regard the JAP stereotype as a veiled anti-Semitic attack, which, like any other bias-motivated activity, must be combated. That this expression of anti-Semitism has been cast in the guise of a joke and thus dismissed as frivolous requires even more vigorous repudiation.

At Syracuse University, Jewish women's groups protested and called on university officials to mount a consciousness-raising effort to discredit the JAP stereotype. The university responded by sponsoring sensitivity-training workshops that addressed the JAP stereotype in the broader context of discrimination.

At the University of Michigan, the response was less public but just as concerned. Today, the JAP stereotype is frequently discussed in seminars and workshops on intergroup relations and discrimination. Hopefully, men (including Jewish men), as well as women, are becoming sensitive to the fact that JAP jokes disguise anti-Jewish contempt whether it comes from non-Jews or Jews.

We have all faced the question of how to respond to ethnic or racial jokes. Suppose you are sitting at a lunch table with a few of your friends. One of your friends, who happens to be non-Jewish, tells you a joke about JAPs. What should you do?

1. Respond with another JAP joke you heard.
2. Say "I really don't think those jokes are funny."
3. Say "I find that kind of humor offensive."
4. Listen to the "joke" coldly, say nothing, and later weigh the incident in determining whether to continue that friendship.
5. Brush it off.

ANTI-SEMITISM ON COLLEGE CAMPUSES

In theory, the last place one would expect to hear anti-Jewish rhetoric is on the nation's college campuses, the citadels of liberality, free speech, and pluralistic interaction. Increasingly, however, the campus has become a cauldron of racial and ethnic conflict. Some examples:

1. In November 1993, at Kean College, in Union, New Jersey, Dr. Khalid Abdul Muhammad, a self-described disciple of Minister Louis Farrakhan, unleashed a venomous diatribe against Jews, calling them the "bloodsuckers of the black nation," as well as against Catholics and gays. The main topic of Muhammad's speech was "the secret relationship between Blacks and Jews," based on a book published by the Nation of Islam. The mostly black audience cheered as Muhammad outlined a Jewish conspiracy: the Jews crucified Jesus, "supplanted" and "usurped" German society, dispossessed the Palestinians, participated in the civil rights movement to exploit Blacks, and "raped black women," he said. Muhammad further claimed that Jews were liars and that Blacks were really the Chosen People. He also ridiculed the pope, the Church, women, and gays, among other targets. In our rage, we Jews little noted that we were the only target that responded to the assault. How come?

2. At the University of Michigan in the mid-1980s, Steve Cokely was invited to speak by a black student organization, following the

notoriety he achieved in Chicago alleging that Jewish doctors were part of a conspiracy to inject black babies with the AIDS virus.

3. At UCLA in 1990, the African-American student magazine *Nommo* published an article culled from *The Protocols of the Elders of Zion*, a classic anti-Semitic forgery. When Jewish students protested to the editors, one of them actually defended the authenticity of the protocols and attacked Jews as a "small group of European people who have proclaimed themselves God's chosen by using an indigenous African religion, Judaism, to justify their place in the world."

4. In 1991, Leonard Jeffries, a professor at CUNY in New York, then chair of the Department of Afro-American Studies, addressed a conference in Albany, New York, in which he denounced whites as inferior devils. He lashed out especially at Jews, charging that they control Hollywood and exploit and denigrate Blacks, dominated the slave trade, and conspired with the Mafia to control Blacks.

On other campuses, Palestinian students have invited speakers who blended their anti-Zionism with anti-Semitism, causing discomfort and anger among Jewish students. In the 1970s and 1980s, anti-Israeli groups also tried to have Hillel Foundations banned from using campus facilities on the grounds that they were Zionist and therefore racist, citing the then existing United Nations resolution equating Zionism with racism.

Should hatemongers be permitted on campus? Why not pass a law that forbids the expression of group hatred? Unfortunately, it is not that simple.

As previously noted, our courts have determined that the First Amendment was drafted to protect the expression of offensive ideas, not merely the bland and the tame. Nazis marching in Skokie, Illinois, and lunatics burning the American flag are two groups protected by the First Amendment of the Constitution. It is better to endure the slings and arrows of occasional verbal bigotry than to tamper with the U.S. Constitution, which provides Jews and other minorities with their ultimate security. (For a more detailed analysis, see chapter 10, "Safeguarding our Civil Liberties.")

Does that mean we have no recourse in the face of anti-Semitic slander? No. It means we cannot stop Jew-baiting through legislation or censorship.

Anti-Semitism can be fought. University officials must be pressed to assume a leadership role. Since the First Amendment only limits government from infringing on free speech, no private university is under any obligation to invite or bar any particular speaker to use its platform. And when the likes of David Duke or Louis Farrakhan do appear on campus and spew their hatred, university officials must be pressed to step up and condemn anti-Semitism and all forms of hatred as cancerous to the free spirit of academia. Students and faculty can also exercise their First Amendment rights to denounce bigotry.

Campus papers should be urged to speak out against the voice of bigotry. Coalitions of decency, representing all ethnic and racial groups, can organize counterdemonstrations or educational events. Truth squads can be organized to rebut falsehoods. Such means, utilized successfully on campuses, may require more effort than passing a problematic law, but that's the price of democracy.

A Real Dilemma: Kwame Toure on Campus

In 1991, a Jewish college student at the University of Colorado called the UAHC for advice. He explained that Kwame Toure (formerly known as Stokely Carmichael), considered by many to be an anti-Semite and an anti-Zionist, had been invited to speak on campus. Jewish students were upset and not sure how to react. Some were demanding that the university cancel Toure's contract. Others argued that censorship was the worst solution, preferring to stage a protest that would educate the student body. What would you have advised?

Response

Anti-Semitism often appears under the guise of anti-Zionism, as evidenced by the former United Nations resolution equating Zionism with racism. The Jewish students were rightly concerned about Toure's coming to campus, but breaking the contract would not have been advisable. If freedom of speech is to be protected for all, then even individuals espousing obnoxious views must be permitted to speak their minds. The Jewish students organized a counterevent—a "teach-in"—aimed at educating the rest of the university community about Toure's viciously hostile views on Israel, Zionism, and Jews. Inviting a persuasive Israeli spokesperson or a knowledgeable American Jewish leader at a subsequent date might be another effective counteraction. Organizing a debate is not advisable because placing a bigot on the forum with a respected figure gives respectability to the hatemonger.

There is also a danger in focusing only on tensions between Jews and other groups. Keeping a sense of perspective is vitally important. There are tensions and social alienation among various minority groups. Breaking down this alienation requires patient efforts. At the Black-Jewish College Conference described in chapter 9, a number of helpful steps were analyzed and detailed, including looking for opportunities to work together on projects of common interest; creating opportunities to socialize and share personal stories; creating dialogues for ongoing problems not only at times of crisis but also at times when things are calm; and seeking opportunities to stand up on issues of concern to the other group. While dealing with the problems of extremist speakers always provides thorny challenges, these problems are far less daunting when they arise in communities or on campuses that have strong track records of ongoing cooperation with a resulting level of trust.

Anti-Muslim stereotyping is also growing in America. Remember when the Oklahoma City bombing occurred and the immediate suspicion was "Middle East Muslim terrorists"? Every Muslim felt the twinge of fear we Jews have always known. And the Muslim community in America will surpass Jews in number early in the twenty-first century. The UAHC's Interreligious Affairs Department and the Religious Action Center have worked especially hard to encourage understanding and cooperation between Jews and Muslims. The UAHC published *Shalom/Salaam: A Resource for Jewish-Muslim Dialogue*, a manual drawn from the experience of scores of our congregations that have such dialogues. The RAC has worked closely with the Muslim community on religious freedom issues, against the genocidal activity aimed at Muslims in Bosnia, and in condemning instances of anti-Muslim hate speech in our own country. One of the coauthors cochairs a national coalition for peace in the Middle East, comprised of leaders from the Protestant, Catholic, Jewish, and Muslim communities.

RESPONDING TO BIGOTRY

One of the lessons of the American experience is that expressions of bigotry must be condemned by leaders of all groups, not merely by representatives of the religious or ethnic group that was maligned. Bigotry is seamless, and it must be countered by leaders across the spectrum of American life.

An example: In October 1997, Pat Robertson, who had earlier outraged Jews with a book that repeated an ancient canard about international Jewish power, insulted Muslims in comments made on his television program, *The 700 Club*. While calling justifiably for an end to persecution of Christians in the Middle East, Robertson said that "to see Americans become followers of, quote, Islam is nothing short of insanity." Jewish and Islamic leaders accused Robertson of denigrating a respected universal faith.

Rabbi David Saperstein sent the following letter to the Christian Coalition leader:

> Having just returned from the Union of American Hebrew Congregations' biennial conference, I did not, until now, have a chance to read of your remarks on the October 27, 1997, edition of *The 700 Club*, in which you said that seeing "Americans become followers of, quote, Islam, is nothing short of insanity." We are, of course, well aware that over the years you have advanced a vision of American society that was often at odds with our own. But these remarks step over the line of decency. Any vision of an ethical, tolerant, pluralistic America is simply irreconcilable with the ugly anti-Islamic animus of your remarks.
>
> That you engaged in such religious bigotry in the name of combating religious persecution compromises all of us engaged in efforts to rebuff that persecution. George Washington spoke directly to such a crabbed

vision of America when he asserted that in this new
nation: "To bigotry no sanction." Religious tolerance
and freedom are indivisible. Our common efforts to
combat religious persecution in other lands is irreconcilable with remarks such as yours.

For the sake of religious decency and for the integrity
of all those involved in the struggle for the religious
freedom you invoked to justify your comments, I call
on you to issue an immediate apology to Muslims and
to our nation.

Islam is one of the great religions of the world. Its
teachings are followed globally by tens of millions of
people. You cite the fact that early African slavers were
Muslim ("Why would people in America want to
embrace the religion of slavers?") to justify your anti-
Islam remarks. Can you not see that the exact same
thing could be said about Christianity or even Judaism
("Who would want to embrace the religion of slave-
holders")? We Jews have been the quintessential
victims of the kind of bigotry that attributes the faults
of the few to the group. That some, over the centuries,
have distorted and misinterpreted the Koran does not
make its followers "insane" any more than the actions
of those who murder doctors in abortion clinics taint
all your own parishioners or all Christians.

As members of a minority religion, we rejoice in the
increasing religiosity of the American people who are
finding their faith in the Islamic, Christian, Jewish,
and other religious movements gaining strength in our
country. But as a people who has experienced the
hatred and bigotry of others, we, too, are hurt by slurs
such as yours against the Islamic faith.

Reverend Robertson, intolerance anywhere is a
threat to tolerance everywhere. Surely, comments such
as yours put off, rather than advance, the day I know
we both pray for—"when all shall live under their vine
and fig tree, and none shall make them afraid."

In his response, Reverend Robertson reaffirmed his original statement. The Religious Action Center went public with the correspondence and major Jewish and Islamic voices joined in protest.

IS ANTI-ZIONISM A FORM OF ANTI-SEMITISM?

Since the 1970s, a new strain of anti-Semitism has appeared, masquerading as anti-Zionism or as "mere" anti-Israeli opinion. This poses a difficult dilemma for Jews. Is criticism of Israel the same as anti-Semitism? If so, how do we explain that during the 1980s, half of Israel's population was critical of former Prime Minister Shamir's policy on the territories and over half of American Jews and American Jewish leaders opposed the establishment of new settlements in the territories? How is it explained that Israelis, while generally supporting the peace process in the 1990s, split down the middle on how much land to give Yassir Arafat and the Palestinian Authority? And what of those American Jews who are bitterly opposed to the peace process? Clearly, criticism of particular policies of the Israeli government cannot be the same as anti-Semitism. But does the same criticism when it comes from non-Jews become anti-Semitism, racism against Jews?

Racism is the assignment of negative attributes, the deprivation of rights, or the imposition of responsibility on members of a particular group of people simply because of their membership in that group. Racism against Blacks, for example, consists of assigning to Blacks negative attributes (e.g., Blacks are violent), denying rights (e.g., Blacks are unqualified for certain jobs), or requiring certain actions not required of others based on group membership (e.g., instituting difficult voter registration procedures for Blacks).

The technical term for racism against Jews is *anti-Semitism*. Occasionally, one hears Arabs dismiss an anti-Semitic indictment: "I can't be anti-Semitic! I'm an *Arab* and *Arabs* are *Semites* themselves." This is nothing less than an intellectually insulting argument. Anti-Semitism is not discrimination against Semites; it is a term of art that means racism or bigotry against Jews.

One classical variant of racism is based on the religious belief of Jews. As cardinal John Henry Newman, himself a persecuted Catholic leader of the nineteenth century, once said: "Religious bigotry is assuming that your first principles are better than someone else's first principles and you therefore have the right to impose negative attributes to others for holding the 'wrong' first principles."

Judaism, however, is more than a religion; it is also a culture, a people, a civilization, and a nation. The national expression of the Jewish people is Zionism. When we refer to anti-Zionists, it does not mean that they oppose an aspect of Zionism or a particular policy of the Israeli government; it means that they simply deny the very legitimacy of Jewish statehood. In doing so, they would deny to Jews, solely *because they are Jews*, the same right to determine their political destiny that is granted to so many other peoples.

In this context, anti-Zionism is indeed anti-Semitism. The most distressing manifestation of this form of anti-Semitism occurred in 1975 when the United Nations General Assembly formally equated Zionism with racism. Since racism in its political form is prohibited by international law, the U.N. resolution declared Jewish nationalism (i.e., Zionism) to be illegitimate and unlawful. This was not only an attack on Israel's elementary right to exist as a Jewish state but an attack upon Jews everywhere.

In the early 1990s, Israel and the United States launched a major international effort to expunge this outrageous resolution. Addressing the United Nations General Assembly on September 23, 1991, American President George Bush called on the United Nations to repeal Resolution 3379, the Zionism-Is-Racism resolution, which he described as "mocking the principles upon which the United Nations was founded." On December 16, 1991, by a vote of 111 to 25 with 13 abstentions, the disgraceful resolution finally was rescinded.

THE DEEPER DANGER

The potential danger of anti-Semitism lies not primarily in the sleazy skinheads, not in the militias, not in vandalism, but in the failure of America to solve its urgent domestic crises: the rotting of our inner cities and the collapse of the public schools in them, the despair of the underclass, the spread of poverty among children, and the epidemics of drugs and of violence. Add to these inflammable conditions a full-fledged economic crisis, and the potential for anti-Semitism in America would be not only serious but likely. So the fate of the Jew is still interwoven with the economic, political, and moral health of the entire society.

The Jewish community has every right and duty to condemn all anti-Semitism, Christian or Muslim, left-wing or right-wing, white or black. We know that throughout our history, anti-Semitic words have often led to pogroms and even worse. But it is also important for Jews not to lose perspective.

We can find no safety in turning inward upon ourselves, severing our links with the general community. We can find safety only if we help America deal not only with the symptoms of anti-Semitism—ignorance, rage, bigotry—but with the root problems of our society. These spawn the evils of bigotry and conflict. Our task as Jews must go beyond the defensive job of countering the attacks upon us. Our task is to help bring about a just and peaceful society.

It has been said that only a person with a broken heart can be truly human. Jewish brokenheartedness has given us the empathy to understand the heart of the stranger. The lesson of the Holocaust is that the slogan "Never Again" must apply not only to Jews but to all peoples.

··· 13 ···

The Changing Jewish Family

THE TRADITIONAL JEWISH FAMILY

The archetypal Jewish family is the nuclear family—mother, father, and children—all of them linked to grandparents and to a large, extended family. This ideal family has inspired some sociologists and historians to conclude that the concept of wholesome family life, derived from Jewish tradition, may well be the crowning gift that Jews gave to world civilization. Implied in this valuation are warmth, closeness, mutual regard, intellectual and cultural aspirations, moral ideals, fidelity, religion, and integrity.

We still honor the ideal of two-parent families, but the reality is that the "traditional" nuclear family has become a minority segment of American families, including Jewish families. Consider the following:

- Only 17 percent of American Jews currently live in families with the father, mother, and children living in the same household.

- Intermarriage rates have surpassed 50 percent in the Jewish community.

- Jewish divorce rates approximate those for the general community; nearly one out of two marriages will end in divorce.

- The Jewish birthrate is so low that we are not reproducing our own numbers.

- Increasingly, there are late marriages, as well as growing numbers of blended families from previous unions.

- The number of single-parent families is increasing.

- The number of gay and lesbian families with (and without) children is growing.

The Jewish family in America is going through drastic and startling culture shock.

THE JEWISH FAMILY IN TRANSITION

Paradoxically, we who gave the world the exalted idea of marriage as a spiritual union (*kiddushin*) and of the home as a sanctuary of peace seem to be in the forefront of legitimizing contemporary movements that are challenging traditional family concepts. These trends include unrestricted sexual freedom, living together without marriage, and the choice of a growing number of married couples to have only one or two children or no children at all. Add to these tendencies the zooming rate of intermarriage and divorce, easy and legal access to birth control devices and abortion, and profound changes in the role of women and gays and lesbians in our society.

None of these developments was intended to weaken the institution of the family. Quite the contrary, some—like the women's movement, gay and lesbian rights, and abortion rights—are seen as means to enlarge freedom and thus strengthen family life in the long run. In the meantime, however, the Jewish family is in crisis as traditional values are being sharply modified.

What shape will the *Jewish* family take? In most American Jewish homes, secular values prevail. Television, sports, computers, and auto-mobiles have more influence on Jewish family life than do Hillel, Deborah, Isaiah, and Moses. More heed is paid to the analyst than to the rabbi or even to God.

Much of the self-centeredness of American culture has seeped into the consciousness of the American Jewish family, displacing the religious and moral underpinnings of yesterday, which commanded marital fidelity and reverence for the elderly and for one's parents. Similarly, alcoholism, recreational sex, substance abuse, as well as spousal and even child abuse, are no longer uncommon among Jews. The extended Jewish family has become a rarity as elderly parents often move to distant leisure villages or are placed in nursing homes far from their children and grandchildren. Are we witnessing a temporary aberration or is the traditional Jewish family becoming an endangered species?

In Jewish literature, the centrality of the family is paramount. "Honor your father and your mother" was one of the ten divine utterances heard at Sinai. The classic books of Jewish law are filled with attempts to spell out the responsibilities of children to their parents and vice versa. The practical implications of the commandments to honor one's parents are discussed in detail, and the responsibilities of parents to their children are even more clear. For example, the father must, among many things, provide for his son's circumcision, ensure that his child receives a proper education, and see that the child finds a suitable mate. All these were considered to be among the most crucial of the father's religious obligations, and any man who failed in them was regarded as a sinner.

WOMEN

The demands of Jewish women for full equality pose a difficult dilemma for traditional Judaism. Despite Jewish heroines like Deborah in the Bible and the traditional praise of the wife and mother as a "woman of valor," it is clear that Jewish tradition casts women in what today is viewed as an inferior position. Compared to most other cultures, however, Jewish tradition was for many centuries relatively more considerate toward women. Husbands were enjoined to honor their wives and to provide for their economic, sexual, and emotional needs. Jewish women were granted greater economic and legal rights than their non-Jewish counterparts in almost any other culture until the Age of Emancipation in the nineteenth century.

Nonetheless, Jewish law is plainly male-oriented. Within the framework of Orthodox *halachah*, women cannot serve as witnesses or as rabbis. Neither can they participate as part of the *minyan*, the traditional quorum of ten people required for public worship. They may attend services only if separated from men behind a *mechitzah*, or partition.

Perhaps the most problematic aspect of family law is the dilemma of the *agunah* ("deserted wife"). When a man leaves his wife without granting a *get* (religious divorce), the woman is still technically married. A second marriage without a *get* would be adulterous. Children of the second marriage would be considered *mamzerim* ("illegitimate") and would be unable to marry a "normal" Jew. This situation is sad enough when a husband disappears or is killed with no witnesses, but the situation often arises in which a husband tries to punish a wife by leaving her an *agunah* or actively delays a *get* for a better deal in a divorce proceeding.

In Israel today, such matters of personal status as marriage, divorce, child custody, inheritance, and others are subject to *halachah* and are administered solely by the Orthodox rabbinate. (See Chapter 6 on Israel.) It does not matter that one is non-Orthodox or even considers oneself "not religious"; there is no civil authority to which one can turn.

As equal rights within Judaism are demanded by women in Israel, in America, and wherever Jews live, the dilemma in reconciling traditional Judaism with the rising assertion of women's rights has begun to be resolved in the Reconstructionist, Conservative, and Reform movements. Conservative Judaism now allows its synagogues to count women as part of a *minyan*, and they may also be called to read from the Torah. In 1985, its Jewish Theological Seminary decided to ordain women rabbis and its cantorial association finally allowed women to join in 1991.

In the smaller Reconstructionist movement, there has long been a strong egalitarian view. The Reconstructionist Rabbinical College admitted women to its rabbinical program from its founding in 1968. By 1996, women served as presidents of both the Reconstructionist Rabbinical Association and the Jewish Reconstructionist Federation, the congregational arm of the movement.

In Reform Judaism, the dilemma of equal religious rights for women has been largely resolved. From its inception, Reform, at least in theory, was based squarely on equality of the sexes. Men and women pray together and are encouraged to participate in all aspects of religious life. The first woman rabbi in history, Rabbi Sally Priesand, was ordained in 1972.

Today, more than half of the rabbinic and cantorial students at Hebrew Union College–Jewish Institute of Religion are women. Increasingly, women are serving as temple presidents, educators, congregational board members, and in positions of national leadership. The picture of legal and functional equality, however, conceals residual sexism in custom and practice that still prevents the full participation of women, even in liberal Judaism. Of the 243 members of the Board of Trustees of the Union of American Hebrew Congregations in 1998, only 65 were women, a decrease in percentage from 1991; and few chairs of important committees are women. The leadership of the UAHC is pledged to improve this record.

In 1997, the First International Conference on Feminism and Orthodoxy, chaired by noted Orthodox Jewish feminist Blu Greenberg, was held in New York City. Organizers expected about 350 participants. Over 1,000 showed up. In 1998, the number of participants more than doubled. The overwhelming attendance at and interest in the conference are evidence of significant changes in women's attitudes within the Orthodox community. Issues discussed at the conference included gender and traditional texts, expanding women's religious roles, reclaiming a mother's name in traditional ceremonies like *Berit Milah*, pre- and postnuptial agreements, domestic violence, modesty laws, creation of women's prayer groups, rabbinic ordination of women, and *get* (Jewish divorce) law.

Women are increasingly creating and attending women's prayer groups (some of which continue after being banned by rabbinic boards) and studying Torah as full-time pursuits. There are approximately sixty Orthodox women's institutes in Israel and several in the United States devoted to the study of Torah. The existence of these institutes and the steadily rising numbers of women actively engaged in study does not mean, however, that there is widespread official acceptance of or support for these efforts. Many movement leaders feel that women are prohibited from this type of study, and as Rabbi Hertz Frankel, dean of an ultra-Orthodox girls' school maintains, "The purpose of the girls' education is to be chasidic housewives and mothers, the pillars of the home...our girls don't care about feminism, about reading the Torah, about getting an *aliyah*."

Rabbi Emanuel Rackman, an Orthodox rabbi who is chancellor of Bar-Ilan University in Israel, is a supporter of equal-opportunity Torah education and of women's rabbinic ordination. He stated in a column for the *Jewish Week* that:

> it is a pity that so many in our day would begrudge [women] what they seek: more of God, more of Jewish learning, more of *mitzvot*, more responsibility, more of the yoke of the law.... These women will prevail. They will one day omit no prayers in their services and enjoy the guidance of ordained women.

What is clear is that the growing numbers of women completing studies at a rabbinic level will bring about irresistible pressure for systemic changes, empowering them to use that knowledge as leaders of their communities.

In 1997, two Orthodox synagogues hired women in "para-rabbinic" roles as congregational interns, and more are in the process of doing so. These interns teach classes, visit sick congregants, help prepare girls for their bat mitzvah ceremonies, counsel women congregants, and deliver "sermonettes." Until these positions were created, careers within the Orthodox religious world were limited to teaching at Jewish day schools or universities. Most highly educated Jewish women sought work in the secular world.

For the first time, there are places—albeit too few and far between—for women to serve as sanctioned educators and leaders in the Orthodox community. While both the quality and quantity of women's education is on the rise, the challenge lies in finding meaningful jobs and, for many, in finding husbands, rabbis, and communities that aren't intimidated by their levels of Jewish scholarship and learning and by the mounting backlash by the intimidating right wing of the Orthodox movement. As Blu Greenberg noted after the 1998 conference, "The open question is, where will these women go from here, what will they be doing?"

GENDER LANGUAGE AND PRAYER

Judaism has a rich liturgical tradition. Many of the prayers in our *siddur* can be traced back to the beginning of the Common Era—almost two thousand years ago. While there have always been minor variations within each community, the basic outline and wording of the prayers went unchanged until the beginning of the Reform movement in the 1800s. At that time, major changes were made—many prayers were abbreviated, repetitive psalms and poems that had been added in more recent centuries were removed, and other prayers were altered to accurately reflect the theology of the movement. Such changes occurred only after careful consideration because the power of the worship experience, at least in part, is based on a perceived eternality of the words we say.

In recent years, debate about prayer language has focused on gender issues, both in reference to humans and to God. The language that we use in our rituals and our prayers creates filters through which we see the world. What has been the impact of thousands of years of describing God as a "He" and using male terms (e.g., men, mankind) to describe people in general?

When *Gates of Prayer* was published in 1975, the editors were careful to ensure that its English translations referred to human beings in a gender-neutral manner (referring neither to males nor females exclusively). However, God was generally referred to in male terms and no Hebrew prayers were altered because of this issue. It was not long after *Gates of Prayer*'s publication that both of these issues were raised.

Now, many Reform and Reconstructionist and several Conservative synagogues have made significant changes to their liturgy, even before new *siddurim* have been published to reflect such differences. These changes include the inclusion of the names of the *imahot* (mothers) along with the traditional *avot* (fathers) in the first blessing of the *Amidah*; changing references to God from third-person singular (where there is no gender-neutral term) to the second person "You"; and adding Miriam's name to Moses' in reference to the *Song of the Sea*.

In the 1980s, the Reform movement adopted a policy that all future prayer books would use only gender-sensitive language in reference to God.

While most rabbis support this policy, several difficult issues have been raised. Is the word "Lord" a male term, or does it refer only to God? If it is deemed a male term, does that necessitate changing the translation of the *Shema* from "Hear O Israel, the Lord is our God, the Lord is One" to "Hear O Israel, the Eternal is our God, the Eternal is One" or, alternatively, "...*Adonai* is our God, *Adonai* is One"? What of quotes in masculine language from the Bible? Can they be changed? What do we do with prayers whose traditional language resonates with people both in Hebrew and English, such the *Avinu Malkenu*, "Our Father, Our King" prayer on Yom Kippur? "Oh, Lord, what is man that You are mindful of him" from the Psalms? Do we change the English, the Hebrew, or both? Do such changes mandate the publication of a new prayer book, despite the cost that this involves? Or is all of this just a form of liberal political correctness?

*A Real Dilemma: Do Jews Have a Right to Use "Traditional"
Gender-Specific Liturgy?*

In 1996, the CCAR published a new edition of *Gates of
Repentance*, the high holiday *machzor* (prayer book) for the
Reform movement. Based on its policy, it eliminated all English-
language male-exclusive references to God in the liturgy. Thus
the term *Avinu Malkenu* was used in the Hebrew and the English
without translation. However, an alternative version was also
included in the back of the book. Here, the words *Avinu Malkenu*
were changed in both Hebrew and English. The Hebrew was
altered to read *Shechinah, M'kor Chayenu* (literally, Divine
Presence, Source of our lives), and in each line of the English
translation, a different divine attribute was used to address God
(e.g., "Motherly Presence, Source of our lives" or "Guiding
Presence, Source of our lives"), depending on the content of that
line of the prayer.

While many rabbis acclaimed these changes, others did not.
Some objected to the gender-sensitive language in principle,
asserting that it distances the Hebrew used for three thousand
years in the Bible and the *siddur*. Others argued that their congregations could not afford to buy all new books and it was wrong to
force them to buy new gender-sensitive books, creating a situation in which part of their congregation would be using one
book, part the other. At the very least, the dissenters wanted the
CCAR to respect their freedom of choice regarding these
significant changes and to continue publishing the old versions
for a few years, so they could stockpile copies for new members
or replace worn-out books. The CCAR Executive Committee
refused to do so, citing its policy to publish only gender-sensitive
prayer books.

Should the CCAR continue to publish nongender-sensitive
prayer books, at least for a limited period of time, since many
congregations use them and either disagree with the changes
made or cannot afford to buy the new books? Or, alternatively,
should the conference hold that this was a matter of principle,
that it needed to guide the movement into more appropriate
prayer language and publish the gender-sensitive prayer book

exclusively? Is this an issue of social justice or only of synagogue liturgy?

Response

At the CCAR's June 1997 meeting, those who objected to the CCAR policy brought forth a resolution that would allow the continued publication of the older version of *Gates of Repentance* for at least one year. This resolution was defeated and the CCAR has continued to publish gender-sensitive prayer books only.

As the CCAR considers publication of a new *siddur* to replace *Gates of Prayer* (for Sabbath, festivals, and daily prayer), one of its guiding recommendations is that "the language of the service must strive to be inclusive and address the diversity of worshipers including gays and lesbians, Jews by choice, differently abled." In addition, it recommends that "the CCAR should consider feminism as an important lens through which plans for the new *siddur* should be examined. Women's experiences and voices must be included in the text. God language is a reflection of theology. How we image God will depend in part on whose voices are included in the text." We might add: how we image women will depend on how we talk about God. As such changes are contemplated, this debate is likely to continue for some time to come.

ZERO POPULATION GROWTH: IS JEWISH SURVIVAL AT RISK?

Jewish anxiety about the future of the Jewish family is intensified by the fear that we Jews may be a vanishing breed. The Jewish birthrate is so low (2.1 children per family) that we are not reproducing even our own numbers, much less making up for the grave loss of one-third of the entire Jewish people in the Holocaust. What makes matters worse is a growing intermarriage rate of about 52 percent and a declining rate of conversion to Judaism (the 1991 Jewish population study indicated that those entering Judaism through conversion [9 percent] and those converting out of Judaism were essentially equal). The study also indicated that contrary to long-held assumptions, only 28 percent of children of intermarriages are raised as Jews; 41 percent are raised as non-

Jews; and 31 percent are raised without any religion. (There was some positive data, however, such as that among synagogue members, the intermarriage rate is only 30 percent.)

Since World War II, the percentage of Jews in the United States in relation to the total population has dropped from 5 percent to 2.4 percent. As a result, we are losing political and cultural influence, and our communal and religious structures are not as strong as they might be. Within a decade, Muslims in America will surpass Jews in number. Will Jewish influence and political clout decline as a result?

What steps can be taken now to protect our future? Some answers are clear: strengthening the Jewish family through the teaching of Jewish parenting skills; family programming in the synagogue; expansion of outreach programs aimed at bringing intermarried families into the life of the synagogue; dynamic adult education programs; more creative efforts in religious schools and youth groups to discourage intermarriage; and greatly expanded Jewish camping programs and youth trips to Israel—programs that have proven to be the most successful efforts in strengthening Jewish identity among our young people.

Other possible solutions raise interesting ethical and political dilemmas. Some Jewish leaders have recommended that communities launch a determined educational campaign to persuade young Jewish couples to have larger families. They argue that we have a moral obligation not "to give Hitler a posthumous victory," and therefore this generation must bring the Jewish population back to a level that will guarantee Jewish survival.

A Real Dilemma: Should Jewish Families Be Encouraged to Have More Than Two Children?

In 1978, the Central Conference of American Rabbis (the Reform rabbinical association) considered the following resolution: "Reform Judaism approves birth control, but we also recognize our obligation to maintain a viable and stable Jewish population. Therefore, couples are encouraged to have at least two or three children."

Reactions were strong and divided. One woman said of the proposal:

I feel that what the CCAR is asking shows a lack of respect for the woman, for the child, and for the family. They are asking Jewish women to become baby machines for the political benefit of the community. Nowhere do they talk about how a woman might feel using her body in this way. Many women and mothers feel burdened and want an opportunity to do more with their lives than simply care for their children and their men. It is asking women once again to subordinate their own needs to that of the community and to become either eternal mothers and housewives or baby makers.

(Mary Gendler, *Women's American ORT Reporter*)

If the Jewish community feels it has a right to consider asking Jewish women to have more children, is it not obligated to provide day-care service to relieve the burden on mothers who aspire to professional careers? Should the wording of the resolution have recognized adoption as a viable alternative?

If you had been a rabbi and a member of the CCAR, would you have voted for this resolution? Why or why not?

Response

The CCAR passed this resolution. Although undoubtedly some Jewish couples have decided to have more than two children for the explicit reasons embodied in the resolution, there has been no noticeable trend of increasing birthrates among liberal Jews. It is interesting to note that while the Orthodox community has a higher birthrate, it has not grown either in absolute numbers or as a proportion of the Jewish community because many choose to become Conservative or Reform Jews.

However, the Reform movement's Outreach program, seeking to enhance the Jewish identification of children of intermarriage, has increased our numbers by keeping within our community children who otherwise would have been lost to Jewish life. The high rate of intermarriage results in potential danger—and potential opportunities. If each couple averages two children and there were no intermarriage at all, for every 100 Jews originally, there would be 50 marriages producing 100 children. If there is a 50 percent intermarriage rate, 50 of those Jews will marry non-Jews, producing 100 children, and the other 50, marrying each other, will produce 25 marriages with 50 children. These statistics argue for yet stronger outreach programs to bring the children of intermarriages fully into the Jewish community.

INTERMARRIAGE: THE BIG DILEMMA

American Jews are obviously deeply concerned about the high rates of marriage between Jews and non-Jews.

What can be done about it? A central debate in the Jewish community has to do with rabbinic officiation at an intermarriage. Orthodox and Conservative rabbis are overwhelmingly opposed, feeling that to put the stamp of Jewish authenticity on such a marriage is to legitimize a trend that threatens Jewish survival and sends a message to young Jews that it is all right to intermarry. They feel that officiating at such a marriage is also an abuse of the trust that the Jewish community places in them at ordination and performing a Jewish ceremony for a non-Jew shows a lack of respect to the non-Jewish partner who has made a conscientious decision not to convert.

Reform and Reconstructionist rabbis are split on the subject, the majority siding with their more traditional colleagues. A growing minority disagrees, contending that the marriage will take place anyway; that it is better not to drive the couple away completely; and that free choice also must be respected. Rabbis who do officiate at such marriages generally require that the couple agrees to raise its children as Jews.

What happens *after* a couple intermarries? Should the Jewish community reach out to the couple, or write it off as lost? Reform Judaism leads the Jewish community in the effort to bring such families into Jewish communal life. The UAHC/CCAR Outreach Commission encourages programs in all Reform temples to involve the intermarried couples and to demonstrate that Judaism is a universal faith, accessible to the non-Jewish partners.

A Real Dilemma: Should NFTY Require Only Jewish Dating?

In 1991, United Synagogue Youth (USY), the Conservative Jewish youth movement, adopted a resolution calling on all its members not to date non-Jews because interdating leads to intermarriage. The proponents of the resolution were gravely concerned about the skyrocketing rate of intermarriage. They felt that if they were committed to the survival of the Jewish family and the Jewish people, they had to do whatever was in their power to discourage the trend toward intermarriage. The most effective way to stop intermarriage was, they felt, to stop interdating. Should NFTY, the youth movement of Reform Judaism, adopt a similar resolution?

Why or why not?

Response

NFTY refused to go along with USY, seeing the issue as an invasion of individual autonomy and personal freedom. They, too, felt that mounting intermarriage was a serious problem but believed the focus ought to be on building stronger Jewish identities, on better education about the problems of intermarriage, and on effective outreach programs to the intermarried families rather than on attempting to mandate dating patterns, which they assessed to be ineffective.

Although NFTY did not pass a resolution on this topic, leaders of NFTY did draft a statement that expressed diverse opinions about the USY resolution. The statement contains the following language:

> The concern for the Jewish community is understood and justified. However, that future rests on issues of Jewish identity rather than blood.
>
> If one interdates and ultimately intermarries, what is important is that the Jewish half of the couple does not see the marriage as cause to stop the development of a Jewish identity...we feel it is important that the children be raised as Jews.

THE RIGHTS OF GAY AND LESBIAN JEWS

The issue of gay and lesbian rights burst into the nation's consciousness in the 1970s. The quest for gay and lesbian rights has become one of the legitimate social revolutions of our time. It is estimated that between 3 and 10 percent of the population might be gay. According to this estimate (*Kinsey Report*, 1947), there were about 26 million gay people in the United States in 1998. Thus it can be inferred that in North America today, perhaps 150,000 Reform Jews and 500,000 members of the larger Jewish community are gay or lesbian.

There is an increasing body of law that bars discrimination on the basis of sexual orientation. In this more tolerant atmosphere, gays, lesbians, and bisexuals exert increasing political power, especially in cities like New York and San Francisco. National leaders, including some members of Congress, now publicly affirm their gay and lesbian identity.

Despite these steps forward, there has been a sharp rise in incidents of gay- and lesbian-bashing, including physical violence. According to government statistics, bias-related violence against gay and lesbian people constitutes the fastest-growing recognized category of hate crime. Anti-gay violence rose 102 percent from 1990 to 1995. In 1996, there were 2,529 reported episodes of anti-gay harassment and violence in fourteen major U.S. cities, a 6 percent increase from 1995. Gay men, lesbians, and bisexuals surveyed by the Philadelphia Gay and Lesbian Task Force in 1995 were victimized at least three times more often than the average rate for the U.S. adult population. Threats and pressures placed upon young homosexuals are thought to have contributed to the disproportionately high suicide rate among gay teens. According to the Department of Health and Human Services, gay and lesbian teens are three times more likely to commit suicide than other teenagers. This statistic does not, however, reflect the additional population of gay teens who commit suicide without anyone ever knowing of their sexual orientation.

While there is a trend toward city and state laws barring discrimination based on sexual orientation, there is no federal protection of gays and lesbians in terms of employment, housing, or public accommodations. In 1996, despite overwhelming popular support, the U.S. Senate narrowly defeated the Employment Non-Discrimination Act (ENDA), a bill strongly supported by the Reform movement, which would have barred workplace discrimination on the basis of sexual orientation. The defeat of ENDA leaves gays and lesbians without federal protection from workplace discrimination.

Fundamentalist religious groups have joined with right-wing political forces in an effort to link homosexual rights with pornography and abortion as part of a "liberal" conspiracy to destroy traditional American family values. Against this bigotry, supporters of gay and lesbian rights have invoked the memory of Nazi persecution, an argument intended to appeal, in part, to Jewish sensibilities. They recall that in addition to moving against Jews and other minorities, the Nazis persecuted gays and Gypsies. It is bitterly ironic that upon liberation by the Allies, many gay concentration camp inmates were transferred to civil prisons to "serve out their terms."

JEWISH VIEWS OF GAY AND LESBIAN RIGHTS

What about the Jewish community? Where does it stand on gay and lesbian rights? In part because of the clear halachic statement that homosexual sex is an "abomination," most Jewish organizations, especially traditional religious bodies, have been slow to address the issue of gay, lesbian, and bisexual rights.

In the last decade, the Reform and Reconstructionist communities have confronted various issues related to gay and lesbian rights. As liberal movements within Judaism, they asserted the inherent dignity and equality of *all* God's children, that we are all—gay, lesbian, and straight—created *b'tzelem Elohim*, in God's image.

A Real Dilemma: Should a Rabbi Perform a Wedding for a Gay or Lesbian Couple?

Two Jewish people, long active in their local temple, decide that they want to get married. Having lived together for several years, they wish to take the next step: celebrating their decision in a religious ceremony. The partners make an appointment with their rabbi. After meeting with the couple, the rabbi says that he is not sure he could perform a marriage between two women.

What could the rabbi do? After all, according to *halachah*, marriage is a legal contract between a man and a woman. In American civil law, this issue is currently being debated. The Defense of Marriage Act (DOMA), passed in 1996 and signed under heavy political pressure into law by President Clinton, required the federal government to define marriage only as the union of one man and one woman. Yet states still possess the authority to recognize same-sex marriages, as a Hawaiian lower court recently did. Without legal recognition of same-sex marriage, gay and lesbian couples cannot benefit from the tax breaks, health insurance, and inheritance laws that a married man and woman receive. But what about a religious Jewish wedding?

The heterosexual ideal is central to traditional Judaism. If a rabbi performs a same-sex ceremony, wouldn't he or she be encouraging homosexuality? Does such a ceremony teach young people that in Judaism homosexual relationships are acceptable and equal to heterosexual relationships?

Isn't marriage about creating a family with children? What about a *ketubah* ("wedding contract"), the *Sheva Berachot* (the "Seven Blessings" said at weddings), or the language *kedat Moshe* ("according to the law of Moses")? What would the reaction of other congregants be? The board of directors? The larger Jewish community? Should the views of congregants affect the rabbi's decision? Does this mean their anniversary will be listed in the temple bulletin or mentioned from the *bimah*?

In 1998, when the CCAR was expected to formally consider this issue, many Reform rabbis in Israel urged the CCAR not to endorse same-sex rabbinic officiation or at least not now, asserting it would be a significant setback for their efforts to achieve formal recognition in Israel. It would, they said, be used by the Orthodox community to paint the Reform movement as a radical extremist sect and would be used by the Israeli government as justification to withhold formal recognition—at exactly the moment when the Reform movement was making real strides in its long struggle for recognition. The battle for recognition, which affects every Reform Jew, is too important to be jeopardized by taking a formal position on this issue at this time, they argued. Supporters of the resolution argued that this was a matter of principle that could not and should not be put aside for political expediency. Further, there would always be some reason to postpone acting on this issue and angry controversy has met every Reform initiative. Better to "bite the bullet" and take action now. What position should the CCAR have taken? What weight should the CCAR have given to the views of the Israeli rabbis who asked the CCAR not to pass this resolution at this time?

Response

In the 1990s, both the UAHC and the CCAR passed resolutions endorsing full civil rights for gay and lesbians, including formal support for same-sex civil marriage. Both resolutions stopped short of endorsing same-sex religious marriage, and neither the UAHC nor the CCAR had yet developed explicit policy on this issue by the time this book went to press, thus leaving it to the judgment of the individual rabbi.

While the vast majority of Reform rabbis warmly welcome gays and lesbians as congregational members, at present only a few Reform rabbis perform such weddings. Others oppose such weddings, some have never been asked, and yet others do not have a formal position on the issue. The CCAR is currently studying the issue.

Those rabbis who perform weddings between homosexuals feel that such couples are committed to creating a strong Jewish household and apply the same criteria they use to evaluate a heterosexual couple. They look not to *halachah* but to the aggadic concepts of the infinite value and equality of all people, asserting that the values of love and sanctity could flourish as easily in a gay marriage as in a heterosexual marriage. By changing a few words of the traditional ceremony (as rabbis have long done for heterosexual couples desirous of an egalitarian ceremony), some rabbis feel they can perform with integrity a Jewish wedding for a gay or lesbian couple.

Others cannot justify performing a gay or lesbian wedding, either because they do not accept homosexuality as a legitimate way of life or are *not* prepared to deviate so radically from the

Jewish tradition and the rest of the Jewish community.

In contrast, many Reconstructionist rabbis do officiate at gay and lesbian wedding ceremonies. The Reconstructionist Rabbinical Association's *Rabbi's Manual* contains a sample wedding ceremony for use with gay and lesbian couples. As might be expected, almost no Conservative or Orthodox rabbis would officiate at such ceremonies.

As to the concerns raised by Israeli rabbis, CCAR rabbis seemed split on the issue. Some suggested that passing a resolution that did not call for rabbinic officiation but acknowledged the value of such marriages and affirmed the autonomy of rabbis to follow their individual consciences on the issue of officiation might meet everyone's needs. Critics who favored rabbinic officiation argued that that would be a sellout, while opponents argued that such an affirmative resolution would still give the Orthodox rabbinate additional ammunition to attack Reform Judaism. The CCAR postponed a decision.

Even within more halachically based Jewish communities, some argue that a contemporary understanding of sexual orientation must be a new one, based on modern knowledge, that simply did not exist in the biblical framework, most notably, that sexual orientation may be a reflection of genetic character and not a matter of choice. This is especially crucial since in biblical times, while people were involved in homosexual relationships and engaged in homosexual sex, individuals did not identify publicly as gays or lesbians nor did they live exclusively gay lives. Therefore, biblical prohibitions speak to specific sexual acts rather than to the people or to sexual orientation.

Similarly, just as the legal and social status of categories of people has changed as our understanding of them developed, so, too, must we reevaluate the biblical injunction against homosexual sex. For example, deaf and disabled people were relegated to certain forms of inferior status because deafness was mistaken for mental retardation, and the physically disabled were not considered whole or competent. Respected rabbis sanctioned the shunning of lepers. Today, many Orthodox Jews recognize the harsh impact of those erroneous assumptions and have sought ways to adapt the *halachah* accordingly. So, too, the argument goes for those who regarded homosexuality as inferior or a matter of a "wrong" choice.

The UAHC has formally supported both civil rights in the larger society and full integration into the Reform movement for gay and lesbian Jews. With much care and serious discussion, Reform Judaism was the first American Jewish movement, starting as early as 1974, to accept into its ranks congregations with an outreach to the gay and lesbian community.

Recognizing that much remains to be done, Rabbi Alexander M. Schindler, then president of the UAHC, eloquently stirred the Jewish community on this issue in his 1989 Biennial address to the Union of American Hebrew Congregations:

> ...In most mainstream congregations, we have not extended our embrace to include gay and lesbian Jews. We have not dispelled the myth of the "corrupting homosexual," of the counselor and/or teacher who would fashion children in his or her sexual image. And we have not consciously included gay and lesbian parents as part of the Jewish family circle....
>
> In our denial, in our failure to see one another as one family— indeed, as one holy body—we forget Jewish history, we opt for amnesia. We who were beaten in the streets of Berlin cannot turn away from the plague of gay-bashing. We who were Marranos in Madrid, who clung to the closet of assimilation and conversion in order to live without molestation, we cannot deny the demand for gay and lesbian visibility.
>
> ...In all of this, I am working to make the Reform Jewish community a home: a place where loneliness and suffering and exile end; a place that leaves it to God to validate relationships and demands of us only that these relationships be worthy in God's eyes; a place where we can search together—through the written Torah and the Torah of life—to find those affirmations for which we yearn.

In its 1987 and 1989 resolutions on gay and lesbian Jews, the UAHC affirmed its commitment to full inclusion of gay and lesbian Jews in all areas of synagogue life. The UAHC has urged all of its congregations to (1) encourage lesbian and gay Jews to share and participate in worship, leadership, and the general congregational life of all synagogues; (2) continue to develop educational programs in the synagogue and community that promote understanding and respect for lesbians and gays; and (3) employ people without regard to sexual orientation.

Reform Judaism has affirmed the right of a person to be ordained as a rabbi or invested as a cantor irrespective of his or her sexual orientation, but many congregations have been reluctant to employ an openly gay rabbi to serve a heterosexual congregation. Only recently have openly gay rabbis been hired for the pulpits of heterosexual Reform congregations.

Raw bigotry can target gays and lesbians as easily as it can Blacks, Jews, Asians, women, disabled persons, or any other vulnerable group. Just as Reform Judaism has been on the cutting edge in affirming the rights of gays and lesbians—including the right to serve as a rabbi—so, too, Reform Judaism is called upon to educate and sensitize our members to our own fears of homosexuals. We must also be more vigorous in repudiating any hate crimes, indeed any discrimination, against gays or lesbians in our own communities.

Domestic Violence

Family violence in America has reached epidemic levels. Consider the following statistics:

- One in every three female children and one in every six male children in the United States will be sexually abused by the age of eighteen. In 85 percent of these cases, the abuser is someone known to and trusted by the victim.

- One in every twenty-five elderly persons in the United States will meet with physical abuse at the hands of his or her adult children.

- In the United States, at least 1 million children are physically abused by their parents or caretakers every year. Two thousand die from physical abuse and neglect.

- Three-to-four million women in the United States are victims of domestic violence each year.

- Forty-four percent of women who are murdered are killed by their husbands or male friends.

- Fifty-two percent of all married women in the United States experience at least one act of violence at the hands of their husbands.

- Four thousand women are beaten to death every year.

- Every fifteen seconds, a woman in the United States is battered.

- Thirty percent of women seeking treatment in hospital emergency rooms are victims of wife-beating.

- In homes with spousal abuse, children are abused or seriously neglected at a rate of 1500 percent of the national average.

Although domestic violence may plague Jewish families with slightly less frequency than non-Jewish families, the Jewish community has been reluctant to acknowledge its presence in our homes. Historically, the family unit has been both the source of strength and the pride of the Jewish people. To admit that such abuse occurs within our homes poses an enormous threat to our cultural identity and self-image.

Our tradition emphasizes the dignity of each human life and the sanctity of the home; further, it mandates us to protect the vulnerable. Yet our tradition also defines women as the property of their husbands and fathers. We are commanded to honor our parents, but how can one honor parents who are abusive? We must confront and reconcile these contradictions and produce a coherent social framework for dealing with abuse when it occurs in our community.

Child Abuse

Studies show that child abuse can be transmitted from generation to generation; child abusers were often abused children. Many such abusers vowed that they would never subject their children to the treatment they received, yet many revert to the types of behavior that they knew growing up—even though it had caused their own suffering.

Child abuse is found in families with varied incomes and educational backgrounds. The greatest impediments to overcoming domestic violence are denial and silence. As long as Jewish leaders cling to the assumption that child abuse is not a Jewish problem, Jewish children will continue to be molested, physically and emotionally, without effective community intervention.

Teachers, youth directors, and rabbis need to be trained to identify victims of abuse and provide help. They must be sensitive to those subtle types of violence that wound and tear but leave no physical scars. Victims of abuse must be taught that there are people to whom they can safely turn: parents, rabbis, counselors, and confidential hot lines. Although victims of abuse are certainly in need of counseling and often must be removed from abusive situations, the perpetrators of abuse are in need of help as well. We as a community must be willing to address the problem and to commit to the support and rehabilitation of all parties concerned. Hopefully, we can help prevent such abuse from being passed to the next generation.

Spouse Abuse

Rabbis have recognized the problem of spouse abuse for centuries; an eighth-century Babylonian text makes specific reference to a husband abusing his wife. Female abuse of male victims and spouse abuse among gay and lesbian couples are also not unheard of. Only in recent years, however, have female victims come forward and reported the crime. The vicious cycle of spouse abuse is a difficult one to end. Socioeconomic factors play a large role in the ability of a woman to leave her abusive husband, particularly if there are children involved. If the husband is a professional or is seen as a "pillar of the community," it has traditionally been difficult for the wife to find anyone to believe her. She will be encouraged to keep it quiet, told that she is making it all up or that it's not as bad as she's making it seem, or advised to ignore it in the interest of *shelom bayit*, of keeping peace in the home. Although women continue to join the workforce in greater and greater numbers, many women are wholly dependent on their husbands' income for financial solvency. Often, abusers will not allow their wives to work as a means of controlling them and making sure that they remain dependent and cannot leave. This creates a real problem when women, particularly women with children, want to leave. Where will they go? How will she pay for food, housing, clothes, childcare? Who will hire a woman with no marketable skills? The myriad issues that accompany spouse abuse must be fully examined in order to provide women with the resources they need to be able to leave their batterers.

Spouse abuse takes many forms, including forced social isolation, verbal harassment, sexual abuse, and battering. Studies show that as is the case of child abuse, violence against one's spouse is almost as common in the Jewish population as in the general American population.

A 1980 Los Angeles study, based on more than two hundred completed questionnaires from congregants of nine Orthodox, Conservative, and Reform synagogues, reported 22 incidents of spouse abuse, 4 incidents of sexual abuse, 11 incidents of forced social isolation, and 118 incidents of violent acts toward children. In total, 30 percent of the respondents reported either having experienced or having known of violence in Jewish families.

Sadly, the study also found that victims of abuse most often kept knowledge of the violence within a close circle of family and friends. A few told private therapists. Only four respondents spoke to a rabbi about the abuse.

Many abused Jewish women who call hot lines do not identify themselves as Jewish to their counselors, and many abused Jewish women can afford to, and prefer to, stay in hotels rather than in battered women's shelters, which remain the primary source of statistical information on spouse abuse.

Clearly, there is still a great deal of shame associated with admitting that abuse can occur within a Jewish household. A mythology seems to be at work that prevents us from addressing this unpleasant reality. Because the characteristics of a batterer or a battered woman do not fit our image of a Jewish couple, it is difficult, almost impossible, for us to believe that this is a Jewish problem. The result is massive denial, even in the face of such celebrated headline cases as the fatal battering of little Lisa Steinberg in New York City by her violent adoptive father in 1987 and the tragic story of the Chasidic mother in Brooklyn who beat her son to death in 1992.

EMERGE, a men's counseling group that works with batterers, reports that one-third of the men it counsels are professionals: doctors, lawyers, even clergy. Particularly in cases such as these, the wife's accusation is often met with disbelief by people in the community who know only the public image of the abuser.

As long as we perpetuate the myth that such violence does not occur in Jewish homes, the road to recovery will remain long. Even as women increasingly report their abuse, sexual assault remains the nation's least-detected crime.

The sooner we engage in the debate and place these issues on our communal agenda, the sooner we will bring relief to legions of silent victims and bring hope to those who are confused, ashamed, and do not know where to turn. The UAHC Department of Jewish Family Concerns is involved in precisely this quest.

DATE RAPE

In the emerging awareness of the widespread occurrence of acquaintance rape and date rape, we see a particular challenge to young adults. Date rape involves, among others, Jewish women as victims or Jewish men as perpetrators. In fact, because of the particular focus on college campuses and the disproportionate number of Jewish women and men attending higher educational institutions, there is a specific Jewish dimension to this issue.

Consider the following hypothetical situation, adapted from an article "'Friends' Raping Friends," published by the Association of American Colleges:

Phil and Cindy: The Same Story but Two Different Points of View

> *Phil:* I still don't know what happened. Cindy and I had been dating for about two months and, while we had not slept together yet, I had certainly made it clear that I was very attracted to her and eventually expected to have sex with her. We were supposed to go to a party and when she showed up in this sexy low-cut dress, I thought maybe this was her way of saying she was ready.

At the party, we drank some beer, which made her sort of sleepy and sensual. When she said she wanted to go lie down and have me come snuggle with her, what was I supposed to think? Of course I thought she wanted to have sex. Granted, she did protest a little when I started to undress her, but I just figured she wanted to be persuaded. Lots of women feel a little funny about being forward and want men to take responsibility for sex. I don't know. We had sex, and it was fine. I took her home from the party, and I thought everything was OK. But ever since then she refuses to talk to me or go out with me. I thought she really liked me. What happened?

Cindy: I'll never forget that night as long as I live. Phil and I had been dating a while, and he had always acted like a perfect gentleman. Well, we had done our share of kissing, but he never gave me any reason not to trust him. The night of the party I wore this gorgeous dress that I borrowed from my roommate. It was a little flashier than I normally wear, but I thought it was very flattering. At the party I had some beer, and it made me tired so I wanted to lie down. Maybe I shouldn't have suggested we both lie down together, but it felt weird to go upstairs by myself and leave Phil all alone. The next thing I knew, he was all over me, forcing me to have sex with him. It was horrible. I didn't want to scream and make a fool of myself with all those other people in the next room, but I tried to fight him off. I guess I was just too wiped out to be very effective. After a while I just stopped struggling. Needless to say, I never want to see Phil again. He seemed like such a nice guy. What happened?

Was this rape? How could Cindy and Phil see the same experience in such shockingly contrasting ways? The best way to avoid such misunderstandings is to set one basic ground rule in sexual relations: when one partner says no *at any time*, the decision of that partner must be fully respected. No means *no*, not "maybe," not "if," not "whatever"!

YOUTH SUICIDE

Suicide is the third-leading cause of death among young people between the ages of fifteen and twenty-four. In the United States, eighteen young people commit suicide every day. For each of these successful suicides, there are a hundred unsuccessful attempts. There are an estimated 500,000 attempted youth suicides annually in the United States. Almost every student in high school or college today knows at least one person who has attempted suicide. Although precise statistics are unavailable, it appears that these figures apply proportionally to the Jewish community as well. Teen suicide has increased 200 percent since 1964. This trend is a tragic indication that many young people are feeling deeply alienated from their families and other support systems in our society.

Why do young people choose to commit suicide? Often, they believe that their feelings of loneliness and stress are unique and hopelessly irresolvable and they will not be understood by others. While an individual is unlikely to commit suicide in response to a single incident, such factors as the death of a sibling, the strain of dealing with a parent's financial failure, a breakup of a romantic relationship, involvement with drug abuse, or concern over homosexual feelings may elevate stress in teens to the point of contemplating suicide. Although divorce per se has not been shown to be a direct factor in adolescent suicide, "pathological divorce," in which parents fight over the children or use them as pawns, may in some cases be such a factor. It is therefore important for young people to learn how to deal with stressful situations and feelings without becoming so overwhelmed that they consider suicide as a solution.

The UAHC has responded to this frightening trend in a variety of ways. Beginning in 1985, it established a Task Force on Youth Suicide Prevention, created under the auspices of the Yad Tikvah ("Hand of Hope") Foundation with the goal of encouraging congregations, camps, and youth groups to become involved in the vital work of suicide prevention. Also in 1985, the UAHC Press published Dr. Sol Gordon's best-selling *When Living Hurts*, an in-depth discussion of suicide prevention geared especially to young people. The UAHC also distributes a suicide prevention kit that includes programming options for religious schools, camps, and youth groups. The kit was sent to rabbis to implement suicide-prevention programming in their synagogues.

How can friends as well as adult supervisors of children (parents, counselors, teachers, rabbis, youth directors) help? Primarily by being observant and willing to listen. While signs of depression, of sudden loss of appetite, of changes in sleeping patterns, of repeated unexplained bruises, of crying jags, of a decrease in concentration or deterioration of grades might well have varied—and often innocent—causes and explanations, they should never be ignored. They are all symptoms that *may* mask more serious problems: physical abuse, drug and alcohol use, and emotional problems that could lead to suicide. A responsible adult should be informed, and that adult should look into the matter. Above all, even passing references to suicide should never be considered idle chatter but should be addressed directly and caringly by a responsible adult.

In addition to its proactive emphasis on preventative programming and counseling, the task force has published a booklet, *It's Not Over When It's Over: The Aftermath of Suicide*, which is a guide to rabbis on how to comfort suicide survivors. Often, the sense of shame, guilt, and anger surrounding the suicide makes the grieving process especially difficult for its survivors.

The recent epidemic of suicides and attempted suicides is especially disturbing because of the immense value our religion ascribes to human life. Traditional Jewish law views the taking of one's life as *chet* ("sin")—morally wrong and prohibited. A suicide is traditionally buried on the periphery of a Jewish cemetery, a significant distance from the other grave sites. In addition, no mourning rites are traditionally observed for one who commits suicide, unless the individual is considered mentally incompetent.

Although Reform Judaism concurs that suicide is wrong, we think that the Jewish tradition emphasizing compassion and concern for the surviving family supersedes other considerations. Therefore, in the Reform tradition, rites of burial and mourning customs are observed for the deceased who has committed suicide, and every effort is made to avoid attaching stigma to the victim and the family.

··· 14 ···

A Jewish Ethical Will for the 21st Century

There's a remarkable Jewish tradition that many of our ancestors practiced and preserved. They would write and pass on to their children an "ethical will." Such wills did not deal with the conveyance of things (land, property, jewelry, or animals) to one's heir. In this ethical will, Jews would take measure of their lives and sum up the values that had been tried and tested through the years, distilling those eternal truths that they wished, above and beyond all worldly possessions, to transmit to their children and to their children's children. And they knew that if their children and their children's children would hearken to their words, Jewish continuity would remain unbroken.

Trust in God, fealty to the faith of our ancestors, justice to one's fellows, charity to the poor and the hopeless, commitment to the community, learning, truth, confidence that the seed of a world of peace and justice is being nurtured beyond the horizon despite the agonies and heartbreak of the day, invincible belief that God's people will be an instrument for the redemption of humanity—these were among the incandescent beliefs that beyond all else Jews sought to implant in the hearts of their children.

Each ethical will spelled out, with individual particularities and nuances, the glories and the burdens of Jewish survival. And now it is our turn and our time.

The twentieth century is waning. A new millennium of the Jewish experiment hovers just ahead. Our duty is not merely to await it patiently or to endure it stoically or even to welcome it actively. Our duty is to enter it wisely with renewed vigor, having plumbed the meaning of our own experience—the experience of people who have endured the depths and witnessed the peaks of the twentieth century—and then to produce our own ethical will, a testament to what we seek to preserve and what we believe needs changing, a testament we can then pass on to the new generations that follow ours, a testament to be read not as a mandate but as a guide, not as the fossilized endgame of Jewish history but as a shaping vision that gives hope and strength and spirit to those who come after us.

For this is the only true immortality: to keep alive for all generations to come a way of life that has endured in grandeur through all the traumas that history has hurled at this people, the Jews, whose unique tale winds through all the recorded history of humankind. To fail in this—to embrace our Jewish destiny but fail to hand it on to generations yet unborn—would be to bequeath a gross posthumous victory to our enemies, to commit an act of moral negligence. No, our task—our privilege—is to seize the future and to shape it according to the best traditions of the past, including those keenest insights we ourselves have added. That is our title deed, our ethical will, our immortality.

Dreams, words, hopes—but how? How can the Jews and all that they—we—have learned be vouchsafed? There can be no guarantees in such an explosive and volatile world, but there are some truths we do know: we know that Judaism—the religious civilization of the Jew—provides the most powerful answer to the mystery of Jewish survival—the answer to why we Jews survive. The faith of the Jew—God, Torah, Israel—has preserved a people, a God-intoxicated people, whose moral vision has graced the world—a people that has sought relentlessly to keep humanity human. So we know that Judaism is both the reason and the purpose of the Jews.

And if we endure, what is it that will distinguish us from the legions of other ethnic, communal, civic, and cultural groups on this planet? The marvels of Jewish intellect and culture, of social justice and civic creativity, of benevolence and charity, of Jewish peoplehood—all these qualities radiate outward from the magnetic core of a historic Judaism. This is what has linked the generations as a distinctive people. Sever the Jewish people from its spinal cord, and it will shrivel into paralysis and be rendered trivial.

The American Judaism of the twenty-first century cannot be a carbon copy of the Judaism of antiquity—animal sacrifice, Temple and Sanhedrin, castes and superstitions. Judaism lives because it evolves and changes to meet the needs of new eras. And today, on the threshold of a new century, Judaism faces challenges of a magnitude undreamt of by the patriarchs and matriarchs: biomedical revolutions and bioethical challenges, the threat of nuclear holocaust and the reality of ethnic war, the danger of pollution of the environment, the wrenching changes in the traditional family, the rising curve of intermarriage, the spread of personal anomie, the hunger for new approaches to Jewish learning, our profound connections with a beleaguered and often problematic Israel, the inchoate yearning for spiritual sustenance, the erosion of politics—all these must be faced by a clear-eyed Jewish community that reveres the past but is not trapped by it, that has instead the courage and capacity to take charge of the challenge and rise to the imperatives of change that an uncertain future demands.

This volume is neither a Jewish catechism nor a Reform *halachah*. It is a wide-ranging summary of the fundamental social justice issues that test our Jewish values. These issues will dominate the headlines of the twenty-first century. There is no specific Jewish "right" answer to most of these dilemmas. But there is a Jewish mandate to care, to study the issues, to be engaged in the work of the community, and to undertake the social action that will help to heal this battered and weary world. There is a recognition that it is a sin—no less than that—to do nothing when moral decisions must be made.

Long ago, we stood at the foot of Sinai. From our encounter with the Divine, we brought forth a message of justice and hope that transformed human history. From that time on, the need for such a transforming vision has never been more urgent than it is now. Today.